science
FOR GCSE

Bob McDuell, Morton Jenkins & Graham Booth

First published by Simon & Schuster Education
Reprinted in 1994

Reprinted in 1996 by
Stanley Thornes (Publishers) Ltd, Ellenborough House,
Wellington Street, Cheltenham GL50 1YW

A catalogue record of this book is available from the British Library

ISBN 0-7487-2498-2

Designed and produced by Gecko Limited, Bicester, Oxon.
Cover design by Iguana Creative Design

Printed & bound in Hong Kong by
Dah Hua Printing Press Co. Ltd.

Acknowledgement is due to the following Examinations Boards for permission to reproduce examination questions:
Welsh Joint Education Committee (WJEC);
Reproduced by permission of the University of Cambridge Local Examinations Syndicate (MEG);
University of London Examinations and Assessment Council (LEAG).

Acknowledgement is due to the following for permission to reproduce photographs:

Key (t = top, b = bottom, l = left, r = right, c = centre)

All-Sport Photographic: 230tl/Jon Nicholson, 242tl/Simon Bruty, 242tr/Gary Mortimore, 242c/David Leah, 242b/Howard Boylan,
Ann Ronan at Image Select: 56br, 74, 96l
Archiv für Kunst und Geschichte, Berlin: 78t & b, 120r, 140, 145, 239t
Australian Information Service, London: 83b
Graham Booth: 249b
Chris Coggins: 101, 12l & r, 13t, 57, 69t, 94br, 96r, 115, 118, 127, 137b, 138tr, cr & br, 139tl & bl, 167t & b, 168, 194, 197l & r, 199 all photos, 200, 209t & b, 210bcr & b, 211, 212t & b, 213, 215t & b, 216, 221tl, tr & b, 230b, 238, 240, 241, 247t & b, 248, 256, 262, 264tr, cl, cr & r, 269
Courtesy of the Colt Car Company, Cirencester/Mitsubishi: 234
Donald Cooper, Photostage: 132/Hansel & Gretel, ENO 1992
The Environmental Picture Library: 86/Alex Clam, 103tr/Jimmy Holmes, 104bl/Alex Clam, 153/Pete Addis, 254br/Philip Carr
Colin Garratt's Steam Locomotives of the World Photo Library/Milepost 92½: 201tr & tl, 236
GeoScience Features Picture Library: 4t, 47, 53, 83t, 122 tl, bl & r, 129r, 141, 178 all photos, 179bl, 277

Greenpeace: 71br
Robert Harding Picture Library: 91/Ian Griffiths, 230tc/Adam Woolfitt, 230 (motorbike)/Ian Griffiths
Michael Holford: 152
Hulton-Deutsch Picture Library: 62bl, 661/Bettmann Archive
Image Select International: 272/NASA, 278 br/NASA
Magnum Photos/Sebastiano Salgado: 99
Courtesy of the Metropolitan Police Service: 28
National Medical Slide Bank/Graves Educational Resources: 30
National Meteorological Library, University of Dundee: 257b
Natural History Photographic Agency: 2t/Stephen Dalton, 2b/Anthony Bannister, 16t/Scott Johnson, 20/Stephen Dalton, 24b/M.I. Walker, 25t/M.I. Garwood, 34tr/W.S. Paton, 45/Henry Ausloos, 46/J. & M.Bain, 68l & r/G.I. Bernard, 102 Janisauvanet, 69cb/Gérard Lacz, 80/Tsuneo Nakamura, 87tr/David Bishop/ANT, 88bl/B. & C. Alexander, 88r/G.I. Bernard, 103bl/Henry Ausloos, 104tl/Stephen Krasermann, 104cl & tr/Marka Wendler, 104br/Jany Sauvanet, 230 (frog)/Stephen Dalton, 245cl/Stephen Dalton
Klaus Paysan at Image Select: 16b, 34bl
Courtesy of PowerGen Photographic: 94tr
Redferns Photography 201c/Fin Costello
Courtesy of the Salt Museum, Northwich, Cheshire Museums Service: 170
The Science Museum, London: 120l
Science Photo Library: 1, 4l & 4br/Dr Jeremy Burgess, 10tr & cr/James Stevenson, 10br/Profs. Motta & Courer–Nottola, University La Sapienza, Rome, 13b/Phillipe Plailly, 15/Biology Media, 23/Alexander Tsiaras, 24t/M.I. Walker, 25b/Claude Nviridsany & Marie Perennou, 31t/Biophoto Associates, 31b/Bettina Cirone, 35/Dr Jeremy Burgess, 40tl/Prof. P.M. Motta & J. van Blerkom, 40tr/Petit Format/Nestle, 40bl/James Stevenson, 49/Simon Fraser, Royal Victoria Infirmary, Newcastle upon Tyne, 52tr/Andrew Syred, 52cl/CNRI, 52bl/John Giannicchi, 56t/Martin Bond, 62tr/Peter Menzel, 67l & r/CNRI, 70/US Dept. of Energy, 71t/John Durham, 71bl/Martin Bond, 76, 77/Jackie Lewn, Royal Free Hospital, 87tl/Dr Morely Read, 88tl/Simon Fraser, 89l & r/Dr Jeremy Burgess, 90/John Mead, 92/Sheila Terry, 94bl/Martin Bond, 95b, 116/David Parker, 119, 129l/John Walsh, 130t & b, 138bl/James Holmes/Rover, 139cl/Pat & Tom Leeson, 142, 143/Los Alamos National Laboratory, 179tr Adam Hart-Davis, 183/Peter Menzel, 189/David Parker, 190/Gordon Garradd, 191/Will & Deni McIntyre, 203/Alex Bartel, 207/David Parker, 210/John Walsh, 217/Dr T.E. Thompson, 221cr/Dr Ray Clark, 226/Martin Bond, 227tr/Tommaso Guicciardini, 227cl/Martin Bond, 245tr/Ray Ellis, 251lt/Heini Scheebeli, 252/David Parker, 254tl/Phillippe Plailly, 255t, 255b/Chris Priest, 257t/Dr Ray Clarke & Mervyn Goff, 258/David Parker, 259/Martin Bond, 264tl & 265/Alexander Tsiaras, 267/Jerrican, 271/ESA/PLI, 273/NASA, 274/Julian Baum, 276tl & 276tr/NASA, 276bl/Earth Satellite Corporation, 276br/US Geological Survey, 278tl/John Sandford, 278tr, bl & bc/NASA, 279tr/NASA, 279tr/Harvard College Observatory
Frank Spooner Pictures: 69ct, 69b, 95t, 180, 222
Courtesy of Stanley Thornes: 251b, 262br, 268
Topham Picture Source: 249t
Courtesy of Vauxhall Motors: 243
Zefa: 56bl, 100, 137t, 139tr, 150, 230tr, 237, 239b

Picture Research by Suzanne Williams

INTRODUCTION

Science for GCSE is intended to help students preparing for the higher level GCSE examinations. These papers generally test levels C, B, A and A*. This introduction will help you tackle level A and A* questions.

Firstly, do not be put off just because you are told that questions are level A or A*. Depending upon the subject of the question, the amount of information given, the style of response required and the marking scheme used by the examiner, a question at level A or A* can seem easier than a question at a lower level.

The wording of questions at higher level is critical and you should ensure that your answer is the type of answer required for the particular question you are answering. The following terms may appear on your examination paper.

Define: If you are asked to define a term you are required to give only a short formal statement.

State: Here you are required to give a concise answer with little or no supporting argument. This might be, for example, a numerical answer which you can give by looking at the information in the question.

State and explain: Again this suggests that you should give a concise answer with only a brief reference to theory.

Outline: This requires a brief answer giving just essentials.

Predict: Where 'predict' is used in a question you are not expected to produce your answer by recall but by making a logical connection between other pieces of information. Such information may be wholly given in the question or may depend on answers to an earlier part of the question. Again, a concise answer with no supporting statement is required.

Deduce: This is used in a similar way to 'predict' but some supporting evidence is required, for example a reference to a law or principle or the necessary reasoning.

Suggest: This is used in two main contexts – either to imply that there is no unique answer, or to show that you should apply your knowledge to an unfamiliar situation.

Find: This general term can be interpreted as 'calculate', 'measure' or 'determine'.

Calculate: Where this is used a numerical answer is required and the working should be shown.

On the paper there should be a space for the answer to each part and a maximum mark which can be awarded for each part. Use the space as a guide to how much you should write, but continue your writing elsewhere if you think you need more space. If a part has four marks, it is likely that you need to make four points.

You may be expected to know some equations for the examination. These equations are shown in colour throughout the book, and listed on page 280.

Good luck!

LIFE AND LIVING PROCESSES

1 ENERGY AND LIFE

By the end of this section you should be able to

- understand the concept of potential energy
- understand that energy is transferred in living organisms
- recall that adenosine triphosphate can transfer energy to other molecules by the loss of a phosphate group.

ACTIVITY IN LIVING THINGS

Movement

There is a constant activity in living things. Hearts beat, muscles contract and stomachs digest food. Plants that spend all their lives rooted in one spot are also active. They grow taller and stouter. Flowers open and close. Stems twist and turn so that leaves face towards the Sun, fig 1.1. Roots reach out towards water. Even when there is no apparent motion, microscopes reveal that cytoplasm within cells is always moving.

Fig 1.1 Stems of climbing plants such as ivy twist and turn so that leaves can face the Sun

Heat, light and electricity

Besides motion, cell activities produce heat. Small electric currents run along nerve cells, and some organisms can produce light, fig 1.2. Motion, heat, electricity and light are all forms of **energy**. Cells change energy from one form into another, but cannot make energy. All life's energy comes from fuel in the form of food.

Fig 1.2 Some animals such as this glow worm can turn chemical energy into light energy

WHAT IS ENERGY?

Energy is the 'push' that makes things happen. It is the ability to do work (see page 228) and can be classified in two ways.

Potential and kinetic energy

If you wind up the spring motor of a clock, the tightly wound spring has stored or **potential** energy. As the spring unwinds and causes wheels and gears to move, the moving parts have **kinetic** energy.

When wood burns it undergoes a chemical change in which stored energy is released. The cellulose in the wood is broken down into carbon dioxide and water. The chemical potential energy in the bonds is rapidly converted to heat and light energy.

Respiration

Living organisms also produce heat energy from chemical energy in a process similar to burning called **respiration** (see page 6). However, instead of letting the energy escape rapidly, cells save it to be used for many purposes and release it slowly.

STORING AND RELEASING ENERGY WITHIN CELLS

ATP

There is a transfer of energy in every living process. Some reactions release energy and others store it. These two types of reactions are linked by special chemicals. The most important of these chemicals is **adenosine triphosphate (ATP)**. This molecule is like a storage battery. In the ATP molecule, three phosphate groups (P) are bonded to adenosine (A)

A–P–P–P

Releasing energy from ATP

The most important chemical fact about ATP is that the bond to the last phosphate group can be broken and the phosphate group separated from the rest of the molecule and joined to other compounds. When this bond is broken, energy is released which can be used to drive other reactions. The loss of one phosphate group converts ATP into **adenosine diphosphate (ADP)**

$$A–P–P–P \longrightarrow A–P–P + P$$
$$\text{ATP} \qquad\quad \text{ADP} \quad\;\; \text{phosphate}$$

The compound that receives the phosphate group from ATP can either use the energy for some chemical reaction, or hand the phosphate on to another chemical for more permanent storage.

Storing energy in ATP

In order to store energy, ADP reacts with a phosphate group and ATP is recycled. This reaction takes in energy.

$$ADP + P \rightarrow ATP$$

ATP may be described as the energy currency of the cell. The energy stored in the phosphate bonds can be converted to all the forms of energy required in cells.

The significance of ATP may be seen in the storage of energy during photosynthesis (see page 4) and in the release of energy in respiration (see page 6).

Q1 Suggest why ATP is described as the 'energy currency' of the cell.

Q2 When energy is released from ATP (adenosine triphosphate), chemical bonds holding the phosphate groups to the adenosine are broken. Suggest the name of the group of chemicals responsible for breaking the bonds.

Q3 Fig 1.3 shows two sets of apparatus set up to compare the energy content of sugar and margarine. The foods were burned. The temperature change in water was noted in **A** after all the food had burned, but in **B** the temperature change after 2 minutes was noted. The results are shown in the table.

	Apparatus A	Apparatus B
temperature rise from burning sugar	14 °C	6 °C
temperature rise from burning margarine	21 °C	18 °C

a State *four* ways by which the apparatus set up in **A** is an improvement on that shown in **B**.

b The energy production measured from the foods burnt in **A** was expected to be greater. Suggest *three* reasons why the energy production appeared less than that expected.

c Suggest how the apparatus in **A** could have been improved to produce a more accurate result. [8]

(WJEC Common Syllabus (Biology) June 1986 Q18)

▼ **Fig 1.3**

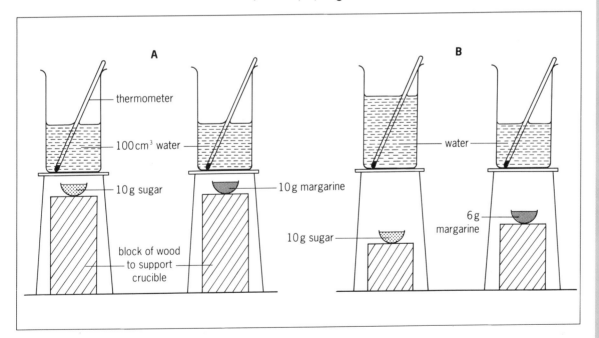

2 PHOTO-SYNTHESIS

By the end of this section you should be able to

- understand the life process of photosynthesis
- explain how a leaf is adapted for photosynthesis
- understand limiting factors of photosynthesis.

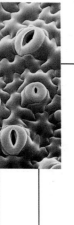

Fig 2.1 Plants can make kilograms of sugar

PRODUCING SUGAR

Sugar is the basic fuel for all living things. It can be converted into other food molecules. Every day, year in and year out, century after century, living things burn up tonnes of sugar. Where does it all come from?

A chemist in a well-equipped laboratory can produce a few crystals of sugar after many hours and much expense. While the chemist links one carbon atom to another in a series of complex reactions, the trees outside the laboratory window use sunlight to produce kilograms of sugar from carbon dioxide and water. From the sugar the tree makes other carbohydrates, and also fats and protein, figs 2.1 and 2.2.

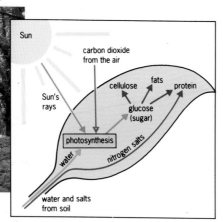

▲ Fig 2.2 Products of photosynthesis in a leaf. Fats and carbohydrates are formed from glucose. Nitrogen salts from the soil are needed to make proteins

What is photosynthesis?

In the cells of green parts of plants, carbon dioxide and water are changed into glucose (sugar) in a series of reactions called **photosynthesis**. Oxygen is produced as a by-product.

$$6CO_2 + 6H_2O \rightarrow C_6H_{12}O_6 + 6O_2$$

carbon dioxide + water → glucose + oxygen

The structure of the leaf

Carbon dioxide diffuses into the leaves through pores on their undersides called **stomata**, fig 2.3. Inside the leaf are the mesophyll layers of cells. The **palisade mesophyll** layer is where most photosynthesis takes place. The cells here contain large numbers of **chloroplasts**, the sites of photosynthesis. The **spongy mesophyll** layer contains many air spaces so that the carbon dioxide can get to the cells that need it for photosynthesis. Fig 2.4 shows the structure of a leaf, and fig 2.5 shows a chloroplast.

The photosynthesising cells produce oxygen, and this diffuses out through the stomata. The water needed for the process comes from the soil and is transported in the **xylem** vessels of the veins. The **phloem** vessels transport the sugar made by photosynthesis, and other substances, around the plant. There is more about stomata and transport in plants on page 51.

▼ Fig 2.4 How a leaf is adapted for photosynthesis. Carbon dioxide enters through the stomata and diffuses between the mesophyll cells, which are packed with chloroplasts. These cells are arranged near the top of the leaf so they capture plenty of sunlight.

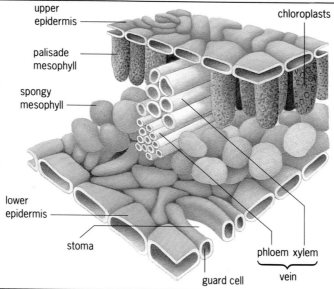

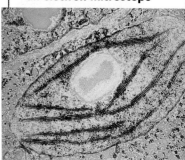

▼ Fig 2.5 A chloroplast from a pea plant seen with an electron microscope

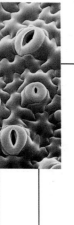

▲ Fig 2.3 This electron micrograph shows the minute pores or stomata on the under surface of a tobacco leaf. The stomata open and close according to conditions of light, humidity, etc.

LIGHT AND LIFE

Energy is required for photosynthesis, and this comes from sunlight. The green plant's power to capture energy holds the key to life, because only green plants can make their own food. Animals have to eat plants or other animals to obtain food – they cannot make their own.

The energy in light is measured in units called **photons**. When sunlight passes through a glass prism, it separates into a spectrum of colours (see page 252). The light is separated according to the frequencies of the waves, and waves of different fferent amounts of energy.

How photosynthesis takes place
Chlorophyll, the green pigment of plants present in chloroplasts, absorbs the photons of red and blue light best. It reflects green light, which is why it looks green. When a photon of red light strikes a chlorophyll molecule, it is absorbed. The photon is 'captured'.

The trapped light energy from the Sun helps to add a phosphate group to a molecule of ADP and form ATP. The energy from sunlight is also used to split a molecule of water into oxygen and hydrogen.

The hydrogen is collected by an 'acceptor' molecule called **nicotinamide adenine dinucleotide phosphate (NADP)** and carried to carbon dioxide in a complex series of reactions ending in the formation of glucose.

So the process can be summarised as two reactions

1 in the **light reaction**, water is split into hydrogen and oxygen and ATP is formed from ADP. NADP is converted to $NADPH_2$ (a carrier molecule for hydrogen).

$$H_2O \xrightarrow[\substack{ADP \\ NADP}]{sunlight} \tfrac{1}{2}O_2 + ATP + NADPH_2$$

2 in the **dark reaction**, hydrogen from the carrier molecule $NADPH_2$ is added to carbon dioxide to form glucose.

$$CO_2 \xrightarrow[\substack{ATP \\ NADPH_2}]{} C_6H_{12}O_6$$

The glucose can be converted into all the other carbohydrates found in plants. It can also be used as a basis of fat formation and, in the presence of nitrogen from nitrates, can be the beginning of protein formation.

LIMITING FACTORS FOR PHOTOSYNTHESIS

A **limiting factor** is one which affects the rate of photosynthesis. An increase in the quantity of the factor will cause an increase in the rate of photosynthesis.

The rate of photosynthesis is affected by a number of limiting factors, including light intensity, concentration of carbon dioxide available and temperature.

Activity
As oxygen is given off during photosynthesis, the rate of its production can be used as a measure of the rate of photosynthetic activity. By counting the bubbles produced in a given time using the apparatus in fig 2.6, the main limiting factors of photosynthesis can be investigated. Note that sodium hydrogencarbonate can be used as a source of carbon dioxide in this experiment.

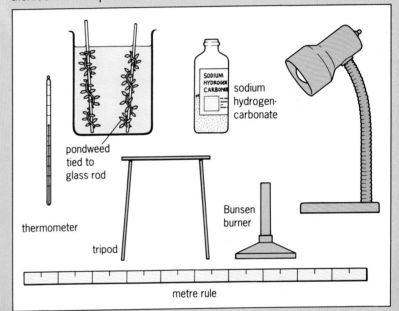

▲ Fig 2.6

1 Investigate the effects of the following variables on the rate of photosynthesis
   a light intensity **b** concentration of carbon dioxide **c** temperature.
2 Plot your results as graphs. Evaluate your results in terms of **a** valid conclusions **b** possible sources of error and **c** possible improvements to your design.
3 **Extension:** design investigations
   a to find the temperature at which photosynthesis takes place most rapidly (the **optimum** temperature)
   b to compare rates of photosynthesis in yellow, red and blue light. (Coloured sheets of transparent plastic or cellophane could be stuck to the beakers.)

3 RESPIRATION

By the end of this section you should be able to

- understand the life process of respiration
- explain how the lungs are ventilated
- explain how lung structure and blood circulation aid gas exchange
- know the difference between inhaled and exhaled air.

RELEASING ENERGY FROM GLUCOSE

The glucose made during photosynthesis is the fuel for all cells. The release of energy from this fuel is called **respiration**. When oxygen is used in this process (**aerobic respiration**) all of the available chemical energy in the glucose molecule is released. When oxygen is not used (**anaerobic respiration**), not all the energy is released.

Aerobic respiration can be summarised as

$$C_6H_{12}O_6 + 6O_2 \rightarrow 6CO_2 + 6H_2O + E$$
glucose + oxygen → carbon + water + energy
dioxide

Note that this reaction is like the 'opposite' of photosynthesis. As with photosynthesis, this equation merely shows the reactants and the products in the reaction. There is no indication of the complex chemistry involved or the form of energy released.

The energy is in the form of molecules of ATP, which are produced in stages. The energy in glucose is not released all at once, as the equation implies.

Anaerobic respiration in plant cells and fungi can be summarised as

$$C_6H_{12}O_6 \rightarrow 2CH_3CH_2OH + 2CO_2 + E$$
glucose → ethanol + carbon + energy
dioxide

Or in animal cells and some bacteria as
$$C_6H_{12}O_6 \rightarrow 2CH_3CHOHCOOH + E$$
glucose → lactic acid + energy

Providing the raw materials

Before energy can be released in cells, fuel and oxygen must be carried to them. In plant cells these are readily available as products of photosynthesis. In animals such as humans, the glucose is carried in the blood **plasma** from the intestine where it is absorbed after digestion of food, pages 12–15. The oxygen is carried as **oxyhaemoglobin** in red blood cells.

Q1 The apparatus shown in fig 3.1 can be used to illustrate the process by which energy is released inside living cells. After 10 minutes the wax candle had completely burned away, the anhydrous copper sulphate turned blue (cobalt chloride would have changed from blue to pink) and the limewater turned milky (bicarbonate indicator would have changed from red to yellow).

a Name the process in which energy is released in living cells.
b The wax candle is made of carbon, hydrogen and oxygen. Name the compound made of the same elements from which energy is released in cells.
c Suggest the purpose of the ice.
d What caused the anhydrous copper sulphate to turn blue or the cobalt chloride to turn pink?
e What caused the limewater to turn milky or the bicarbonate indicator to change to yellow?
f In plant cells, a waste product of the energy release process can be made use of by certain parts of the cell. Name these parts.

[6]
(WJEC Common Syllabus (Biology) June 1986 Q23)

HOW OXYGEN GETS INTO THE HUMAN BODY

Oxygen from the air diffuses into the blood in the air sacs of the lungs, fig 3.2.

Respiration and breathing

A popular misconception is that the words 'respiration' and 'breathing' mean the same thing. Simply put, respiration is a chemical process that releases energy as already described. Breathing is a physical process to bring about the exchange of gases needed for respiration at a **breathing surface**. Oxygen is taken in and carbon dioxide removed. This exchange takes place by the process of diffusion.

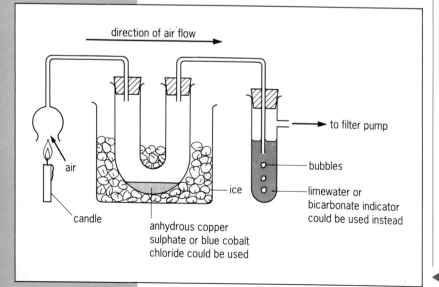

direction of air flow

to filter pump

bubbles

ice

limewater or bicarbonate indicator could be used instead

air

candle

anhydrous copper sulphate or blue cobalt chloride could be used

◀ **Fig 3.1**

6

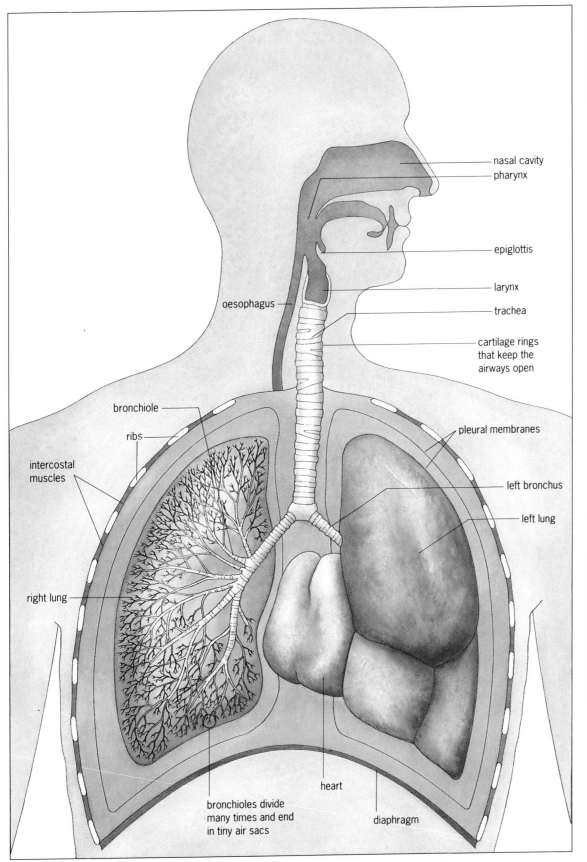

nasal cavity
pharynx
epiglottis
larynx
trachea
cartilage rings that keep the airways open
oesophagus
bronchiole
ribs
intercostal muscles
pleural membranes
left bronchus
left lung
right lung
heart
bronchioles divide many times and end in tiny air sacs
diaphragm

▲ Fig 3.2 The human 'respiratory system' – where gaseous exchange takes place

Breathing in and out

In humans, gases are made to reach the breathing surface by a pumping action of the chest and diaphragm, fig 3.3.

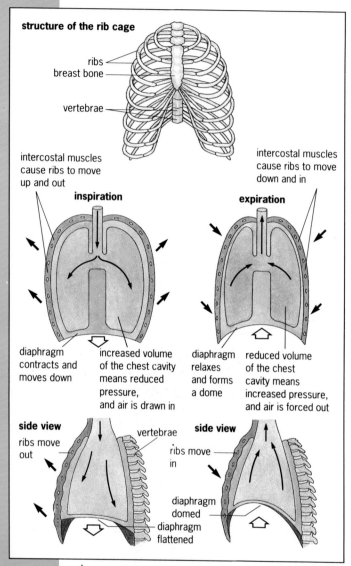

▲ **Fig 3.3 The mechanism of breathing**

During 'breathing in' (**inspiration**), the diaphragm changes from its normal dome shape to become flattened. The rib cage pivots at the vertebrae and the ribs are attached to the breast bone by pliable cartilage. The intercostal muscles between the ribs cause the rib cage to move up and out. In this way the volume of the air-tight chest is increased and the pressure inside decreases. Once the pressure inside is less than atmospheric pressure, air is sucked into the lungs.

Breathing out (**expiration**) involves the opposite movements of the diaphragm and the rib cage. It is also helped by the elastic nature of lung tissue which allows it to contract and squeeze air out.

Control of breathing

The rate of inspiration and expiration is controlled by part of the brain which responds to the amount of carbon dioxide in the blood. When cells speed up their rate of respiration, the concentration of carbon dioxide in the blood rises above the normal level.

The breathing centre in the brain then sends an urgent message along nerves to the diaphragm and intercostal muscles telling them to work harder. This continues until the concentration of carbon dioxide in the blood is reduced to normal once again.

Conversely, if the blood contains too little carbon dioxide, the breathing centre tells the muscles of the rib cage and diaphragm to work more slowly.

Exchange of gases at the breathing surface

Once the air enters the windpipe or trachea, it begins its journey along the branching tubes of the bronchioles, which end in tiny moist bubble-like **air sacs**, fig 3.4. Diffusion takes place when gases are in solution, which is why the air sacs are moist. The walls of the air sacs are so thin that oxygen can diffuse in solution through them and through the walls of the capillaries into the blood. Here it joins with the haemoglobin of the red blood cells and can be carried to the cells that need it. The waste gas carbon dioxide diffuses in solution from the blood into the air sacs to be breathed out. The table shows how the exchange of gases results in different compositions of the air breathed in and the air breathed out.

Gas	Composition as a percentage of volume	
	Inhaled air	**Exhaled air**
oxygen	20.70	14.6
carbon dioxide	0.04	3.8
water vapour	1.26	6.2
nitrogen	78.00	75.4

How the breathing system is adapted

The features which make the human breathing system good at gaseous exchange include

1 an enormous surface area provided by the air sacs (about 70 m²)
2 a rich supply of blood capillaries
3 thin-walled air sacs
4 a moist surface
5 a pumping action to renew the air at the surface.

Fig 3.4 Gaseous exchange in the alveoli

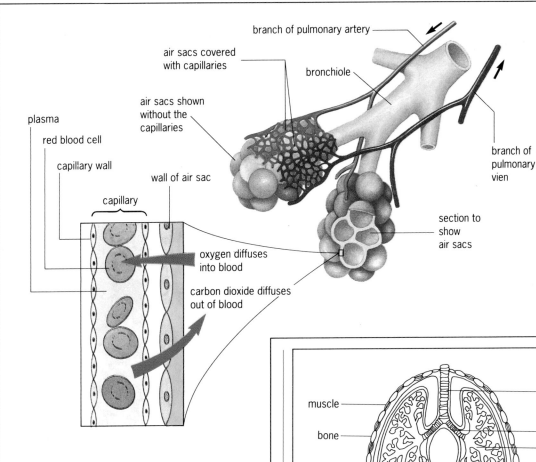

Fig 3.4 Gaseous exchange in the alveoli

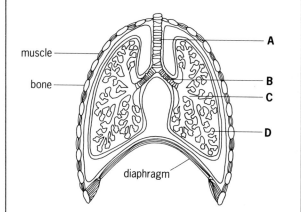

▲ Fig 3.5

Q2 Fig 3.5 shows the breathing organs inside the human chest.

a Write labels for structures **A**–**D**. [2]

b Explain how air is moved *into* the lungs during breathing. Details of the path followed by the air are not required. Use the words *diaphragm*, *rib-cage*, *volume* and *pressure*. [4]

c Fig 3.6 shows how increasing the amount of carbon dioxide in the air breathed in affects a person's breathing.

   i By how much does the amount of air breathed in per minute change when carbon dioxide increases from 1% to 5%? [1]

   ii Suggest what happens to breathing as the concentration of carbon dioxide in air breathed in increases. [1]

   (WJEC Modular Science 1991 Q3)

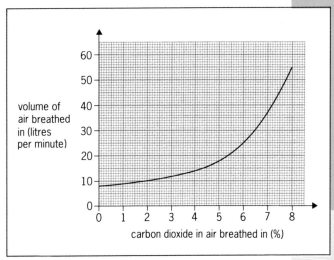

▲ Fig 3.6

4 PAYING TO DIE

By the end of this section you should be able to

■ describe the effects of tobacco on the respiratory and circulatory systems.

Between 1990 and 1991, the Government collected over 4000 million pounds in taxes from smokers. The Health Service spends over three million pounds a week on treatment of smoking-related diseases, and in addition, the Government pays out sickness benefit, widow's pensions and social security benefits to the families of victims of the smoking habit.

50 million working days per year are lost by industry because of ill health caused by smoking. About 20% of all accidental fires are caused by discarded cigarette ends.

◄ **Fig 4.1 You can see the mess cigarettes make outside the body – what do they do to the insides of people's lungs?**

WHY SMOKE?

So why do people smoke? Often, because they find it difficult to stop once they have started. Tobacco contains **nicotine**, which is an **addictive drug**.

A much more difficult question to answer is 'Why do people start to smoke?' The tobacco industry makes a few people very rich and kills a great many others. The art of advertising has reached such a degree of sophistication that it can achieve its aim without people realising that they are being 'sold' products. Vast sums of money are spent on advertising a desirable image of smoking, and it works! The Health Education Council tries to counteract this image, but cannot compete with the sums of money spent on advertising by the tobacco industry.

THE EFFECTS OF SMOKING ON THE BODY

What's in cigarettes?
Cigarettes contain
1 **tar**, a cancer-causing substance
2 **nicotine**, an addictive drug
3 carbon compounds which can form the poisonous gas, **carbon monoxide**
4 **acreolin** which is an irritant and causes coughing.

If you wanted to make a poisonous 'cocktail', you would be hard pressed to improve on the above list!

The greater the level of smoking, the higher is the death rate in otherwise similar groups of people.

Tissue damage and lung cancer

Most of smoking's harmful effects are due to tissue damage, fig 4.2. Smoking causes abnormal cells to develop in the lungs, some of which may lead to **lung cancer**. There are 1000% more deaths from lung cancer among smokers compared with non-smokers.

Air sacs rupture and arterioles become thickened in a smoker's lung. **Cilia**, fig 4.3, normally clean the respiratory tract and help prevent infection. In the trachea and bronchi, cilia are destroyed by smoking.

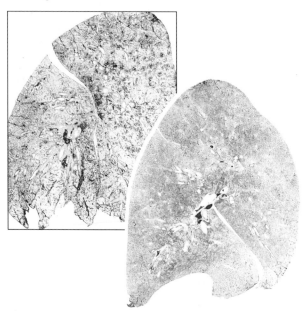

▲ **Fig 4.2 Sections of the lung of a smoker, showing deposits of tar caused by smoking, and a healthy lung (right)**

▲ **Fig 4.3 Tiny hairs called *cilia* normally keep the trachea and the rest of the respiratory tract clean by moving foreign particles away. This is a false colour scanning electron micrograph of a bronchiole**

Other causes of death

There are 500% more deaths among smokers than non-smokers from bronchitis and emphysemia. The death rate is also much higher among smokers resulting from cancers of the tongue, larynx and oesophagus, and from peptic ulcers and circulatory diseases.

Even an unborn fetus may suffer if its mother is a heavy smoker.

Smoking and pregnancy

Smoking during pregnancy reduces the oxygen available to the developing fetus, resulting in stunted development. This is particularly important in the later stages of development when the rate of growth of the brain and nervous system is at its maximum.

Carbon monoxide

Oxygen is carried around the body bound to haemoglobin in the blood. Carbon monoxide binds to haemoglobin and prevents it carrying oxygen. Small amounts of carbon monoxide can lead to dizziness and headaches, while high concentrations can kill due to the inability of the blood to carry oxygen.

Carbon monoxide is produced by traffic exhausts as well as being inhaled during smoking (see page 95).

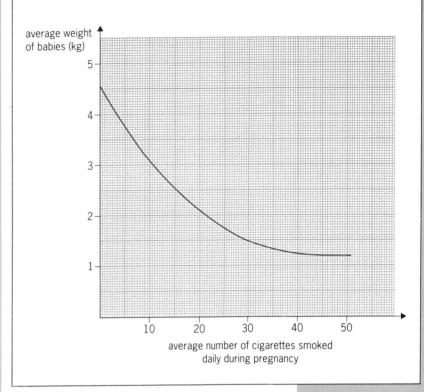

▲ **Fig 4.4**

Q1 Fig 4.4 shows the results of a survey carried out to investigate the effects of smoking by pregnant women on the birth weight of their babies.

a From the graph, state the effect of smoking on the birth weight of babies.
b State the average weight, shown on the graph, of a baby born to a mother who smokes 20 cigarettes a day.
c Name *one* harmful substance present in cigarette smoke.
d State *two* ways in which smoking can damage the health of a smoker. [14]
(WJEC Common Syllabus (Biology) 1985 Q6 (part))

Q2 The table shows the percentage of carbon monoxide in the blood of city taxi drivers.

a Suggest two main sources of carbon monoxide in the air inhaled by taxi drivers.
b Which source is likely to cause the high value of 5.8% carbon monoxide in the blood of day drivers?
c Explain the difference in the blood concentration of carbon monoxide in day and night non-smoking drivers.
d State how carbon monoxide affects the normal functions of blood. [5]
(WJEC Common Syllabus (Biology) 1986 Q21)

Type of driver		Mean concentration of carbon monoxide in blood (%)	Range of concentration (%)
day drivers	non-smokers	2.3	1.4–3.0
	smokers	5.8	2.0–9.7
night drivers	non-smokers	1.0	0.4–1.8
	smokers	4.4	1.0–8.7

5 FUELLING THE BODY'S MACHINERY

By the end of this section you should be able to

- relate energy values of foods eaten to body condition
- recall the main types of food molecules and their structures.

UNITS OF ENERGY

We need food as fuel to release energy by respiration to drive all life's processes. Energy is measured in **joules**, where one joule is enough energy to move a force of one newton through a distance of one metre. This unit of energy is so small that its use is limited and it is more usual to speak of kilojoules (kJ), where 1 kJ = 1000 J. There is another unit which is still sometimes used to measure energy, called the **calorie**. One calorie is the energy needed to raise the temperature of 1 g of water through 1°C. Again, this is a very small quantity of energy, so kilocalories (kcal or Cal) are more often used. The kilojoule is the internationally accepted unit, though kilocalories are still used on some food containers to indicate the **energy content** of the food. This energy content is determined by burning a measured amount of the food in controlled conditions and measuring the amount of heat energy produced.

DIFFERENT KINDS OF FUEL

Foods which give us most energy per gram are **fats** and **carbohydrates**. Some energy can be obtained from **proteins. Vitamins** and **minerals**, although essential in our diet, do not provide us with energy directly. A healthy, balanced diet should consist of roughly 60% carbohydrate, 20% fat and 20% protein, with small amounts of vitamins and minerals.

Carbohydrates

Carbohydrates include **sugars** and **starches**. They are all compounds of carbon, hydrogen and oxygen, and all have twice as many hydrogen as oxygen atoms in their molecules.

The simplest carbohydrate is **glucose**. It is sweet and soluble and found in many fruits. Glucose is the building block for other carbohydrates. For example, two glucose units make **sucrose** – the 'sugar' you put in your tea.

glucose $\quad C_6H_{12}O_6$
sucrose $\quad C_{12}H_{22}O_{11}$

You can see that a molecule of sucrose is almost twice as big as a molecule of glucose.

Starches and **cellulose** are other types of carbohydrates. These have giant molecules compared to sugars. They are insoluble and are made of long chains of glucose building blocks. Starch is a common carbohydrate in plants. When pure, it is very much like flour. Foods containing starch are very important as staple diets throughout the world. For example, rice, wheat, maize and potatoes are all rich in starch.

Cellulose makes up the cell walls of plants. We cannot digest cellulose, but it is important as fibrous roughage in the digestive system.

▲ **Fig 5.2 Some foods rich in fat**

Fats and oils

The molecules of **fats** and **oils** (together known as **lipids**) also contain carbon, hydrogen and oxygen. They are arranged in a different way within the molecules compared with carbohydrates. The building blocks of lipids are called **glycerol** and **fatty acids**.

It is recommended that fat should provide us with about 30% of our energy. Unfortunately, most people in Britain obtain at least 38% of their energy from fat. We should therefore eat less fat. Also, some scientists who specialise in diets suggest that we ought to eat less of the kinds of fats called **saturated**. These are in animal and dairy foods. It is possible that saturated fats cause deposits of fatty **cholesterol** in our blood vessels. This may cause heart and circulatory problems later in life. Many people now use margarine and vegetable oils containing **polyunsaturated** fats instead of butter and cream. Polyunsaturated fats are present in plant oils and do not lead to cholesterol deposits.

Fig 5.1 Some foods rich in carbohydrate

Storing carbohydrates and lipids

If the body has more carbohydrate or fat than it needs, some of this can be changed into substances that can be stored. (This is not the case with excess protein.)

Carbohydrate is stored in the body as **glycogen**. This is stored in the liver and the muscles. Any further surplus can be changed into fat.

Any fat which is not used up to give up its energy or to form other substances for the body is stored in fat cells. This 'fat' collects around organs and under the skin. Some acts as a useful insulator against heat loss and helps the survival of animals which live in cold climates. It can be used for energy when the animal is short of food. However, too much stored fat makes a person overweight and this may lead to a variety of health risks.

Proteins

▲ **Fig 5.3 Some foods rich in protein**

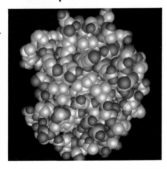

► **Fig 5.4 Proteins are made up of building blocks called amino acids linked in long chains. The chains are folded up like this to make a protein molecule**

Protein molecules are long chains made of building blocks called **amino acids**. Each amino acid contains carbon, hydrogen, oxygen and nitrogen, and sometimes phosphorus or sulphur.

Proteins are used for growth and repair of tissues. All **enzymes** are proteins and so all chemical reactions which are controlled by enzymes depend on proteins.

If the body is short of carbohydrate and lipids for energy, it can use proteins instead. However, if the body has more protein that it can use immediately, it is chemically changed and then excreted (see page 19).

Q1 The table below shows the foods present in a meal eaten by Jane, a fifth form girl, at lunchtime.

   a From the table calculate the total energy value of this meal.

   b i If Jane's total daily energy requirement is 9600 kJ, what further energy requirement will she need on this day?

     ii What proportion of her daily energy need is provided by this meal?

   c i Name the food in this meal which has the richest protein content.

     ii Explain why it is important for Jane to have sufficient protein in her diet.

   d Explain the importance of iron and vitamin C in the diet.

   e Explain what would happen if Jane's daily energy intake regularly exceeded 9600 kJ.

   f The recommended ratio of carbohydrate to fat in a balanced diet is 5:1. State their approximate ratio in this meal.

   g The table shows the absence of one very important constituent of the diet. Name this substance and state its importance in the diet. [11]

(WJEC Common Syllabus (Biology) 1987 Q16)

Food	Weight eaten (g)	Energy value (kJ)	Protein (g)	Fat (g)	Carbohydrate (g)	Iron (mg)	Vitamin C (mg)
beefburger	80	1200	10	24	6	1	0
chips	180	1890	7	18	65	2	18
beans	200	500	9	1	18	2·7	3·5
rhubarb tart	150	1800	5	25	60	1	1
ice cream	60	460	2·5	14	24	0	0
lemonade	300 ml	550	0	0	30	0	0

6 DIGESTION

By the end of this section you should be able to

- understand the life process of digestion
- understand that digestion is brought about by the action of enzymes
- relate the structure of the small intestine to the absorption of the products of digestion.

Fig 6.1 Digestion in the human alimentary canal ▼

BREAKING DOWN THE MOLECULES

The need for digestion

After you have finished your dinner, your meal is still on the outside of your body! This is because your digestive system is a long tube through your body, connected to the outside world at both ends. Before the protein, carbohydrate, fat, minerals and vitamins can be used by your body, the meal has to get inside your cells.

In order to be absorbed by living cells, food must first be broken down to smaller, water-soluble substances. The carbohydrates must be broken down to simple sugars, the fats to glycerol and fatty acids, and the proteins to amino acids.

Digestion and absorption

This breakdown of large molecules into smaller simpler ones is called **digestion**. The products of digestion, the smaller molecules, can then be **absorbed** into cells and used for respiration or for other purposes. Fig 6.1 shows the human digestive system and the **enzymes** (see page 157) that digest food, and fig 6.2 shows how the products of digestion are absorbed.

TYPES OF DIGESTION

Intracellular digestion

Single-celled animals such as *Amoeba*, fig 6.3, surround their food and form food vacuoles separated from the cytoplasm by a membrane. Enzymes are secreted by the cytoplasm and diffuse into the vacuoles where digestion occurs. The products of digestion then diffuse into the cytoplasm. Digestion within a food vacuole like this is called **intracellular digestion.** This kind of digestion occurs in plants, single-celled animals and sponges.

▼ **Fig 6.2 Structure of the ileum, where the products of digestion are absorbed into the blood. The muscle layers enable the ileum to move and mix the digested food, and the villi can move**

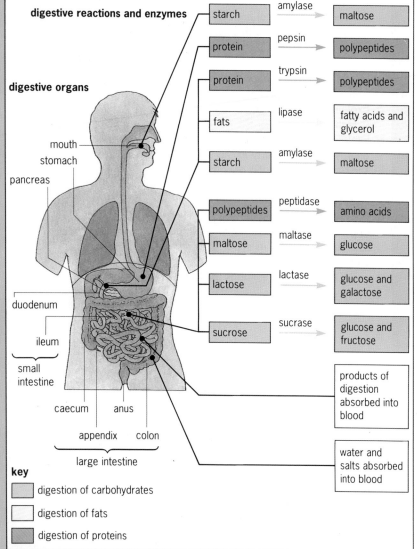

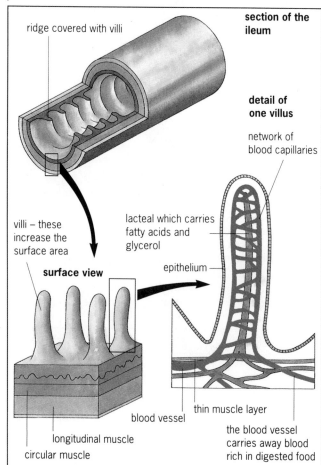

14

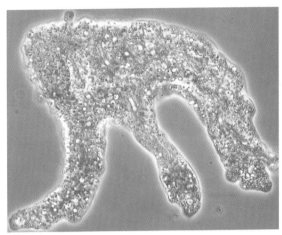

▲ Fig 6.3 *Amoeba* carries out intracellular digestion. Three pseudopodia are reaching out to find food particles and engulf them

Extracellular digestion

Intracellular digestion is not suitable for digesting the food of organisms that 'eat' relatively large pieces of food. The cells of bacteria and fungi secrete enzymes directly onto their food. The food is digested outside the cell and then the products absorbed. This type of digestion is called **extracellular digestion**, and is not limited to bacteria and fungi. A few green plants have leaves that can trap insects to be used as food. One of the most dramatic is the Venus flytrap. Its leaves close on a fly, which is digested by enzymes secreted by glands in the leaves.

Most animals combine both intracellular and extracellular digestion. With the development of the digestive tract, digestion chiefly becomes extracellular, because the food we swallow still lies, in effect, outside our bodies.

Q1 We produce an enzyme in our mouth which digests starch. A scientist measured the amount of this enzyme in three groups of people who eat different foods. The results were

Group	Food eaten	Amount of enzyme in mouth (units per cm³)
A	mixed diet of meat, vegetables, fruit and cereals	101
B	mainly meat	22
C	mainly starchy cereals	248

a How does the type of food eaten affect the amount of enzyme produced? [1]

b The following information was obtained from an experiment involving the digestion of starch by this enzyme.

Temperature (°C)	Amount of starch digested in one minute (g)
5	32
25	164
35	216
45	204
65	36

i Plot a graph to show these results using graph paper. [5]

ii What does the graph tell you about the effect of temperature on starch digestion? [1]
(WJEC Modular Science 1990 Q1)

Q2 Seven groups of pupils carried out an experiment in which they used identical thin slices of boiled egg white. These were placed in test tubes in water baths at different temperatures. Into each test tube a small amount of dilute hydrochloric acid and some enzyme were added, fig 6.4.

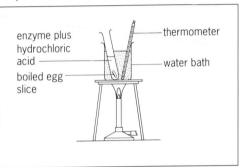

◄ Fig 6.4

The time taken for the egg white to disappear was recorded for each test tube. Here are the results.

Temperature (°C)	15	20	25	30	35	40	45
Time taken for egg white to disappear (min)	4.2	3.1	1.5	1.0	1.0	2.2	2.9

a Use the results to draw a graph. Plot the points and connect them with a line. [4]

b Write *one* conclusion made from your graph. [1]

c In what part of the digestive system would you expect to find an enzyme similar to the one used in the experiment? [1]

d Explain why the egg white disappears.

e Explain why the egg white disappears faster at 30°C compared with 45°C. [1]
(WJEC Modular Science 1989 Q1)

LIFE PROCESSES

7 DIGESTIVE ORGANS

By the end of this section you should be able to
- recall the main types of digestive organ
- understand how food is prepared for digestion
- understand the role of bacteria in digestion by ruminants and by humans.

TYPES OF DIGESTIVE ORGAN

Food pouches

Jellyfish and many flat- and roundworms carry out extracellular digestion in a digestive **pouch**. Food enters the cavity and undigested remains leave through the same opening. The tissue lining these simple digestive cavities is made up of cells that secrete digestive enzymes into the cavity. Once the food is partially broken down, particles are engulfed by cells of the lining tissue. Digestion is then completed within food vacuoles of the cells.

Extracellular digestion makes it possible for these animals to eat large pieces of food. By comparison, the food used by *Amoeba* and other single-celled animals must be small enough to be surrounded and engulfed by a single cell.

Digestive tracts

Earthworms, somewhat more complex than the flat- and roundworms mentioned above, and more complex animals have **digestive tracts** that are tubes with openings at both ends.

Parts of the digestive tract are often quite different in form in various animal groups, but many of the parts are almost alike in function. The main differences between the digestive tracts of an earthworm and a human are that
1. the digestive part of the human canal is lengthened to provide a larger absorbing surface
2. the human tract has a more elaborate blood supply to carry away absorbed products
3. the human has a **liver** which acts as a vast workshop of enzymes where food may be stored, sorted or prepared for oxidation or excretion.

PREPARING FOOD FOR DIGESTION

'Chewing' and 'swallowing'

Food is prepared for digestion in many different ways. The earthworm and birds grind their food in a muscular **gizzard** containing small stones. Lobsters, crabs and some insects have mouthparts like knives and forks, which break the food into bits before it is swallowed, fig 7.1. The starfish turns its stomach inside out, and digests its food before swallowing it. Snakes swallow their prey whole, fig 7.2, and digest it over a long period of time. Fish and snakes have teeth adapted for catching their prey, while mammals have biting and grinding teeth.

▲ **Fig 7.1 The mouthparts of a crab are like knives and forks, and are used to shred food**

▲ **Fig 7.2 Snakes swallow their prey whole**

THE ROLE OF BACTERIA

Chewing the cud

Digestion in some **herbivorous** animals (that eat vegetable matter such as grass), including cows, sheep, goats, camels, deer and antelopes, differs from that of most creatures. Their teeth are adapted for grinding up their food well, while those of **carnivorous** animals are adapted for catching and tearing their prey, fig 7.3. The ground-up plant food goes first to the **rumen**, one section of a four-chambered stomach, fig 7.4. Afterwards the food is returned to the mouth and the animal 'chews the cud'. In the rumen, the food is acted on by some very large bacteria which digest cellulose of the plant cell walls. Mammals cannot digest this material themselves and so rely on the bacteria to do it for them. This is an example of **symbiosis**, where two organisms of different species live together for mutual benefit. Similar bacteria live in the large intestine of the horse and other non-ruminant herbivores.

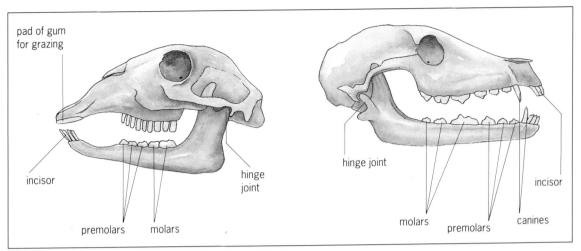

▲ **Fig 7.3 The teeth of a mammal are specialised for a particular function. The teeth of a herbivore such as a sheep (left) are adapted for grazing and grinding, while those of a carnivore such as a dog (right) are adapted for catching and tearing prey**

Bacteria in the human gut

Humans cannot digest cellulose, and for us it acts as bulk for the intestinal muscles to act on, and helps them to pass undigested food or **faeces** to the anus for **egestion**. Faeces also contain worn-out blood pigments that enter the intestine in bile, secreted by the liver. Half the weight of faeces may be bacteria that lived and multiplied in the intestine, and are now dead. Such bacteria do not harm the host. Many make vitamins that the host cannot make for itself. However, it is possible that intestinal bacteria may cause disease in other parts of the body, or in the intestine of a host not accustomed to them.

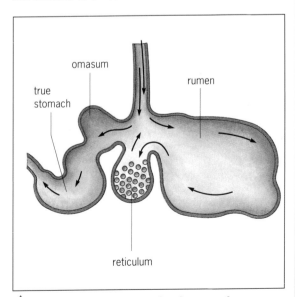

▲ **Fig 7.4 In a ruminant, food enters the rumen where it is acted on by bacteria mixed with digestive juices. It then passes to the reticulum and is returned to the mouth to be chewed. Chewed cud then passes to the omasum and then to the true stomach**

Q1 Fig 7.5 shows the lining of part of the alimentary canal (digestive system).

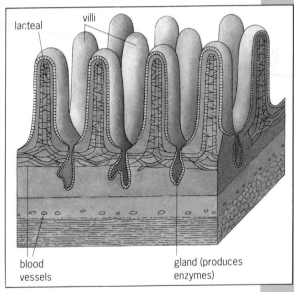

▲ **Fig 7.5**

a Name the part of the alimentary canal which has such a lining. [1]

b If the surface area of a single villus is 5 mm², what is the total surface area of all the villi shown? [1]

c **i** State *two* functions carried out by this part of the alimentary canal. [2]

 ii What can you observe on the diagram to help you answer the last question **ci**? [2]

(WJEC Modular Science 1991 (part))

8 EXCRETION

By the end of this section you should be able to
- understand the life process of excretion
- compare different methods of excretion
- describe the mammalian excretory system.

All living cells eventually die. Cells must constantly maintain a balance between the processes that produce order and structure, and those that destroy cells.

THE NEED FOR EXCRETION

The activities that feed cells must be balanced by **excretion** – the carrying away of wastes and by-products that cells cannot use. These chemicals would poison the cell if allowed to build up. Carbon dioxide and water are produced in excess by cells that are not photosynthesising. Urea, ammonia and uric acid are all nitrogen-containing by-products of protein reactions in cells.

Excretory systems

In mammals and other complex animals with blood systems, excretory products are carried in the blood. A specialised **excretory system** removes them and so tends to keep the composition of the blood nearly constant. This is essentially different from elimination by **egestion** (see page 17) which is the removal of undigested material from the digestive system.

Excretion in plants

Plants as a rule do not have an organised excretory system. Carbon dioxide and oxygen diffuse in and out through the stomata as necessary, depending on whether photosynthesis is taking place. Water usually evaporates (**transpires**) from the underside of leaves and is replaced by water from the soil. Other excretory products may form crystals in cells.

METHODS OF EXCRETION IN ANIMALS

Apart from carbon dioxide, the main waste products in animals are nitrogen compounds such as ammonia, formed when amino groups are removed from amino acids that are not needed by the body.

Excretion by diffusion

Ammonia is highly soluble in water, so one way of getting rid of it is by diffusion. Simple sea animals have body fluids with a composition similar to sea water. Ammonia diffuses freely out of the cells.

Similar freshwater animals have body fluids with a higher concentration of dissolved materials than their surroundings. Water tends to flow into their cells by a process called **osmosis**. Water and dissolved waste therefore have to be excreted. *Amoeba* pumps out excess water from a **contractile vacuole**, fig 8.1.

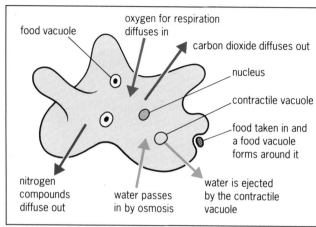

▲ **Fig 8.1 The contractile vacuole of *Amoeba* expels water from the cell**

Simple excretory systems

In more complex animals, beginning with the flatworms, an excretory system is present. It consists of tubes called **nephridia** branching among the tissues and opening to the outside, fig 8.2. Cilia maintain an outward current of the excreted material.

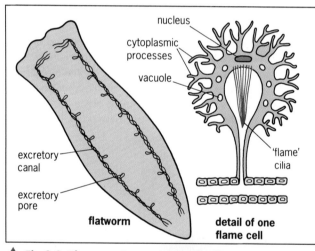

▲ **Fig 8.2 The excretory system of a flatworm consists of a simple system of branched tubes called nephridia, each ending in a flame cell. The flickering cilia give the cell its name**

In annelids and molluscs the system is more intricate. Capillaries surround the nephridia. Waste products diffuse out of the blood into the excretory tube and pass to the outside.

Lobsters, crabs and their relatives have a special method of excreting ammonia. They get rid of some dissolved waste through a pair of small **excretory glands**, but most nitrogen-containing material is used to make their exoskeleton.

Marine fish swallow water and excrete mineral salts through special cells in their gills.

Uric acid

In animals that lay eggs on land, such as insects, reptiles and birds, ammonia and carbon dioxide are combined to make **uric acid**, a substance that is not very soluble. In the developing egg, waste nitrogen accumulates as uric acid which is discarded at hatching. In the adults, dissolved waste is concentrated to a solid urine, passed to the end of the digestive tube and expelled with the faeces.

THE MAMMALIAN EXCRETORY SYSTEM

In higher animals such as mammals, excretion of nitrogen compounds is carried out by the **kidneys**, fig 8.3, and the excreted fluid containing the waste nitrogen compounds and excess salt is called **urine**.

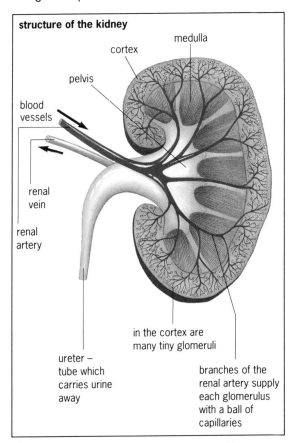

structure of the kidney

medulla
cortex
pelvis
blood vessels
renal vein
renal artery
in the cortex are many tiny glomeruli
ureter – tube which carries urine away
branches of the renal artery supply each glomerulus with a ball of capillaries

▲ **Fig 8.3 The structure of the mammalian kidney**

Urine contains **urea**, the main form in which nitrogen is excreted in mammals. Urea is a very soluble and relatively harmless substance that can be carried in less water than is needed to carry the same amount of ammonia.

What happens in the kidney?

By the pressure of the heartbeat, arterial blood is forced through the capillaries in the **glomerulus**, fig 8.4. This acts as a filter, and small soluble

molecules including urea pass through the capillary walls into the **Bowman's capsule**. Large molecules such as proteins remain in the blood, unless the kidney is damaged or diseased. As the filtrate passes along the tubule and through the loop of Henlé, the cells take back useful substances including glucose, some salts and some water and return them to the blood. Urea and other waste molecules remain in the filtrate. This is now urine, which passes into the **bladder**, fig 8.5.

▼ **Fig 8.4 How the kidney functions – detail of one nephron**

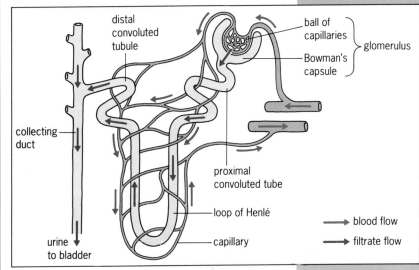

distal convoluted tubule
ball of capillaries
glomerulus
Bowman's capsule
collecting duct
proximal convoluted tube
loop of Henlé
urine to bladder
capillary
→ blood flow
→ filtrate flow

◄ **Fig 8.5 The human urinary system**

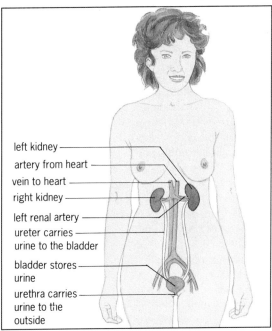

left kidney
artery from heart
vein to heart
right kidney
left renal artery
ureter carries urine to the bladder
bladder stores urine
urethra carries urine to the outside

There is more about the control of the kidneys on pages 48–9.

 Q1 Explain this statement

'Plants excrete oxygen during the day and excrete carbon dioxide during the day and night.'

9 RESPONSE AND MOVEMENT

By the end of this section you should be able to

- understand the life process of movement
- compare different methods of movement.

METHODS OF MOVEMENT

Animals must move in search of food in order to survive. Methods of movement vary. We move using similar principles to other land-living vertebrates, the action of **muscles** on a **skeleton**. Single-celled animals rely on properties of the cytoplasm to move their cells around. Some animals such as earthworms rely on the fact that liquid is incompressible. They force liquid forward within their bodies by the action of muscles, fig 9.1. Many invertebrates move without the aid of a skeleton.

Fig 9.1 Many invertebrates such as earthworms move without the aid of a skeleton ▶

MOVEMENT IN MAMMALS

Control

Muscles provide the power for our movement, but that power has to be harnessed and controlled to provide the wide variety of physical activities that we carry out. This variety depends on the arrangement of the body's movable parts – mainly the limbs and the trunk. These elements are linked in ways which allow movements in various planes.

The starting point for any movement is a **nerve signal**. If the movement is **voluntary**, then the signal results from a conscious decision to move a part of the body. Movement could also be an **automatic response** to some **stimulus**, such as pain, tickling, loss of balance, etc. This kind of movement may happen without our making a conscious decision. It involves the detection of the stimulus by a **receptor**, such as cells sensitive to touch, pain or light, for example. The organ that brings about the response is called the **effector**, a muscle or set of muscles when the response is a movement. There is more about this on page 24.

Whether a movement is voluntary or automatic, the nerve signal is the beginning of a carefully controlled sequence of events in the body involving nerves, muscles, joints, the brain and the inner ear.

Muscles

Muscles bring about the movements of bones. Muscles which move the skeleton (**skeletal muscles**, fig 9.2) have long slender cells which can **contract** or shorten. Muscle fibres contract when supplied with energy from adenosine triphosphate (see page 2), after being activated by a **nerve impulse**. Muscle fibres may also be stimulated by heat, light, chemicals, pressure and electricity.

Nerve cells carry these impulses to the muscles. The nerve cells branch, and each branch stimulates a few muscle fibres, fig 9.3. The combination of nerve cells and muscle fibres is called a **motor unit**, and the point where the nerve fibre joins the muscle fibre is the **motor end plate**.

When stimulated, each fibre contracts. The strength of each fibre's contraction is always the same, but the amount of contraction of the whole muscle depends on how many motor units are called into action. The more units that contract, the greater the movement. In this way, we can control movements to be very precise or very forceful.

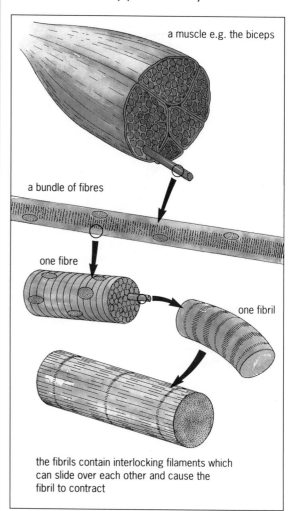

a muscle e.g. the biceps

a bundle of fibres

one fibre

one fibril

the fibrils contain interlocking filaments which can slide over each other and cause the fibril to contract

▲ **Fig 9.2 The structure of a voluntary (striped) muscle**

20

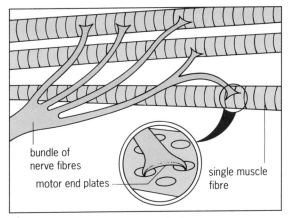

Fig 9.3 Nerves transmit their messages to muscles at motor end plates

bundle of nerve fibres

motor end plates

single muscle fibre

How muscles produce movement

Muscles are attached to bones via **tendons**. A muscle will be attached to two different bones, and when it contracts, it moves the bones at a joint, like a lever.

It is usually the case that the contraction of one muscle to move a part of the body is accompanied by the relaxation of another muscle. For example, bending the elbow by contracting the **biceps** muscle at the front of the upper arm means that the muscle at the back (the **triceps**) must **relax** or lengthen to allow the arm to be pulled up, fig 9.4. This is called **antagonistic action** – members of a pair of muscles act in opposition to bring about movement.

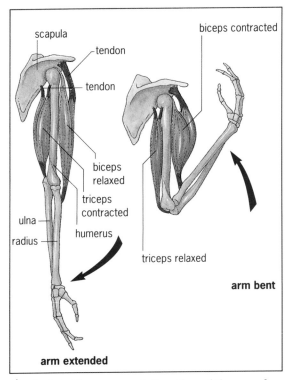

scapula

tendon

tendon

biceps contracted

biceps relaxed

triceps contracted

ulna

radius

humerus

triceps relaxed

arm bent

arm extended

Fig 9.4 The antagonistic action of the muscles of the upper arm

Activity
How strong is your arm?

1 Place your arm on a flat surface as shown in fig 9.5 with your upper arm in position X.
2 Fix a forcemeter to an immovable point below the bench as shown.
3 Without moving the upper arm, pull on the forcemeter and record the maximum force you can exert.
4 After resting the arm, repeat the procedure with the upper arm held in positions Y and Z.

Q1 Which is the best position to hold your arm when you lift things? Explain your answer.

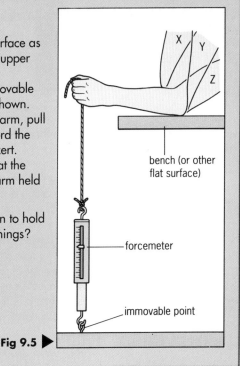

bench (or other flat surface)

forcemeter

immovable point

Fig 9.5 ▶

Q2 **a** The drawings in fig 9.6 (not in sequence) show how our nervous system helps us to respond quickly in dangerous situations, such as a car driver braking suddenly to avoid hitting a child.

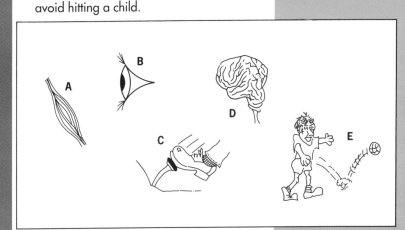

▲ **Fig 9.6**

The diagrams are not drawn to scale.

In the above situation use the letter to identify
i the stimulus
ii the effector
iii the receptor. [3]
b What links all these different parts together in the body? [1]
(WJEC Modular Science 1991 Q5)

LIFE PROCESSES

10 JOINTS

By the end of this section you should be able to
- recall the different types of joint
- recall the structure of a joint.

JOINTS IN THE HUMAN BODY

There are more than 200 **joints** in the human body, each designed to allow a greater or lesser amount of movement about a specific point, fig 10.1. Some joints give a lot of freedom of movement – the hip, for example, which is a **ball-and-socket joint**. Other joints allow only a very restricted range, for example, the knee can only move in one plane – it is a **hinge joint**. (You may think that your knee can move in any direction, but it is the hip joint that plays the major part in the movement of the lower leg. Try to move your knee without moving your hip and you will see just how limited the movement is.)

There are more than 100 joints in the backbone or **vertebral column**. Though the range of movement of the individual joints is small, except for those in the neck, their combined movements can dramatically arch or bend the back.

THE STRUCTURE OF JOINTS

Designed for life

Although the joints may seem to be simple linkages, they have a wide variety of complex structures. Machines can achieve some of the actions of joints quite simply. Rods linked with pins can transmit the force to where it is needed, and rubber pads can protect surfaces in contact. However, rubber perishes, metal corrodes and friction wears away points of contact. In the human body, every joint is designed to last for 70 years or more. To reduce wear and tear, the friction between surfaces is kept to an absolute minimum. As we grow, each joint has to adapt to the increasing size and strength of the body.

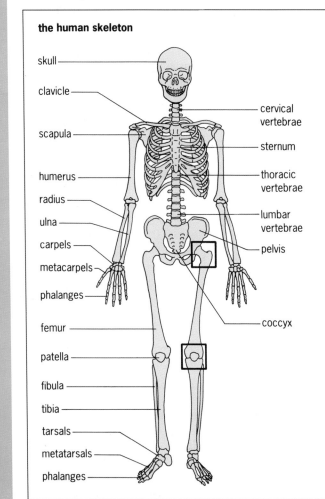

the human skeleton

- skull
- clavicle
- scapula
- humerus
- radius
- ulna
- carpels
- metacarpels
- phalanges
- femur
- patella
- fibula
- tibia
- tarsals
- metatarsals
- phalanges
- cervical vertebrae
- sternum
- thoracic vertebrae
- lumbar vertebrae
- pelvis
- coccyx

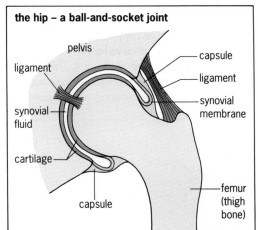

the hip – a ball-and-socket joint

- pelvis
- ligament
- synovial fluid
- cartilage
- capsule
- capsule
- ligament
- synovial membrane
- femur (thigh bone)

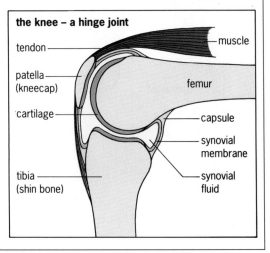

the knee – a hinge joint

- tendon
- patella (kneecap)
- cartilage
- tibia (shin bone)
- muscle
- femur
- capsule
- synovial membrane
- synovial fluid

▲ **Fig 10.1 The human skeleton and two different types of joint**

Fulfilling the design brief

A joint like the knee has a structure that has evolved to overcome all of these problems. The two bones that meet at the hinge are held together by **ligaments**, sheets of a tough elastic fibre called **collagen**. Inside a **capsule** of collagen, the bone ends are cushioned in a closed pocket of lubricating fluid, the **synovial fluid**. When the knee bends the two bones do not come into contact, but are kept apart by the pressure generated in the fluid. The structure of this fluid makes it as good a lubricant as oil in a machine. In the joint, however, the lubricant never has to be drained and replaced because it is recycled. Like many body fluids, the synovial fluid is filtered out of the blood plasma and has some special thickening ingredients added by the cells of the **synovial membrane** that lines the joint.

With joints like the hip, knee and ankle all having this kind of lubrication and suspension, the body can withstand strenuous activity without jarring and damaging the joints. Some of these joints can take the impact strain of up to 20 times the force of gravity without any damage.

When joints wear out

For 70 years or so, this lubrication and suspension system generally works quite well. As we get older, however, movement of the joints can become less smooth and increasingly difficult. Inflammation caused by the disease **arthritis** may occur in some of the joints, producing pain and sometimes damaging the ends of the bones.

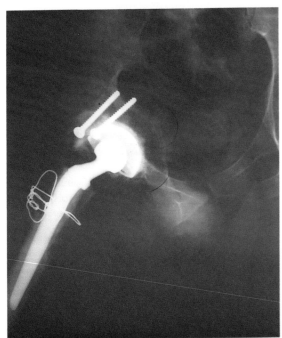

▲ **Fig 10.2 X-ray showing an artificial hip, replacing a hip joint damaged by rheumatoid arthritis**

Q1 Fig 10.3 shows a section through a hinge joint.

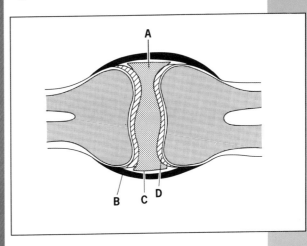

◀ **Fig 10.3**

a Write labels for **A–D**.
b Name *one* example of this type of joint.
c Name the part that
  i acts like oil and lubricates the joint
  ii acts as a shock absorber
  iii produces the lubricant (oily liquid).   [6]
(WJEC Common Syllabus (Biology) 1986 Q3)

Q2

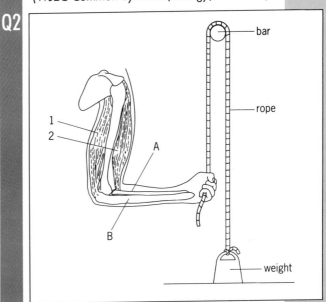

◀ **Fig 10.4**

Fig 10.4 shows some of the muscles and bones in a human arm about to raise a heavy weight.

a Name muscle **1** and muscle **2**.
b State what happens to muscle **1** and muscle **2** when the weight is raised.
c Name the bones of the leg which are equivalent to bones **A** and **B**.
d Explain how *two* internal features of the shoulder joint ensure smoothness of movement.   [5]
(WJEC Common Syllabus (Biology) 1986 Q8)

11 IRRITABILITY

By the end of this section you should be able to
- understand the life process of sensitivity in animals
- compare systems of irritability in different classes of animals.

Living protoplasm has the unique ability of **irritability.** Because of this, all living organisms are able to respond to changes in their external environment which could harm them, in such a way that their internal environment is protected.

STIMULUS AND RESPONSE

Many changes in the external environment **stimulate** living organisms to make **responses.** Animals register many types of changes in their environment with the help of **sense organs.** The same environmental conditions may lead to different types of response from different types of organism. For example, light gives rise to a variety of responses. Some animals, such as moths, fly towards it; others, such as earthworms, prefer darkness. All such responses are to the advantage of the organism and aid survival.

The mechanism of irritability

Changes in surroundings that can be sensed by organisms are called **stimuli**. If, for example, a person unknowingly touches something very hot, the hand is withdrawn very quickly. The skin can sense that it is in contact with something hot. The response that the person makes is due to this stimulus. However, if the person had been given a local anaesthetic in the hand before touching the hot surface, it would not be possible to register the stimulus, and no response would follow. A response is always preceded by a stimulus.

Irritability can be summarised as follows
1 A stimulus is received by a **receptor** at a particular point on the body.
2 The stimulus is conducted to other parts of the body.
3 A response is made by an **effector**. The effector may not be located at the part of the organism that received the stimulus.

IRRITABILITY IN ANIMALS

Most animals are able to respond to stimuli in a fraction of a second. This is of great value to a carnivore as it chases its fast-moving prey, or to the prey which has to defend itself against the lightning attacks of the predator. Speed of response is vital.

Nervous systems and sense organs

The speed with which animals are able to respond to stimuli is due to the nature of their nervous tissue. This links all the sense organs to all the organs of response, via the **central nervous system**. Messages can pass from our fingertips, for example, to the central nervous system and out to a responding muscle in a fraction of a second.

The larger and more complex animals have much more elaborate sense organs and nervous systems than the simpler ones. The cnidarians such as *Hydra* have nerve cells dotted about their bodies, fig 11.1. This nerve net links their special touch-sensitive cells to all the body cells. If something touches *Hydra*, part of its body may withdraw, or, if the stimulus is strong, the whole animal may move.

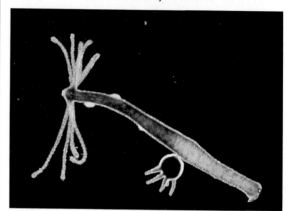

▲ **Fig 11.1** *Hydra* **has nerve cells dotted about its body**

The flatworms, for example *Planaria*, have small primitive eyes on the upper surface near the head, fig 11.2. Nerves radiate out from these organs to all parts of the body.

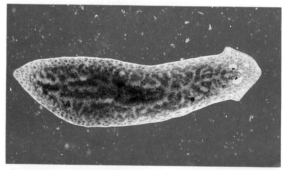

▲ **Fig 11.2 Flatworms have small primitive eyes**

A similar pattern is found in almost all animals where a 'brain' is present. In these animals, well-developed nerve tissue links all the sense organs to the 'brain' which is in turn linked to all the organs of response. In this way, the 'brain' is able to coordinate the responses the body makes to the many stimuli received by the sense organs.

The invertebrates have a variety of special organs. Some have very sensitive 'feelers', like the antennae of arthropods, fig 11.3; others have well-developed eyes. The insects are among the most highly developed invertebrates. They possess two large compound eyes, fig 11.4, and can make lightning responses to danger.

▲ **Fig 11.3 Arthropods such as this beetle often have long sensitive 'feelers' called antennae**

▲ **Fig 11.4 Compound eyes allow insects to see all around them**

Among the vertebrates, perhaps the greatest specialisation is shown by the birds and mammals. The eye of a hawk is an amazing organ of sight. Watching sparrows chasing one another demonstrates how quickly one bird can register and respond to the movements of the other.

Q1 Fig 11.5 shows the changes in the size of the pupils of a cat's eyes over 24 hours.

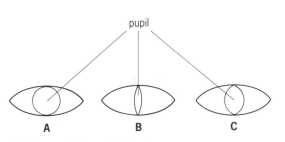

this diagram is drawn half life size

▲ **Fig 11.5**

a Copy and complete the table below. [3]

Eye	Maximum width of pupil (mm)	Possible time of day (dim light, bright light, darkness)
A		
B		
C		

b When a light is shone into the eye a rapid response is recorded.
  i What type of reaction is this? [1]
  ii What is the stimulus in this case? [1]
c The basic organisation of nervous control is shown below.

receptor → central nervous system → effector

Name
  i a receptor **ii** an effector
  iii part of the central nervous system. [3]
  (WJEC Modular Science 1991 Q5)

Q2 30 pupils were involved in an experiment to find out which areas of the tongue were most sensitive to sweet, sour, salt, and bitter liquids. The table below shows the number of pupils who indicated that they could taste the various liquids when the liquids were each placed on the different areas of the tongue.

Parts of tongue	Liquid A (sweet)	Liquid B (sour)	Liquid C (bitter)	Liquid D (salt)
back	2	12	28	8
front	27	10	12	22
side	8	29	10	21
middle	1	2	0	1

a Which area of the tongue appears to be most sensitive to the
  i bitter liquid **ii** sweet liquid?
b Explain why it is more difficult to tell from the results which area is most sensitive to the salt solution than it is to tell which area is most sensitive to the sour solution.
c State, with a reason, which area of the tongue seems to be *least* sensitive to chemical stimuli.
d Chemical stimuli from food on the taste buds of the tongue may start a reflex action. Name the effector in this reflex.
e State *three* ways in which this reflex is different from the response made by a plant's stem that has received light from one side. [9]
(WJEC Common Syllabus (Biology) 1984 Q7)

By the end of this section you should be able to

- explain the coordination of body activities through nervous control
- explain the mechanism of reflex actions.

THE BRAIN AND SENSE ORGANS

The sense organs and nervous system of humans are as highly developed as those of any other animal. Our brain is more advanced than that of any other creature. Our specialised sense organs include eyes, ears, nose, tongue and skin. The skin is sensitive to touch, and contains several types of sensory cell, each sensitive to heat, cold, pain or pressure. The organs listed above make up what are commonly called the **five senses**, but we are also sensitive to other stimuli. Special sense cells can register hunger or thirst. We are also able to tell when we are off balance by means of a gravity-sensitive organ in the inner ear.

Control of automatic responses

When something stimulates an invertebrate's sense organ, a response follows automatically. We can also make automatic responses to stimuli. However, we can often override an automatic response by conscious efforts. It is also possible for us to learn new responses. For example, our natural reaction when swallowing distasteful medicine is to spit it out, but we can overcome this response to the stimulus received by the tongue and make ourselves swallow. We can learn to catch an object thrown at us rather than avoid it.

REFLEX ACTIONS

The automatic responses that the human body makes to stimuli detected by the sense organs are called **reflex actions**. One of the best known reflex actions is the **knee-jerk response**. If the ligament just below the kneecap is tapped, then the knee joint straightens for a moment. Other widely known examples are the dilation of the pupil of the eye when a person goes into a dimly lit room, and the secretion of saliva when food is anticipated.

The mechanism of reflex actions

The sense organs of the body are linked, via the **central nervous system** (brain and spinal cord), to organs that effect a response. For example, when we smell food, this stimulus is carried along the **nerves** which pass from the nose back to the brain, and then out to the salivary glands. The whole circuit of nerve tissue between the sense organ and the organ of response is called a **reflex arc**.

Fig 12.1 shows the reflex arc involved in the knee-jerk response. When the hammer hits the ligament, several stretch-sensitive cells in the muscle are stimulated. This leads to a **nerve impulse** passing up the **sensory** or **afferent nerves** of the leg and all the way to the **spinal cord**. The fibres of these sensory nerves are parts of nerve cells or **neurones** whose cell bodies are gathered in a group called a **ganglion**. Thus the impulse reaches

Fig 12.1
The reflex arc of the knee-jerk response

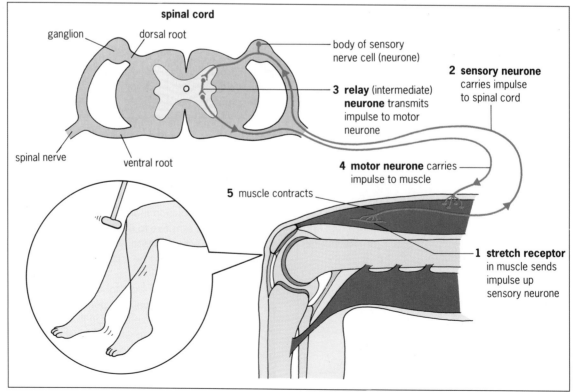

spinal cord

ganglion

dorsal root

body of sensory nerve cell (neurone)

3 relay (intermediate) **neurone** transmits impulse to motor neurone

2 sensory neurone carries impulse to spinal cord

spinal nerve

ventral root

4 motor neurone carries impulse to muscle

5 muscle contracts

1 stretch receptor in muscle sends impulse up sensory neurone

the central nervous system. A **motor** or **efferent nerve** fibre leads from the spinal cord to the organ of response, which in this case is the muscle of the leg. The sensory and motor nerve fibres are connected in the spinal cord by a **relay neurone**.

The ends of nerve fibres do not quite touch each other in the central nervous system. The impulse is transmitted across the gap (**synapse**) between the nerve fibres by production of a transmitter substance, **acetyl choline**.

Thus, armed with a variety of sense organs which are able to register many kinds of stimuli, and the means of transmitting these very quickly to the organs of response, humans and other mammals are very well equipped to defend themselves against changes in the external environment which could harm them.

Q1 Fig 12.2 shows some of the structures involved in a simple reflex action. The hand is about to touch a drawing pin.

a Write labels for structures **A–D**.
b State what happens to muscle **R** when the forearm is raised.
c List, in order, the nerve fibres along which the impulse (message) must travel from the hand to the muscle.

d Name the type of joint found at the elbow.
e State another example of a reflex action which is used to protect the body. [6]
(WJEC Common Syllabus (Biology) 1984 Q9)

Q2 Imagine that you are walking along a sunlit pathway, and you enter an area of dark woodland. You fail to see a tree root in front of you and you trip and fall over, bruising your knee.

a Name one stimulus suggested in the above statement. [1]
b What type of response occurs to the eye on entering the woodland? [1]
c State precisely what changes occur in the eye when you go into the wood. [2]
d Why would you not see a tree root immediately after going into the wood? [1]
e How does the sensation of pain from the knee reach the brain? [1]
f Why is it necessary for the body to be able to respond to this type of situation? [1]
g State *one* difference between this type of response and the response obtained by the action of hormones. [1]

◄ **Fig 12.2**

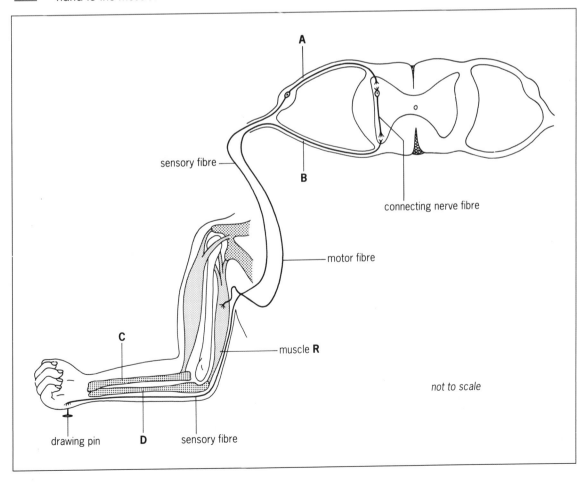

A

sensory fibre

B

connecting nerve fibre

motor fibre

muscle **R**

C

not to scale

drawing pin   D   sensory fibre

13 DRUGS AND THE NERVOUS SYSTEM

By the end of this section you should be able to
understand the effects of alcohol and other drugs on the nervous system and the rest of the body.

WHAT IS A DRUG?

A **drug** is any substance which interferes with the normal functioning of the body. Some drugs may become **addictive** – once people start to take them they find it difficult to stop, because they experience **withdrawal symptoms**.

Some drugs are extracted from plants and are called **natural** drugs. Others are synthesised in laboratories and are called **synthetic** drugs. There are natural drugs in coffee, tea, cocoa and the kola nut, from which cola drinks are made. The drugs in these drinks prevent sleep and cause emotional excitement. They are called **stimulating** drugs.

ALCOHOL

Heating up and drying out

Alcohol or **ethanol** can be absorbed into your bloodstream within two minutes of being swallowed. It is carried to the cells and passes through their membranes. In the cells it is oxidised, releasing heat and raising the blood temperature. This in turn stimulates the heat control centre of the brain (see page 50) and causes increased blood circulation to the skin. While the skin radiates heat, the internal organs are not receiving an adequate supply of blood. During oxidation, alcohol produces water. This is excreted by the skin to control temperature and, as a result, the body suffers dehydration and concentrates wastes in the kidneys.

Over the limit?

Not all the alcohol taken in is oxidised. Part is released into the lungs as vapour. This causes breath odour and is the basis of the **breathalyser** test for drivers, fig 13.1. Some goes to the skin and is added to sweat. Some passes to the kidneys and leaves in the urine.

Fig 13.1
Alcohol breath odour is the basis of the breathalyser test

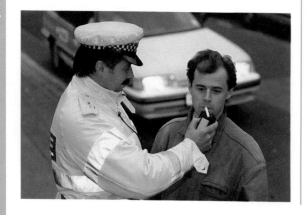

Alcohol is absorbed by all the body organs, but some organs are affected more than others.

Drinking too much

Alcohol has an **anaesthetic** or numbing effect on the nervous system. The brain is affected, leading to changes in emotional control, blurred vision, slurring of speech and dizziness. In the final stages of drunkenness, the brain cortex stops working, leaving the person unconscious. Heart action and breathing rate slow down and, in extreme cases of **alcoholic poisoning**, will stop altogether, leading to death.

Long-term effects of alcohol abuse

Vitamin-deficiency diseases are common among people who persistently drink too much, because they will eat little food during long periods of heavy drinking. The liver therefore gives up its stored glycogen and swells as carbohydrates are replaced by fats. Over a long time, this leads to **cirrhosis**. The liver hardens and shrinks as the fats are used. Cirrhosis occurs eight times more frequently in heavy drinkers than in others.

Excessive use of alcohol can also affect the stomach leading to **gastritis**, a painful swelling of the stomach lining.

NARCOTICS

Narcotics are potentially addictive drugs. They produce sleep and relieve pain. The use or possession of all unprescribed narcotics is illegal.

Opium and **cocaine** form the basis of the most common narcotics. Opium comes from the juice of the white poppy. **Morphine** and **codeine** are both made from opium. **Heroin** is a synthetic compound made from morphine.

Cocaine comes from the leaves of the South American coca plant (not to be confused with the cacao plant which produces cocoa beans) and is used to deaden nerves. Dentists often use substances made from cocaine to deaden areas when filling cavities in teeth or during extractions.

Abuse of narcotics

The misuse of narcotics may stem from similar circumstances to the misuse of alcohol. People who take heroin may feel better about their problems at first. They go into a dream world, but the effects soon wear off. Another dose is needed to get the dream-like feeling back again. Eventually a craving builds up. The user has to take more and more heroin to get the same effect, as the body begins to develop a **tolerance** for the drug. Ten times the original dose may eventually be needed and the user will become addicted.

When the effects of heroin begin to wear off, the withdrawal symptoms are serious. Temperature and blood pressure increase. Sweating, vomiting and diarrhoea occur. The addict's resistance to disease is lowered. The body's cells now need the drug and the user becomes so desperate for a supply of the drug that rational thought is impossible and the person's complete lifestyle degenerates.

OTHER DRUGS

Tranquillisers

Tranquillisers can reduce emotional anxiety, relieve pain or make you sleep. They are often prescribed by doctors. They are not addictive in the same way as narcotics are, but people can come to depend on them psychologically.

Barbiturates are synthetic drugs which are sometimes abused. Barbiturates can be deadly when combined with alcohol.

Stimulants

Amphetamines are stimulant drugs. They are used in 'pep pills'. People often take them to stay awake. They impair judgement and vision and may produce hallucinations. Amphetamines are not physically addictive, but users become emotionally dependent on them.

Psychedelic or 'mind-expanding' drugs

Psychedelic drugs are chemical compounds that affect the mind. They change sensory perception and cause hallucinations. The most common psychedelic drugs are **LSD**, **mescaline** and **psilocybin**. Mescaline comes from the mescal or peyote cactus. Psilocybin is prepared from certain mushrooms.

LSD is **d-lysergic acid diethylamide.** It easily diffuses into the brain via the bloodstream and is very powerful even in extremely small doses. During pregnancy, it can diffuse through the placenta and into the fetus, where it can cause damage to chromosomes. Physical reactions to LSD seem to vary, as do users' emotions. Heart rate and blood pressure may increase. Suicides and mental breakdown have been attributed to this drug.

Marijuana

Marijuana comes from the flowers, leaves and seeds of *Cannibis sativa*, the Indian hemp. It can be eaten but is usually smoked like tobacco. It is psychologically addictive. It is rapidly passed from the blood to the brain.

Lung cancer and a condition leading to the birth of deformed children are possible consequences for users of this drug.

Solvents

Solvent abuse has become a serious problem among young people. The habit is deadly. Solvents which are abused in this way include kerosene, paint thinner, glues and lighter fuel. After inhalation these solvents diffuse into the bloodstream and the user feels dizzy and loses coordination. Slurred speech, blurred vision, loss of colour vision and sickness are other symptoms. Solvent inhalation often leads to unconsciousness and death. Users invariably suffer permanent liver, kidney and brain damage.

Q1 Before going to lunch at 1 p.m., Dennis had a glass of sherry. During lunch he drank two glasses of wine and a brandy. He returned to work at 2 p.m. and worked until 5.30 p.m. On leaving work Dennis drank two pints of beer and at 8 p.m. drove home.

Fig 13.2 shows the level of alcohol in Dennis's blood from lunchtime onwards.

▼ **Fig 13.2**

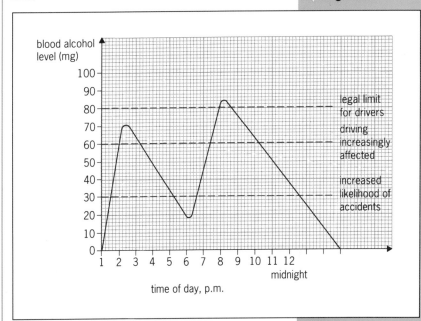

a From the graph, state the time when
  i the alcohol level in Dennis's blood was at its highest
  ii he was most likely to have an accident at work.
b If Dennis had not drunk any beer, when would his blood alcohol level have probably returned to zero?
c Until what time should he have delayed driving home to be within the legal limit for drivers?
d Assuming that he got home, state when his blood would have no alcohol in it.   [5]
(WJEC Common Syllabus (Biology) 1984 Q10)

14 CHEMICAL CONTROL

By the end of this section you should be able to

- explain the coordination in mammals of the body's activities through hormonal control
- understand how hormones can be used to promote fertility, growth and development in plants and animals
- be aware of the implications of the use of hormones.

CHEMICAL CONTROL IN ANIMALS

Endocrine glands

Some glands, like the salivary glands, pour secretions into the digestive tract through **ducts**. We call these **exocrine glands**. **Ductless** glands secrete chemicals directly into the bloodstream. The blood carries these secretions to all parts of the body, and they may influence all organs. Ductless glands are called **endocrine glands**.

The secretions from ductless glands are called **hormones**. Hormones regulate the activities of all the body processes. The positions of the major human endocrine glands are shown in fig 14.1.

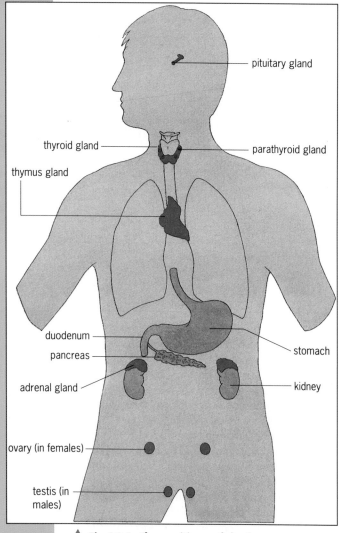

pituitary gland

thyroid gland

parathyroid gland

thymus gland

duodenum

pancreas

stomach

adrenal gland

kidney

ovary (in females)

testis (in males)

▲ **Fig 14.1 The positions of the human endocrine glands**

THE THYROID GLAND

The hormone produced by the **thyroid gland** regulates certain processes related to growth and the oxidation of glucose. The hormone is called **thyroxine**. This substance has the highest concentration of iodine found in any substance in the body.

Thyroid disturbances

If the thyroid gland is overactive, it produces a condition called **hyperthyroidism**. The rate of glucose oxidation increases and the body temperature rises. The heart rate increases together with the blood pressure.

Surgery used to be the only treatment for hyperthyroidism, but now effective drugs such as thiouracil are used to neutralise the effects of excess thyroxine. Another treatment uses radioactive iodine. This is absorbed by the thyroid gland and its cells are killed by the radioactivity. Some of the gland is destroyed as a result.

If the thyroid gland is underactive, the symptoms are opposite to those of hyperthyroidism. This condition is called **hypothyroidism** and results in physical or mental retardation. The heart beat slows and often the heart enlarges.

Hypothyroidism can be treated with thyroid extract. This can be extracted from the thyroid glands of sheep and is the least expensive of all commercial endocrine preparations. However, genetic engineering could increase its supply (see page 84).

Sometimes the thyroid gland does not function properly during infancy. This results in **cretinism** which causes stunted growth, both physically and mentally, fig 14.2. Treatment must be given during critical stages of development to be successful.

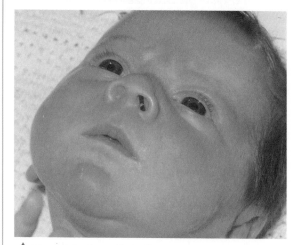

▲ **Fig 14.2 If too little thyroxine is secreted, a person may suffer from cretinism which causes stunted growth both physically and mentally**

Sometimes the thyroid gland enlarges. The most common cause of this is iodine deficiency and the enlargement is called **goitre**, fig 14.3. People who live near the coast and eat a lot of sea food rarely have this condition because sea food is rich in iodine. In areas where there is not much iodine in the soil, iodine can be added to the diet as iodine compounds in table salt.

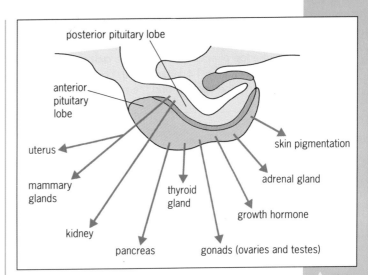

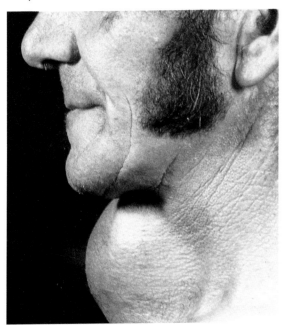

▲ **Fig 14.3 This goitre is the result of a disease called Grave's disease**

THE PARATHYROID GLANDS

There are four **parathyroid glands** embedded in the back of the thyroid, two in each lobe. They secrete **parathyroid hormone** which controls the body's use of calcium. A constant balance of calcium is needed for bone growth, muscle and nerve activity.

THE PITUITARY GLAND

The **pituitary gland** is a small gland, about the size of a pea. It is located at the base of the brain, fig 14.4. The pituitary used to be called the 'master gland' because its secretions affect the activity of all other endocrine glands. It is now known that other glands in turn affect the pituitary.

Secretions of the pituitary gland

Two lobes make up the pituitary gland, the **anterior** and the **posterior**. The anterior lobe secretes several different hormones. One of these is **growth hormone**. Growth hormone controls the growth of your skeleton (see page 43).

The anterior lobe also secretes **gonadotrophic hormones**. These influence the development of your reproductive organs. They also affect the hormone secretions of the ovaries and testes. The gonadotrophic hormones work together with sex hormones to produce changes in your body during adolescence.

The anterior lobe also secretes hormones which stimulate the secretion of milk by the mammary glands, and others which stimulate other endocrine glands such as the thyroid and the adrenal glands.

The posterior lobe release two hormones. One is **oxytocin**, which helps regulate blood pressure and smooth muscle contraction. During childbirth oxytocin is secreted in large amounts. Sometimes it is given to help the uterus contract. The other hormone is the **antidiuretic hormone**, **ADH**, which regulates water reabsorption in the kidneys (see page 19).

Pituitary disturbances

◀ **Fig 14.5 If too much growth hormone is secreted, a person may grow to more than 2.5 m**

The most common disorder of the pituitary involves growth hormone. If too much of this hormone is secreted, bones and tissue grow too fast. A **giant** might result with a height of 2.5 metres or more, fig 14.5. Similarly, a deficiency of this hormone results in **dwarfism**.

On the top of each kidney are the **adrenal glands** (see fig 14.1, page 30). Each is made of two parts, the **cortex** and the **medulla**, fig 14.6.

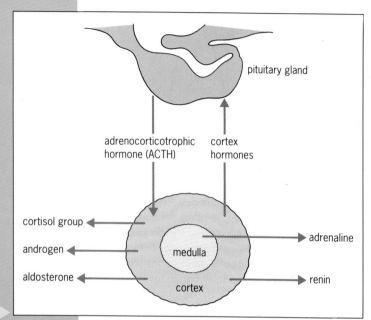

The adrenal cortex

The cortex secretes hormones called **corticoids**. These hormones control carbohydrate, fat and protein metabolism. They also affect balance of salt and water in the body. The adrenal cortex releases other hormones that control production of some types of white blood cell and the structure of connective tissue.

If the adrenal cortex is damaged or destroyed, a person develops **Addison's disease**. Such people get tired easily and lose weight. Their circulation fails and their skin colour changes. They can be helped by treatment with a corticoid called **cortisone**.

The adrenal medulla

The medulla secretes **adrenaline**. This can cause sudden body changes during anger or fright. Because the adrenal glands have this effect, they are called the 'glands of emergency'. High concentrations of adrenaline in your blood have the following effects:

1 You become pale, because the blood vessels in your skin constrict. If you have a surface wound, you will lose less blood because of its diversion from the body surface. At the same time, more blood is supplied to your muscles, brain, heart and other vital organs.
2 Your blood pressure rises, because the blood vessels in your skin constrict.

3 Your heart beats faster.
4 Your liver releases some of its stored carbohydrate. This provides material for increased activity and oxidation.
5 Your rate and depth of breathing increases.

Fig 14.7 shows the action of the **pancreas**. There are special cells in the pancreas called the **islets of Langerhans**. These cells secrete **insulin**. Insulin enables the liver to store carbohydrate in the form of glycogen. It also controls the oxidation of glucose.

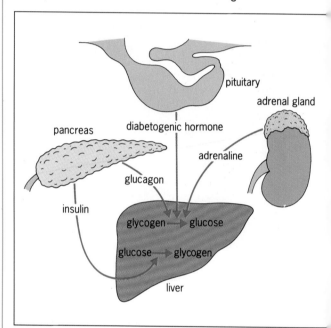

▲ Fig 14.7 The functions of the pancreas, also controlled by the pituitary

Diabetes mellitus

A person who does not secrete insulin is unable to store or oxidise sugar properly. So the tissues are deprived of fuel and sugar collects in the blood. Cells in the kidney tubules (see page 19), which usually reabsorb glucose from the filtrate into the blood, fail to cope with the high concentration and glucose is lost in the urine. This condition is called **diabetes mellitus**.

Diabetes mellitus is caused by a combination of factors. It may not be just the failure of the islets of Langerhans to make insulin. The disorder is also affected by the activity of the pituitary, thyroid and adrenal glands, as well as the liver. People who are overweight are more likely to develop this condition. Diabetes mellitus can also be hereditary.

Treatment is by injection of insulin, either as an extract from domesticated animals or as a product of genetic engineering (see pages 84–5).

Hypoglycaemia

Too much insulin results in a condition called **hypoglycaemia**, or low blood sugar. Excess insulin makes the liver store sugar that is needed by the cells. This can result in coma and death.

The insulin given to diabetics has to be carefully controlled to avoid inducing hypoglycaemia.

Q1 Three children were given a strong glucose (sugar) drink and their blood glucose levels were measured over the next two hours. The results are shown in fig 14.8.

a What is the maximum blood glucose level reached by Mary? [1]

b If the blood glucose level reaches above $10 \, mmol/dm^3$, then glucose is lost from the kidneys into the urine.
  i Of what condition is this a symptom?
  ii Give *one* more symptom of this condition.
  iii Which children are suffering from this condition?
  iv Bill's urine was tested 120 minutes after drinking the sugar. Explain the presence of glucose in his urine if his blood glucose was only $6 \, mmol/dm^3$. [4]

c Look at the treatments below and say which treatment fits *each* person best. Match the letters to the name in a copy of the table below.
  A Reduce the amount of carbohydrate in the diet.
  B Regular injections of insulin.
  C No treatment at all.

Name	Treatment
Mary	
Bill	
Jim	

[3]

(WJEC Modular Science 1991 Q3)

▼ **Fig 14.8**

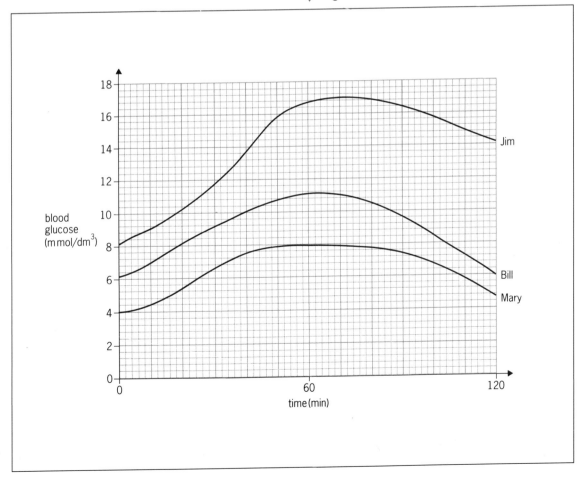

THE OVARIES AND TESTES

The **ovaries** of the female and the **testes** of the male have a dual function. We usually think of these organs as the producers of eggs and sperms (see pages 36–9). However, certain cells of both the ovaries and the testes do the work of endocrine glands.

The sex hormones

The ovaries secrete female hormones called **oestrogen** and **progesterone**. Cells in the testes make the male hormone, **testosterone**. This particular hormone can now be made artificially. The cortex of the adrenal glands also produces male sex hormones in both males and females. A woman's ovaries normally secrete enough oestrogen to neutralise the effects of the male sex hormones from the adrenal glands.

Secondary sex characteristics

Sex hormones affect the development of **secondary sex characteristics**. These are changes which appear as an individual develops from a child to an adult. They begin with the maturation of the ovaries and testes during the stage called **puberty**.

Many secondary characteristics appear in humans. As a boy approaches puberty, his voice 'breaks' (gets deeper). His beard appears, with a general increase in pubic hair and hair in the armpits. The chest broadens and deepens. Rapid growth of the long bones add to his height.

As a girl matures, her breasts develop and her hips get broader. Fat is deposited under the skin in those areas, and hair develops around the pubis and in the armpits. Around the same time, **menstruation** begins (see page 39). All these physical changes are accompanied by major mental and emotional changes.

In other vertebrates, secondary sex characteristics take many forms, such as the bright feathers of most male birds, fig 14.9, and the antlers of deer, fig 14.10.

Fig 14.9 ▶ The bright feathers of male birds are secondary sexual characters

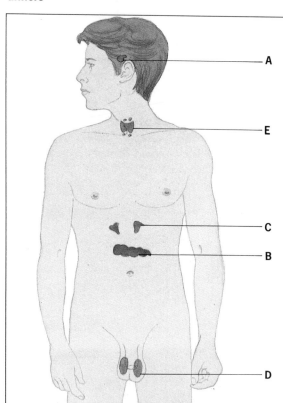

▲ **Fig 14.10 Some mammals also show secondary sexual characters, such as this stag's antlers**

▲ **Fig 14.11**

Q2 a Write labels for glands **A–E**, fig 14.11.
b Select any *one* of the glands labelled and
  i name a hormone produced by it
  ii state the function of the hormone.
c Explain how hormones reach their destination.
d Name a gland which produces both digestive enzymes and a hormone.
e State the difference between the structure of a hormone-producing gland and a salivary gland. [9]
(WJEC Common Syllabus (Biology) 1983 Q15 (modified))

CHEMICAL CONTROL IN PLANTS

Plant hormones

Plant growth is affected by external factors such as light and temperature. It is also regulated by the internal influence of **hormones**. Plant hormones are very active chemical substances secreted inside the plant. The production of these hormones may be influenced by external conditions. This interplay of factors makes a complex growth-control mechanism.

Hormones differ from other plant secretions in that they are produced in certain parts of the plant and then translocated to other parts. There they influence the growth, division and elongation of cells.

Auxins

The most widely studied plant hormones are called **auxins**. They mostly cause cells to get longer and larger. They also act in the development of flowers and fruits. Auxins are sometimes called growth hormones, though they are really **growth regulators** since they may either speed up or slow down the growth processes.

The main natural auxin that plants produce is called **indoleacteic acid (IAA)**. Large amounts of IAA are secreted in growing parts of plant organs. These include the tips of shoots and young leaves, flowers and fruits. IAA may also be secreted in cambial cells (around the stems and roots) and in the root tip. It is then translocated from these places to other parts of the plant.

Effects of auxins

Different parts of the plant react differently to auxins. A high concentration of auxin seems to stimulate stem growth. Root tissues are affected in the opposite way. Root growth may be inhibited by high auxin concentrations.

Experiments with oat seedlings show the activity of auxins in the tip of the growing shoot. The oat's primary shoot is enclosed by a protective sheath called a **coleoptile**, fig 14.12. As the seedling grows, the shoot normally pierces the tip of the coleoptile. If the tip is removed, no further growth occurs. But if the tip is replaced on the shoot, growth will begin again, fig 14.13. Thus auxins must be secreted by the coleoptile tip. These auxins move down into the growing cells, making them elongate.

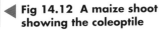

◀ Fig 14.12 A maize shoot showing the coleoptile

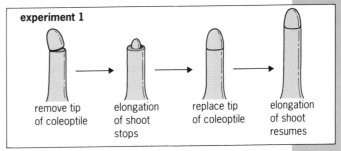

experiment 1

remove tip of coleoptile → elongation of shoot stops → replace tip of coleoptile → elongation of shoot resumes

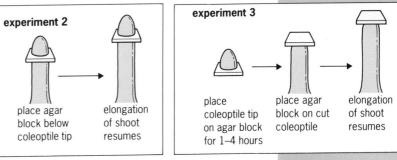

experiment 2

place agar block below coleoptile tip → elongation of shoot resumes

experiment 3

place coleoptile tip on agar block for 1–4 hours → place agar block on cut coleoptile → elongation of shoot resumes

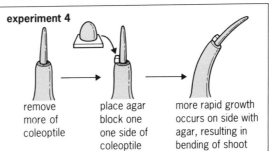

experiment 4

remove more of coleoptile → place agar block one one side of coleoptile → more rapid growth occurs on side with agar, resulting in bending of shoot

Fig 14.13 Investigations with auxins

Q3 **a** Biotechnologists have made weedkillers containing plant hormones. These can reduce the numbers of weeds without killing grasses. A 10 m² lawn was sprayed with such a weedkiller. Here are the results.

Name of weed	Number of plants		
	Before treatment	2 weeks after treatment	4 weeks after treatment
daisy	47	13	16
buttercup	20	5	2
clover	24	12	15
speedwell	16	12	12
dandelion	5	4	5

i Which weed was most easily controlled by this weedkiller?

ii Suggest *one* reason for your answer.

iii Compare the results for clover and speedwell.

iv Some resistant weeds have a thick cuticle. Explain how this could affect the reaction to the weedkiller.

(WJEC GCSE Biology 1990 Q18 (part))

15 HUMAN REPRODUCTION

By the end of this section you should be able to

- understand the life process of reproduction in mammals
- name and outline the functions of the reproductive organs in mammals
- understand the role of hormones in human reproduction
- understand how the environment of the embryo is kept constant in humans.

SEXUAL REPRODUCTION

Sexual reproduction is the union of two **gametes** (sex cells) to form a **zygote**. The zygote is capable of growing into a mature form that resembles both its parents but is different from them – it is unique. This combination of unlike genes from two different parents can produce almost endless variety. Organisms that reproduce asexually cannot develop much variety.

The significance of variation

The variation brought about by sexual reproduction may produce small but favourable adaptations. These may improve the adaptation of the species from one generation to the next.

Asexually reproducing organisms may sometimes produce favourable characteristics by **mutation** (see page 68). But the species is not as likely to adapt within a one-parent system. Sexual reproduction produces greater chance of variation, which improves the chances that a species will adapt and survive. This is explained further on pages 68 and 83.

THE MALE REPRODUCTIVE SYSTEM

The human male **gonads** (sex organs) are the **testes**. They are located outside the main body cavity in a pouch of skin called the **scrotum**, fig 15.1. Here the temperature is slightly below normal body temperature and is ideal for the development of the male gametes, the **spermatozoa** or **sperms**.

Within the testes are tightly coiled tubes called **seminiferous tubules**, fig 15.2. The cells lining these tubules divide by meiosis (see page 54–5) to form sperms, sex cells containing half the normal number of chromosomes. Ciliated cells of the seminiferous tubules then move the sperms to the **epididymis**, a storage area.

Eventually, the sperms leave the epididymis through a duct called the **vas deferens**. This duct carries the sperms past the **seminal vesicles**. A short tube connects the seminal vesicle to the **urethra** by passing through the **prostate gland**. A small organ called **Cowper's gland** also opens into the urethra. The seminal vesicles, the prostate gland and Cowper's gland all release secretions into the tubes as the sperms pass by.

Semen is made up of sperms and these secreted fluids. The urethra is the duct for the passage of semen out through the penis. The urethra also carries urine from the bladder for excretion.

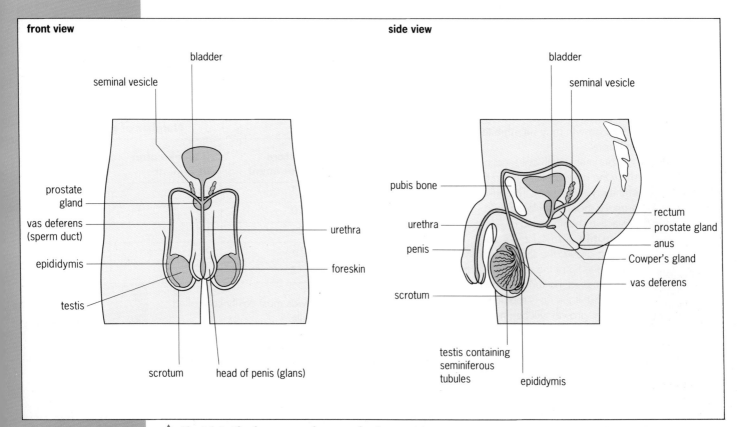

▲ **Fig 15.1 The human male reproductive system**

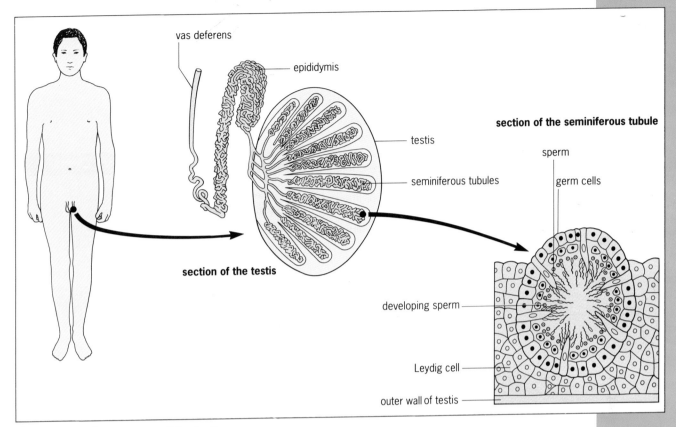

vas deferens
epididymis
section of the seminiferous tubule
sperm
germ cells
testis
seminiferous tubules
developing sperm
Leydig cell
outer wall of testis

section of the testis

▲ Fig 15.2 **The structure of the testis**

THE SPERM CELL

The human sperm cell is very small compared with the human ovum. The head of a sperm is flattened and oval shaped, fig 15.3. It contains the nucleus which is **haploid** – it has half the normal number of chromosomes (see page 54). The tail acts like a whip to move the sperm. The short middle part is the energy-releasing area of the cell. Energy is released by respiration from fructose sugar, a carbohydrate found in semen.

It takes as many as 130 million active sperms to ensure sufficient density for fertilisation of one ovum (see page 40). However, only one sperm will eventually fuse with a single ovum.

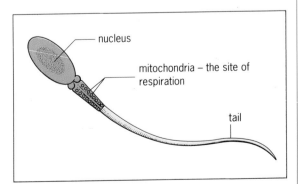

nucleus
mitochondria – the site of respiration
tail

▲ Fig 15.3 **Sperm cell magnified 1000 times**

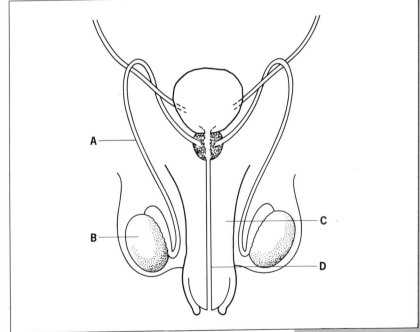

A
B
C
D

▲ Fig 15.4

Q1 Fig 15.4 shows the male human reproductive system and part of the urinary (excretory) system.

Write labels for parts **A–D**.   [2]

(WJEC Modular Science 1991 Q2 (part))

LIFE PROCESSES

THE FEMALE REPRODUCTIVE SYSTEM

The female has a pair of **ovaries** in the body cavity, fig 15.5. These are about 3.5 cm long and 0.5 cm wide.

The ovaries produce the female gametes, the **ova**, by meiosis (see pages 54–5). An ovum is haploid – it contains half the normal number of chromosomes. One ovum is released each month, from one of the ovaries. The ovum is drawn into the **oviduct** or **Fallopian tube**. These tubes are not connected directly to the ovaries. They are lined with ciliated cells which draw the ovum into the tubes. The Fallopian tubes lead to the **uterus** (womb).

The uterus is a hollow, muscular organ with thick walls. It is lined with a mucous membrane containing small glands and many capillaries.

If the ovum is not fertilised, it passes through the neck of the uterus, the **cervix**. The cervix opens into the **vagina** which receives the erect penis during intercourse. The baby passes through the vagina during birth.

THE FEMALE REPRODUCTIVE CYCLE

The development of an ovum each month is coordinated with changes in the uterus. These changes are controlled by **hormones** (see page 34). Female mammals are born with all the ova they will ever release already in their ovaries. They begin to release these ova periodically once they reach sexual maturity. Human ovaries usually produce one ovum in the course of a 28-day cycle of activity.

Changes in the ovary

The cycle is started by a hormone called **follicle-stimulating hormone (FSH)**, produced by the pituitary gland. This causes one of the ovaries to form a **follicle** in which the ovum develops, fig 15.6. As the ovum becomes mature, the follicle fills with fluid containing another hormone, **oestrogen**.

▼ **Fig 15.5 The human female reproductive system**

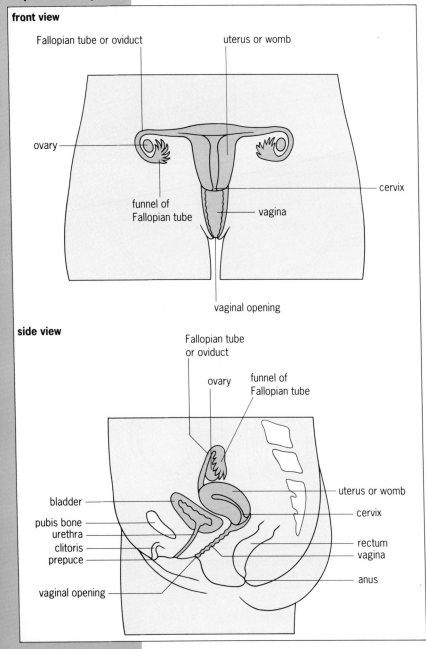

front view

- Fallopian tube or oviduct
- uterus or womb
- ovary
- funnel of Fallopian tube
- cervix
- vagina
- vaginal opening

side view

- Fallopian tube or oviduct
- ovary
- funnel of Fallopian tube
- bladder
- pubis bone
- urethra
- clitoris
- prepuce
- vaginal opening
- uterus or womb
- cervix
- rectum
- vagina
- anus

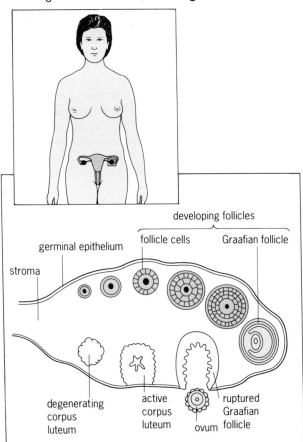

- developing follicles
- germinal epithelium
- follicle cells
- Graafian follicle
- stroma
- degenerating corpus luteum
- active corpus luteum
- ovum
- ruptured Graafian follicle

▲ **Fig 15.6 Changes in the ovary**

The release of the ovum from the follicle is called **ovulation**. After ovulation, the follicle becomes yellowish in colour. The follicle is now called a **corpus luteum**. The development of the corpus luteum is controlled by another hormone from the pituitary gland, **luteinising hormone (LH)**. The corpus luteum now produces the hormone **progesterone**. If the ovum is not fertilised, the corpus luteum degenerates and stops producing progesterone.

Changes in the uterus

Progesterone maintains the growth of the mucous lining of the uterus. If the ovum is not fertilised, no more progesterone is produced, and the inside lining of the uterus detaches and sloughs off. The breakdown and discharge of the soft uterine tissues and the unfertilised egg is called **menstruation**.

The complete cycle

The complete cycle has four distinct stages:
1 menstruation, averaging four days
2 the follicle stage, from the end of menstruation to the release of the ovum, between 10 and 14 days
3 ovulation, the release of a mature ovum from the ovary
4 the corpus luteum stage, from ovulation to menstruation, about 10 to 14 days.

Fig 15.7 summarises the female reproductive cycle.

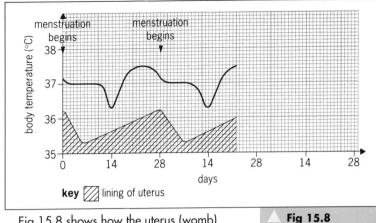

Q2

Fig 15.8 shows how the uterus (womb) lining varies in thickness during the menstrual cycle. Also shown is the variation in body temperature. In the second month fertilisation occurs.

a Copy and complete the chart to show what happens to the body temperature and the thickness of the uterus lining in the third month.

b Name the process which takes place about the same time as the drop in body temperature about the fourteenth day of the cycle. [3]

(WJEC Modular Science 1990 Q2 (part))

▲ **Fig 15.8**

▼ **Fig 15.7 Hormonal control of the menstrual cycle**

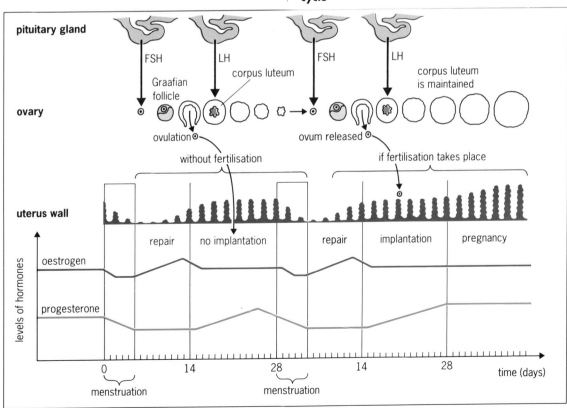

FERTILISATION

Sexual intercourse and fertilisation

During **sexual intercourse** the erect penis is inserted into the vagina. **Ejaculation** occurs and sperms are discharged in semen through the man's urethra which is close to the woman's cervix. The sperms swim up through the uterus towards the Fallopian tubes. If an ovum is present in a Fallopian tube at this time, **fertilisation** is likely to occur. The sperm fertilises the ovum by penetrating it. At that time, the tail separates from the rest of the sperm. The head and the middle part enter the ovum, and the nuclei of the sperm and the ovum unite to form a **zygote**. A membrane immediately forms around the zygote. This prevents any other sperm entering.

Implantation

Fertilisation causes several important changes in the female's body, fig 15.9. The corpus luteum continues to produce progesterone, which causes the lining of the uterus to thicken. Many additional small glands and blood vessels form in the lining of the uterus. This builds up and prepares the uterus to receive the zygote which will be embedded in the uterus wall in a process called **implantation**.

Fig 15.9
Fertilisation

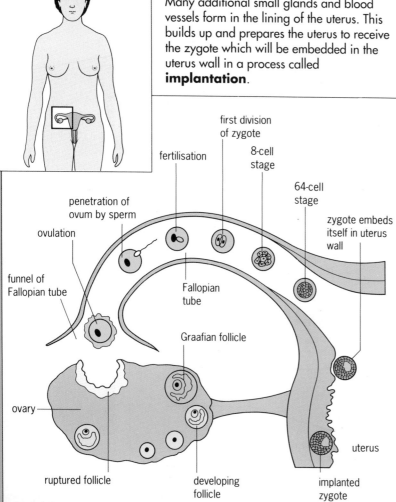

DEVELOPMENT OF THE EMBRYO

The zygote reaches the uterus in 3–5 days. During this time, the zygote continues to grow. It has become a ball of cells with a fluid-filled cavity. Some of its cells will become the **embryo**. In humans, this stage lasts from 6–8 weeks after fertilisation. At the end of this time the embryo is about 2 cm long. Its growth rate then increases rapidly and it starts to take on a human embryonic form. From this point until birth, it is called a **fetus**. Fig 15.10 shows stages in the development of the embryo and fetus.

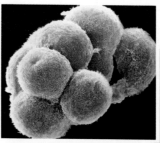

4 days

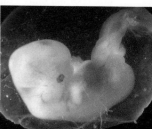
5–6 weeks

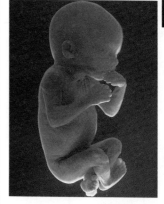
5 months

Fig 15.10 An embryo becomes a fetus and is fully developed at 9 months

Attachment of the embryo

As the zygote passes down the Fallopian tube to the uterus, a membrane called the **chorion** forms around the mass of dividing cells. The chorion develops many small, finger-like projections called **chorionic villi**. Enzymes produced by the villi allow them to sink into the uterine wall. The villi are in close contact with the capillaries in the lining of the uterus, providing nourishment for the embryo.

The amnion and placenta

Soon another membrane, the **amnion**, develops. The amnion forms a cavity around the developing embryo and secretes a fluid called **amniotic fluid**. This protects the embryo from injury, keeps it moist and equalises the pressure around it.

The third membrane to form is the **yolk sac**. The human yolk sac is small and not significant. However, in animals that hatch from eggs, the yolk provides food for the embryo.

The fourth membrane is the **allantois**. In humans it is only present for a short time. In birds and reptiles, it acts as an embryonic lung.

When the chorionic villi lodge in the wall of the uterus, the capillaries break down and form blood spaces (**sinuses**) around the villi. Food and waste exchange occurs between mother and embryo by diffusion through the thin membranes of the villi. There is no direct connection between the blood of the mother and embryo. The area where the chorionic villi meet the mother's blood supply within the uterus is called the **placenta**. In time the area that attaches the embryo to the yolk sac and allantois lengthens into the **umbilical cord**, fig 15.11. The developing embryo is connected to the placenta by two umbilical arteries, one umbilical vein and the allantoic duct.

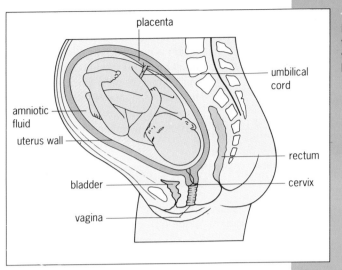

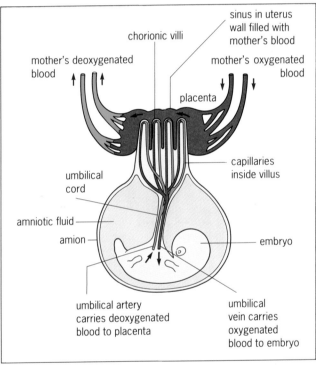

▲ **Fig 15.11 The formation of the placenta**

BIRTH

Fig 15.12 shows a fully developed fetus ready to be born. **Birth** occurs about 40 weeks after fertilisation.

The smooth muscles of the uterus begin to contract. The membrane of the amnion breaks and the amniotic fluid passes out through the vagina. This is called 'the breaking of the waters'. Muscles in the cervix relax so that the opening can become larger. More uterine contractions force the child out from the uterus, usually head first.

The baby is still attached to the placenta by the umbilical cord. The cord is tied and cut immediately after birth so that the child will not lose blood through the umbilical vessels. After the child is born, the placenta and remains of the amnion are expelled as the **afterbirth**.

Changes to the baby at birth

Until the baby is born, it receives both oxygen and nourishment through the placenta. As the fetus grows, the movement of its thoracic (chest) muscles draws a special fluid into its lungs. The lungs expand because of this fluid. The first cries of the baby remove the fluid and fill its lungs with air.

Another important change takes place at birth. In the fetus, the blood does not circulate through its lungs. Instead, the blood leaves the right ventricle and passes through a vessel called the **ductus arteriosus** which takes blood to the aorta. At birth, the ductus arteriosus closes. Now the blood must flow through the pulmonary arteries to the lungs. The new supply of blood helps the lungs expand as the baby begins to breath air.

Occasionally, the ductus arteriosus fails to close off. When this happens, not all of the blood passes to the lungs. The oxygen content of the blood then falls below normal. In severe cases, the baby's skin will have a blue colour. Surgery is sometimes needed to tie off the vessel.

While blood is circulating in the fetus, there is an opening between the atria of the heart called the **foramen ovale**. A membrane grows over this opening, normally closing it completely soon after birth. If the opening does not close, oxygenated blood will mix with deoxygenated blood. If this happens, surgery may also be needed.

Q3 a Explain the rôle of
   i the amniotic fluid **ii** the placenta
      in the protection of the fetus. [2]
b State *two* ways in which the content of the blood in the umbilical vein differs from the content of the blood in most other veins. [2]
      (WJEC Modular Science 1991 (part))

16 GROWTH

By the end of this section you should be able to
— understand the life process of growth
— understand how cells specialise to form tissues.

Growth depends on increasing the numbers of individual cells. Every organ is made up of cells, and an adult human is made up of about 30 million million cells! Since we all start from one cell, the zygote, an enormous amount of multiplication has obviously taken place.

SPECIALISATION

An increase in numbers of cells comes about by **cell division** (see page 53). Each cell splits into two, usually identical, cells. These cells will have identical genes, but each cell may subsequently develop into a very different part of the body. This is called **specialisation**.

While two cells in the earlier stages of an embryo are identical, they both contain all the information necessary to become any type of cell. The future paths of these cells will diverge.

Forming tissues

At an early stage in the development of an embryo, three layers of cells form. They each give rise to different **tissues**. A tissue is a group of cells specialised to carry out the same function, for example skin or blood. The three layers are

- the **ectoderm** which gives rise to skin, nerves and hair (or scales or feathers)
- the **mesoderm** which gives rise to blood, bone and muscle, excretory organs and reproductive organs
- the **endoderm** which gives rise to the lining of the digestive system, digestive glands and lungs.

▼ **Fig 16.1 The three basic layers from which all our tissues develop**

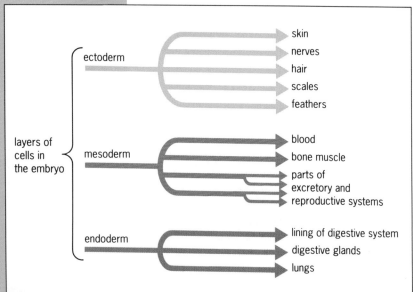

Fig 16.1 illustrates this process of specialisation. The layers seem to develop along their paths by each switching off the irrelevant part of the genetic blueprint (see pages 62–5) and leaving active only the relevant genes. The tissues become specialised for particular tasks like developing power in muscles, passing on messages in nerves or making useful chemicals for the body's needs in liver. So a small blob of identical cells changes over time into a highly organised, fully functional organism.

GROWTH IN HUMANS

At birth, a baby is generally between 27 and 30% as tall as the adult he or she will become. The size of a newborn mammal is a compromise between the largest size that can develop in the uterus and the smallest size that is likely to survive.

Fig 16.2 illustrates growth in humans, and fig 16.3 how this growth is controlled by hormones.

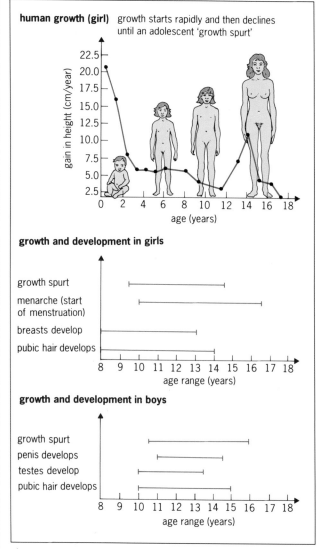

▲ **Fig 16.2 Growth from infancy to adulthood**

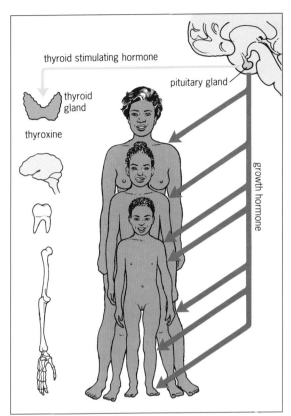

▲ **Fig 16.3 Hormonal control of growth. Thyroxine acts on the brain, teeth, bones and metabolism, while growth hormone influences all body systems**

Puberty is the time when the secondary sex characteristics develop (see page 34). These characteristics are shown in fig 16.2. Puberty happens over a range of ages.

GROWTH AND LIFE SPAN

We can divide the life span of any organism into five stages

1 beginning
2 growth
3 maturity
4 decline
5 death.

After an organism is formed, it goes through a period of relatively rapid growth. This growth period may last for minutes, weeks, months or years, depending on the organism.

As the organism grows larger, the rate of growth decreases. Finally **maturity** is reached. During this period, growth is reduced to just the repair and replacement of the organism's cells or chemicals.

At last, the organism reaches a point at which it can no longer repair or replace all damaged or worn out materials. This marks the period of **decline** which ends in **death**.

How long can an organism live? The answer differs greatly for different organisms. Certain insects live only a few weeks. Five years is old for some fish. A horse may reach 30 or more. The California redwood tree can live for thousands of years! For humans, an average life span in the UK is about 70 years.

If we could continue to organise and replace worn out cells and substances, we could extend our life span. We are only beginning to learn about these processes. With advances in genetic engineering (see pages 84–9), who knows what the future might hold?

Q1 The table below shows the average height for boys at various ages during their growth.

Age (years)	Height (cm)
0 (birth)	50
4	105
8	125
12	145
14	160
16	186
18	187

a Plot these results as a graph and join the points. [4]
b From the graph deduce
  i the age at which puberty occurs
  ii the average height for boys at age 7 years. [2]

(WJEC Modular Science 1991 Q2 (part))

Q2 The growth rate of teenagers is shown by the graphs in fig 16.4.

 Fig 16.4

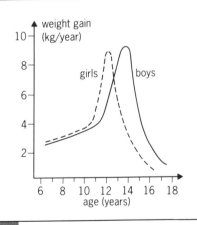
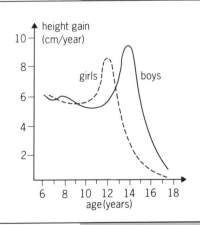

a State the two-year period when
  i girls gain most weight
  ii boys gain most height.
b Explain how some teenagers should change their diet after this growth spurt to avoid becoming overweight.
(WJEC Common Syllabus (Biology) 1984 Q8 (part))

17 REPRODUCTION IN PLANTS

By the end of this section you should be able to

- understand the life process of reproduction in plants
- name and outline the functions of the reproductive organs in plants
- recall the different methods of pollination and their adaptations.

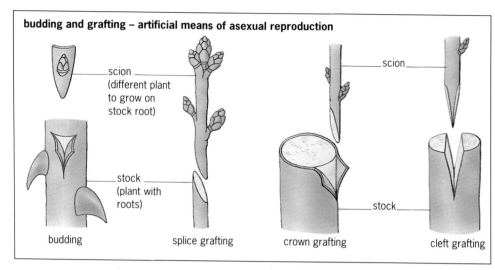

budding and grafting – artificial means of asexual reproduction

scion (different plant to grow on stock root)

stock (plant with roots)

scion

stock

budding

splice grafting

crown grafting

cleft grafting

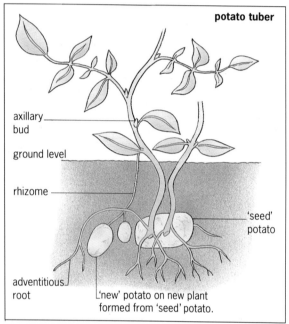

potato tuber

axillary bud

ground level

rhizome

adventitious root

'seed' potato

'new' potato on new plant formed from 'seed' potato.

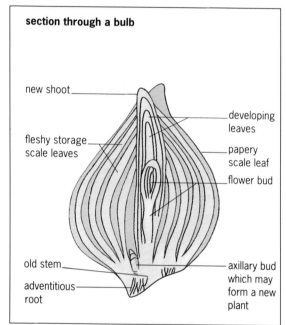

section through a bulb

new shoot

fleshy storage scale leaves

old stem

adventitious root

developing leaves

papery scale leaf

flower bud

axillary bud which may form a new plant

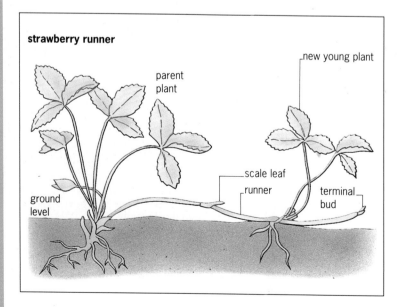

strawberry runner

parent plant

new young plant

scale leaf

runner

terminal bud

ground level

Plants can reproduce by **asexual** means during the growing season, fig 17.1. However, in order to survive, most plants reproduce **sexually**.

Fig 17.1 Some methods of asexual reproduction in flowering plants

44

SEXUAL REPRODUCTION

Sexual reproduction results in **seeds**, which carry new combinations of genes into the next generation. Seeds usually have combinations of genes from different parent plants. As in sexual reproduction in animals, variations come about through the different recombinations of chromosomes and genes during fertilisation. These variations, no matter how slight, may better adapt a species to new conditions in a changing environment.

Flowers

Flowers are the reproductive organs of higher plants. They are branches whose leaves have modified and act as specialised floral parts.

Flowers start the development that leads to the formation of fruits and seeds. Some flowers are large and colourful, like roses, orchids, lilies and tulips. Other flowers, such as those of trees and grasses, are not usually noticed.

THE STRUCTURE OF A FLOWER

Typical flowers, like geraniums or apple blossoms, have many parts, fig 17.2. They grow from a flower stalk or **pedicel** whose tip is the **receptacle**. The outer ring of floral parts is formed by several leaf-like **sepals**. The sepals protect the flower bud and support the other parts when the bud opens.

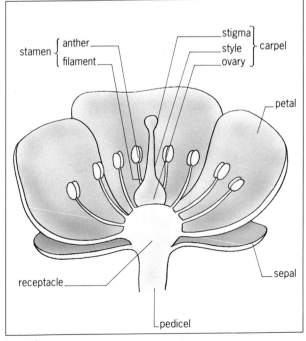

▲ **Fig 17.2 The parts of a flower**

Inside the sepals are the **petals**. The petals are often brightly coloured to attract insects. They also protect the inner parts. In some flowers such as the tulip, the sepals and petals are the same colour.

In the centre of the flower are the two structures directly involved in reproduction. They are the **stamens** and the **carpel**. Each stamen is a slender **filament** with a sac at the end called the **anther**. The anther produces **pollen grains** which are vital to reproduction.

The carpel is usually shaped like a flask. It has a sticky top called a **stigma**, supported by a slender stalk or **style**. The swollen base, the **ovary**, is attached to the pedicel. Inside the ovary are the **ovules** which later become seeds. There may be one to several hundred ovules, depending on the kind of flower.

Variations in flower structure

Flowers vary greatly in colour, size and shape. Many have both stamens and carpels in the same flower. Others have them in separate flowers on the same plant, such as oak trees and corn. Still others have separate male and female plants. Willow and holly are familiar examples.

▲ **Fig 17.3 Sunflowers look like single flowers but are really a cluster of little flowers**

Some flowers that look like single flowers are really a whole cluster of flowers, for example the sunflower and daisy, fig 17.3. They have dense clusters of reproductive flowers at the centre. Around these are petal-like structures that attract insects.

Pollen formation

If you look at a cross-section of the developing anther, you can see four chambers called pollen sacs, fig 17.4. While the flower is developing, each pollen sac is filled with cells which eventually become **pollen grains**.

In each pollen grain, the nucleus divides to form the **tube nucleus** and the **generative nucleus**. The wall of the pollen grain thickens to protect its contents. When mature, the pollen sacs burst open, and the pollen grains are ready for **dispersal**.

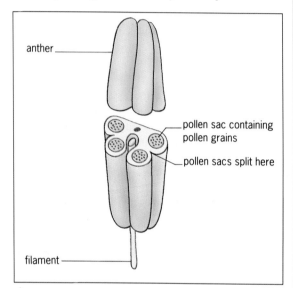

anther

pollen sac containing pollen grains

pollen sacs split here

filament

▲ **Fig 17.4 Section through the anther**

Ovule formation

While pollen grains are forming in the anthers of a flower, there are also changes in the ovary. An **ovule** starts as a tiny knob on the ovary wall. Gradually a pair of protective layers forms around the ovule. It is completely enclosed except for one tiny hole called the **micropyle**.

A single ovule cell now divides and becomes an oval **embryo sac**. This sac goes on developing until it is ready for fertilisation. In order for fertilisation to take place, pollen must get to the stigma of the carpel. This can happen in several different ways, as described below.

POLLINATION

Pollination is the transfer of pollen from an anther to a stigma. In some plants, pollen goes from the anther to the stigma within the same flower. Pollen may also go to the stigma of another flower on the same plant. This is called **self-pollination**. If pollen from flowers on one plant pollinates flowers on another plant, this is called **cross-pollination**. For cross-pollination to take place the pollen must be carried to the second plant. Insects, wind or less commonly water act as these **agents of pollination**.

Insect-pollinated flowers

The most common insect pollinators are bees. Moths, butterflies and some flies may also be important to some types of flowers.

Insects go to flowers in search of sweet **nectar**, secreted by glands in **nectaries**, usually at the base of the **petals**. Bees swallow the nectar, mix it with saliva, and turn it into honey.

The bee's plump, hairy body makes it an ideal pollinator. As it crawls into the flower to get nectar, its body rubs against the anthers and picks up pollen. When it visits the next flower, some of this pollen rubs off on the stigma. A new supply of pollen also brushes onto the bee from this flower.

The brightly coloured petals, fig 17.5, and sweet smell of the flowers help insects to locate them. The bright stripes on some petals may act as 'honey guides'.

▲ **Fig 17.5 Wild pansy – an insect-pollinated flower**

Wind-pollinated flowers

Wind-pollinated flowers are often found in clusters near the ends of branches. Usually there are no petals, and there is rarely any nectar. Often the stamens hang outside the flower and produce large amounts of light, dry pollen grains. Examples are grasses, willow and plantain, fig 17.6.

▲ **Fig 17.6 Couch grass – a wind-pollinated flower**

FERTILISATION

What happens after the pollen lands on the stigma? First, a chemical from the stigma stimulates the pollen grain to form a **pollen tube** that grows into the stigma's surface. As the tube gets longer, it grows through the soft tissues of the style. Finally it reaches the micropyle of the ovule, fig 17.7.

The generative nucleus moves from the pollen grain into the pollen tube. As it does so, it divides and forms two **male gamete nuclei**.

After the pollen tube passes through the micropyle, it digests part of the embryo sac's thin wall. The tip of the tube breaks open, and the two male gamete nuclei are released into the embryo sac. The tube nucleus now disintegrates.

One of the male gamete nuclei unites with the ovum to **fertilise** it. This produces the **zygote**. The other male gamete nucleus unites with a nucleus in the embryo sac to form the **endosperm nucleus**.

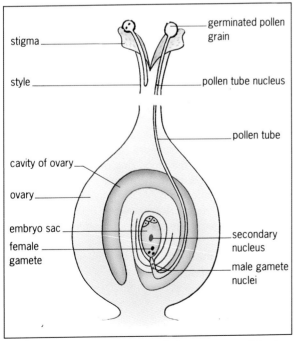

▲ **Fig 17.7 Fertilisation of the egg (ovum) in the embryo sac**

The zygote develops into an embryo plant. The endosperm nucleus forms the **seed endosperm** which contains food for the developing embryo.

Q1 Fig 17.8 shows parts of two different flowers.

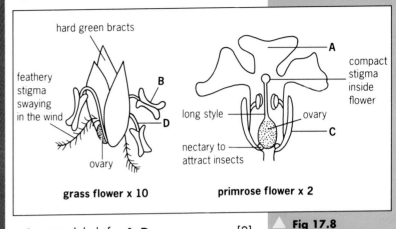

▲ **Fig 17.8**

a i Write labels for **A–D**. [2]
  ii Explain the function of the feathery stigma in the grass flower. [1]
b Explain how pollen of the grass flower is carried to another grass flower. [1]
c Where will a seed be produced in the primrose flower? [1]
  (WJEC Modular Science 1991 Q4 (part))

Q2 a The following words describe the life cycle of a flowering plant. Use these to fill in the boxes on a copy of fig 17.9 in the correct order. The first box has been filled in for you.

Flower, germination, pollination, seed dispersal, fertilisation.

▼ **Fig 17.9 The life cycle of a flowering plant**

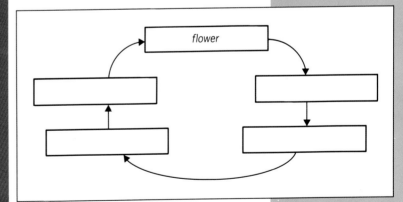

b Explain why
  i flowers pollinated by *insects* have large coloured petals and sticky, heavy pollen grains
  ii flowers pollinated by *wind* have small petals or no petals and light, dry pollen grains. [2]
    (WJEC Modular Science 1991 Q1)

18 HOMEOSTASIS IN ANIMALS

By the end of this section you should be able to

▶ understand how homeostasis and metabolic processes contribute to maintaining the internal environment of animals, including the significance of water relations, temperature regulation and solute balance.

All the activities of organisms are coordinated as if 'they were directed by unseen guides', said Claude Bernard, a famous nineteenth century scientist. He conceived the idea of **homeostasis**, or regulation of the internal environment.

The 'unseen guides' are the chemical compounds called **hormones** (see page 30). Endocrine glands usually maintain a careful balance between the different hormones secreted by animals. Too much or too little of any hormone can upset that balance.

NEGATIVE FEEDBACK

An automatic check on the concentration of materials in the blood is often part of any homeostatic system. This is called **negative feedback**, and can be illustrated by considering **insulin** production for regulating blood sugar (see page 32).

When the glucose concentration in the blood is about to increase above 0.1%, the pancreas produces insulin. This reduces the blood glucose level to 0.1% again. The reduced concentration acts as a trigger which reduces production of insulin, fig 18.1.

Fig 18.1 Negative feedback controls the production of insulin

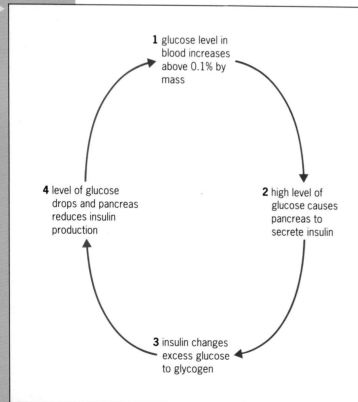

1 glucose level in blood increases above 0.1% by mass

2 high level of glucose causes pancreas to secrete insulin

3 insulin changes excess glucose to glycogen

4 level of glucose drops and pancreas reduces insulin production

If the blood glucose concentration falls, for example after exercise, the pancreas again senses the change and reduces the secretion of insulin. It also secretes **glucagon** which brings about the breakdown of glycogen stored in the liver to form glucose.

WATER REGULATION

The need to control water balance

The regulation of water in the body is essential to maintain the correct concentration of body fluids. For example, if blood cells were in plasma which had a lower concentration of salts than the protoplasm of the blood cells, water would enter the cells by **osmosis** (see page 51). They would swell and burst. If the cells were in plasma with a higher concentration of salts then their protoplasm, water would leave the blood cells.

Automatic control

There is an automatic control mechanism which keeps the water balance relatively constant. When we need more water we feel thirsty, though usually we drink before suffering from thirst.

Our bodies lose water in three ways

- sweating
- breathing
- excreting.

Water balance is adjusted in the tubules of the kidneys (see page 19). The regulation is controlled by the hormone **antidiuretic hormone**, **ADH**, produced by the **pituitary gland**.

Drinking a little water

When water intake is low, very little is absorbed through the wall of the small intestine to the blood. Consequently, the amount of water in blood plasma is decreased and the blood becomes 'more concentrated'. This 'more concentrated' blood circulating through the pituitary gland triggers the pituitary gland to secrete more ADH.

ADH circulates in the blood and eventually reaches the kidneys. Here the membranes of the tubule cells are affected by ADH. They become more permeable and reabsorb more water from the filtrate. Small quantities of highly concentrated urine are excreted.

We also feel thirst if the blood is 'concentrated', so we drink more water.

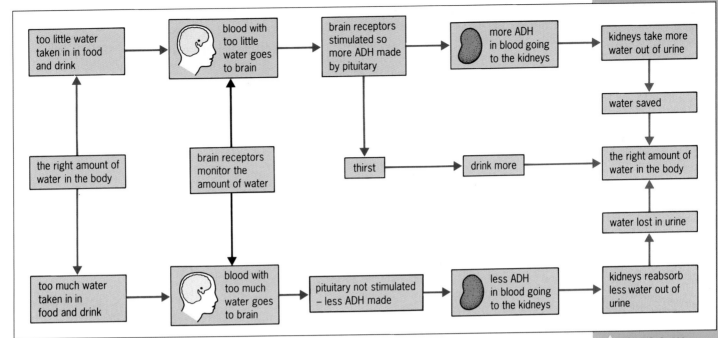

| too little water taken in in food and drink | → | blood with too little water goes to brain | → | brain receptors stimulated so more ADH made by pituitary | → | more ADH in blood going to the kidneys | → | kidneys take more water out of urine |

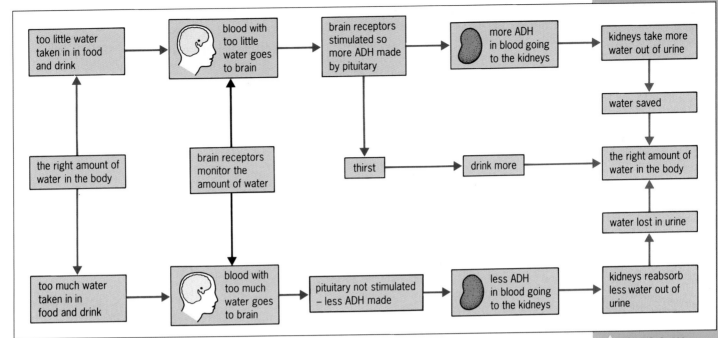

▲ **Fig 18.2 Water regulation in humans**

Drinking a lot of water

When water intake is high, a large volume of water is absorbed through the wall of the small intestine to the blood. Consequently the amount of water in the plasma is increased and the blood is 'diluted'. This 'diluted' blood does not cause the pituitary to produce ADH. The membranes of the kidney tubule cells are not so permeable and little water is absorbed. Large quantities of dilute urine are excreted.

Fig 18.2 shows the mechanism of water regulation.

THE ARTIFICIAL KIDNEY

Kidney machines, figs 18.3 and 18.4, can be used to help with homeostasis when the kidneys become damaged or diseased. The principle of the machine is to take a person's blood, pass it through a filter, and put it back into the person after waste materials have been removed from the plasma. The waste materials would affect the balance of minerals in the body if they were not removed.

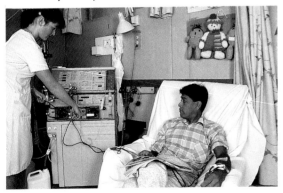

▲ **Fig 18.3 An artificial kidney in use**

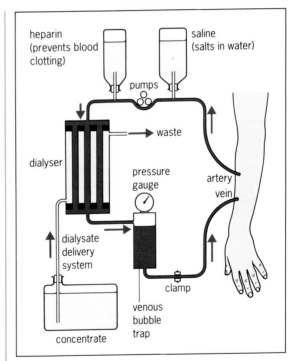

▲ **Fig 18.4 The principle of the artificial kidney**

In many cases a permanent 'shunt' is put between an artery and vein of the arm. The blood is then led from the artery to the artificial kidney and then returned to the vein.

The kidney machine has a **partially permeable membrane**, like visking tubing, to filter the blood. The whole apparatus is placed in a tank containing fluid which takes the waste away after filtration. The fluid has a concentration of salts which is the same as that of blood. The membrane

LIFE PROCESSES

allows water, urea, uric acid, ammonia and salts to pass through, but not larger molecules such as glucose, fatty acids, amino acids and proteins.

Sodium and potassium ions pass freely into the fluid. These ions are essential to the body so their levels must be kept constant. It is difficult to prevent the movement of these ions out of the blood into the fluid. This is why the fluid contains the same concentration of these salts as the blood. These salts can pass both ways across the membrane.

It is possible for people to use kidney machines in their homes. The process of filtration takes from three to six hours and is repeated three times each week.

TEMPERATURE REGULATION

Releasing heat

Heat is continually being produced by the body by the process of respiration. Some of this heat must be transferred from the body to prevent the body temperature rising. The heat is produced because the body is not very efficient in its use of energy from food. 90% of the energy from our daily food intake appears as heat within the body. Most of this heat is released by the liver and muscles.

A constant body temperature

The body temperature of all mammals and birds is kept constant. Such animals are called **homeotherms**, and they can live in a great variety of climates.

There is a balance between heat loss and heat gain to maintain a constant temperature (37 °C in humans). Fig 18.5 and the table below show how this is achieved.

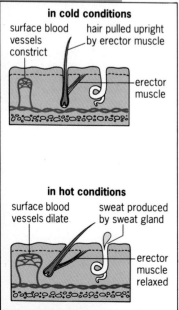

▼ **Fig 18.5 Temperature regulation in humans**

Q1 Tudor and Jasmin ate a quick snack of buns and crisps. Their blood sugar levels are plotted on the graph in fig 18.6. Study the graph, then answer the following questions.

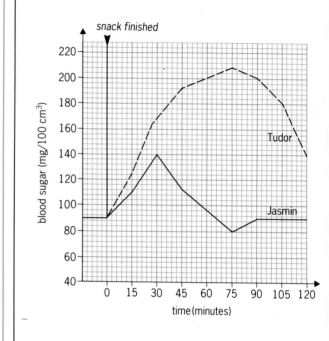

▲ **Fig 18.6**

a How many minutes after the snack does Tudor's blood sugar begin to decrease?

b At what point on the graph of Jasmin's blood sugar does insulin begin to work?

c If Tudor's pancreas cannot produce insulin, state *one* reason for the decrease in the blood sugar level shown.

d After 60 minutes, what was Tudor's blood sugar level? [4]
(WJEC Modular Science 1991 (part))

In cold conditions	In hot conditions
surface blood vessels constrict, so less blood carries heat to body surface	surface blood vessels dilate, so more blood carries heat to body surface
sweat glands stop producing sweat	sweat glands produce more sweat which cools the skin as it evaporates from the surface
hairs are pulled up by erector muscles so a layer of air is trapped against the surface of the skin, providing insulation	hairs drop down against the skin surface so less air is trapped for insulation
shivering occurs by the action of skin muscles which release heat as a by-product	no shivering

19 WATER BALANCE IN PLANTS

By the end of this section you should be able to

■ understand how homeostatic processes contribute to maintaining the internal environment of plants, including the significance of water relations and solute balance.

TRANSPORTING WATER

When plants evolved to live on land, many changes were necessary in their structure and physiology. Aquatic plants were able to absorb water and mineral salts over their whole surface. When roots evolved for anchorage and absorption, the leaves had to be supplied with minerals and water from the soil.

TRANSPIRATION

Plants rely on evaporation of water from their leaves to draw water and mineral salts to the top of the plant. The process is called **transpiration**. As the water evaporates, it 'pulls' more water up the xylem vessels and in from the soil, fig 19.1. This is called the **transpiration stream**.

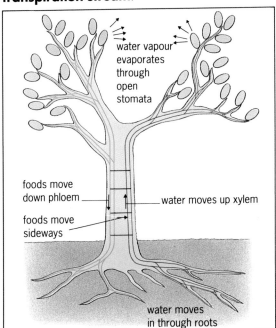

water vapour evaporates through open stomata

foods move down phloem

water moves up xylem

foods move sideways

water moves in through roots

▲ **Fig 19.1 Movement of materials through a typical plant**

However, sometimes water is in short supply. If the rate at which the plant loses water exceeds the rate at which water can enter from the soil, the plant will **wilt** and eventually die. To prevent this, the plant can partially regulate its internal water balance by opening the **stomata** (see page 4) only when it needs carbon dioxide for photosynthesis, and closing them to reduce transpiration for the rest of the time.

When there is no shortage of water in the soil and there is a higher concentration of minerals in the root hair cell vacuoles than in the soil, **osmosis** takes place. This is the passage of water molecules from where they are in high concentration to where they are in low concentration, through a **partially permeable membrane**. This process continues through the root cells until the water reaches the **xylem**, fig 19.2. From here it is carried upwards to the leaves by the transpiration stream. The negative pressure needed to draw the water through the whole plant is generated by evaporation at the stomata. Nearly all of the water passing into the root passes out of the plant through the stomata.

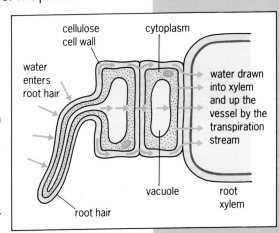

cellulose cell wall

cytoplasm

water enters root hair

water drawn into xylem and up the vessel by the transpiration stream

vacuole

root xylem

root hair

▲ **Fig 19.2 How water passes into a root**

CONTROL OF WATER LOSS BY STOMATA

The stomata usually open during the day and close during the night, fig 19.3. This allows carbon dioxide to pass in for photosynthesis during daylight, and also allows water and minerals to pass up to the leaves for photosynthesis. Transpiration is prevented at night, when no carbon dioxide is needed as no photosynthesis takes place.

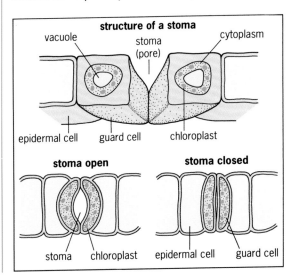

structure of a stoma

vacuole

stoma (pore)

cytoplasm

epidermal cell   guard cell   chloroplast

stoma open

stoma closed

stoma   chloroplast

epidermal cell   guard cell

◄ **Fig 19.3 The opening and closing of a stoma**

20 SITES OF GENETIC MATERIAL

In any study of biology, we recognise variation and consider its implications. However, we must consider its basic cause in more detail.

STUDYING GENETIC MATERIAL

It would be ideal if we could look down a microscope and see the cause of variation, but this is not possible. Characteristics are handed down from one generation to the next through **genetic material**. Those cells which form a link between successive generations, the **gametes**, must contain genetic material and are therefore the best starting point for our study.

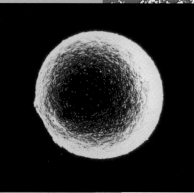

Fig 20.1 A sperm seen through a scanning electron microscope ▸

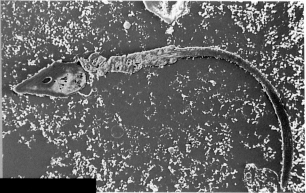

Fig 20.2 The female gamete – a human ovum ▲

The nucleus

Fig 20.1 shows a **sperm**. Like other cells, it has a nucleus and a membrane. Unlike the **ovum** in fig 20.2, it has very little cytoplasm.

Male gametes carry genetic material in the nucleus, which is the head of the sperm. When fertilisation takes place, the nucleus enters the female gamete and fuses with the female nucleus, fig 20.3.

Activity

In this activity you will take a closer look at the nucleus. The best material to use is the growing region of a root tip of garlic. This plant is available throughout the year and is easy to grow. Place the garlic bulb on the top of a test tube containing water. In a few days roots will appear.

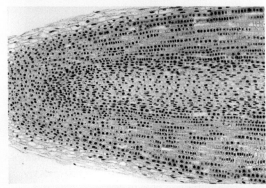

▲ **Fig 20.4 Longitudinal section through a root tip stained to show the chromosomes**

You will be given root tips which have been stained with Feulgen's stain – this reacts with chemicals in the nucleus to produce a pink colour.

1 Cut 2 mm off the end of the root tip using a sharp scalpel. (Take care.)
2 Place the tip on a microscope slide in a drop of 45% ethanoic acid. Use two mounted needles to pull the root tip apart. Try to break down the tissue into very small pieces.
3 Place a cover slip on the material. There should be just enough ethanoic acid to fill out under the cover slip.

▼ **Fig 20.3 Fertilisation – the male and female gametes fuse to form a zygote**

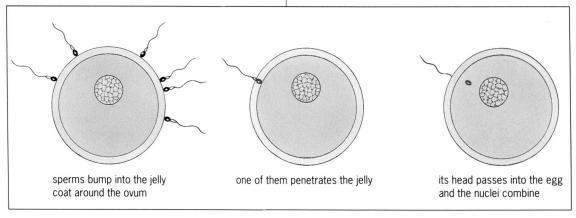

sperms bump into the jelly coat around the ovum

one of them penetrates the jelly

its head passes into the egg and the nuclei combine

4 Rest the slide on some filter paper and put a few layers of filter paper on top of it. Press your thumb straight down on the region of the cover slip. Do not push sideways. This pressing down should flatten the cells and separate the **chromosomes** which carry genetic material.

5 After about 5 seconds, peel off the filter paper. The ethanoic acid should still fill the space under the cover slip.

6 Examine the slide under the microscope. Use the high power objective after focusing under low power. Draw the cells.

You should be able to make out the chromosomes on your slide. Chromosomes contain **genes** – the carriers of genetic information.

Try to find the earliest stage of cell division at which the chromosomes are visible as double structures.

Look at several cells and compare them with fig 20.5.

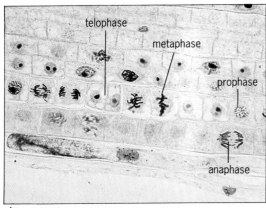

▲ **Fig 20.5 Mitosis in a root tip**

Your observations should tell you that

1 The nucleus is the most likely site of genetic material.

2 The nucleus can contain chromosomes.

3 Chromosomes are only visible in cells which are actively dividing.

CELL DIVISION BY MITOSIS

The type of cell division seen in the activity is called **mitosis**. Apart from the special case of gamete formation, most cell divisions involve mitotic division of chromosomes. Fig 20.5 shows a cross-section of a root tip with cells at different stages in mitosis.

The stages in mitosis are shown in fig 20.6. The nucleus divides in four main stages: **prophase, metaphase, anaphase** and **telophase**.

Prior to mitosis, each chromosome makes a copy of itself – it consists of two **chromatids**. During mitosis, the original and the copy separate and migrate to opposite poles along a spindle. Two daughter nuclei are thus formed. Division of the cytoplasm and the formation of a new cell wall then occurs.

Mitosis results in each new daughter cell having an identical set of chromosomes to the original cell. Mitosis is the means by which all the cells of an organism are derived from a zygote. It also allows organisms to reproduce asexually. Thus all asexually produced offspring from one organism have the same genetic information as that of their parent.

As we have seen, sexually produced offspring arise from the fusion of male and female gametes. The production of these gametes takes place by a special form of cell division called **meiosis**, which we shall loook at in the next section.

◄ **Fig 20.6 Stages in mitosis**

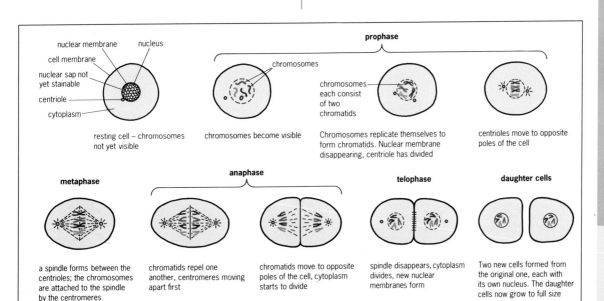

resting cell – chromosomes not yet visible

chromosomes become visible

Chromosomes replicate themselves to form chromatids. Nuclear membrane disappearing, centriole has divided

centrioles move to opposite poles of the cell

a spindle forms between the centrioles; the chromosomes are attached to the spindle by the centromeres

chromatids repel one another, centromeres moving apart first

chromatids move to opposite poles of the cell, cytoplasm starts to divide

spindle disappears, cytoplasm divides, new nuclear membranes form

Two new cells formed from the original one, each with its own nucleus. The daughter cells now grow to full size

VARIATION, INHERITANCE AND EVOLUTION

53

21 GAMETES AND FERTILISATION

By the end of this section you should be able to

■ understand how genetic information is passed from generation to generation.

The largest known cells are the female gametes, the ova. They contain little except cytoplasm – their bulk is mostly water and stored food. The important part of the ovum is the nucleus.

Sperm cells, the male gametes, are hundreds or even thousands of times smaller than ova. They are little more than a nucleus attached to a vigorous tail. During fertilisation, the sperm's nucleus joins the nucleus of the ovum to form the nucleus of a new and separate cell.

CHROMOSOMES IN THE GAMETES

The nuclei of both kinds of gamete contain fewer chromosomes than other cells in the body of the same organism. The reason for this becomes clear when we think what would happen if they did not. Cells in the human body have 46 chromosomes. If each gamete also had 46, then fertilisation would result in a baby with 92 chromosomes, and its children would have 184 chromosomes, etc. Yet all normal cells in human bodies have 46 chromosomes.

Human cells normally contain **23 pairs** of chromosomes – they are **diploid**. One of each pair comes from the mother's ovum and the other of each pair comes from the father's sperm. These combine in the zygote, and mitosis ensures that each new cell of the embryo gets a full set of chromosome pairs.

Microscopic studies of developing human sperms and eggs show that they have only **23 chromosomes**, one from each pair. They are **haploid**. How does an organism produce cells with half the number of chromosomes?

MEIOSIS

Of all the countless millions of cells in our bodies – and those of other organisms – only ovum- and sperm-producing cells divide in a way that splits up the chromosome pairs. The process is called **reduction division** or **meiosis**.

What happens during meiosis?

We shall follow meiosis as it occurs in an organism that has only two pairs of chromosomes, fig 21.1. The first step in meiosis is similar in some ways to mitosis. Each chromosome pairs with its opposite

Fig 21.1 Stages in meiosis

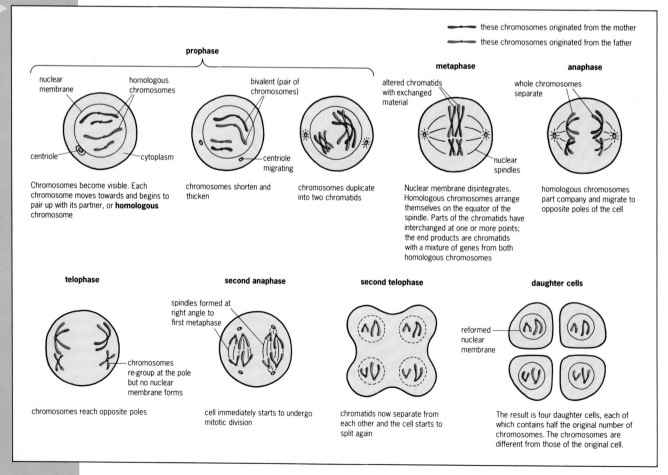

these chromosomes originated from the mother

these chromosomes originated from the father

prophase

nuclear membrane

homologous chromosomes

centriole

cytoplasm

Chromosomes become visible. Each chromosome moves towards and begins to pair up with its partner, or **homologous** chromosome

bivalent (pair of chromosomes)

centriole migrating

chromosomes shorten and thicken

chromosomes duplicate into two chromatids

metaphase

altered chromatids with exchanged material

nuclear spindles

Nuclear membrane disintegrates. Homologous chromosomes arrange themselves on the equator of the spindle. Parts of the chromatids have interchanged at one or more points; the end products are chromatids with a mixture of genes from both homologous chromosomes

anaphase

whole chromosomes separate

homologous chromosomes part company and migrate to opposite poles of the cell

telophase

chromosomes re-group at the pole but no nuclear membrane forms

chromosomes reach opposite poles

second anaphase

spindles formed at right angle to first metaphase

cell immediately starts to undergo mitotic division

second telophase

chromatids now separate from each other and the cell starts to split again

daughter cells

reformed nuclear membrane

The result is four daughter cells, each of which contains half the original number of chromosomes. The chromosomes are different from those of the original cell.

54

partner across the middle of the nucleus, and each chromosome duplicates itself. There is a double chromosome for each original, the halves of which are chromatids as in mitosis. Now the nuclear membrane disappears as in mitosis, but unlike mitosis each *chromosome* member of a pair goes to the new cells, not each chromatid. At this point we have the makings of two cells, each containing two double chromosomes, one from each original pair.

A brief resting period follows, then begins a new wave of nuclear events, during which the chromatids in the double chromosomes break apart and each chromatid becomes a separate chromosome as in mitosis. Then the cells divide again. There are now four cells, each with two chromosomes, one member of each pair of chromosomes in the original.

The significance of meiosis

Both sperm and egg cells are formed by meiosis. When the sperm unites with the egg, each provides half the total number of chromosomes for the new individual.

Because of the interchange of parts of chromatids during meiosis, each egg and sperm produced by meiosis is unique. A zygote is formed by the combination of two unique gametes, so all zygotes are also unique.

The advantage of sexual reproduction lies in the fertilised egg which makes each new life just a little different from either of its parents. This **variation** among offspring may produce one individual that is well adapted to changing conditions in the environment.

Once the egg has been fertilised, all further cell divisions produce cells with the full number of chromosomes – they are mitotic divisions. Eventually the new organism will reach maturity, and its time will come to reproduce. Its reproductive organs will then produce sperms or eggs and the cycle of life will have come full circle.

Q1 a Fig 21.2 shows a cell dividing by mitosis. Write labels for parts **A, B** and **C**.
b What will eventually happen to part **C** as mitosis continues?
c Draw one of the new cells produced by the mitosis shown in fig 21.2.

Q2 The diagrams in fig 21.3 show cells, and the number of chromosomes in their nuclei. Choose the correct word from the list to describe each diagram. [4]

mitosis meiosis ovum sperm fertilisation
(WJEC GCSE Human Biology 1991 Q17)

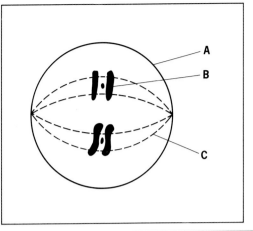

◀ **Fig 21.2**

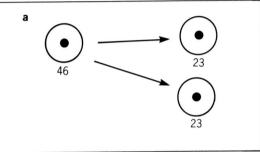

◀ **Fig 21.3**

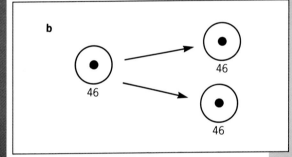

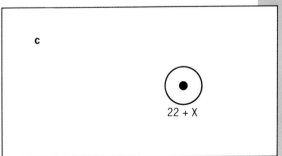

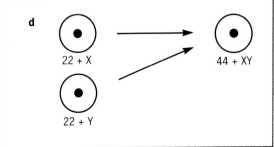

VARIATION, INHERITANCE AND EVOLUTION

22 INHERITANCE

By the end of this section you should be able to

- understand the applications of the study of genetics
- recall the work of Mendel and its significance.

We have seen that the connection between one generation and the next consists of an ovum and a sperm cell. Within these tiny units of living matter are the plans for the next generation.

WHAT IS INHERITANCE?

The sperm fertilises the ovum, and then one of the most remarkable series of changes known to science begins. The instructions within the human cell control the development of the embryo into a human, rather than into an elephant or a mouse. This control is present for every other organism that reproduces sexually.

The instructions for development are in the form of chemical messages. The way in which these messages are passed from one generation to the next is called **inheritance**. The study of inheritance has become a branch of science called **genetics**.

Applications of genetics

Today most people have heard of the term 'genetics'. Genetic engineering, genetic counselling and genetically inherited diseases are terms which are often used in newspapers, radio and television.

You have probably heard of genetics being used in medicine. There are many disorders that can be passed from parents to their children through genetic inheritance. If you were a farmer or a gardener, you would be interested in genetics as applied to methods of passing useful characters from one generation to the next, in **selective breeding**.

SELECTIVE BREEDING

For thousands of years selected pedigree animals have been prized. Such animals have had a recorded ancestry for many generations. The dairy farmer wants selected pedigree cattle that are known to give high milk yields from which to breed milking cows, fig 22.1. The hunter wants a pedigree dog bred from parents with suitable character traits. Similarly, pure lines of cultivated plants are needed by arable farmers. Characters such as grain yield (fig 22.2), fruit yield and disease resistance in plants are desirable qualities that can be maintained through selective breeding. (There is more about selective breeding on pages 86–7.)

▲ **Fig 22.2 Wheat yield has been increased through selective breeding**

Understanding inheritance

Although humans have learned a great deal about selective breeding, we do not pretend to understand the process completely. Some attempts at breeding to produce particular characteristics have had little or no success. We know that selective breeding sometimes gives the results we want, but sometimes it does not.

Inheritance is obviously involved in selective breeding, but how the process operates remained a mystery until the nineteenth century.

It might seem difficult to believe, but the whole science of genetics began with a monk experimenting with pea seeds in 1865. Using this unlikely material and a great deal of patience, this Augustinian monk, Gregor Mendel, set out the first principles of inheritance. For his unique contribution to science, he is often called the 'father of genetics'.

22.1 A herd of pedigree dairy cows ▶

◀ **Fig 22.3 Gregor Mendel, the 'father of genetics'**

THE WORK OF GREGOR MENDEL

Careful planning

Although Mendel performed very few experiments that had not been done before, he succeeded where others had failed. Possibly his success was due to the unusual combination of skills he brought to the task. He was trained in mathematics as well as in biology. With this background, he planned experiments that at the time were novel in three respects

1. Instead of studying a small number of offspring from one mating, Mendel used many identical matings. He therefore had enormous numbers of offspring to study.
2. As a result of having large numbers to study, he was able to apply statistical methods to analyse the results.
3. He limited each cross to a *single* difference, a single pair of contrasted characters at a time.

People who had carried out genetic crosses with plants and animals before Mendel did not concentrate on one character at a time. Mendel always used **pure-breeding** stock, individuals which received similar genes from both parents and always produced the same characteristics generation after generation, like pedigree cows. In previous experiments pure-breeding stock had not been used and characters were often masked by each other.

Why the garden pea?

Mendel selected garden peas for his experiments because he knew they possessed many varieties which could be studied. The plants are easy to cultivate and cross, and the generation time is reasonably short. Finally, and of great importance, the plants are self-pollinating (see page 46).

▲ **Fig 22.4 Pea seeds – the plant on which the science of genetics was based**

Fig 22.5 shows the structure of the pea flower. Pollen from the anthers falls onto the stigma of the same flower. This happens before the flower opens fully. Pollen tubes develop from the pollen grains and the male gamete travels down to the female gamete in the ovary to fertilise it.

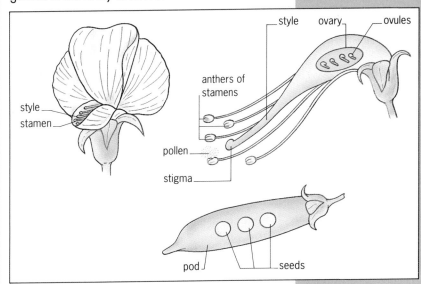

▲ **Fig 22.5 Pollination and the pea flower**

Cross-pollinating pea plants

In order to pollinate one pea flower with pollen from another plant, the anthers are removed from the flower before its own pollen is mature. Later, when the stigma is ready to receive pollen, it is dusted with pollen taken from some other chosen pea flower. In this way the parents of the next generation can be controlled. Cross-pollinating is sometimes called **crossing**.

MENDEL'S EXPERIMENTS

Mendel first made sure that the plants he started with were all pure-bred for the character he was studying. He did this by letting the plants fertilise themselves for a number of generations. The offspring of each generation were studied to make sure they were all like one another and like the parent plant.

Then Mendel made hundreds of crosses by dusting the pollen of one kind of plant on the stigmas of plants of another kind. For example, he pollinated plants from a type whose seeds were always round with pollen from a type whose seeds were always wrinkled.

In every case he found that all the offspring resembled one of the parents, and showed no sign of the character of the other parent. Thus all the crosses between plants with round seeds and plants with wrinkled seeds produced offspring whose seeds were always round. One character seemed to 'dominate' the other. Mendel therefore called this character the **dominant** character.

VARIATION, INHERITANCE AND EVOLUTION

Mendel's results for the first generation

Mendel used seven pairs of contrasted characters. His characters are shown in the table below.

Character	Dominance
seed shape	round seed dominant to wrinkled seed
seed colour	yellow seed dominant to green seed
seed coat colour	coloured seed coat dominant to white seed coat
pod shape	inflated pod dominant to wrinkled pod
pod colour	green pod dominant to yellow pod
flower position	axial flower dominant to terminal flower
stem length	long stem dominant to short stem

Analysing the results

When a cross is made between two plants which are pure bred for contrasted characters, for example round seed versus wrinkled seed, the parents are the **P1 generation**. The offspring are the **first filial** or **F1 generation**. These labels will help us follow the steps in Mendel's thinking.

He let the F1 plants pollinate themselves (he **selfed** them). This produced the **F2 generation**. The dominant character appeared in 75% of the F2 generation, while 25% of the other character reappeared. Since the other character had receded into the background for a generation, he called it **recessive**. He also noted no 'in between' forms. The new seeds were either round or wrinkled, or the plants tall or short, etc. – just like the P1.

Mendel's results for the second generation

Mendel's results are shown in the table below. The 75% : 25% or 3 : 1 ratio is obvious in all cases.

Characters crossed	F1	Selfed	F2	Ratio
round × wrinkled seed	all round	round × round	5474 round 1858 wrinkled	2.96 : 1
yellow × green seed	all yellow	yellow × yellow	6022 yellow 2001 green	3.01 : 1
coloured × white seed coat	all coloured	coloured × coloured	705 coloured 224 white	3.15 : 1
inflated × wrinkled pods	all inflated	inflated × inflated	882 inflated 299 wrinkled	2.95 : 1
green × yellow pods	all green	green × green	428 green 152 yellow	2.82 : 1
axial × terminal flowers	all axial	axial × axial	651 axial 207 terminal	3.14 : 1
long × short stems	all long	long × long	787 long 277 short	2.84 : 1

23 MONOHYBRID INHERITANCE

By the end of this section you should be able to
- understand the principles of a monohybrid cross involving dominant and recessive alleles.

The type of crosses carried out by Mendel involved studying a single character at a time. Today we call this **monohybrid inheritance**.

INTERPRETING MENDEL'S WORK

Mendel made his greatest contribution to genetics by explaining his observations. He began by using symbols to represent the characters he was dealing with. His mathematical training encouraged him to use symbols rather than written descriptions.

Genes

For example, Mendel assumed that the character for tall plants was caused by a **dominant factor**. He used a capital **T** to symbolise this factor. The character for short plants, the only alternative to tall plants, was caused by a **recessive factor**, which he denoted as **t**. In 1910, many years after Mendel's work, the factor was given the name **gene**.

Alleles

Next, Mendel assumed that every plant had a **pair** of factors (genes) for each character. These pairs of genes are today called **allelomorphic pairs** or **alleles**. An allele is one of two alternative forms of a gene which may occupy the same part of a chromosome. For example, if **T** represents tall and **t** represents short, the allelomorphic pair may be **TT** or **Tt** or **tt**. **T** and **t** are at the same place on corresponding chromosomes in a pair.

Mendel was convinced of the existence of alleles because some parent plants with the dominant gene produced some offspring with the recessive gene. Therefore, every F1 plant in his crosses must have had *both* types of gene, though only the dominant one was expressed. The F1 plant could be represented by **Tt**.

Mendel also assigned a pair of genes per character even to pure-breeding plants. A plant from parents that bred true for tall plants was therefore **TT**. Similarly, a plant from parents that bred true for short plants was **tt**.

Phenotypes and genotypes

These paired symbols representing the genes of an organism are today called its **genotype**. When an organism has identical factors in its genotype (for example **TT** or **tt**), it is known as **homozygous**. If it has different factors (for example **Tt**), it is known as **heterozygous**.

The character displayed by an organism is called its **phenotype**. For example, both a **TT** and a **Tt** plant have the same phenotype – they are both tall.

TESTING HYPOTHESES

Using this logic, Mendel was now able to test his hypothesis about genes. If he knew the genotype of each parent, he could predict the kinds and proportions of gametes each parent could produce. From this, he could predict the kinds and proportions of the offspring.

If every plant had a pair of genes for each character, was there any rule about how these genes were passed on to the next generation? Mendel thought about the short plants that appeared in the F2 generation. These could not carry the dominant gene **T**. They must have received the recessive gene **t** from the F1 parent. Remember the F2 generation was produced by self-pollinating the F1 generation.

The next question was: how frequently do gametes that carry **t** occur among all the gametes produced by the F1 **Tt** parents? Mendel reasoned back from the proportions of **tt** short plants in the F2 generation. These amounted to $\frac{1}{4}$ of the entire F2 generation. So the frequency of **t** in the ova and pollen grains produced by the F1 generation should be $\frac{1}{2}$ (since $\frac{1}{2} \times \frac{1}{2} = \frac{1}{4}$). This means that half the gametes of a **Tt** plant would carry **T**, and the other half **t**.

Working backwards – an illustration

Fig 23.1 (overleaf) shows one of Mendel's experiments with peas. If a pure-breeding tall variety was crossed with a pure-breeding short variety, all the offspring were tall. When two of these plants were crossed, three tall offspring were produced for every short one.

Mendel saw that these results could be explained if the characteristics were inherited as 'particles'. Each plant had two of these particles, and one was dominant to the other. In this case the tall character (**T**) was dominant to short (**t**). His interpretation of the results is shown in fig 23.2.

The law of segregation

Mendel thus arrived at a general rule – the **law of segregation**

'The two members of each pair of genes must separate when gametes are formed, and only one of each pair can go to each gamete.'

If a parent is **TT**, its gametes will all inherit one or other of its **T** genes, but not both. If the parent is **tt**, its gametes will all inherit one of its **t** genes. If the parent if **Tt**, half the gametes will inherit its **T** gene, and the other half will inherit its **t** gene.

Fig 23.1 One of Mendel's experiments with tall and short pea plants

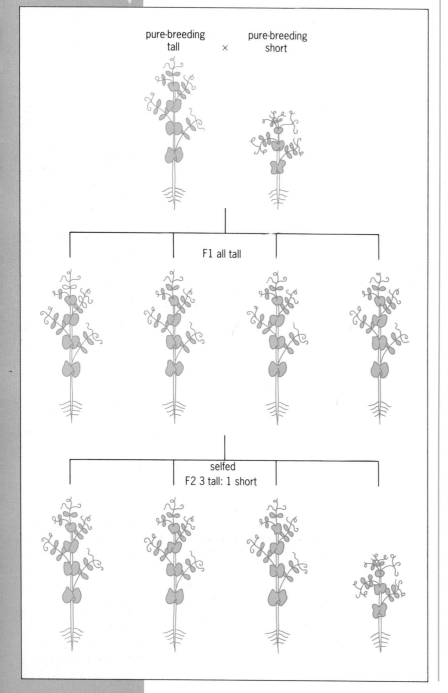

Q1 Gregor Mendel formulated his first law of genetics which states 'Of a pair of contrasted characters, only one can be represented in a gamete by its germinal unit'.

a Give the modern name for 'germinal unit'.
b State where these 'germinal units' are found in the gametes.
c A red-haired woman marries a brown-haired man, and all the children are brown haired. Explain this genetically.

▼ **Fig 23.2 A graphic explanation of Mendel's results**

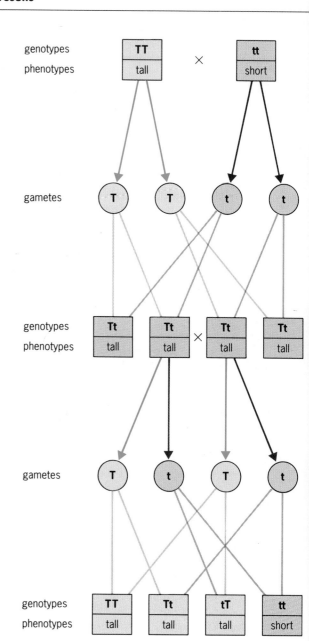

Q2 Fig 23.3 is part of a family tree showing the distribution of brown eyes and blue eyes.

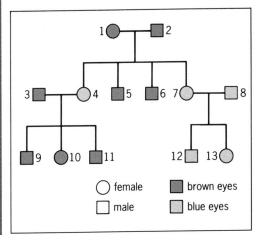

▲ **Fig 23.3**

a Which number represents a man who is homozygous for blue eyes?
b Which number represents a woman who must be heterozygous?
c Which of the eye colours is controlled by a dominant gene?
d Which part of the family tree enables you to answer part **c**?

Q3 In humans, the gene for tongue rolling, **R**, is dominant to the gene for the inability to roll the tongue, **r**.

a Using these symbols, give the genotypes of the children that could be born from a marriage between a heterozygous father and a non tongue-rolling mother.
b State whether the children would be tongue-rollers or not.

Q4 Alex was interested to see how eye colour was inherited in his family, so he wrote down the colours of the eyes of all his family. The information and his deductions are given in fig 23.4. Unfortunately, he could not finish it. Copy the diagram and fill in the gaps.

a Write the correct words for the numbers 1–17.
b From the results, state the dominant eye colour.
c Also from the results, state what 'recessive' means.
d How many factors for eye colour do the gametes shown contain?

Q5 **a** A little boy wanted to breed grey coloured mice so he bought a white male mouse and a black female mouse from a pet shop and mated them, thinking that the two colours would blend (mix). He was very disappointed when the young all turned out to be black!
 i Why were all the young black rather than white?
 ii Why were no grey mice produced?
 iii Do you think he would have had a different result if the male had been black and the female white?
 iv How could the boy produce white mice?
b In peas, tall plants are dominant to short plants.
 Let **T** represent the gene for tallness and **t** the gene for shortness. Each plant has two genes so can be **TT**, **Tt** or **tt**.
 i Why do we use a capital 'T' (large T) to represent tallness?
 ii Give letters to represent the genes of the *short* plants.
 iii Give letters to represent *two* possible sets of genes of the tall plants.

▼ **Fig 23.4**

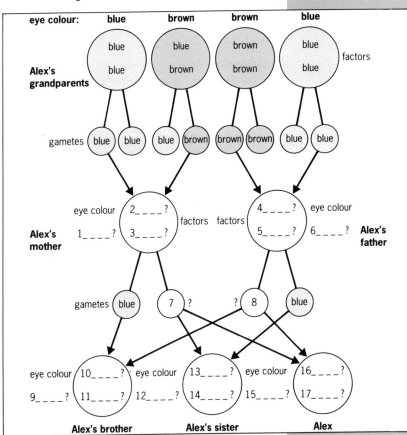

24 CHROMO-SOMES & GENES

By the end of this section you should be able to

- understand how genes are distinguished by the order of base pairs on the DNA molecule
- understand how DNA replicates and controls protein synthesis.

An organism's characteristics are passed down from generation to generation by **genes**. But what are genes, where can they be found and what do they actually do?

NUCLEIC ACIDS

Life is a series of chemical reactions. Quite early in the history of genetics, scientists knew that genes must be chemicals.

Proteins are the essential chemicals found in living cells. Early geneticists knew that genes were contained in chromosomes in the nuclei of cells, and guessed that they were proteins.

By 1950, it became clear that it was not the protein in chromosomes that passed on the code of life from generation to generation. It was another component of chromosomes – **nucleic acids**. These are some of the largest and the most fascinating of all life's molecules. Two forms of nucleic acid are known – **deoxyribonucleic acid (DNA)** which is found in all chromosomes, and **ribonucleic acid (RNA)** which is found in both the cytoplasm and the nuclei of cells. It was DNA that carried the genetic code.

THE STRUCTURE OF DNA

The structure of the DNA molecule was discovered in 1953 by the American James Watson and the English scientist Francis Crick, working at the Cavendish Laboratory in Cambridge.

Fig 24.1 James Watson and Francis Crick

Nucleic acids, like proteins, are made of many units strung together. DNA has a 'ladder-like' structure of two long **sugar–phosphate chains** joined together by connecting **bases** (the 'rungs'). The ladder is twisted to form a three-dimensional **double helix** as shown in fig 24.2. Fig 24.3 shows a model of a molecule of DNA.

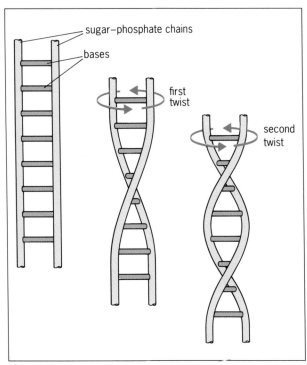

▲ **Fig 24.2 The double helix of the DNA molecule**

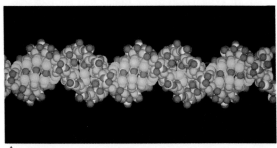

▲ **Fig 24.3 A model of DNA – the spheres represent atoms**

The base pairs

Watson and Crick discovered that the rungs of the ladder are made of four different bases: **guanine**, **cytosine**, **thymine** and **adenine**. The bases fit together as shown in fig 24.4. Guanine only pairs with cytosine, and thymine only pairs with adenine.

The differences between one DNA molecule and another depend on the pattern of these base pairs. This order determines how genes produce their effects in organisms. For example, the order of base pairs which produces blue eyes is different from the order of base pairs which produces brown eyes. The DNA contains the **genetic code** which tells an organism how to develop.

A strand of DNA can be over 10 000 base units long, so there is an almost unlimited number of possible arrangements of base pairs. Therefore there is an almost unlimited number of possible genes in plants and animals.

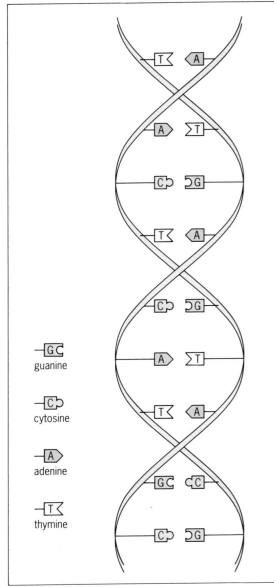

▲ Fig 24.4 The structure of DNA

GC
guanine

C
cytosine

A
adenine

T
thymine

HOW DO GENES WORK?

How do genes control the development of an organism?

Genes are units on the DNA molecule. They make up a code on the DNA molecule that determines which chemical reactions will take place in a cell, and at what speed.

The growth and development of a cell is determined by the type and speed of these chemical reactions taking place within it. This is controlled by enzymes, which are proteins. The genetic code has its effect by determining which proteins are made (synthesised) in the cell. Hence, by controlling protein synthesis, DNA controls the life of the cell, and so the development of the organism.

Q1 A method called DNA fingerprinting lets us compare the genetic material in different people.
A person's DNA is separated into 'bands' by this method.
Only identical twins have exactly the same DNA.
Fig 24.5 shows bands of DNA for eight people A to H.

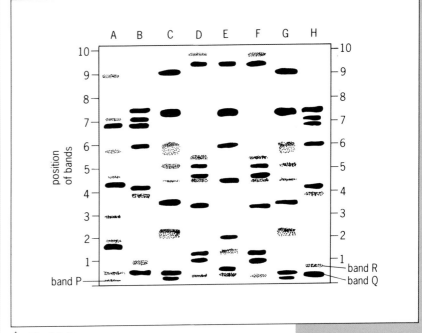

▲ Fig 24.5

a i Copy and complete the table below to give the number of 'bands' for each person. The first one has been done for you. [2]

Person	A	B	C	D	E	F	G	H
Number of bands	11							

ii So that the data can be used by a computer, the positions of the bands are given numbers using the scale on the side of the diagram.
The readings are taken from the middle of each band starting from the bottom. Copy and complete the data for person A in the table below. Band P has been done for you. [2]

0.3								

(question continues on page 65)

VARIATION,
INHERITANCE
AND EVOLUTION

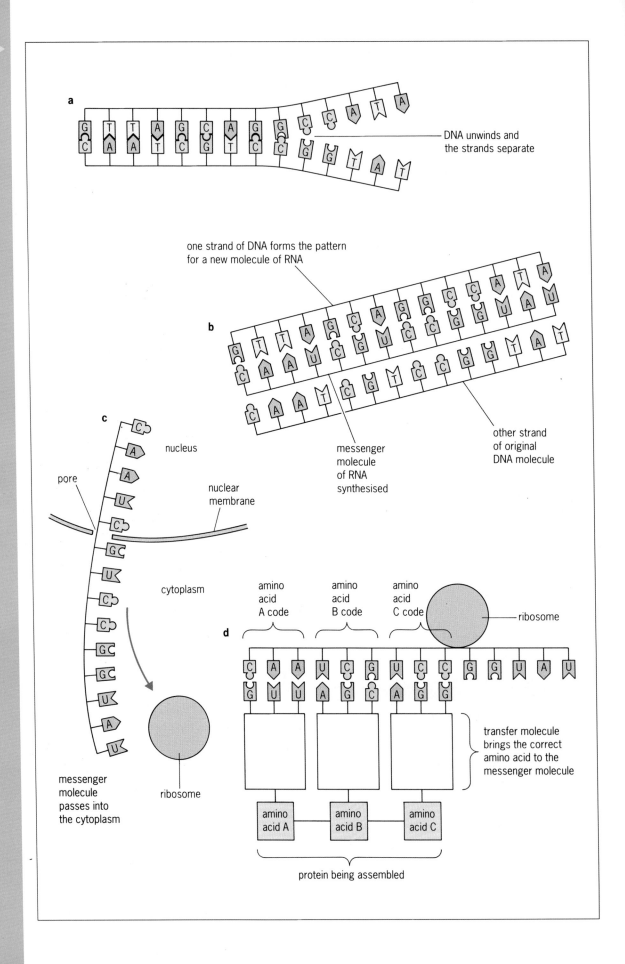

Fig 24.6 How the DNA code is read and determines the structure of a protein

a — DNA unwinds and the strands separate

one strand of DNA forms the pattern for a new molecule of RNA

b

messenger molecule of RNA synthesised

other strand of original DNA molecule

c

nucleus

pore

nuclear membrane

cytoplasm

messenger molecule passes into the cytoplasm

ribosome

d

amino acid A code

amino acid B code

amino acid C code

ribosome

transfer molecule brings the correct amino acid to the messenger molecule

amino acid A

amino acid B

amino acid C

protein being assembled

b i D and F are identical twins. State *two* ways in which the bands show this. [2]

ii Give the letters of *two* other pairs of identical twins shown in fig 24.5. [2]

iii Give the letters of two people who are not shown as a pair of identical twins. Give *one* reason why we can tell this from the diagram. [2]

(LEAG GCSE Human Biology 2 1991 Q4 (part))

HOW DOES DNA CONTROL PROTEIN SYNTHESIS?

Coding for amino acids

Proteins are made of building blocks called **amino acids** (see page 13). The amino acids are linked together in chains. The different orders in which different amino acids are linked together determines the type of protein synthesised.

DNA is able to regulate how the amino acids are arranged in a protein. The types and arrangement of the bases in the DNA molecule act as a code that determines which amino acids are linked together in what order. Thus, by determining the form and arrangement of these building blocks, DNA controls protein synthesis.

The synthesis of proteins

The following is a very simplified account of how DNA is used for making proteins in the cell.

1 The long 'twisted ladder' molecule of DNA unwinds and splits along its length between the bases, fig 24.6**a**.

2 One half of the molecule now acts as a pattern for the formation of a **messenger molecule**. This consists of RNA, and is made up of new bases found in the chemical mixture inside the nucleus. These strings of bases line up opposite their partners on the original half of the DNA. In this way, they form a single strand of RNA. The result is that the code originally present in the DNA is now also on the RNA messenger molecule, fig 24.6**b**.

3 The messenger RNA molecule then passes through a pore in the nuclear membrane to structures in the cell cytoplasm called **ribosomes**, fig 24.6**c**.

4 The code on the messenger RNA molecule then determines which amino acids from the cytoplasm of the cell become linked together, and therefore determines the type of protein synthesised, fig 24.6**d**.

The role of RNA molecules

Once attached to the ribosome, the **messenger RNA** molecule acts as a template. The message coded for in the sequence of bases on the original DNA molecule is translated into the sequence of amino acids, which in turn form a particular protein molecule.

Another type of RNA, **transfer RNA**, occurs in the cytoplasm of the cell. Every transfer RNA molecule contains three bases which can pair with three bases on the messenger RNA, fig 24.6**d**. Each transfer RNA molecule brings its own amino acid, corresponding to the three-base code, into line so that chain of amino acids is built up. Thus a whole protein molecule can be made.

Once a transfer RNA molecule has brought its amino acid into the corrrect position in the chain, it is free to operate again. In fact, a transfer RNA molecule can carry out this process three times every second.

DNA REPLICATION

The discovery that DNA carries the code of life was an enormous step forward in molecular biology. The next step was to find out how the molecule replicates itself.

We saw on page 53 that before a cell divides, the chromosomes duplicate themselves. As we have just learned, a chromosome consists of a long chain of DNA, and this is what duplicates itself.

The two long strands of DNA separate and then the free bases present in the cell nucleus align themselves with the separated strands, the bases pairing guanine with cytosine and thymine with adenine as before. This results in two new double helices, each with the same order of base pairs as the original, fig 24.7.

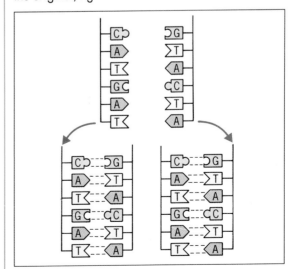

▲ **Fig 24.7 The mechanism of DNA replication**

25 SEX CHROMOSOMES

By the end of this section you should be able to
- understand how the sex of an individual is determined by the sex chromosomes in the gametes of the parents
- understand the principle of sex-linked inheritance.

THE DISCOVERY OF THE SEX CHROMOSOMES

The discovery of special chromosomes which determine the sex of an organism took place in 1910. An American geneticist, Thomas Hunt Morgan, fig 25.1, was studying the genetics of the fruit fly, *Drosophila melanogaster*. You may have seen this small fly hovering around over-ripe fruit, sometimes in vast numbers. Just as Mendel's significant discoveries were made using very common but perhaps unlikely organisms, so Morgan's discoveries were equally important.

Fig 25.1 ▶ Thomas Hunt Morgan, 1866–1945

Morgan's experiments

Among thousands of red-eyed flies raised under laboratory conditions, Morgan found one **mutant** fly (see page 68) with white eyes. This fly was a male, and was mated with a normal red-eyed female. The F1 generation consisted entirely of red-eyed flies. By following Mendel's logic, this meant that the gene for white eyes was recessive to the gene for red eyes.

Next, members of the F1 generation were mated to produce the F2 generation. The results agreed with Mendel's observations on peas, that is, a 3:1 ratio of red-eyed flies to white-eyed flies. However, Morgan noticed that all of the white-eyed flies were males. The gene for eye colour was in some way linked to the sex of the animal. White eye colour is controlled by a **sex-linked gene**.

X and Y chromosomes

A clue to this puzzle was seen in the chromosomes. It was already known that there is a difference between the chromosomes of male and female *Drosophila*. Of the four pairs of chromosomes in each cell, three pairs are identical in males and females. The other pair contains two different sorts of chromosomes. Straight, rod-shaped chromosomes are called **X chromosomes**. Females have two X chromosomes. Males have one X chromosome and one hook-shaped chromosome called the **Y chromosome**, fig 25.2.

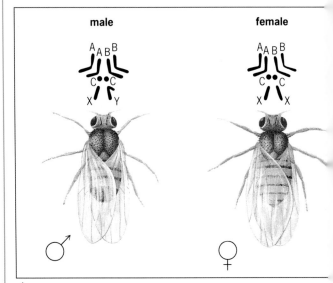

▲ **Fig 25.2 Sex chromosomes in the fruit fly**

The significance of Morgan's work

When combined with a knowledge of meiosis, Morgan's observations led to an important conclusion.

Males produce two different kinds of sperms. Half their sperms carry an X chromosome and the other half carry a Y chromosome. Females, on the other hand, produce one kind of ova, all containing one X chromosome. Both ova and sperms, of course, also carry one chromosome of each of the other pairs.

Because of their connection with the sex of the flies, the X and Y chromosomes are called **sex chromosomes**. All other chromosomes are called **autosomes**.

SEX DETERMINATION

The discovery of two kinds of sex chromosomes suggested that perhaps they would provide an explanation for the determination of sex. Flies with two X chromosomes are always females. Those with an X chromosome and a Y chromosome are always males. The sex of a fly then depends whether the ovum (with an X chromosome) is fertilised by a

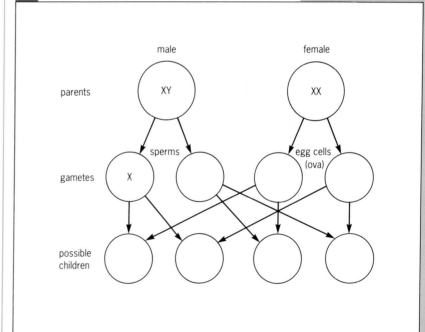

Fig 25.3 Sex determination in the fruit fly

sperm with an X chromosome or one with a Y chromosome. Thus it is the male fly's sperm that determines the sex of the offspring, fig 25.3.

Sex chromosomes in other species

Since the time of Morgan, experimental and research techniques have been improved. It is now possible to show that a similar difference in one pair of chromosomes is common among all animals. Most plants do not have separate sexes. However, those with separate male and female individuals have sex chromosomes.

The human pattern of sex chromosomes is similar to that of the fruit fly. Humans have 23 pairs of chromosomes, fig 25.4. Twenty-two pairs of these are autosomes (non-sex chromosomes), and one pair consists of the sex chromosomes. The Y chromosome is very small compared with the X chromosome. We can explain sex determination in humans in the same way as in fruit flies.

Not all animals have sex-determining sperms. Birds and butterflies have males with XX chromosomes and females with XY chromosomes, so it is the female gamete that determines the sex of the offspring.

Q1 **a** Use the symbols X and Y to fill in the blank circles in a copy of fig 25.5 showing sex inheritance. [3]

▼ Fig 25.5

b Explain the difference between the following pairs.
  i genotype and phenotype [1]
  ii gene and allele [1]
  [Total 10 marks]
(LEAG GCSE Human Biology 1 1990 Q14)

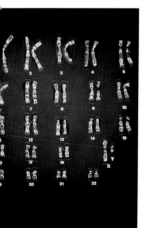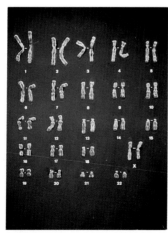

▲ **Fig 25.4 The chromosomes of the human male (left) and female (right)**

26 VARIATION AND MUTATION

By the end of this section you should be able to

- understand different sources of genetic variation
- explain how genetic variation is brought about by reshuffling of chromosomes and gene mutation.

No two living things are exactly alike. If you look casually at a group of organisms of one species, you might think that they were all the same, but people who are familiar with particular organisms soon learn to distinguish between them. Plants can vary just as much as animals.

HEREDITY

A boy tends to resemble his sister or his parents more closely than his more distant relatives. He resembles his relatives more closely than his unrelated friends. These resemblances are due mainly to **heredity**, or the combination of genes on his chromosomes. The resemblance of identical twins is due totally to heredity – their chromosomes contain the same genes. (Identical twins are formed when the fertilised ovum splits and forms two zygotes instead of one, so identical twins are genetically identical.) The differences that enable us to tell one twin from another are due to environmental influences.

Variation

Separation of chromosomes in meiosis (see pages 54–5), and the random way in which they recombine, produces **variation**. Even the simplest of organisms has hundreds of genes, and complex organisms have thousands. A tremendous amount of variation is possible from this number of genes. Furthermore, crossing over of chromatids in meiosis increases the possibility of variation by making new combinations of genes. The mixing of chromosomes from two different organisms at fertilisation ensures that all individuals are unique.

Environmental factors

Other factors apart from heredity affect the development of an organism. A pea plant may inherit tall genes, but will not grow to its full height in poor soil.

MUTATION

Regardless of how many times different genes are combined into new arrangements, the results are all variations on an existing pattern. However, a change in the genes themselves – a **mutation** – will give a new type of pattern. A mutation occurs when the order of base pairs on the DNA molecule becomes altered for some reason (see page 65).

Mutations of the fruit fly

One of the first mutations studied was in the fruit fly, *Drosophila melanogaster*. Thomas Hunt Morgan (see page 66) found that in a strain of pure-bred red-eyed flies, there was one with white eyes, fig 26.1. This mutation was caused by a sudden change in one of the many genes controlling eye colour. Since then hundreds of fruit fly mutations have been found and studied.

▲ **Fig 26.1 A normal red-eyed fruit fly and a mutant with white eyes**

What is a mutation?

Mutation involves a change in the chemical structure of a gene. Mutations can result from a mistake in gene duplication. For example, in replication, one DNA strand might pick up the wrong base and so produce a new arrangement. Since genes control the manufacture of proteins, the new gene might make a different protein, or be unable to make a protein at all. This could result in a change of body characteristic, or the introduction of a new characteristic.

Most mutations are recessive, and are masked by dominant normal genes. Thus, except for some sex-linked genes (see page 66), mutations do not show up until two of the mutant genes occur in the same individual. The individual will then be homozygous for the mutant gene.

Mutations and evolution

Some mutations produce only minor changes in body chemistry. If it is an unfavourable change for the organism it will probably be lost, because the organism with the mutation is unlikely to survive and have offspring which will inherit the mutant gene. Sooner or later, however, the mutation will occur again.

A few examples of mutations are shown in figs 26.2–5. Although we speak of 'mutant' genes and 'normal' genes, the genes we now call 'normal' were once mutants. Because they were favourable, they have been passed on from generation to generation and have become part of the normal collection of genes. Mutation is all part of the process of evolution (see page 78).

▲ **Fig 26.2 A normal orange and a mutant without seeds**

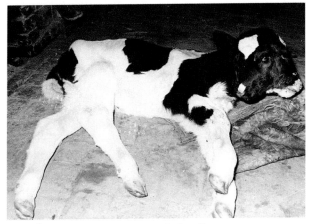

▲ **Fig 26.3 A two-headed calf**

▲ **Fig 26.4 Canadian mutant cats with no hair**

▲ **Fig 26.5 One-eared rabbits**

Q1 Penicillin is an antibiotic which normally kills certain types of bacteria. Fig 26.6 shows how a bacterium might produce a population which is resistant to penicillin.

▼ **Fig 26.6**

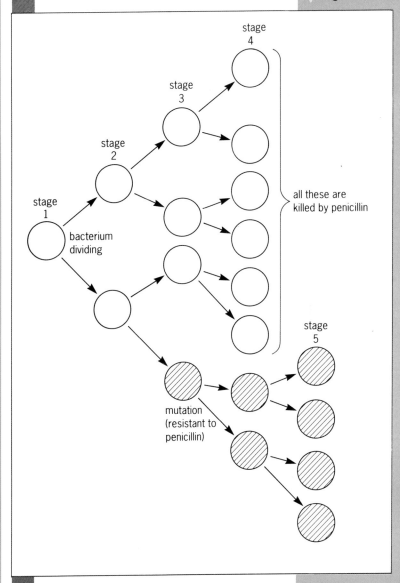

a Name the type of reproduction shown in the diagram. [1]

b i Between which *two* stages has the mutation taken place?

ii What is meant by a 'mutation'?

iii What percentage or fraction of the bacteria shown survive penicillin treatment at stage 4?

iv Why do mutations show up more frequently in bacteria than in humans? [4]

c In the theory of evolution, what is the importance of mutations? [1]
(WJEC Modular Science 1991 Q4 (part))

27 RADIATION AND GENETICS

By the end of this section you should be able to

▸ explain how radiation can bring about mutations and cell damage.

All living things are exposed to a certain amount of radiation (see pages 140 – 42). The two main sources of this radiation are

1 cosmic rays from space
2 radioactive materials in the Earth's crust.

This **background radiation** is, in part, responsible for the mutations that occur in all organisms.

HOW DOES RADIATION AFFECT LIVING TISSUES?

We can think of radiation as being a series of rapidly fired mini-bullets. These bullets hit the molecules that make up organisms. These molecules can be damaged by radiation. If DNA is damaged in this way, then the code which is normally inherited can be destroyed or altered, causing mutations.

Ionisation

Radiation leaves decaying nuclei (see page 140) with enormous energy. All types of radiation can **ionise** materials in their path. Thus any biological molecule hit by radiation may be ionised and therefore destroyed. This in itself is enough to cause considerable damage to a living cell.

Radiation and mutation

It has been known for a long time that an increase in radiation causes an increase in the mutation rate. In other words, it causes an increase in the rate at which genes are altered.

This knowledge has been used in genetic experiments to produce mutations in experimental organisms. This treatment has produced some useful plant varieties. It is also known that there is no level of radiation that is so low that it brings about no change in mutation rate – radiation always has an effect. These findings have important significance for us in the modern nuclear and technological age.

Increasing levels of radiation

The human race has increased the background radiation levels in several ways. First, there has been an increase in the use of X-rays for medical purposes. There was an increase in the testing of nuclear weapons, fig 27.1. The dumping of radioactive waste from nuclear power stations is a problem which has not been solved with modern technology.

▲ **Fig 27.1 These soldiers watching a nuclear weapon test in 1953 were unaware of the dangers of the radiation to which they were being exposed**

It must be emphasised that this increase in radiation is only a fraction of the naturally occurring background radiation. However, we have seen that any increase will increase the mutation rate.

HOW THE DAMAGE IS DONE

Radiation may damage a cell by **direct action** or by **indirect action**. The result of direct action is damage to a molecule, for example damage to a molecule of DNA by an electron or other atomic particle passing through it.

Indirect action is the change in a large molecule brought about by highly active pieces of molecules (**free radicals**). Free radicals are formed by the action of radiation on water molecules. Fig 27.2 shows the various particles that are produced when water molecules absorb radiation energy. Although these highly active pieces of molecules are very short lived, they can do a lot of damage to any large molecules that are near them. If they are near to DNA then changes in genes or mutations will result.

70

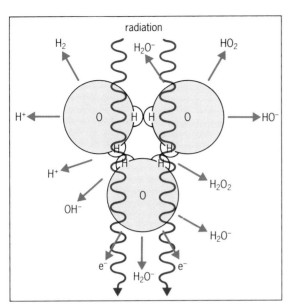

▲ **Fig 27.2 Many highly reactive products are formed when water molecules absorb radiation energy. The ions, free radicals and molecules are short lived, but are reactive enough to damage other molecules in the body**

TYPES OF RADIATION AND THEIR EFFECTS

We shall look at the biological effect of alpha-particles, beta-particles, and X-rays and gamma-rays (see page 141).

Alpha-particles

Alpha-particles spread their energy very quickly. They form an enormous number of ions and fragments of molecules.

There is little danger from alpha-particles unless they get inside the body. The skin easily stops the particles entering from outside sources. However, if an organism takes in food containing an alpha-radiation source, the body cells will become contaminated and the alpha-particles become a serious hazard.

The most actively dividing tissues in the body are the blood-producing bone marrow, the liver, the testes and the ovaries. If alpha-particles get into these tissues they can do two kinds of damage:

1 the bone marrow and liver cells will be affected, which will shorten the life of the person
2 any harm done to the sex organs will be inherited via the DNA in the gametes and passed on to future generations.

Products from nuclear reactors are one source of alpha-particles and pose a serious problem. For example, plutonium-239 is a long-lasting alpha source which can easily enter food chains. Once in the body, it accumulates in the bone and is suspected of causing anaemia and **leukaemia**. Leukaemia is a form of cancer which affects blood cells in the bone marrow. Leukaemia occurs when mechanisms which control blood cell manufacture break down. An imbalance in the correct proportions of red cells, white cells and platelets then occurs, fig 27.3.

Nuclear waste leaked from the Sellafield reprocessing plant in Cumbria (fig 27.4) has been detected in the Irish Sea. Fish are now tested for radiation contamination, and grass and mud samples (fig 27.5) near power stations are also analysed to check that the radiation levels are not too high.

▲ **Fig 27.4 The Sellafield nuclear reprocessing plant in Cumbria**

Beta-particles

Beta-particles are high-speed electrons and can penetrate the skin. They are also a hazard if a beta source is taken internally.

Strontium-90 and caesium-137 have attracted considerable attention because they readily accumulate in living organisms. For example, fish caught in the North Sea have been found with caesium-137 in their flesh. Strontium-90 is similar to calcium and becomes localised in bones. Beta emissions can damage the red bone marrow and cause anaemia and leukaemia. Caesium-137 is absorbed by all cells.

X-rays and gamma-rays

X-rays and gamma-rays have great penetrating power. They are a massive hazard even when their source is outside the body. Great care must be taken to minimise exposure when X-rays are used. Again, the most actively dividing tissues – developing embryos, for instance – are most sensitive. X-raying pregnant women is rarely carried out for this reason – ultrasound imaging is used instead (see pages 250 – 51).

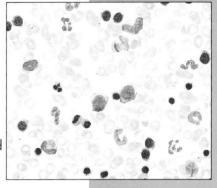

▼ **Fig 27.3 Sample from the bone marrow of a leukaemia patient, showing white blood cells stained**

▲ **Fig 27.5 Collecting plutonium-contaminated mud for monitoring near British Nuclear Fuels, Sellafield**

VARIATION, INHERITANCE AND EVOLUTION

28 RADIOACTIVITY AND THE ENVIRONMENT

By the end of this section you should be able to

- explain the implications of nuclear waste disposal and nuclear accidents for the environment.

NUCLEAR WASTE

One of the main environmental concerns today is disposal of nuclear waste from power stations.

Half-life

Some radioactive waste chemicals have extremely long **half-lives** (see page 142). This is the main consideration when deciding on methods of disposal. The half-life is the time that it takes for the radioactivity emitted by the chemical to be reduced by half. A radioactive substance can be thought of as decaying away over a period of time.

The table below shows the half-lives of some important radioactive elements. Some of these may enter our environment as a result of human activities.

Element	Half-life
carbon-14	5760 years
phosphorus-32	14.3 days
sulphur-35	87.2 days
calcium-45	165 days
strontium-90	28 years
iodine-131	8.04 days
caesium-137	30 years
plutonium-239	24 400 years

Plutonium's radiation is made up of alpha-particles. Note the vast difference between the half-life of this element and those of the others in the list!

METHODS OF DISPOSAL

The production of highly radioactive waste is a problem with all technologies which use radioactive materials, including nuclear power stations. The waste must be disposed of safely in places where it cannot be recovered.

Three main sites for the disposal of solid, high-level waste have been suggested

1 the surface of the deep ocean floor
2 under the surface of the land
3 under the surface of the ocean floor.

Whichever method or combination of methods is used, there may always be routes by which radiation will return to the environment.

Dumping at sea

Fig 28.1 shows the possible routes radiation could take if waste leaked from containers stored on or under the ocean bed.

The total radiation that affects the human environment is given in the following table.

Source of radiation	Approximate percentage
naturally occurring from rocks and outer space	87.0
medical uses	11.5
luminous watches, etc.	0.9
weapons testing	0.5
waste dumped at sea	0.1

NUCLEAR ACCIDENTS – CHERNOBYL

In 1986 an accident at the Soviet Union's largest nuclear power station released a cloud of radioactive material high into the atmosphere. The winds then blew this cloud across Poland and Scandinavia. These countries were showered with radioactive chemicals. The direct risks to health were inhalation and skin irradiation, but there were other indirect risks. There were restrictions on the consumption of fresh vegetables and milk in several countries.

In March 1989, articles like the following appeared in science magazines.

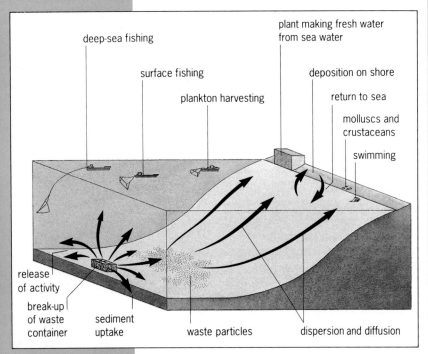

deep-sea fishing

surface fishing

plankton harvesting

plant making fresh water from sea water

deposition on shore

return to sea

molluscs and crustaceans

swimming

release of activity

break-up of waste container

sediment uptake

waste particles

dispersion and diffusion

Fig 28.1 Possible routes for radiation from nuclear waste on the ocean floor to humans

HEADLESS CALVES BETRAY THE LEGACY OF CHERNOBYL

The effects of the world's worst nuclear accident at Chernobyl are becoming clear at farms just outside the 30km exclusion zone around Chernobyl. There has been an alarming increase since 1986 in the number of deformed animals being born on a farm 50km from Chernobyl. This farm, which has 350 cows and 87 pigs, has records of only three deformed pigs born in the five years before the accident and no deformed calves. In 1987, 37 pigs and 27 calves were born with serious deformities. During the first nine months of 1988, a further 41 deformed pigs and 35 deformed calves were born. Some calves lacked heads, limbs, eyes or ribs. Most of the pigs had deformed skulls.

Radiation at the farm was 148 times as high as background level. Food is still delivered to the area from elsewhere. However, local people still consume home-produced milk, fruit and vegetables. Cattle still eat locally produced fodder.

Concern is now growing about the possible effects on people. For instance, women from the area are advised not to have children. The average annual number of new cancer cases, especially of the lip, has doubled since the accident.

Farmers use pressurised cabins on tractors to protect themselves from radioactive dust from the fields. Medical workers have found the thyroid glands of more than half of the children were affected by radiation.

Q1 Explain how radioactive materials get into milk and vegetables.

Q2 Besides the potential hazards of accidents in nuclear power stations, state another problem which arises from generating electricity by nuclear means rather than by using tidal or solar energy.

Q3 One of the radioactive materials was iodine-131. Explain the link between this and its accumulation in the thyroid glands of people affected by the radiation.

Q4 Give a genetical explanation for the birth of deformed animals that took place two years after the accident.

Q5 Radiation from nuclear accidents and explosions may cause mutations. The table below shows the effect of the atomic bomb dropped on Hiroshima on leukaemia, a blood cancer often caused by mutation.

a Plot the information as a histogram.

Distance from explosion centre (m)	0–999	1000–1499	1500–1999	2000–2499	2500–2999
Leukaemia cases per 10 000 people	131	33	9	2	1

b What is the relationship between the number of leukaemia cases and the site of the explosion?

Q6 In 1986 a radioactive cloud was blown across Northern and Western Europe, after the Chernobyl disaster, in which many people died or were exposed to radiation. Study the map in fig 28.2 and answer the questions.

▼ **Fig 28.2**

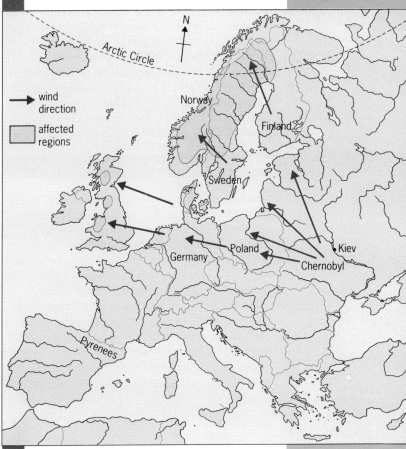

a What caused the Chernobyl disaster?
b In which direction were the prevailing winds blowing?

Several regions of Britain were seriously affected. In North Wales, Cumbria and parts of Scotland, high levels of radiation were recorded. As a result of these levels of radiation the effects on flocks of sheep were monitored. A ban on the movement and the sale of sheep from flocks in the area was imposed.

c Tests on the fleeces of some of the sheep showed low levels of radiation, but meat from them showed much higher levels. How would you explain the difference in these observations?
d Similar tests were carried out at regular intervals since the incident. They all show higher levels of radiation than would normally be expected. Give a possible reason for this result.

29 INHERITED DISORDERS

By the end of this section you should be able to

understand how certain disorders are inherited in humans

As we have seen, scientists are far from understanding all the mutations that interfere with the way the body works. However, it is possible to classify at least two types of genetic effect. One group consists of mutations that stop the body making certain essential proteins, for example enzymes, hormones or proteins which make up the structure of cells.

The second group is related to the first in that it often involves the lack of certain enzymes. However, the main problem is the accumulation in the body of chemicals which would normally be broken down. An example of this type is a mutation leading to an accumulation of a chemical called phenylalanine in the blood. This results in the condition known as **phenylketonuria (PKU)**, described on page 76.

HAEMOPHILIA

Inherited inability to synthesise certain proteins can be seen in various forms of blood disorders in humans. Perhaps the best known example of a genetically controlled blood defect is **haemophilia**. This is a condition in which the blood fails to clot, or else it clots very slowly. People with extreme cases of haemophilia can bleed to death from normally minor injuries.

The chemistry of blood clotting is very complicated and involves over a dozen different enzyme-controlled reactions. If one or more of the enzymes is not made by the body, then blood clotting is hindered or perhaps (in rare cases) prevented all together.

A royal complaint

Haemophilia is a genetic defect with a royal history. The gene for the problem became so widely distributed in European royalty during the nineteenth and twentieth centuries that the course of history was affected, particularly in Spain and Russia.

The gene for the condition probably first appeared as a mutation in Queen Victoria, fig 29.1, since there is no record of haemophilia in her ancestry. Because of marriages among the royalty of Europe, the gene became distributed in a number of royal families. Fig 29.2 shows the pedigree of the distribution of haemophilia in Queen Victoria's descendants. Note that the present royal family of Great Britain is free of the gene.

▲ **Fig 29.1 Haemophilia first appeared in the royal family as a mutant gene in Queen Victoria**

Fig 29.2 Haemophilia in the royal family

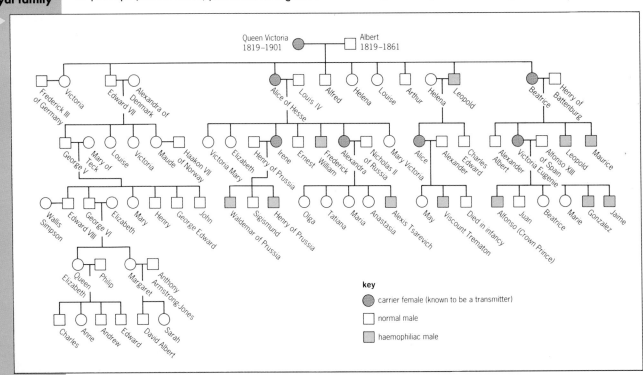

Men only

Haemophilia only appears in males, except in very rare circumstances, although the condition is inherited from the mother. This form of inheritance is called **sex-linked recessive**. This means that the gene is carried on the X chromosome. Males have only one X chromosome, whereas a female has two X chromosomes. Thus in females the recessive condition is masked by the normal gene on the other X chromosome. The Y chromosome in the male does not have the normal gene to mask the recessive condition. If an affected male becomes a father, then all his daughters will be carriers and all his sons normal (they will receive their X chromosome from their normal mother).

Let **Hb** represent the gene for haemophilia. The condition can only be carried on the X chromosome. Therefore an affected male must be $X^{Hb}Y$. A normal female will be XX.

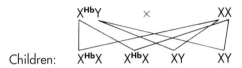

Children: $X^{Hb}X$ $X^{Hb}X$ XY   XY

2 carrier females: 2 normal males

If a carrier female marries an unaffected male and becomes a mother, then the chances are that half her sons will be affected and half her daughters will be carriers

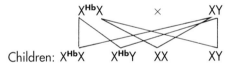

Children: $X^{Hb}X$ $X^{Hb}Y$ XX   XY

1 carrier: 1 affected: 1 normal: 1 normal
female   male   female   male

Genetic counselling

The problem is that there is no foolproof method of telling a carrier daughter from a normal daughter. Obviously, it is extremely difficult to give guidance on family planning to such women. A genetic counsellor can only say with confidence that all daughters of an affected man will be carriers. The daughter of a haemophiliac female carrier cannot be identified as a carrier herself until she has given birth to a haemophiliac son.

In approximately one-third of all patients no history of the condition can be detected in the family ancestry. This may be due to the transmission through several generations of female carriers without an affected male being born. Furthermore, all record of a previously affected male could be lost to the memory of that family. Alternatively, the condition may have arisen by a gene mutation.

It is not possible to provide accurate statistics for all countries, but in Europe and North America the incidence of haemophilia is approximately one per 8000 to 10 000 of the population. There have been major improvements in treatment of the condition and the chances of survival have undoubtedly improved in recent years. Also, the number of recognised patients is increasing, leading to more meaningful counselling.

Q1 What ratios of normal, carrier and haemophiliac chidren would be expected from a marriage between

   a a haemophiliac man and a carrier woman
   b a normal man and a carrier woman?

Q2 Queen Victoria had a haemophiliac son, Leopold, Duke of Albany, and three normal sons, among whom was Edward VII. Prince Albert was not a haemophiliac.

   a What was the Queen's genotype with respect to this gene?
   b Could she have had haemophiliac daughters?
   c Has this haemophiliac gene been passed on to the present British royal family?

Q3 What advice would a practising counsellor on genetics offer to a woman who, while having no haemophiliac symptoms herself, informed him that her father was a haemophiliac? She is married to a normal man but is concerned about the chances of this condition being passed on to her children.

CYSTIC FIBROSIS

Possibly the most common human genetic disorder is **cystic fibrosis**. This is an inherited condition which affects the pancreas, page 32, and the bronchioles of the lungs, page 7. It results in failure of the pancreas to function properly, intestinal obstruction and malfunction of the sweat glands and salivary glands. Cystic fibrosis is one of the most common fatal diseases of childhood.

Inheritance of cystic fibrosis

The disease is inherited as a recessive gene in the following way.

Let **C** represent the gene for a normal pancreas and bronchioles. Let **c** represent the recessive gene for cystic fibrosis.

A person suffers from the disease only if he or she has two genes for cystic fibrosis, that is the genotype **cc**. A person with the genotype **Cc** is a carrier of the disorder but does not suffer from the disease. There is therefore a one in four chance of a child suffering from the complaint if two carriers have a child.

carrier man   carrier woman
Cc   ×   **Cc**

gametes	C	c
C	CC	Cc
c	Cc	cc

The condition occurs once in about 2000 births. It accounts for between 1% and 2% of admissions to children's hospitals. Many children die as a result of pneumonia, though some survive to adulthood.

Q4 **N** is the gene for normal pancreas and lungs. Unaffected people have the genotype **Nn** or **NN**. **n** is the gene for cystic fibrosis. In a copy of the box below, show how two people with normal pancreas and lungs could have a child with cystic fibrosis.

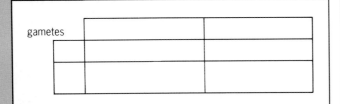

NEUROFIBROMATOSIS

Neurofibromatosis or **NF** for short is an inherited disease that affects about 18 000 people in the United Kingdom. About 200 babies are born with the condition each year. It varies in severity from just a few coffee-coloured skin spots to life-threatening tumours. Indeed, many people do not even realise they have it.

NF is caused by a mutant gene on the human chromosome number 17 (see fig 25.4, page 67). How this causes the many features of the disease is not known. The most common sign is the growth of small nodules on the skin which tend to develop at puberty.

The first symptoms are coffee-coloured patches on the skin, fig 29.3. These are followed by brown spots on the iris of the eye. At the beginning of puberty, nodes develop. They increase in number throughout life but they rarely cause major health problems. It is the complications of the disease which are more serious. These include short stature, curved spine and learning difficulties. In 1% of cases victims suffer from large facial tumours. There is a 2–3% chance of nodules becoming cancerous.

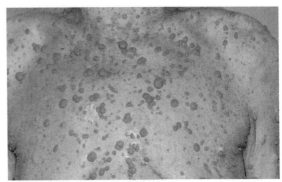

▲ **Fig 29.3 Neurofibromatosis**

PHENYLKETONURIA

There is an enzyme which sufferers of **phenylketonuria** cannot make. This enzyme is responsible for changing an amino acid called **phenylalanine** to another amino acid that is used by the body. Phenylalanine occurs in meat, fish, cheese, eggs, wheat and butter. In the absence of the enzyme which acts on it, phenylalanine accumulates in the tissues of the body, fig 29.4. Some is converted into a dangerous chemical which causes damage to the central nervous system. This leads to a person being mentally retarded.

Phenylketonuria is due to a single mutant gene. About one in 15 000 babies suffers from the problem and synthetic substitutes for protein must be given in the diet.

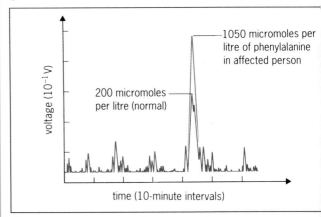

▲ **Fig 29.4 A technique called electrophoresis separates the substances in blood. The high peak shows excess phenylalanine in a phenylketonuria sufferer**

HUNTINGTON'S CHOREA

In 1872 an American doctor, Fraser Roberts, wrote the following observation in his notebook: 'The boy George Huntington, driving through a wooded lane in Long Island while accompanying his father on professional rounds, suddenly saw two women, mother and daughter, both tall and very thin, both bowing, twisting and grimacing'. Fifty years later George Huntington made a major contribution to science by describing and studying the inherited disease, now known as **Huntington's chorea**.

It is an inherited disease characterised by involuntary muscular movement and mental deterioration. The age of onset is about 35 years. The majority of those affected can therefore produce a family before being aware of their own condition. It is transmitted by a dominant gene and both sexes can be equally affected. An estimate of its frequency is roughly 5 in 100 000.

Inheritance of Huntington's chorea

Affected people are heterozygous. Let **HC** represent the gene for Huntington's chorea and **hc** represent the normal gene.

affected mother   normal father

HChc   ×   **hchc**

gametes	hc	hc
HC	HChc	HChc
hc	hchc	hchc

There is a one in two chance that a child will be affected.

Theoretically, two parents could be affected and a homozygous **HCHC** child could be produced. The effect of this would probably be lethal. The gene is so rare that it is most unlikely to occur in the homozygous condition.

SICKLE-CELL ANAEMIA

Sickle-cell anaemia is an often fatal condition which is quite common in West Africans. If there is a low level of oxygen in the blood, the red blood cells of a person suffering from this disorder collapse into a sickle shape, fig 29.5, and may form blockages in blood vessels.

The disease is inherited as a single mutant recessive gene. If a child inherits the gene from both parents it has only a 20% chance of surviving into adulthood. In sufferers, the gene that controls the formation of haemoglobin is not formed properly. The haemoglobin in the sickle-shaped cells is not very good at carrying oxygen.

▲ **Fig 29.5 Deformed and normal red blood cells from a sickle-cell anaemia sufferer**

A mutation that confers an advantage

You might think that, over thousands of years, the mutant gene would have disappeared from human chromosomes because sufferers would die before having children. However, under certain circumstances, it is an advantage to have some sickle-shaped red blood cells. The reason is that people who are heterozygous for the mutant gene are likely to suffer the effects of the malarial parasite.

Inheritance of sickle-cell anaemia

Let us represent the gene for normal haemoglobin as **Hb** and the gene for sickle-cell haemoglobin as **HbS**. A normal person will have the haemoglobin genotype **HbHb**. A person with the sickle-cell disorder will have the genotype **HbSHbS** and will usually die. However, a person with the genotype **HbSHb** can survive and will be resistant to malaria. If two people, each with the genotype **HbhSHb,** have a child, then the predicted genotypes of the children can be shown as follows

heterozygous parents

HbSHb × **HbSHb**

gametes	HbS	Hb
HbS	HbSHbS	HbSHb
Hb	HbHbS	HbHb

It can be seen that there is a one in four chance of a child having the sickle-cell disorder (**HbSHbS**). There is a one in two chance of a child being a carrier of the sickle-cell gene but probably surviving (**HbSHb**). There is a one in four chance of the child being normal for the haemoglobin gene (**HbHb**).

30 EVOLUTION

By the end of this section you should be able to

▸ understand the relationships between variation, natural selection and reproductive success in organisms and the significance of these relationships for evolution.

One of the first people to collect evidence for the process of **evolution** was the English naturalist, Charles Robert Darwin (1809–82), fig 30.1.

▼ **Fig 30.1 Charles Darwin, the great British naturalist**

DARWIN'S THEORY OF EVOLUTION

In the nineteenth century, Darwin introduced a startling new theory to the world. It was an explanation of how all living organisms had come into existence.

A common ancestor

Darwin's theory was that all organisms were descended from either one or a very few simple forms of life. Over a period of millions of years, these original forms of life branched out. Gradually they developed new characteristics that helped them to survive. All known species came into existence as a result of these changes.

The highest of all these forms of life is the human species. This explanation of how new kinds of organisms have developed by **natural selection** (see page 83) is called the **theory of evolution**.

The Origin of Species

Darwin first explained his theories to a group of scientists in London. His ideas were so new and startling that few of the scientists accepted them. A year later, in 1859, Darwin published his book, *The Origin of Species*. In this book he showed that plants and animals could not possibly have been created in their present form. They must have gone

through a long process of development and change – evolution.

In *The Origin of Species* Darwin also described the method of evolution. He showed not only that it was a fact but also how evolutionary processes actually worked.

The acceptance of the theory

As the years passed, more and more scientists accepted Darwin's ideas. Later, discoveries of chromosomes and genes confirmed his belief that all present-day organisms have descended from either one or a few original forms of life. These discoveries have also proved that new species do not come into existence quickly. They develop very slowly, over millions of years – just as Darwin suggested.

THE GREAT BRITISH NATURALIST

Darwin's whole life was devoted to scientific research. His interest started in his youth, when his hobbies were hunting for beetles, collecting minerals and watching birds. Darwin's father wanted him to become a doctor but Darwin changed the course of his studies after beginning medicine. He began studies to become a clergyman but found that this career did not suit him either.

Shortly after his graduation from Cambridge University, Darwin received an offer that was to change his life, and also change the way the whole world thought about evolution.

A voyage of discovery

Darwin was invited to go on a trip around the world on the British Royal Navy ship HMS *Beagle*, fig 30.2. The ship was making a voyage of scientific discovery to survey little-known areas of the world. Darwin was offered the job of naturalist.

▲ **Fig 30.2 HMS *Beagle***

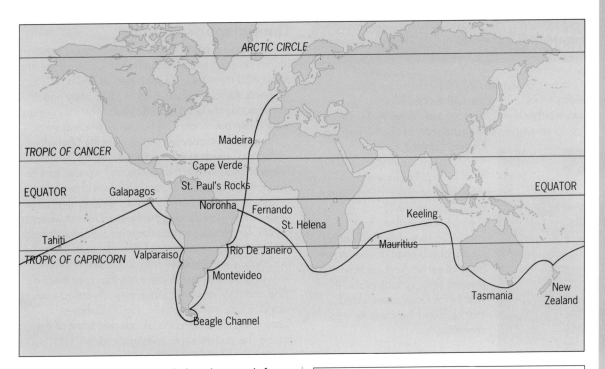

ARCTIC CIRCLE

TROPIC OF CANCER

Madeira

Cape Verde

St. Paul's Rocks

EQUATOR   Galapagos   EQUATOR

Noronha

Fernando

Keeling

St. Helena

Tahiti   Mauritius

TROPIC OF CAPRICORN   Valparaiso   Rio De Janeiro

Montevideo   New
                                                  Zealand
                                    Tasmania

Beagle Channel

Darwin was 22 when he sailed on the *Beagle* from Plymouth in 1831. He returned in 1836. The voyage, shown in fig 30.3, was a revelation to Darwin. It enabled him to study vast numbers of creatures that he had never known existed. In the rocks of remote countries he discovered fossils of species which had since become extinct, fig 30.4. These fossils showed Darwin that forms of life went through many changes. The patterns of life he saw around him and in the rocks had a profound effect on Darwin. They made him think that gradual changes in life took place over many thousands of years.

The work continues

Darwin began to form his ideas of evolution in the Galapagos Islands in the Pacific. When he returned home his notebooks were filled with his observations and his boxes were filled with specimens. For the next 20 years he continued his studies of evolution. Then, when he had reached conclusions as a result of his careful observations, he wrote down his ideas in *The Origin of Species*.

Darwin produced seventeen books on a large variety of scientific subjects. He wrote all but two of them in the study of his home in the village of Downe, 20 miles from London. His study was packed with books, papers, stuffed animals and specimens from his voyage.

Darwin conducted endless experiments in his study and in the greenhouse in his garden. He studied the way in which orchids attract bees and the way sundew plants trap fruit flies. Watching colonies of earthworms during the night, he discovered that the worms react to light. His interests covered every kind of living organism. He wrote books on a variety of

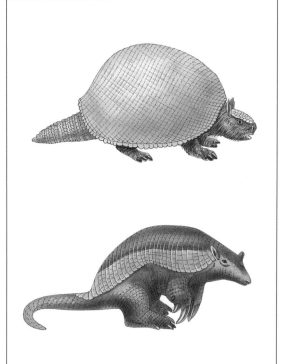

subjects ranging from the earthworm to coral reefs, including a four-volume work on barnacles.

But Darwin's most famous work was his theory of evolution. It revolutionised the sciences of botany, biology and zoology. It brought new ideas into the studies of religion and astronomy, history and psychology. The truths about the history of life which Darwin perceived have affected every branch of science. Every one of them has benefited from his work.

VARIATION, INHERITANCE AND EVOLUTION

DARWIN'S WORK ON THE GALAPAGOS ISLANDS

▼ **Fig 30.5 A Galapagos tortoise**

Charles Darwin was 26 years old when HMS *Beagle* took him to the Galapagos Islands. He had already been on board for over three years. He had explored jungles and grasslands of South America. He had climbed the high mountains of the Andes, and had filled his notebooks with thousands of observations about plants and animals.

These observations had convinced him of the truth of his theory of evolution. However, he had not yet worked out how the process actually took place. It was in the Galapagos Islands that he found the clues he was searching for.

The Galapagos Islands

The Galapagos Islands are a cluster of lonely volcanic islands on the Equator, in the Pacific Ocean. They are about 650 miles from the mainland of South America. Although discovered in 1535, they had remained uninhabited for 300 years. The only visitors were a few buccaneers and crews of whaling ships.

The name 'Galapagos' comes from the Spanish 'galapago' which means giant tortoise, fig 30.5. These animals live on the islands and were to feature as important animals in Darwin's ideas of evolution.

Darwin remained on the islands for only five weeks. They were among the most important weeks of his life, for he realised that these isolated islands held the key to the mystery of evolution. Because the Galapagos were isolated from the rest of the world, he was able to study the creatures that lived there as if he and they were in a laboratory. He called each island 'a little world in itself'. Fig 30.6 shows Darwin's route around the islands and some of the species he studied in his investigations.

Fig 30.6 ▶ The *Beagle* took Darwin to four of the Galapagos Islands

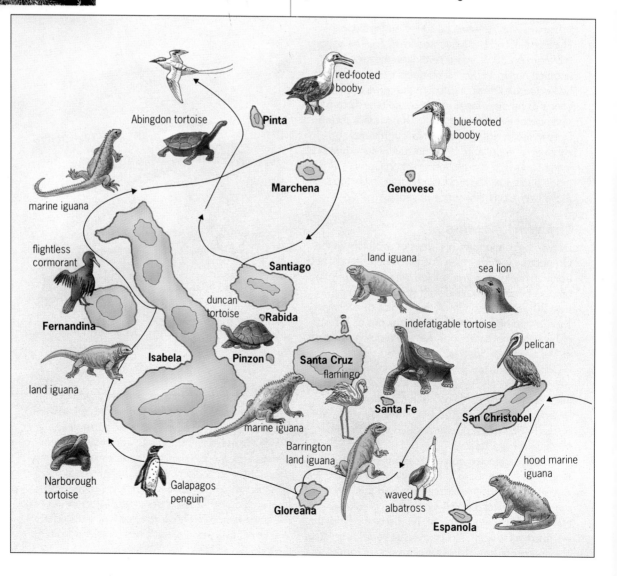

Where did the animals come from?

Darwin was puzzled by the fact that living creatures inhabited the Galapagos at all. Most of the animals were unique – they could not be found anywhere else in the world. The islands were of volcanic origin, so he was sure that the animals had not originated on the islands. Also, some of the island creatures were very similar to those found on the mainland. Yet the islands were more than 600 miles from the mainland. How, then, had these creatures managed to reach the Galapagos?

Darwin's first idea was that a land bridge might have once connected the islands to the mainland. The animals could have reached the islands by crossing the bridge. He gave up this idea as soon as he noted that frogs and toads were absent from the islands, and that hardly any mammals lived there. If there had been a land bridge then these types of animals would have reached the islands and thrived there.

By sea or air

Darwin's conclusion was that life had arrived from the mainland by way of sea or air, fig 30.7. This would explain the abundance of reptiles but the absence of amphibians. Reptiles have eggs protected by shells, but amphibian eggs only have jelly surrounding them. Reptiles like lizards and tortoises could have laid eggs which survived the ocean journey, while frogs' and toads' eggs would have died.

Darwin performed many experiments to test his theory that life had reached the Galapagos in a hit-or-miss fashion across the ocean. His aim was to discover which kinds of eggs and seeds could survive the long journey by water or air. He kept seeds in water for several months and found that some would still germinate. He grew plants from seeds dropped by birds and from seeds embedded in the mud on birds' feet. The results confirmed his belief that plants had come to the islands from the mainland.

A variety of species

During his time on the Galapagos, Darwin was particularly impressed by the enormous variety of reptiles and birds that he found on the islands. He noticed that the individual types of various species differed from one island to another. Since the climate and soil on different islands were similar, why had they arisen?

It was the vice-governor of the Galapagos who first called Darwin's attention to the way the animals inhabiting different islands varied from each other. He said that by looking at a tortoise he could tell which island it came from. However, it was not the tortoises but the finches which led Darwin to discover how different species of creatures come into existence.

▼ **Fig 30.7 How some animals reached the Galapagos Islands from the mainland**

The Galapagos finches

Darwin had observed 13 different varieties of finches, fig 30.8, on the Galapagos. He suggested that these must all have descended from some birds which had flown to the islands or been blown there in a storm.

There were no other land birds on the islands. Therefore, without enemies or rivals, the finches were able to develop freely into many different species. On each island, the special features that were best suited to their environment were passed on from one generation to the next. In some finches, slender curved beaks for probing flowers had evolved; in others, strong parrot-like beaks useful for cracking seeds had survived.

▼ **Fig 30.8 The 13 varieties of finch found on the Galapagos Islands. They vary in beak shape, diet and plumage**

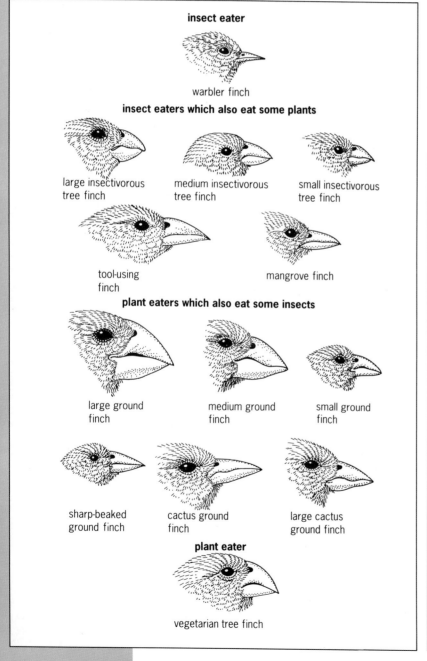

insect eater

warbler finch

insect eaters which also eat some plants

large insectivorous tree finch

medium insectivorous tree finch

small insectivorous tree finch

tool-using finch

mangrove finch

plant eaters which also eat some insects

large ground finch

medium ground finch

small ground finch

sharp-beaked ground finch

cactus ground finch

large cactus ground finch

plant eater

vegetarian tree finch

How different species develop

It was this discovery which gave Darwin his first clue to the central part of his theory of evolution. In *The Origin of Species* he explained that there were two main factors which decide how creatures change and develop. The first is the physical surroundings in which they live. Organisms that have survived have gradually developed the characteristics they need to exist in their environment. The second factor is the other organisms living in the environment. Survivors develop characteristics needed to conquer their prey and avoid their enemies.

Although the climate and terrain were similar on all the Galapagos Islands, the animals and plants had begun to develop differently. Each slight change in one organism led to changes in others, so the process of evolutionary change continued. On the Galapagos Islands the differences had become so great that Darwin was able to make one of his most important discoveries.

The Galapagos today

In 1957 a group of scientists working with international conservation groups recommended that some of the islands be set apart as sanctuaries. A unique 'laboratory' of evolution now exists on the islands – the Charles Darwin Memorial Station. Here, many scientists of all nationalities strive to answer questions relating to evolution.

Q1 Giant tortoises are found on the Galapagos Islands. Each island has its own particular form of the tortoise but they are of two main types, shown as **A** and **B** in fig 30.9. Type **B** can survive where there is bare soil but type **A** needs a good supply of ground plants.

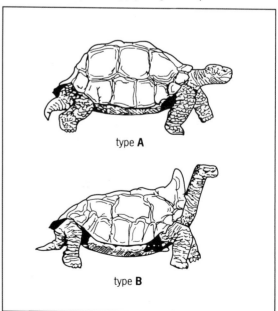

type **A**

type **B**

▲ **Fig 30.9**

a List *two* features shown by type **B** which would help it survive on islands with only bushes and no ground plants. [2]

b Type **B** probably developed from type **A** by a mutation. What is a *mutation*? [1]

c Name *one* factor in the environment which could cause mutations. [1]

(WJEC Modular Science 1992 Q5 (part))

NATURAL SELECTION

Darwin worked out that organisms best suited to their environments, and best suited to avoid predators, would be more likely to survive and produce offspring, so their favourable characteristics would be passed to their offspring. This is called **natural selection** and results in a gradual change in characteristics to **adapt** the organism to its environment.

We shall now develop the idea of natural selection in the way that Charles Darwin did. He used three facts and made two deductions from them.

Population explosions

The first fact was stated in 1798 by Thomas Malthus in his *Essays on Population*. Malthus explained that animals and plants have a tendency to multiply at a geometrical rate, that is, in numbers that run 2, 4, 8, 16, 32, and so on. The offspring always tend to be more numerous than the parents. We have only to look at the human 'population explosion' to see this in action.

Automatic control

The second fact is that while all living organisms *can* increase their numbers at a geometrical rate, they seldom do. Few species, apart from humans and some animals and plants dependent on us, have been observed to increase so rapidly for very long. The species that have done so have often been presented with new opportunities by humans, for example, the gulls feeding on our refuse dumps, fig 30.10, and the rats feeding in our sewers. Another example was seen in the rabbit which was introduced to Australia. There it had no natural enemies and in a few years became a national nuisance, fig 30.11.

The struggle for existence

From these two facts, Darwin deduced a 'struggle for existence'. More accurately, organisms are in competition for a chance to reproduce. Almost everywhere in nature, organisms produce more young than can possibly survive to the age at which *they* can reproduce. They must compete for food and for all their other needs. For example, we are not completely over-run with flies despite their enormous

breeding rate – many flies die before reproducing due to lack of food or other hardships.

Variation and natural selection

The third fact is that all living things vary. We have seen this in our studies of genetics.

From this Darwin deduced a mechanism of **natural selection**. The principle of natural selection states that there is competition for existence between individuals which vary among themselves. Thus some individuals must be more likely to succeed than others. Those with favourable characteristics will be more likely to survive and reproduce than those with unfavourable characteristics.

A great deal of variation is inherited. Favourable inheritable characteristics have a better chance of being passed on than unfavourable variations, because the organisms carrying the characteristics are more likely to survive and reproduce.

Evolution of a new species

Natural selection is the principal cause of **evolution**. As organisms adapt by natural selection, they eventually become so different from others of their original species that they can no longer breed with them. A new species has **evolved**. Natural selection is not a physical force with an obvious purpose, but a process that occurs completely by chance, like evolution itself. It is a process that has made, through millions of years, the human brain, the bird's eye and the bat's ear – all from simple cells.

31 GENETIC ENGINEERING

By the end of this section you should be able to

▶ understand the principles of genetic engineering.

The principle of **genetic engineering** relies on isolating a useful gene from one organism and putting it into another of a different species. For example, scientists often isolate genes from human chromosomes which control the production of certain hormones. They put these useful genes into bacteria or yeasts.

The human genes are transferred to the bacteria or yeast to increase production of the hormone. The microbes multiply very rapidly and can be cultured relatively cheaply. In fact, they can provide almost unlimited amounts of substances that are practically unobtainable in bulk in any other way.

THE PROCESS OF GENETIC ENGINEERING

Cutting out the gene

The process starts with biological 'scissors' called **restriction enzymes**. These cut chunks of DNA at points on the chromosome to isolate sections where useful genes are known to exist. Restriction enzymes enable scientists to cut out very precisely the gene that is needed. It may be one out of hundreds on a particular chromosome.

Inserting it into a plasmid

The next stage is to put the gene into a bacterium. It is not put directly into the bacterial chromosome. Instead, genetic engineers use a circle of DNA called a **plasmid**. These are normally present in bacteria but are largely independent of the rest of the cell. Plasmids, like chromosomes, carry bacterial genes which control the microbe's metabolism.

The plasmid is cut open with restriction enzymes and the foreign gene inserted. The break is sealed with another enzyme called a **ligase** (an enzyme which binds chemicals together). This process makes a mixed molecule called **recombinant DNA**.

Inside the microbe

The altered (**infective**) plasmids are then mixed in a test tube with bacteria which do not have any plasmids. Some plasmids move inside these bacteria. The infective plasmids carry the foreign gene inside the cell where it can instruct it to make the required protein. The process is shown in fig 31.1.

Large-scale production

The process is regarded as a success only when the gene is **expressed**. This means that the host cell obeys the instructions carried by the foreign gene and makes the human protein.

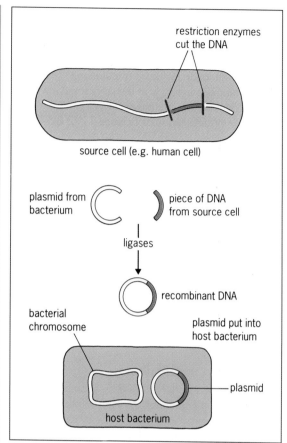

▲ **Fig 31.1 Summary of genetic engineering – a piece of DNA from a source cell is combined with a plasmid to form recombinant DNA. The plasmid is put into the host bacterium where it controls the bacterium's cell chemistry**

If this happens, then the microbe can be cultured – it is given the right food and temperature conditions to encourage rapid reproduction. The new microbes also make the human protein, so it can be produced on a large scale. The new microbes are clones (see page 87).

GENETICALLY ENGINEERED INSULIN

The hormone **insulin** is made by the islets of Langerhans in the pancreas (see page 32). Insulin keeps the concentration of glucose in the blood at a constant level. Some people do not produce enough insulin and so cannot control their blood glucose level. They suffer from **diabetes mellitus**, which is controlled by the injection of insulin.

Until recently the insulin used for this treatment was taken from the pancreas of various mammals. It was difficult to produce enough insulin in this way. Scientists have solved the problem of mass production by using genetic engineering. The method is summarised in fig 31.2.

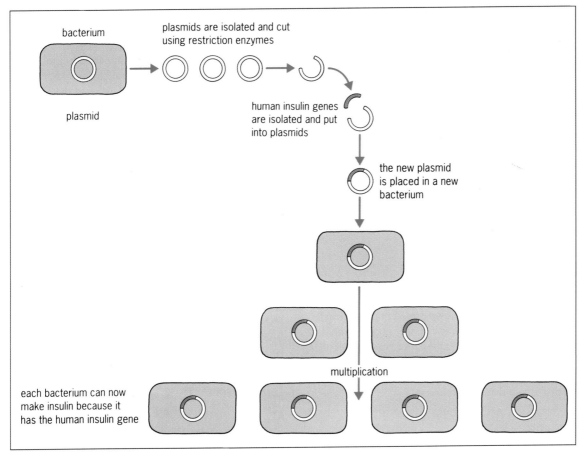

▲ **Fig 31.2 Producing insulin by genetic engineering**

Built-in pesticides

Biologists have grown a tobacco plant that makes its own pesticide. The genes of a tobacco plant have been modified so that the plant makes a poison that kills insects.

The gene which controls the production of the toxin has been isolated from a bacterium and put in a plasmid. It has been inserted into the tobacco plant in two ways

1 the cellulose cell walls of some of the leaf cells were broken down so that the plasmid could pass freely into the cytoplasm
2 fragments of the stem were wounded and treated with preparations containing the genetically altered plasmids.

Q1 Explain how the cellulose cell walls of the tobacco cells might have been broken down.

Q2 Explain why there might be possible dangers to the environment as a result of this technique.

Mutants down under!

The releasing of genetically engineered microbes into the environment to help plant production is about to spread to Australia. An Australian scientist wants to soak the roots of almond seedlings in a solution of genetically altered bacteria to treat crown gall disease in roots. After completing the four-month experiment, he will sterilise and dispose of the affected soil.

Q3 Explain why the scientist intends to sterilise the soil before disposing of it.

Q4 Suggest how sterilisation could be carried out.

Q5 Discuss why environmentalists might oppose the introduction of mutant bacteria into the surroundings.

Q6 Suggest how bacteria might be able to combat crown gall disease (a disease caused by a bacterium) in plant roots.

32 SELECTIVE BREEDING AND AGRICULTURE

By the end of this section you should be able to

- understand how selective breeding can produce economic benefits and contribute to increased yields
- understand the basic principles of selective breeding and cloning and how these give rise to social and ethical issues.

CEREAL CROPS

The grasses or **cereal crops** provide the staple diet for most of the world's population. Humans have cultivated cereals since the earliest records of history. More people eat rice than any other food. Wheat, maize, oats, barley, rye and millet make up the bulk of the rest of the world's cereals.

However, farmers do not want to waste time and money sowing seeds if their yield will be poor or if there is a high chance of pests and diseases destroying them.

Developing new varieties

For many years farmers have aimed at producing the 'perfect' crop. Today, an enormous range of varieties of cereals are available to the farmer as a result of **artificial selection** over many generations. New varieties are developed by planned **hybridisation** (crossing two different varieties).

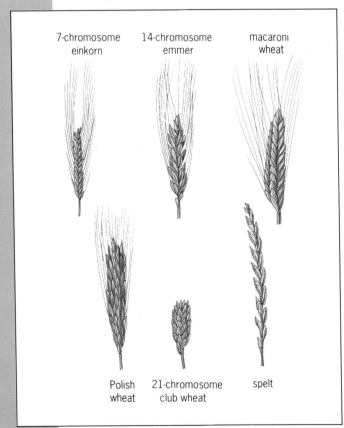

7-chromosome einkorn   14-chromosome emmer   macaroni wheat

Polish wheat   21-chromosome club wheat   spelt

▲ **Fig 32.1 Most authorities agree that there are 13 wheat species in addition to the wheat used for bread. The six shown here are all cultivated today**

The aim of hybridisation is to concentrate as many desirable features as possible in a single variety. One variety of wheat, for instance, may have good milling properties but poor resistance to fungal disease. Another may resist fungi but provide a low yield of grain. A third might not thrive in dry conditions but may give good baking flour when well irrigated.

New varieties are constantly being developed by plant breeders. Fig 32.1 shows some varieties of wheat. To the basic properties already mentioned are added others that vary according to the climate and soil in which the wheat is to be grown. Also, the season of planting may differ. Some varieties are planted in autumn, others in spring.

Increased world production

The improvement in varieties is largely responsible for the enormous increase in world production of wheat during the last 50 years, fig 32.2. Hybridisation and selection of varieties of rice has boosted yields by 25%. Rice breeding is a slower process than wheat breeding, but promises to give even higher yields in the future.

▲ **Fig 32.2 Rice breeding at a research station in the Philippines**

Q1 Some barley plants can be attacked by a fungus whilst others are resistant to this fungus. In an investigation by a plant breeder, it was found that those plants that were susceptible produced offspring which were all susceptible when self-fertilised. A resistant plant produced a mixture of resistant plants and susceptible plants when self-fertilised.

a How would the plant breeder obtain a stock of barley plants which were all resistant to the fungus?

b Assuming that resistance is controlled by a single gene, what must be the genotype of the resistant stock?

MASS PRODUCTION

Once a plant breeder has produced a 'tailor-made' hybrid plant with all the required desirable properties, the breeder will want to satisfy the market demand for the product. This means production of vast numbers of plants. The plants must all be identical with regard to the desirable genes that they carry.

Asexual reproduction – cloning

All organisms produced asexually from the same parent have the same genotype. They are called **clones**. Clones are produced by mitosis (see page 53) which gives rise to two genetically identical cells.

The plant breeder uses cloning to produce identical plants. The basis of plant cloning is the production of whole plants from parts of plants by asexual means, as in vegetative reproduction (see page 44). This eliminates the possibility of different genes being introduced via sexual reproduction. The different genes may not be the ones required in the 'tailor-made' variety.

Many varieties of fruits and flowers are maintained for generations in this way. Desirable characters can be precisely genetically controlled.

Cloning from cultures

Recently some commercially important plants have been mass produced using a cloning technique from **tissue cultures**. Between the 1960s and 1980s research into production of oil palms took place, fig 32.3. Today many people in the tropics are benefiting from this form of **biotechnology**. Large numbers of people rely on the oil palm for food and detergents either directly or because of exporting its products. Once the desired hybrid variety of oil palm was produced, clones were made from it.

A small part of the growing point from the parent plant is collected. It is then grown in sterile conditions on agar jelly. It is supplied with the best conditions of minerals, hormones and temperature for growth. Mitosis produces identical cells. These are then separated. Each cell can develop into a new plant with the same desirable genes found in the parent plant. The process can be carried out in laboratories anywhere in the world and then the young plants can be exported to the tropics for growth in plantations.

At present, most plants produced in this way tend to be decorative flowering plants for the horticultural industry. However, some fruits such as peaches and raspberries are also grown by this method. Perhaps 'tailor-made' cereal crops will be produced in the same way in future. In this way the problem of world food shortage could be tackled by producing hybrids which could survive in places where, at present, no crops grow.

Fig 32.3 Both the leaves and the fruit of the oil palm are used. The oil is extracted from the fruits at this plant in Ecuador ▶

Q2 Scientists have discovered that they can produce animals with identical genes by cloning. One way to do this is to remove the nucleus from an unfertilised egg cell and replace it with a nucleus from a body cell. The egg cell with its new nucleus can then grow into a new individual.

a Give the *main* differences in the amount of genetic material between the nucleus which has been removed and the one which has replaced it. [2]

b Early cloning experiments were done on the eggs of frogs and toads. This was done because it was easier than using eggs from animals such as rabbits and sheep. Suggest and explain *one* reason why this was easier. [2]

c Domestic sheep differ from their wild relatives because their coats are made mainly of soft wool and lack the straight hair that normally hides the soft wool of the wild forms.
As a result of artificial selection, over 50 separate breeds of sheep are now recognised in the British Isles. The East Friesian sheep are renowned for their milking capacity. The short wool sheep grow quickly and produce good meat. Shetland sheep have soft fine wool that is used to knit shawls and warm clothing. Use the information in the above passage and your knowledge of natural selection to explain the difference between natural selection and artificial selection. [7]
(WJEC Modular Science 1992 QA3 (part))

33 GENETIC ENGINEERING IN THE FUTURE

By the end of this section you should be able to

appreciate the social and ethical issues raised by genetic engineering.

We have come a long way since Mendel carried out his meticulous experiments on garden peas. The applications of genetics today result in many life-saving developments, either directly or indirectly. However, like most branches of science, abuse of knowledge can lead to criticism and potential dangers.

DANGERS OF GENETIC ENGINEERING

Escape of dangerous mutants

A fear that many people have is that harmful genes concentrated in a population that is bred in the laboratory may 'escape'. They could then affect natural populations in the wild.

An example of this has received publicity lately. Fish farmers, fig 33.1, have designed salmon by artificially selecting genes that control desirable qualities for the market. In doing this, the genes responsible for homing behaviour have been suppressed. If these salmon escape into the natural population, they could introduce mutated genes and destroy the normal homing behaviour in the wild salmon, fig 33.2.

Fig 33.1 Fish farming could bring about the spread of mutant fish

Fig 33.2 Mutant genes could prevent salmon reaching their normal breeding grounds

Taking precautions

Many of these potential problems are largely hypothetical. For example, genetically altered disease-causing organisms are most unlikely to escape from laboratories. Great care is taken to stop such accidents happening. For example, when transferring useful genes into a plasmid, biotechnologists also include 'safety genes'. These safety genes mean that the altered cells can only grow in the laboratory. For example, they may require a certain type of food that would not normally be present in the wild. Also, a gene is built in that only allows the cell to grow in the presence of a certain antibiotic. Without the antibiotic, as in the wild, they could not survive.

PLANTS OF THE FUTURE

Plants which fertilise the soil

Crops of the **legume** family, which includes most plants which have pods as fruits such as peas or beans, are exceptional. They have their own built-in 'fertiliser factories'. These are colonies of **nitrogen-fixing bacteria** in their roots, fig 33.4, that can change nitrogen from the atmosphere into a form that can be used by plants. Plants need nitrogen to make proteins. (There is more about the nitrogen cycle on pages 111–12.)

▲ **Fig 33.3 Leguminous plants have pods as fruits**

If genetic engineers could transfer the ability of the legumes to fix nitrogen into other crops, such as wheat or rice, the economic implications would be enormous. The environment would benefit too. The 'home-grown' bacterial fertilisers, unlike artificial fertilisers, do not leach out of the soil to pollute groundwater and rivers.

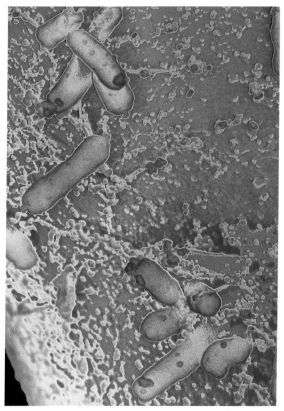

▲ Fig 33.4 Nitrogen-fixing bacteria live in the roots of leguminous plants

A specific relationship

Before scientists can transfer the nitrogen-fixing ability to other crops, they need to understand the relationship between the bacteria and their plant hosts. When the bacteria infect roots of legumes, the plants respond by developing small outgrowths or **nodules**, fig 33.5. Within these, the bacteria enjoy an anaerobic environment, supplied with food by the plant.

The relationship is very specific. A given variety of bacteria can infect only certain groups of legumes. These are called **cross-innoculation groups**. Legumes in the same cross-innoculation group make the same types of chemicals. For example, peas all belong to one cross-innoculation group which also includes vetches and lentils. Clovers belong to a separate group of legumes. So clovers cannot be infected by the same strain of bacterium as peas.

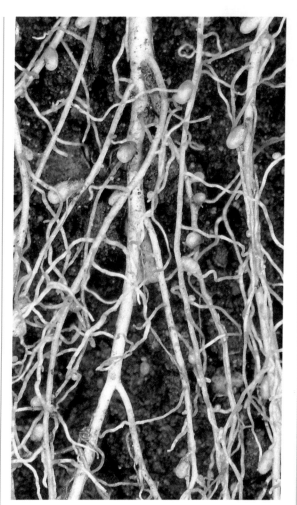

▲ Fig 33.5 Root nodules on clover roots

Genetic engineers have succeeded in altering the bacteria which normally infect peas so that they will now infect clover. The next stage perhaps will be to alter the bacteria so they will be able to infect cereal crops – a truly giant step forward.

Q1 In what form does nitrogen normally enter a plant?

Q2 Explain why you could describe a legume as a 'fertiliser factory'.

Q3 Describe the problems which arise when too much artificial fertiliser is used on crops.

Q4 What is meant by the term 'anaerobic environment'?

Q5 Explain how the bacteria are able to obtain food from the host plant.

Q6 The account describes an example of **symbiosis**. Explain what is meant by this term.

By the end of this section you should be able to

- understand that the impact of human activity on Earth is related to the size of the population, economic factors and industrial requirements
- understand the basic scientific principles associated with a major change in the biosphere.

Pollution can be defined as the upsetting of natural balanced habitats by the introduction of new materials or excess amounts of existing ones. Our planet is remarkably well equipped to cope with all pollution of natural origin. However, the air, land and water that we use are all under attack by human chemical and biological 'warfare' – the by-products of progress.

REASONS FOR POLLUTION

The part played by human activities in the pollution of our environment is very complex. The problems of pollution do not have simple answers, but ignorance has been a major cause of pollution. The ecological balance of habitats is so complex that we will probably never fully understand it.

An escalating problem
The amount of wastes produced by us is increasing so rapidly that some minor items which were of little importance only 20 years ago are becoming a serious threat today, for example chlorofluorocarbons (see page 177).

The real difficulty is that pollution is largely a social as well as technological problem. It arises from a combination of human growth, greed and ignorance.

It has taken a long time for scientists to identify problems of pollution and then to find solutions. It has taken longer for the problems to be appreciated by the public and politicians. Meanwhile, the amount of pollutants and their effects go on increasing.

Developing knowledge
There are few pollution problems for which there are no technical solutions, although some of the solutions are very expensive. To an increasing extent, wastes are being made harmless at their source or they are converted into usable material in recycling.

More people – more development – more pollution
Reducing the growth rate of the world's population is without doubt the most urgent need of our time. However, this idea challenges some basic aspects of our religious and moral codes, which rarely change quickly.

Technological development inevitably produces pollution. The curbing of economic growth is fine in principle for those who already have a large share of the material goods of life. But even in wealthy countries there are many people who are desperately trying to improve their material standard of living. The need for development is more extreme in the developing countries, where some people do not have enough to eat. Clearly the less fortunate people in the world will not be satisfied until they have a fairer share in the material things of life. Even if population growth were to remain static, satisfying these needs will necessitate vast increases in agricultural and industrial production all over the world.

A simple example illustrates this problem. If every person in the world bought a two-page newspaper and used three sheets of toilet paper each day, it would be necessary to obtain from our forests four times as much wood pulp as at present. Since the paper industry is one of the biggest consumers of water and poses one of the greatest pollution hazards, fig 34.1, the problems associated with even a small general rise in the world's standard of living are obvious.

▲ **Fig 34.1 Paper mills use mercury and are among the worst polluters**

POLLUTION FROM AGRICULTURE

Modern agriculture threatens the environment by producing wastes which eventually enter water supplies. Agriculture is becoming more and more intensive to supply enough food for the growing population and is producing correspondingly more waste.

Excess fertilisers
Manufactured fertilisers are washed from the soil into rivers and lakes, increasing the level of nutrients in the water. This may not seem to be a serious problem, but any change in the chemical composition of the environment can damage it.

▲ **Fig 34.2 Phosphates and nitrates are needed for agriculture, but they are entering rivers in increasing amounts**

A river must contain a small quantity of nutrients if it is to maintain life. However, an excess of nutrients can be destructive. Indeed, many rivers are today damaged by an excess of nutrients, while none has ever been damaged by a deficiency.

Fertilisers are essential to productive farming in most areas, fig 34.2. Some farmers use natural organic manures which are not washed out of the soil, but they usually have to supplement these with chemical fertilisers. Phosphates and nitrates from chemically fertilised soils are washed into the rivers.

Eutrophication

High levels of nitrate and phosphate in water cause a condition called **eutrophication**. Microscopic plants multiply rapidly and turn the water opaque, reducing the light reaching bottom-living plants. These plants die and decay. Putrefying bacteria which live on dead material flourish, and use oxygen from the water. Consequently, the other aerobic species are deprived of oxygen and die.

Pesticides

Most wastes from agriculture are nutrients of one sort or another, but there are also residues from **pesticides**. Pesticides cause another major threat to the environment. Organochlorine-based insecticides, for example **DDT**, cyclodienes and dieldrin, do not break down quickly but accumulate in body fats of animals that ingest them. Consequently, they rapidly spread through food chains. Small amounts of these chemicals in the body fats of healthy people do not seem to be poisonous. However, the accumulative effects can be disastrous.

A success story

When DDT was first made in the 1940s, it was considered as one of the greatest inventions. Its inventor was awarded a Nobel Prize. In the next 25 years, DDT alone was responsible for eliminating the threat of malaria from the lives of a thousand million people throughout the world. This is an achievement unparalleled in the history of public health. DDT has also been used to stop the spread of other insect-borne diseases such as typhus and yellow fever.

The bubble bursts

However, like so many interferences with nature, the widespread use of DDT has had its side effects. First, accumulation of DDT in waterways and in plants and animals has led to toxic levels being built up through food chains, fig 34.3 (overleaf).

Second, strains of certain species of insect which are immune to DDT have evolved due to the natural selection of types which could break down DDT in their bodies and make it harmless. This ability is passed on to further generations until the species becomes immune.

Despite many efforts and new technology, we still have not succeeded in completely eliminating any species of important disease-carrying insect.

Q1 Study the three passages **a–c** below.

a DDT, a pesticide, was sprayed by British farmers on crops to kill insect pests. It was found that a decrease in some bird populations followed the use of DDT. The pesticide was found in the muscles, fat and eggs of many birds. Carnivores like the sparrowhawks and herons had more DDT than herbivores like pigeons.

b In the UK it was estimated that over 175 million pounds' worth of crops were saved every year in the 1960s by using pesticides – enough food for over 3 million people.

c The control of the mosquito with insecticides such as DDT has reduced malaria in over 50 countries and saved millions of lives.
(Various governments have banned the use of DDT in their own countries.)

Use your knowledge, together with the information given in each of the passages, to write an account of the advantages *and* disadvantages of using pesticide. Suggest alternatives for pest controls. [9]
(WJEC GCSE Biology 1992 Q19)

HUMAN INFLUENCES ON THE EARTH

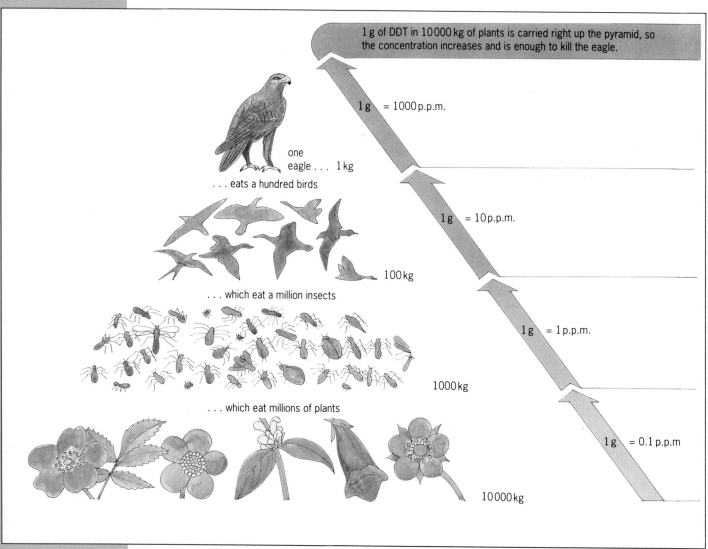

1 g of DDT in 10 000 kg of plants is carried right up the pyramid, so the concentration increases and is enough to kill the eagle.

1 g = 1000 p.p.m.

one
eagle . . . 1 kg

. . . eats a hundred birds

1 g = 10 p.p.m.

100 kg

. . . which eat a million insects

1 g = 1 p.p.m.

1000 kg

. . . which eat millions of plants

1 g = 0.1 p.p.m

10 000 kg

▲ **Fig 34.3 DDT accumulates in living tissue – toxic levels are built up through food chains**

The **greenhouse effect** caused by a build-up of carbon dioxide in the atmosphere is described on page 177.

COMBUSTION OF FOSSIL FUELS

Our industries are another source of potentially dangerous pollution. Combustion of fossil fuels is by far the biggest source of waste gases in the world.

The greenhouse effect
All fossil fuels consist mainly of carbon and hydrogen. These elements burn in the presence of oxygen and make carbon dioxide and water. The **greenhouse effect** caused by a build-up of carbon dioxide in the atmosphere is described on page 177.

◄ **Fig 34.4 Emission of sulphur dioxide from power stations causes acid rain**

Acid rain

Most coals and fuel oils also contain sulphur. When these are burned, the sulphur is released as **sulphur dioxide**. This results in sulphuric acid dissolved in rain. Emissions of sulphur dioxide from combustion are thus causing **acid rain** over the world's biggest cities.

Unfortunately, the problem does not stop there. Prevailing winds carry rainclouds with their acidic cargo many miles from the source of pollution, fig 34.5. Often the acid rain then falls on the countryside, acidifying soils and lakes. The soil of many forests has been affected in this way. Aluminium ions are made available to the roots of the trees by the acid. This results in the death of the trees.

In acidified lakes and streams, the gills and eggs of many fish are affected by the acid, thus causing death. Acid lakes can become completely clear as all life dies.

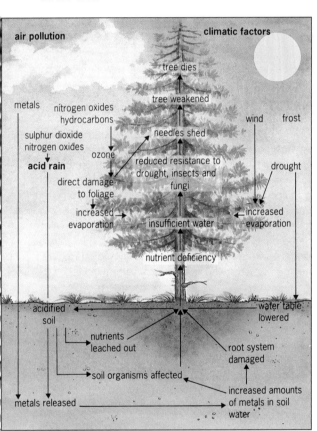

▲ **Fig 34.5 The various ways in which air pollution affects vegetation. The effects are experienced far away from the source of the pollution**

Oxides of nitrogen are also products of industrial combustion and provide us with similar problems to sulphur dioxide. They contribute to acid rain.

Q2 Study the map in fig 34.6 and the account before answering the questions.

◄ **Fig 34.6**

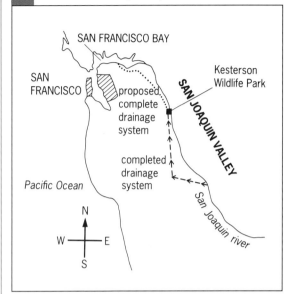

Case history

Soil near the San Joaquin Valley was irrigated (watered) so that it could be used to grow crops. By 1968, millions of tonnes of poisonous chemicals, which were in the rocks in the valley, had been washed out and trapped in the soil. The poisons included the metal called selenium. High levels of selenium were found in the blood of cattle in the area. Crops had only 6 parts per million. In 1975, the authorities began building drains to carry the used irrigation water to San Francisco Bay. Money ran out for this scheme in 1980 and the used water was poured into lakes in the Kesterson Wildlife Park. By 1984 nearly all the fish were killed in these lakes. Also, many birds produced deformed chicks in the area.

a Describe how the case study shows how people have
  i attempted to increase food supply [1]
  ii upset the balance of nature in trying to increase the food supply [1]
  iii encountered problems which they have not solved. [2]
b Explain, using your knowledge of food chains, why the wildlife was affected. [3]
c Suggest why the citizens of San Francisco might object to the building of the drainage system. [1]
(WJEC GCSE Biology 1989 Q18)

35 CONTROLLING POLLUTION

By the end of this section you should be able to

▶ understand how knowledge and public awareness have led to increased activity to prevent pollution and describe methods of pollution control.

As our knowledge about the effects of pollutants increases, along with public pressure and awareness of environmental issues, we are taking more steps to deal with pollution and cut down emissions of the most harmful substances.

AIR POLLUTION

Power stations

Power stations are the main sources of waste gases in the atmosphere. Scientists are devising processes for removing the sulphur from the waste gases, which will reduce the effects of acid rain. In some processes sulphur is changed to ammonium sulphate; in others it is converted into sulphuric acid and removed before it reaches the atmosphere.

Electrical generators are driven by steam turbines (see page 206) which may use coal, oil or natural gas to heat their boilers. Now some stations are using nuclear reactors, fig 35.1, to heat the boilers, with a resulting decrease in waste gases.

▼ Fig 35.1 Nuclear power stations result in less air pollution – they do not emit waste gases

Fossil fuel power stations have chimneys which are very tall so that winds can disperse waste gases more easily. Combustion efficiency has been increased in recent years to reduce carbon monoxide and soot production. However, coal and oil contain minerals which remain as ash after burning the fuel, and some of this ash is carried into waste gases. **Electrostatic precipitators** (see page 225 and fig 35.2) are used to remove dust particles from the gases.

▲ Fig 35.2 Electrostatic precipitators (the white structures) added on to Ferrybridge 'C' power station

Photochemical smog

In the 1940s, the world experienced a new form of pollution. In Los Angeles, a white mist formed which irritated people's eyes, noses and throats. By the 1960s, this form of pollution was common in many cities throughout the world. It was **photochemical smog**, caused by hydrocarbons, oxides of nitrogen and ozone combined under the influence of sunlight. These substances come from a variety of sources, mainly traffic and industry. Today, our weather forecasts frequently include information about air quality.

Traffic

Cars and other traffic are serious polluters of the environment, fig 35.3. Pollution did not concern the early motor manufacturers. It was more important for engines to run smoothly without 'pinking'. The addition of **lead tetraethyl** reduced this problem and made the engines more efficient in terms of miles travelled per gallon of petrol. Today, we know of the hazards of lead from car exhausts. It is breathed in and can eventually be circulated to our nervous systems where it may cause damage.

▲ Fig 35.3 Car exhausts produce carbon dioxide, carbon monoxide, oxides of nitrogen and lead pollution. Unleaded petrol and catalytic converters cut down pollution but do not reduce the carbon dioxide emissions

Unleaded petrol is now being used by more and more people. Leaded petrol will probably be a thing of the past in the next generation or so.

Carbon monoxide is also a serious health hazard from traffic exhausts. It is a colourless, odourless gas which, once in your bloodstream, competes with oxygen for haemoglobin in your red blood cells (see page 11). It can thus starve the cells of oxygen and high concentrations rapidly cause death.

Carbon monoxide in exhausts can be reduced by more than a half through better design of car engines to improve combustion. Addition of **catalytic converters** to exhaust systems reduce the levels of carbon monoxide and oxides of nitrogen emitted.

WATER POLLUTION

Industry and our water supplies

Some of the worst problems of water pollution throughout the world are those which result from the poisonous **heavy metals**. Certain manufacturing processes produce vast quantities of effluent containing such wastes. While these may be discharged in concentrations too low to harm us, they tend to build up through food chains, just like DDT (see pages 91–2). Mercury, lead, zinc and cadmium are heavy metals which poison the enzymes within our cells. As they pass through food chains they accumulate in such high concentrations that animals at the ends of food chains die.

Oil spills

Crude oil or **petroleum** is an essential fuel for many processes of modern life (see pages 166–7). As more and more is transported by sea, accidental spillages occur more often. Thousands of spillages occur throughout the world each year. It is only the major ones like the *Exxon Valdez* in Alaska and the *Braer* in Shetland that make newspaper headlines.

Small amounts of oil are broken down by bacteria and do not do much damage. However, the growing quantity of oil entering the sea causes concern. Oil is unsightly on beaches and can smother larger marine animals, fig 35.4. The effects of oil on links in food chains are probably even worse than the direct action of the oil on larger animals.

Detergents are sometimes used to break up oil slicks but they have to be used cautiously as the chemicals in the detergents can be almost as damaging to wildlife as the oil itself, fig 35.5.

◀ **Fig 35.4 A Western grebe smothered in oil**

▲ **Fig 35.5 Detergents disperse oil, but must be used with care – they can be almost as damaging as the oil itself**

Q1 **a** Fig 35.6 shows the level of lead in samples of dust taken from a road over a ten year period.

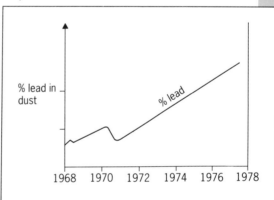

% lead in dust

% lead

1968   1970   1972   1974   1976   1978

◀ **Fig 35.6**

The number of vehicles using the road per year is given in the table.
Using the graph and the table, state *one* piece of evidence which suggests that lead dust comes from motor vehicles.
b Explain how motor vehicles are responsible for this type of pollution.
c State *two* ways by which this type of pollution could be reduced.
d State *one* other air pollutant produced by motor vehicles. [6]
(WJEC GCSE Biology 1990 Q18)

Year	Number of vehicles using the road in thousands
1968	10
1970	15
1972	16
1974	22
1976	30
1978	35

36 DEALING WITH HUMAN WASTE

By the end of this section you should be able to
- understand the implications of discharging organic waste into waterways
- recall how sewage is treated before being discharged.

Through history, humans have treated rivers like sewers and lakes like cesspools, fig 36.1. These natural systems struggle to cope with the pollution of human waste. There are microbes in rivers and lakes which break down moderate amounts of organic matter. However, they can quickly be destroyed by detergents, sewage and effluent from industry. If we do not increase our efforts to keep fresh water pure, we shall soon face desperate problems.

FATHER THAMES INTRODUCING HIS OFFSPRING TO THE FAIR CITY OF LONDON.

(A Design for a Fresco in the New Houses of Parliament.)

DIPHTHERIA.   SCROFULA.   CHOLERA.

▲ **Fig 36.1 Humans have treated rivers like cesspools for centuries. This is a cartoon from the nineteenth century about the polluted River Thames**

MANAGEMENT OF WATER

Our management of sewage disposal and water treatment have progressed considerably since the nineteenth century.

Sewage systems confine much of human waste such as faeces in pipes so that it does not enter groundwater or pollute the surrounding soil. Sewage systems pass wastes to central treatment plants where they can be safely disposed of.

Water treatment procedures have been created to ensure that water supplied to homes and industry is safe to use.

TREATMENT OF SEWAGE

The need for sewage treatment

About 400 litres of sewage and waste water are produced per person per day in large cities in the UK. Only about half a litre of this is the solids such as faeces which could cause a health risk. The problem stems from the variety of bacteria which live on the solids. Many of them are harmless to humans but can still cause pollution. If they enter rivers or lakes they multiply rapidly and use up the oxygen in the water. This is disastrous to all the aerobic organisms in the water as it leads to **eutrophication** (see page 91). Because of this and other health hazards, untreated sewage can no longer legally be dumped in open pits or poured into water sources in Britain. It must first be treated at a sewage works, fig 36.2.

▲ **Fig 36.2 Today effluent is treated at a sewage works before being discharged to a river**

Primary treatment

First the sewage is passed through wire screens. These collect large objects which would otherwise damage the pumps. Then the sewage flows through grit channels. Here grit and gravel are collected which were small enough to pass through the screens. The particles are relatively heavy and settle to the bottom of the channels. They may be washed and used in industry.

Most of the remaining solids are organic. They are pumped into large **sedimentation tanks** where they settle to the bottom. A sediment called **sludge** is formed.

The processes just described make up **primary treatment**. Some cities do little more than this with their sewage. If they are on the coast they remove the sludge and pump the effluent into the sea. **Chlorine** is added which kills harmful bacteria, thus reducing the health risk.

Secondary treatment

Secondary treatment may be needed in other places where the effluent goes into small rivers or streams which would otherwise be affected by the sewage.

From the sedimentation tanks the sewage passes into a **trickling tank**. This contains a bed of stones about 180cm deep. On the stones is a slime of microbes. These are mainly useful bacteria which live on dead matter. The sewage trickles onto the stones from a pipe. The bacteria break down the organic matter to form harmless chemicals.

Any remaining solids settle out in a **humus tank**. By now, up to 95% of the solids in the sewage have been removed.

Chlorine is again added to kill any organisms that are still present. The effluent can then be safely pumped into streams. Finally, the solid sludge collected during the treatment is put in large **digestion tanks**. These are heated to speed up the action of bacteria inside. The bacteria break down the sludge into harmless material in 30 days. The purified sludge may be dried and sold as fertiliser.

Fig 36.3 illustrates the sewage treatment process.

Microbes and sewage treatment

The microbes which are important in sewage treatment are

- **bacteria** which break down cellulose
- **fungi** which break down industrial wastes in acid conditions and destroy nematode worms
- **algae** which produce oxygen, helping to kill harmful anaerobic bacteria.

The captivated sludge process

In the 1980s a novel method of waste water treatment became popular. Traditional biological processes use percolating filters or **completely mixed activated sludge** methods. Activated sludge is solid matter from sedimentation tanks mixed with bacteria and protozoa. The mixture is aerated and passed to percolating filter beds. It then becomes completely mixed activated sludge and thrives, killing harmful anaerobic microbes.

The new **captivated sludge** process no longer needs settling tanks to separate the treated effluent from activated sludge. Surplus activated sludge can be automatically taken out of the reactor whenever necessary.

In the traditional system the microorganisms are present as films. They can move freely in the waste water. Settling tanks are therefore necessary to separate the films of microorganisms from the treated effluent. The microorganisms are then pumped back to the reactor vessel. In the captivated sludge process, small foam pads are placed in the reactor vessel. These are colonised by microorganisms and never leave the reactor vessel.

Q1
  a Name *one* chemical, excreted by humans, which is present in sewage. [1]
  b i What type of useful organism is found in both the aeration tanks and the sprinkler tank of a sewage works? [1]
  ii What do these organisms do to the sewage? [1]
  c Explain why air is needed in the aeration and sprinkler tanks. [2]
  d Name the useful gas formed in the sludge digester and suggest a possible use for it. [2]
  e Suggest why untreated sewage should not be discharged into rivers. [2]
    (MEG GCSE Human Biology 2 1991 Q4 (modified))

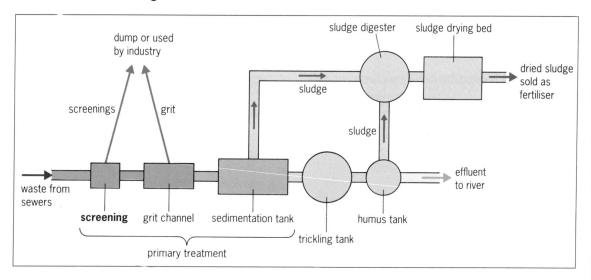

Fig 36.3 The treatment of sewage

37 WORLD POPULATION GROWTH

By the end of this section you should be able to

— know how population growth and decline is related to environmental resources

— understand that the impact of human activity on Earth is related to the size of the population, economic factors and industrial requirements.

The world population is growing at an alarming rate, fig 37.1. The Earth has enough resources for careful, sustained development, but the simultaneous explosion of both population and consumption could upset the global balance if prompt action is not taken.

The impact on the environment of continued growth at current levels of consumption will be disastrous. While known reserves of resources such as minerals have actually increased, future shortages are likely among resources such as water.

▼ **Fig 37.1 The human population explosion**

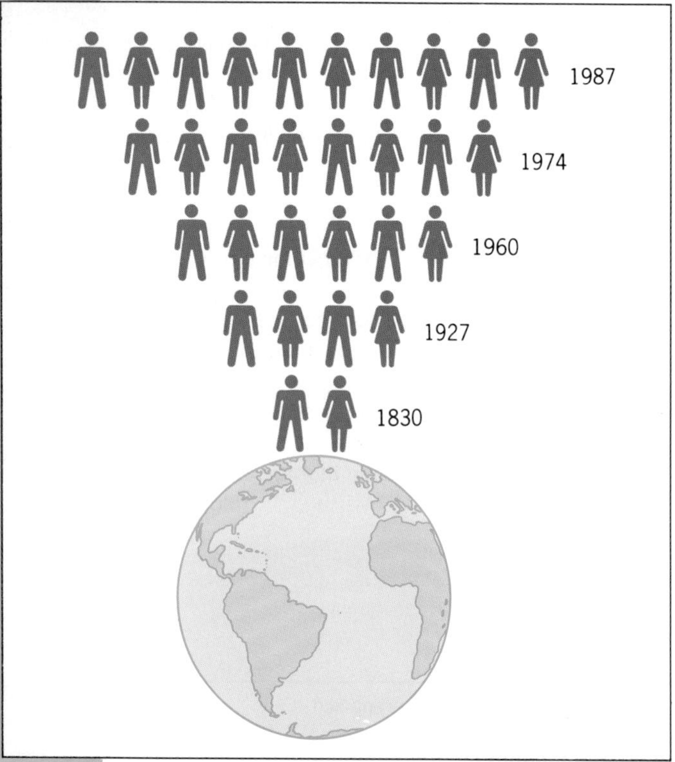

The medium projection is a 'desirable goal'. However, if people continue to increase their consumption of resources as they have in the past, development will be brief and the consequences disastrous. Water shortages could hold back development in many African countries by the year 2025. By 2050 up to four-fifths of today's wildlife reserves could be needed for human use. One solution might be for individual governments to aim to balance population growth with the available resources of the environment.

REASONS FOR POPULATION GROWTH

The reasons for present growth trends in our population are complex, but the most important factors have probably been

- improved medical care
- improved hygiene
- control of disease-causing organisms
- improved agriculture.

Medical care and hygiene

Infant mortality has been reduced dramatically in recent years. In earlier times, at least half of all babies died before becoming adults. Today in the affluent countries, more than 95% reach the age of 21. The epidemics of infectious diseases of the past are almost unknown in the developed countries of the world today.

Pesticides and agriculture

The use of insecticides – DDT in particular (see pages 91–2) – has a record for saving human life which is probably unequalled by any other single factor. More than a billion people alive at the end of this century will owe their lives insecticides.

Better agriculture and methods for storing and distributing food have reduced the effects of famine, but **climatic factors** are largely beyond our control. Famines still cause important problems. Our production of polluting greenhouse gases may possibly make these problems worse in the future.

ESTIMATES OF WORLD POPULATION GROWTH

The United Nations Fund for Population Activities (UNFPA) predicts that the world population will reach almost 10 billion by the year 2050 – almost double today's population. Growth will continue for another century to 11.6 billion before the population starts to fall. This is the 'medium' projection that the UN considers most likely. The 'high' projection puts the total at 12.5 billion in 2050 with continued growth to 20.7 billion.

CONSEQUENCES OF GLOBAL WARMING

The greenhouse effect

The **greenhouse effect** is a predicted situation in which the planet becomes surrounded by a blanket of **greenhouse gases** such as carbon dioxide, sulphur dioxide and oxides of nitrogen (see page 177) would not allow heat to escape, resulting in **global warming**. The burning of fossil fuels inevitably leads to the production of greenhouse gases and global warming.

Famine

Dried-up fields and empty grain stores are likely consequences across much of the Third World by 2050, fig 37.2. The United Nations have made a study of global warming caused by excess production of carbon dioxide. It suggests a decline of between 10% and 15% in grain yields in Africa, tropical America, India and South East Asia. This will lead to a substantial increase in famine. Most of the world's food crops, including wheat, rice, soya beans, sorghum and millet, could be affected. The study assesses the implications of changes in climate predicted by computer models. The models assume a doubling of carbon dioxide concentration in the atmosphere.

Two major models have been developed. They differ over what might happen to crops in the richer northern countries. One suggests that crop yields could increase in some places as hotter summers become more frequent. The other model suggests abandoned fields and declining harvests, especially in North America. This finding contradicts other studies which suggest that US agriculture will be largely immune to damage from global warming.

Declining yields in North America could have a worldwide impact. Changes in grain production in North America would greatly raise grain prices worldwide. Some predictions suggest a resulting rise of 400 million people at risk from hunger. This would increase the number of people at risk to more than a billion within 50 years – one in eight of the world's likely population by that time.

Preventing famine

To prevent hunger on this scale, the world must make breakthroughs in biotechnology, creating new crops adapted to hotter climates and drier soils (see page 86). There will also be a need for major irrigation and land reclamation schemes. But probably the best way of coping with global warming would be to reduce population growth.

Water supplies

It is likely that there will be increased demand for water to irrigate fields in most of Europe. In the South East of England, water supplies are already stretched to the limit. In the early 1990s, continued diminished rainfall highlighted this problem. Massive water transfer projects may be the only way to supply water from the wet hillsides of Scotland and Wales to the increasingly dry and heavily populated South East.

Rising seas

The melting of icecaps at the poles could result from global warming, causing the sea level to rise. Two out of three of the world's cities with more than 2.5

million people are on the coast. Tens of millions of farmers could be forced from large river deltas such as the Nile, Yangtze, Indus and Ganges, where some 100 million people live, as salt water invades crops.

Migration

Changes in the environment brought about by global warming may lead to a significant change in the distribution of the population. If predictions about global warming are correct, the world faces a totally unprecedented migration, 40 times greater than those at the end of the Second World War.

FEEDING THE GROWING POPULATION

Thanks to the development of new disease-resistant plants, better farm management and better pest control, we may be able to cope with some predicted increases in demand. However, distribution of food to countries that need it is often frustrated by political barriers and cost.

Consequences of increased food production

- More mouths will need more food from our shrinking available land.
- More pesticides or alternative pest control will be needed. Crop losses of more than 45% are often due to pests.
- More fertilisers will be needed for intensive agricultural methods.
- More water will be needed for irrigation. Better methods of recycling water will therefore be necessary.

As we saw on page 90, these requirements will inevitably result in pollution problems.

▲ Fig 37.2
Possible future effects of global warming include dried-up fields and large-scale migration

38 POPULATION AND BIRTH CONTROL

By the end of this section you should be able to

- understand the need for world population control
- describe different contraceptive measures, their method of working and their relative effectiveness.

In order to prevent the problems of famine and pollution caused by the population explosion, should the world consider **population control**? We would not think it ethical to enforce population control, but some voluntary measures need to be encouraged.

BIRTH CONTROL

Programmes to encourage the use of **contraception** are being introduced in many developing countries. There are several different methods of preventing pregnancy, so that families can be planned and parents can limit the number of children they have. However, effective birth control cannot be achieved in a short period. Educational programmes are necessary to overcome cultural resistance and ignorance. Also, 45% of the population in developing countries are under the age of 15. When these children enter the reproductive period of life, they will add further pressure to the growing population.

If birth control is reasonably effective, the population of developing countries may grow to around 4 billion by 2000. This is a 60% increase on present levels. If the programmes have no success, the population may grow to more than 6 billion – an increase of 140%.

REVERSIBLE METHODS OF CONTRACEPTION

Withdrawal

In the world as a whole, male **withdrawal** remains the most common method of contraception. This involves withdrawing the penis from the vagina during sexual intercourse just before sperms are released by ejaculation (see page 40). This is not a very reliable method of contraception as some sperms can escape unknown to the man.

Douching

Douching or washing the inside of the vagina following intercourse is also not an effective method. Sperms pass through the neck of the womb or cervix very rapidly, and these cannot be washed out. The sperms responsible for fertilisation are probably the first through.

The condom

The **condom** or sheath is by far the most widespread mechanism of contraception in use. This is a rubber sheath placed over the penis which collects the sperms. The condom also has the advantage of reducing the possibility of contracting or passing on sexually transmitted diseases.

▼ **Fig 38.1 Some methods of contraception (clockwise from left) spermicidal cream, a cap, spermicidal pessaries, 'the pill', a condom and a fertility thermometer used in the rhythm method**

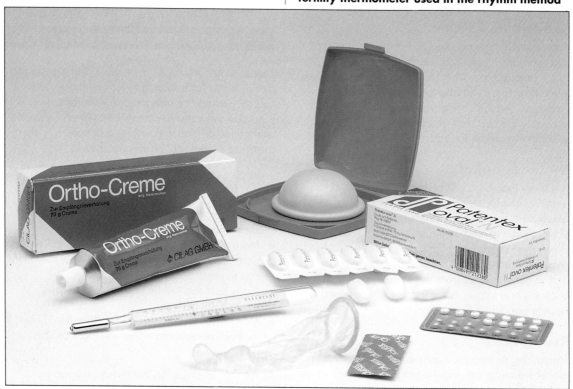

The cap or diaphragm

The **cap** or **diaphragm** is a rubber dome placed over the cervix. It prevents sperms entering the uterus. Used properly, the diaphragm is as effective as the condom.

Spermicides

Spermicides (chemicals that kill sperms) are used in the form of creams and foams. They are not very effective on their own, but may be used in conjunction with a sheath or cap.

The rhythm method

The **rhythm method** depends on the female reproductive cycle (see pages 38–9). An ovum is released 14 days before the next menstrual period occurs. Fertilisation is more likely around the time of ovulation. The rhythm method involves not having intercourse for several days around this time. The rhythm method is not very reliable but is preferred by some couples for religious reasons.

The IUD or coil

Intrauterine devices (**IUD**s) have come to be widely used since the late 1950s. Like many medical inventions, the IUD was used before its mechanism of action was understood.

Usually, the device takes the form of a simple loop or spiral placed in the uterus. The IUD is made of an inert material which causes no inflammation. IUDs appear to work by causing the migration of white blood cells from the bloodstream into the uterus. Here the white cells probably destroy the ovum between the time of fertilisation and implantation (see page 40).

IUDs are effective and do not need repeated attention once inserted, but can give rise to heavy and prolonged menstrual bleeding.

The contraceptive pill

The **contraceptive pill** or **oral contraception** has also increased in popularity since the 1950s. 'The pill' contains a combination of ovarian hormones. These hormones prevent the release of the ovum in the same way as ovulation is stopped during pregnancy (see pages 38–9).

Since its introduction, the number of users of the pill has reached an estimated 40 million throughout the world. As experience with the pill has grown, a number of side effects have been observed. Some such as nausea (a feeling of sickness) may not be very important, but others such as increased incidence of **thrombosis** (blood clots) may be very serious.

The pill is the most effective reversible method of contraception, and risks of death due to unwanted pregnancies arising from the use of other methods may equal or outweigh the risk of death due to thrombosis.

The relative effectiveness of reversible contraceptives

The methods are listed here in decreasing order of effectiveness (most effective first)

- the pill
- the IUD
- the diaphragm }
- the condom }
- spermicides alone
- withdrawal or rhythm method
- douching.

Using any of these reversible methods, a couple can still have a family when the chosen contraceptive method is stopped. However, there are **irreversible methods** of birth control.

IRREVERSIBLE METHODS OF CONTRACEPTION

Male and female **sterilisations** are becoming increasingly widely used. These are surgical techniques. In a woman, the **Fallopian tubes**, page 38, are closed in an abdominal operation. On a world scale the use of this method is limited by medical resources.

Sterilisation of a man is carried out by cutting the **vas deferens** (see page 36). This is a simple operation called a **vasectomy**. It can be completed in 10 minutes.

Neither operation interferes with the sexual activity of the person concerned. The ovaries and testes continue to make sex hormones which pass into the bloodstream and control sexual behaviour. The blocked ova and sperms are reabsorbed by normal bodily processes.

Q1 The table below shows the success rate for various contraceptives.

Method of contraception	Pregnancies in 1 year/ 100 women	Side effect
contraceptive pill	0.003	increase in thrombosis (clots)
IUD (intrauterine device)	1–5	excess bleeding
cap (diaphragm)	7–12	none
condom (sheath)	7–14	none
safe period	18–24	none

a Which method of contraception is the most effective?

b Which method is also effective in stopping the spread of venereal disease?

c Research is continuing to find a 'male' contraceptive pill. What effect would this pill have in order to be successful?

39 CONSERVATION

By the end of this section you should be able to

- understand the basic scientific principles associated with a major change in the biosphere
- appreciate the need for conservation measures and describe some of these measures.

The word 'conservation' conjures up varying images to different people. Conservationists usually aim to protect environments or species.

THE PUBLIC IMAGE OF CONSERVATION

Conservation has in the past been placed rather low on governments' lists of official concerns. Conservationists are sometimes associated with opposition to progress, and may be seen as resisting all development. The result of much conservationist campaigning has not been to stop development, but to persuade many developing countries that conservation is irrelevant, harmful and antisocial. So development has continued regardless of conservationists, resulting in damage to the environment that considered conservation could have helped prevent.

THE WORLD CONSERVATION STRATEGY

With the launch of the World Conservation Strategy (WCS) in 1980, it was hoped to improve the image of conservation. The Strategy recognises the need for development, without which a large proportion of the world's population will remain poor. It argues that for development to be long lasting, it must rely on established conservation principles.

Conservation and development

Conservation and development are in fact dependent on each other. This is illustrated clearly in underdeveloped countries where the dependence of communities on living organisms is direct and immediate. For the 500 million people who are malnourished, or the 1500 million people whose only fuel is wood, dung or crop waste, conservation is the only thing between them and misery or even death.

Unhappily, people on the margins of survival are compelled by their poverty to destroy the few resources available to them. They strip trees for fuel until the plants wither and die. Villagers are forced to burn dung and stubble. The 400 million tonnes of dung and crop wastes that rural people burn each year are badly needed as fertiliser to maintain soils already being eroded, fig 39.1. The organic material being burned would bind the soil so that it would remain.

▲ **Fig 39.1 Deforestation has resulted in soil erosion in the Amazon rainforest**

Defining conservation

The WCS defines **conservation** as the management of human use of the biosphere so that it may yield the greatest lasting benefit to present generations, while maintaining its potential to meet the needs of future generations. Thus conservation, like development, is for people. Development aims to achieve improvements largely through the use of the resources of the biosphere. Conservation aims to achieve these improvements by ensuring that such use can continue. The aim of the WCS is the blending of conservation and development to ensure that changes to our planet secure the survival and well-being of all people.

CONSERVING SPECIES

As humans have developed they have lost the direct contact with nature which used to be necessary for survival. We sometimes forget that, however varied nature is, it is not inexhaustible, and some species cannot cope with the changes we make to their environments.

The conservation of as many species as possible, together with their habitats, is a matter that should concern us all. Furthermore, the losses suffered over the last 200–300 years have been so great that just preserving the present situation is not enough. For many countries that would simply mean isolating a few small remains of natural landscapes from the process of industrialisation, leaving only the more resilient everyday species elsewhere. There would be no room for the more sensitive species, the specialists of the living world such as the koala bear.

Preserving habitats

Nature conservation means preserving nature in its original form so that all species have a suitable habitat in which to live. Once a species has been completely destroyed by the removal of its habitat, nothing can bring it back. This has happened to the wild horse, a few specimens of which can still be seen – but only in zoos. Much as we might wish to see these animals in their natural surroundings, this is impossible because their natural habitat has disappeared.

There are a number of mammals and birds which have only relatively recently come under pressure and have managed to survive to the present day in some countries. Lynx, fig 39.2, bear and wolf disappeared from most of Europe and the bearded vulture ceased to breed in the Alps some 100 years ago. They were exterminated by our forefathers because they were regarded only as competitors. However, these animals still live in other places such as North America.

▲ **Fig 39.2 The lynx is now extinct in many of its former ranges**

Repairing the damage

We obviously have no right simply to eliminate species, and we have an obligation to repair the damage already caused by our ancestors. For some species, it is possible to preserve or restore the original variety and natural state of their habitats. Other species may be artificially transported back to habitats they would not return to of their own accord.

TRADING IN ENDANGERED SPECIES

Law enforcement and CITES

In February of one year, special agents of the US Fish and Wildlife Service seized more than 17 000 furs on a ranch in Texas. Smuggled across the Rio Grande, the 2.5 tonne haul included 1556 bobcats for European markets. The ranch owner and four smugglers were arrested.

▲ **Fig 39.3 Western Europe is a major market for furs**

One month later, French nature conservation authorities seized eight chimpanzees, three pythons and two crocodiles illegally shipped to Bordeaux. The importer was fined and the animals taken back to West Africa.

In April, West German customs officers seized 3600 rare cactus plants from passengers on a single aeroplane at Frankfurt. 141 rhinoceros horns were also on board. Court proceedings were carried out against these smugglers.

Finally, in August, Indian customs inspectors seized 150 000 snake skins and 500 otter furs, ready to leave Calcutta for Frankfurt.

This is a single year's record of international law enforcement action and represents just the tip of a giant iceberg. The law enforcement relied on the Convention on International Trade in Endangered Species of Wild Fauna and Flora (CITES). The convention became law in 1975. It now has over 60 member countries, including most of the important exporters and importers of wild animals and plants.

The aim of the convention is to establish worldwide controls over trade in endangered species and their products. It recognises that this sort of trade is one of the major threats to the survival of species.

Europe as a market for furs

Europe is the centre of trade in endangered species. Germany alone accounts for 60% of the world's fur imports. Adding to this the markets of the UK, Belgium, Switzerland, Holland, France and Italy, Western Europe accounts for 80% of the market for all endangered species of wild cats, that is, about 0.5 million fur skins per year, of various wild cats from the ocelot to the lynx.

Ivory

Ivory imports recorded by customs officials in 1977 totalled 180 tonnes. This represented 10 000 dead elephants! Today, the trade is considerably less, but poachers still destroy large numbers of elephants for their tusks.

◀ Fig 39.4 The horn of the rhinoceros has long been prized, leading to danger of extinction

Fig 39.5 Ivory carvings seized by customs at Munich ▶

Whaling

Some nations are still active in whaling, fig 39.6, and Europe also remains a major consumer of whale products. More than 11 500 tonnes of whale oil, mainly from Japan, were imported to Europe in 1978 – more than 2000 dead whales were needed for this. Fortunately, most nations have reduced their demand for whale products in the 1990s but many whales still suffer in agony due to human greed.

Fig 39.6 Some nations still carry out whaling ▽

Crocodile skins, snake skins and turtle shells

Together with Japan, Western Europe is the main market for crocodile skins, fig 39.7, the vast majority of which are taken from the wild. Up to 50% of this harvest is unusable or lost. Of the estimated 2 million crocodile skins which are traded each year, 1.2 million (60%) go to Western Europe. The European share of snake skins and turtle shells is equally high.

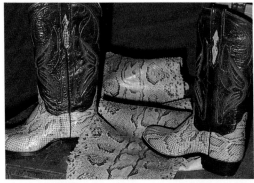

▲ Fig 39.7 Reptile skins are used for boots, handbags and luggage

Exotic animals and plants

Europe also maintains its lead in the traffic of exotic live animals and plants. The customers are pet traders, safari zoos, scientific research centres and private collectors for every imaginable species. Tourists have become the main clients for various wildlife products, fig 39.8, which are now exported as mass souvenirs from developing countries.

▲ Fig 39.8 Turtle shells illegally on sale to tourists at Martinique

SAFEGUARDING NATURAL HABITATS

Most countries in Europe now have nature conservation laws and protected areas. Protected areas differ greatly in extent – the Greenland National Park is almost uninhabited and its environment alters only under the effects of climatic changes, whereas the Camargue Reserve at the mouth of the Rhone in France is subject to many external influences.

The International Union for Conservation of Nature (IUCN) has produced a report reviewing the various types of habitat protection that exist throughout the world. These are described below.

Scientific reserves

These are free from any human interference or internal artificial influences. They are areas set aside exclusively for scientific research and often protect species or habitats which are important for their biological value (for example, wetlands). Their size is determined by the area which can be preserved intact.

National or state parks

These parks serve some of the same purposes as reserves, that is, conservation of the environment and its species. Their regulations do not exclude the public or the provision of access roads. The parks are generally zoned to meet the aims of strict conservation, recreation and education. Most National Parks in the United States prohibit human activities, though this is not the case in European parks – for example, managed herds of reindeer are grazed in the protected parks of Sweden.

Beauty spots or sites of national interest

These sites, which are often spectacular, include gorges, canyons, waterfalls and caves. They are protected in the same way as historic monuments but are accessible to the public.

Managed nature reserves and sanctuaries

These reserves are designed to protect a species or a group of species. Examples include forestry, game and fishing reserves. In such cases the species must be managed to ensure that they are preserved. An example is the grasslands of Mont Ventoux in France which have particularly interesting plants which are maintained by the grazing of sheep, without which the environment would rapidly change.

Man-made landscapes and protected landscapes

Landscapes which have been shaped by agricultural activities are destined to disappear once their economic value ends. Protecting such environments involves maintaining or reviving human activity. The regional natural parks in parts of Europe are good examples.

Q1 The table below shows how the numbers of tigers in India have changed over 60 years. During that period, 88% of India's forests were destroyed and the prices paid for tiger skins became very high. In order to save the tiger from extinction, the World Wildlife Fund launched an appeal called OPERATION TIGER. In 1990, one-third of India's tigers were protected in tiger reserves.

Year	1930	1960	1972	1979	1984	1990
Population of tigers	40 000	2000	1800	3105	4005	4320

(Data by permission of W.W.F. UK Data Support for Education Services)

a i How many tigers were outside protected areas in 1990?
  ii Suggest, with a reason, when OPERATION TIGER was launched.   [2]
b Use all the information given and suggest *two* explanations for the decrease in tigers between 1930 and 1972.   [2]
c The use of satellites has shown that the removal of forests was 15 000 km² per year by 1986. If this rate continued, what area was removed between January 1986 and December 1990?   [1]
(WJEC GCSE Biology 1992 Q5)

Q2 Read the following newspaper article and answer the questions.

Why the frogs have hopped it

The main pond in the village for spawn was close to the brook. After the Anglian water authority 'cleaned it out' the water table fell.

For a few years the dwindling number of frogs tried to breed in the brook itself but failed.

Just a few years ago the pond was the summer home of numerous newts.

They, too, have declined, possibly because of salty water washing in from the roads. The other ponds in the parish are also frogless.

There is some hope that frogs will return to the village. Last summer the water authority dug the old brook pond deeper and it now holds water once more.

Spawn for the restored pond came from several sources: from a garden pond in a neighbouring village, from an old pond that was to be filled in and from a flooded field several miles away. Already hundreds of tadpoles have hatched and later, I hope, the small frogs will successfully leave the water to fend for themselves.

a State a characteristic of the Class Amphibia which is mentioned in the article.
b Suggest a reason why frogs failed to breed in the brook.
c State *two* ways by which Man is trying to conserve frogs.
d i Name the pollutant which is probably killing the frogs.
  ii Explain concisely how this pollutant kills amphibians.   [8]
(WJEC Common Syllabus (Biology) 1983 Q12)

40 ECOLOGICAL PYRAMIDS

By the end of this section you should be able to

- understand pyramids of numbers and pyramids of biomass
- understand how materials for growth and energy are transferred through an ecosystem
- understand how food production involves the management of ecosystems to improve the efficiency of energy transfer, and that such management involves a duty of care.

In order to study a community it is often useful to look at **feeding relationships**. These may be illustrated by diagrams called **ecological pyramids**.

WHAT IS AN ECOLOGICAL PYRAMID?

Trophic levels
Ecological pyramids show organisms in several feeding layers, called **trophic levels**. The first trophic level, at the base of the pyramid, consists of plants. Plants are called **producers** because they produce food by photosynthesis, page 4. The other trophic levels are made up of **consumers**, so called because they feed on other organisms rather than making their own food. Consumers include animals, fungi and most bacteria. Consumers may be

- **herbivores** (which feed only on plants) in the second trophic level – **primary consumers**
- **first carnivores** (which feed on herbivores) in the third trophic level – **secondary consumers**
- **second carnivores** (which feed on first carnivores) in the fourth trophic level – **tertiary consumers**.

Some carnivores may eat a varied diet and may eat both herbivores and other carnivores, so may be in more than one trophic level. **Omnivores** feed on both plants and animals and so will also be in more than one trophic level.

The shape of the pyramid
The number of organisms in each trophic level is smaller than the number in the level below. This gives the pyramid its shape. The number of trophic levels in a pyramid is limited, and there are rarely levels higher than second carnivores because there is not enough food for them (see page 109).

TYPES OF ECOLOGICAL PYRAMID

There are three types of ecological pyramid

- a **pyramid of numbers** which shows the number of organisms per unit area or volume in each trophic level
- a **pyramid of biomass** which shows the dry mass of organic material per unit area or volume in each trophic level
- a **pyramid of energy** which shows the flow of energy through the community and is expressed in units of energy per unit of time for a unit area or volume.

Pyramids of numbers
Fig 40.1 shows how a **pyramid of numbers** is plotted. It is similar to a bar chart, but the bars are horizontal and stacked on top of each other. Fig 40.2 shows pyramids of numbers for grassland and woodland. Notice that the shapes are quite different. The base of the woodland pyramid of

Fig 40.1 A pyramid of numbers is plotted in a similar way to a bar chart

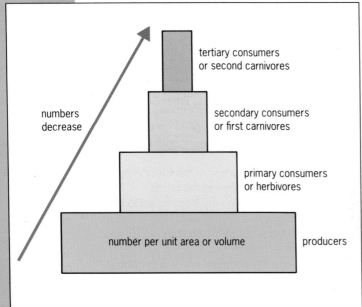

numbers decrease

tertiary consumers or second carnivores

secondary consumers or first carnivores

primary consumers or herbivores

number per unit area or volume   producers

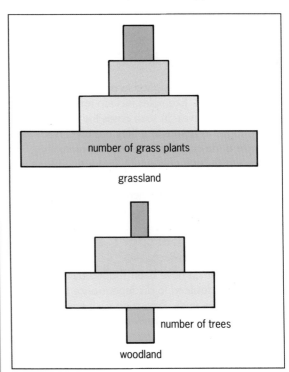

number of grass plants

grassland

number of trees

woodland

▲ **Fig 40.2 Pyramids of numbers for a woodland and a grassland community are quite different in shape**

numbers is much smaller than the first trophic level. This is because one tree can support thousands of first consumers, for example insects. The diagram therefore does not look much like a pyramid shape and is misleading, as it does not take into account the relative sizes of the organisms.

Pyramids of biomass

Fig 40.3 shows a **pyramid of biomass** for a woodland community. This is plotted by measuring the dry mass of organic material or **biomass** in each trophic level.

Organisms contain different amounts of water. They are dried out before weighing because their dry mass gives a more accurate reading of the amount of living material in each trophic level.

When the dry mass of individuals in each trophic level is plotted, the pyramid is a more normal shape, giving a better description of the woodland community. Even so, biomass pyramids can also be unusual shapes if producers are much smaller in size and change in numbers more quickly than the consumers they support. Such an example is seen in an ocean community, where the biomass of plankton changes seasonally, fig 40.4.

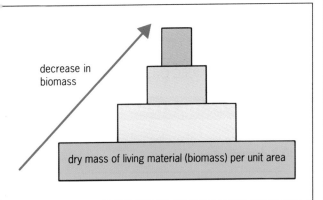

▲ **Fig 40.3 A pyramid of biomass for a woodland community**

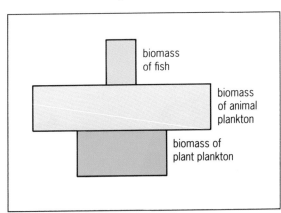

▲ **Fig 40.4 The seasonal change in plankton biomass can result in a pyramid of biomass with an unusual shape**

Pyramids of energy

The energy that flows through a community begins with sunlight, which is used by producers for photosynthesis. The chemical energy produced at the first trophic level flows through the community as consumers feed.

The transfer of chemical energy from one level to the next is never 100% efficient. At each level, some energy is used for the everyday processes of living organisms. This is 'lost' energy which does not reach the next trophic level. So the amount of energy decreases as it flows through the community. Fig 40.5 shows a pyramid of energy, illustrating this energy flow and energy loss. The pyramid tapers to a point.

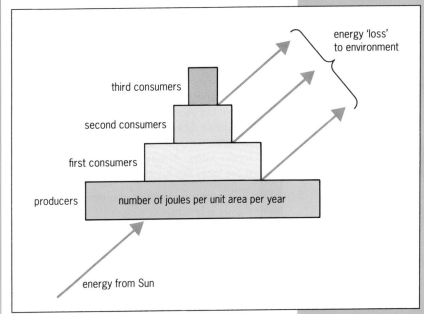

▲ **Fig 40.5 The energy is dispersed as it flows through a food chain**

LIMITING THE LINKS IN A FOOD CHAIN

The number of links in a food chain is limited by the chemical energy available. As the amount of chemical energy at each trophic level becomes smaller, so does the amount of living material that can be supported by that level. When the chemical energy dwindles to nothing, the pyramid ends.

The pyramid of energy, therefore, gives the best picture of the relationships between producers and consumers. Whereas pyramids of numbers and biomass record the organisms supported in each trophic level at any one time, the energy pyramid shows the amount of food being produced and consumed in a given time. Its shape is therefore not affected by differences in size or changes in numbers of individuals.

Activity

Design an investigation to compare pyramids of numbers in a grassland and a woodland.
You will need a sweep net, a quadrat, a beating tray, a hand lens, identification guides and knowledge of the feeding habits of some common insects.
Design your investigation with the following in mind

- standardisation of areas to be studied
- standardisation of methods of catching organisms
- the importance of taking average numbers when counting
- the importance of repeating the investigation (or using class results)
- the importance of clear tabulation of data
- the importance of accurately plotting pyramids of numbers on graph paper to the correct scale.

Write up your investigation using the headings 'plan', 'results', 'discussion' and 'evaluation'.

Q1 Sea anglers use lugworm as bait. The lugworm lives in deep burrows in muddy sea shores. Cadmium is a poisonous metal which reaches the surface of the mud as factory waste. When the lugworm feeds, it carries the cadmium to the lower layers of mud where it remains. Within ten years, sea anglers had reduced the population of lugworms on a South Wales sea shore from 60 per square metre to 1 per square metre. A food web for the muddy shore looks like fig 40.6.

The average number of organisms per m² is shown in brackets.

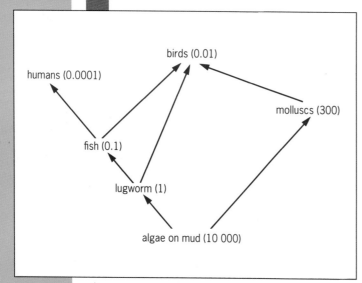

▲ **Fig 40.6**

a Use all the above information and explain *two different* ways in which the reduction of the lugworm population could affect the environment. [2]
b Copy and complete the pyramid of numbers in fig 40.7 using *only* the information given in the food web. At each level, write the name of *one* organism. [4]

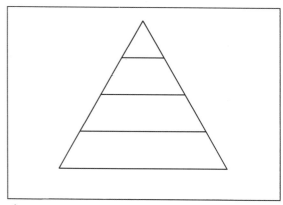

▲ **Fig 40.7**

(WJEC GCSE Biology 1991 Q9)

OUR PLACE IN THE PYRAMID

People live at the tops of ecological pyramids, as fig 40.8 demonstrates.

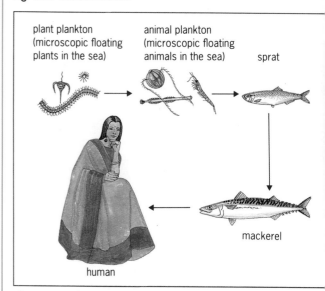

▲ **Fig 40.8 People are at the top of the food pyramid. Sometimes the food chain is several stages long**

Eating tertiary consumers

If humans were to live on mackerel alone, one person would have to catch one mackerel nearly every day, and about 300 mackerel would be needed to support that person for a year.

Each mackerel would eat a sprat every day. Therefore the 300 mackerel required to support a person for a year would themselves eat 90 000 sprats per year. Each sprat would eat some animal plankton – say one animal per day, so the sprat population would consume at least 27 million animal plankton in a year. The animal plankton would require 1000 tonnes of plant plankton. So we can draw a pyramid that looks like fig 40.9.

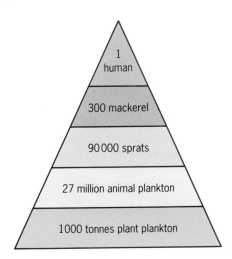

▲ Fig 40.9 A large number of organisms are required at the base of the pyramid to support one organism at the top

The dissipation of energy

The large numbers of organisms towards the base of the pyramid are required to support just one human at the apex because none of the organisms is very efficient at converting food to body tissue. Only about 1% of the Sun's energy striking the sea is converted to chemical energy in plant plankton. The animal plankton are able to convert only about 10% of the plant plankton into animal tissue – most of the plant plankton is undigested or used to provide energy for the plant plankton for swimming, eating and other activities.

Similarly, the human, mackerel and sprats are able to convert only about 10% of their food into human, mackerel and sprat tissue respectively. So the number of animals that can be supported at the top of the pyramid is directly related to the number of layers the pyramid has, because energy is 'wasted' at each layer.

Eating secondary consumers

More people can be supported on this pyramid base simply by shortening the pyramid. Eliminate the mackerel and the sea will produce 90 000 sprats for human consumption. If each person could survive on 10 sprats per day, the sprats would support 30 people for a year.

Eating primary consumers

But sprats alone may be a boring and unbalanced diet. Let us eat animal plankton instead and assume that 100 animals per day would satisfy you. Now 900 people could live on 27 million animal plankton, for example, shrimps.

Eating producers

If we eliminate the last animal link in the food pyramid and eat plant plankton ourselves, the sea would support even more people. About 2000 people, each eating 2 kg of plant plankton per day, could live near the sea that supported only one person who ate mackerel, fig 40.10.

Should we all be vegetarians?

When applied to the land, the same simple rules of food pyramids suggest that the people of over-populated regions of the world should be vegetarians. But in most parts of the richer nations, there is a rich and varied diet that includes large amounts of poultry, beef, lamb, pork and fish.

The rising price of animal protein is pushing us down the food pyramid towards a vegetarian diet. So the size of the human population will be one of the factors determining how much you pay for meat and how often it appears on your table.

In a food pyramid there is a significant loss of available energy from one feeding level to another. Only about 4% of the energy available from the producers is used in growth to produce new tissue in the primary consumers. The rest is used in respiration.

A field of wheat will yield more energy for human consumption than a field of grazing cattle. The cattle will use about 95% of the energy they receive from grass for respiration and excretion, leaving only 5% available for the humans. It is thus more economical for us to be vegetarian than for us to eat meat.

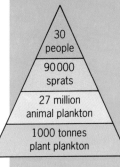

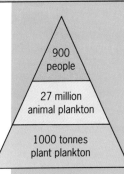

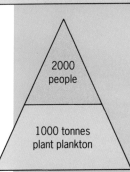

▲ Fig 40.10 About 2000 people each eating 2 kg of plant plankton per day could be supported instead of one person eating mackerel

41 DECOMPOSERS AND CYCLES OF MATTER

By the end of this section you should be able to

■ understand how materials for growth and energy are transferred through an ecosystem

■ understand the role of microbes and other living organisms in the process of decay and in the cycling of nutrients.

We have seen that energy is 'wasted' at each step in a food pyramid – that is, it is no longer available to the consumer of each level. However, this energy is still used by other organisms – the **decomposers**. Without the large numbers of these organisms which survive by breaking down wastes to obtain their energy, we would be buried in a mountain of corpses and animal waste.

TYPES OF DECOMPOSERS

Among the decomposers, which feed on dead material and on the waste products of animals, are two main groups

● **scavengers** that take in their food as solid masses which are digested in the gut (see page 15) or **detritus feeders** that take in very small food particles

● **saprophytes** that secrete digestive enzymes onto dead organisms or waste material and absorb the products of extracellular digestion (see page 15), for example some bacteria and fungi.

Dead organisms can form the starting points of food chains consisting of scavengers, detritus feeders and saprophytes.

DECOMPOSERS AND NATURAL CYCLES

In breaking down the materials contained in the dead bodies of other organisms or their waste, the digestive activity of decomposers produces minerals and water which return to the soil. The result of their activity is called **putrefaction** or **decay**.

Recycling of minerals

The saprophytes play a particularly important part in the circulation of energy and nutrients in the biosphere. As a result of their activities, nutrients 'locked up' in dead remains are released to be made available to green plants again.

The distribution of certain chemical elements throughout the biosphere is very delicately balanced. The soil does not offer an endless supply of minerals to organisms. As a result, many essential elements may be in short supply within a community. For instance, during the millions of years in which life has been established on land, the soil would have become completely emptied of all the minerals which are absorbed by plants if it were not for these minerals being recycled.

▼ **Fig 41.1 The carbon cycle**

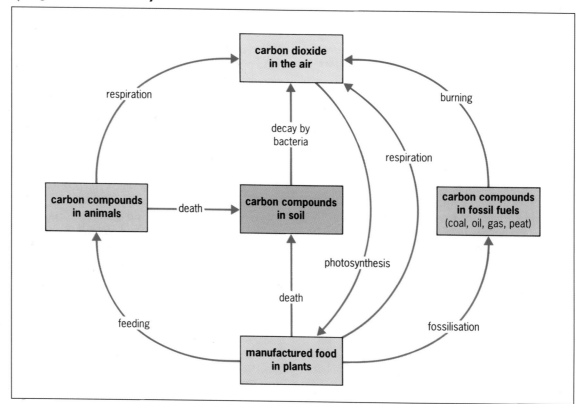

110

Recycling of gases

Similarly, you might expect that the atmosphere could have been emptied of all its oxygen or carbon dioxide. But in fact the concentrations of these gases remain fairly constant. Shortages of these substances are prevented because they are circulated round within a community in a finely balanced cycle of events.

The following examples will illustrate this process.

THE CARBON CYCLE

Organic compounds in plants and animals

Green plants absorb carbon dioxide from the atmosphere and from it form many complex molecules, for instance carbohydrates, proteins and fats. The plant may use the carbohydrate for respiration, when carbon dioxide will be returned to the atmosphere. Or it may build up new plant tissues incorporating the carbon dioxide, which may then be eaten by animals. When this happens, the carbohydrates, proteins and fats of the plant are digested and are either respired or go to build up new tissues of the animal. The carbon atoms which the plant first absorbed from the atmosphere may be passed from a herbivore to a carnivore in a food chain. In this way, the atmospheric carbon is passed through the various parts of a community.

Death and decay

All organisms eventually die, whether they are eaten or not. Their bodies then decay. Therefore, no matter how many times the original atmospheric carbon atoms are passed along food chains, sooner or later they form part of dead matter upon which saprophytes feed. They can then be returned to the atmosphere by the saprophyte during respiration.

All the complex molecules of dead organisms are broken down by saprophytes until only carbon dioxide and water are left. The carbon dioxide passes into the atmosphere and the cycle becomes complete, fig 41.1. As a result, the concentration of carbon dioxide in the atmosphere remains fairly constant.

RECYCLING MINERALS

A similar cycle applies to the circulation of essential minerals. Green plants absorb minerals from the soil at the beginning of a food chain. Saprophytes act on dead organisms or on waste materials and liberate the minerals. The minerals then enter the soil in solution and the cycle begins again.

In the circulation of carbon and minerals around a natural community, all the species play a part. They are all interdependent.

THE NITROGEN CYCLE

Plants and animals need nitrogen to make proteins. They cannot utilise the vast supplies of nitrogen gas in the atmosphere.

Turning nitrogen into nitrates

Some bacteria can combine nitrogen from the air with oxygen to make **nitrates**. Animals obtain their nitrogen ultimately from plants, and plants absorb it from the soil in the form of nitrates, fig 41.2 (overleaf).

The supply of nitrates in the soil is maintained because nitrates are returned to it at approximately the same rate as they are removed. Nitrates are taken from the soil by plants, by some microorganisms or by **leaching**. Leaching happens when minerals are carried in solution from the surface layers of soil to deeper layers where they are out of reach of plants.

Recycling nitrogen

The circulation of nitrogen within a community is similar to the circulation of carbon. Plants absorb nitrates from the soil and the nitrogen becomes part of complex molecules such as proteins. This nitrogen may be passed from plant to herbivore and along the food chain. Saprophytes eventually decompose the dead tissues of all the organisms and so liberate the nitrogen once more. However, they liberate it in the form of **ammonia**. This reactive substance combines with carbon dioxide and water, which are present in the soil spaces, to form **ammonium carbonate**.

The role of bacteria

At this point in the cycle two types of bacteria which are present in all soils play a vital role. One called *Nitrosomonas* is able to obtain all the energy it needs from oxidising ammonium carbonate to **nitrous acid**. The nitrous acid reacts with other salts to produce **nitrites**.

Another bacterium, *Nitrobacter*, oxidises nitrites to **nitrates**. The nitrates can then be absorbed by the roots of plants.

Legumes

Nitrogen is sometimes made available in the soil by plants in the group called **legumes** (Leguminosae) (see pages 88–9). The legumes include pod producers such as peas, beans, clover and lupins. Bacteria called *Rhizobia* live in swellings called **nodules** on the roots of these plants. *Rhizobia* can take nitrogen into their protoplasm. The legumes benefit by absorbing some nitrogen-containing molecules from the bacteria. When the plants die, saprophytes release the nitrogen-containing molecules for use by the plants of the community.

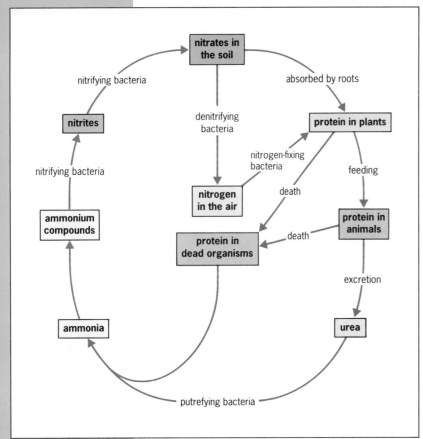

▲ Fig 41.2 The nitrogen cycle

THE PHOSPHORUS CYCLE

Phosphates are important to plants and animals, for example for making fats, nucleic acids, ATP and cell membranes. The ultimate source of phosphate in the ecosystem is crystalline rocks.

Absorbing phosphate

As phosphate rocks are eroded and weathered, phosphate is made available to living organisms, generally as phosphate ions in the soil. These are absorbed by plants through their roots. They reach the leaves and are incorporated into complex organic molecules during photosynthesis.

Excreting phosphate

Phosphates are passed along food chains in the same way as nitrates, with excess being egested in faeces. An extreme example of faecal phosphate is the enormous guano deposits built up by birds on the west coast of South America. These deposits were once a major world supply of phosphate. Phosphate can also be released from forests during forest and grassland fires.

Recycling phosphate

In the detritus food chain (see page 110), large organic molecules containing phosphate are decomposed and the phosphate is liberated as inorganic ions. In this form, it can immediately be taken up by plants incorporated into sediments, either in the soil of land-based ecosystems or in the mud of aquatic ecosystems.

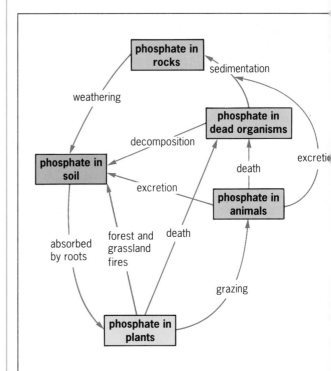

▲ Fig 41.3 The phosphorus cycle

Q1 Household refuse and industrial waste are sometimes dumped in large holes in the ground. They form poisonous chemicals and can cause anaerobic bacteria to grow. Biotechnologists at Bryn Posteg pump air into a pond containing such waste. They also add waste jam from a local factory and phosphates to encourage helpful bacteria. 91% of poisonous ammonia from the waste is removed in this way. This technology depends on the nitrogen cycle shown in fig 41.4.

a Which type of bacteria are encouraged by the treatment at Bryn Posteg? [1]
b Name a substance used by the bacteria present in
　i the air
　ii the jam. [2]
c Explain how these chemicals are used by the bacteria. [2]
d A scientist 'watered' part of a grass plot with ammonium salts produced in the

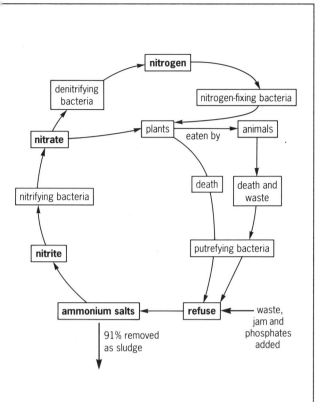

▲ Fig 41.4

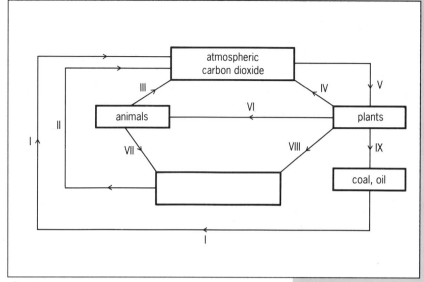

▲ Fig 41.5

process. Three weeks later the grass in that area was darker green and 1 cm taller than the rest of the grass.

   i Name the class of food that plants can make, using the ammonium salts as a source of nitrogen.

   ii Besides colour and height, what other measurement would be more accurate for showing growth? [2]

e Oil is biodegradable. On March 24th 1989, a large oil tanker, the *Exxon Valdez* was wrecked off Alaska. 35 000 tonnes of oil leaked out. It covered miles of beaches and killed thousands of animals.

   i Using similar biotechnology as in Bryn Posteg, describe how you would clean the oil from the beaches.

   ii What problem might you be causing to the environment with your method?

   iii Wave action brings plenty of air to the beaches. What substance produced in the nitrogen cycle could be added to the beach to encourage biodegradation? [3]

      (WJEC GCSE Biology 1992 Q17)

Q2 **a** The carbon cycle is shown by fig 41.5. For each of the processes below, write a number that indicates the position in the diagram where this process takes place.

   i photosynthesis

   ii respiration

   iii combustion

b Name *two* different groups of organisms that could be written in the empty box to complete the cycle.

c A newly built greenhouse contained soil to the depth of 0.5 m on a stone floor. The soil was watered and the greenhouse completely closed for two weeks.

   i Explain what you would expect to happen to the concentration of carbon dioxide in the greenhouse.

   ii If the soil had been burned before being added, what would you expect to happen to the carbon dioxide concentration in the greenhouse after being closed for two weeks?

   iii State *one* reason for replacing old soil in the greenhouse with fresh soil at the start of each season. [10]

(WJEC Common Syllabus (Biology) 1983 Q9)

MATERIALS AND THEIR PROPERTIES

42 MAKING PURE CHEMICALS

By the end of this section you should be able to

- understand that impure materials contain substances that affect the melting point
- describe methods which can be used to purify materials
- select a suitable method to purify a particular impure material.

A pure substance is a single substance and does not contain any other substances or **impurities**. It has a definite melting point. Impurities lower the melting point and cause the substance to melt over a range of temperature.

There are a number of methods which can be used to produce pure chemicals. The method used has to be chosen carefully for each purification and depends upon the properties of the chemicals to be separated.

FILTRATION AND EVAPORATION

Rock salt consists of salt mixed with insoluble impurities such as sand. The fact that the impurities do not dissolve in water is the basis of a method used to obtain pure salt from rock salt.

The crushed rock salt is added to water and the mixture is stirred. The salt dissolves but the impurities sink to the bottom and form a **sediment** or **residue**. The salt solution can be removed by pouring off or **decanting**.

Alternatively, the salt solution can be removed by **filtering** (fig 42.1). The solid impurities remain on the filter paper and the solution, called the **filtrate**, passes through.

Fig 42.1 Filtering – a means of separating sand and salt solution ▶

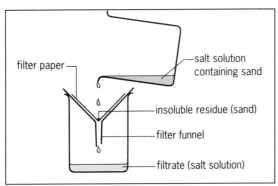

- filter paper
- salt solution containing sand
- insoluble residue (sand)
- filter funnel
- filtrate (salt solution)

Solid salt can then be recovered from the salt solution by **evaporation** (fig 42.2).

Fig 42.2 Evaporation of salt solution ▶

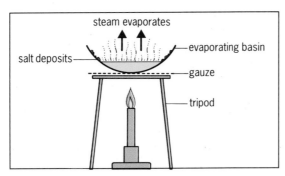

- steam evaporates
- evaporating basin
- salt deposits
- gauze
- tripod

Q1 Evaporation of salt solution using the apparatus in fig 42.2 is often too rapid.

Suggest methods which could be used to evaporate the salt solution more slowly.

Activity

Devise a method for separating a mixture of three substances, X, Y and Z. The following table summarises some of the properties of X, Y and Z.

Substance	Solubility in cold water	Solubility in hot water
X	insoluble	soluble
Y	insoluble	insoluble
Z	soluble	soluble

OBTAINING A SOLVENT FROM A SOLUTION

Evaporation is used to obtain a solute, for example salt, from a solution. The solvent can be recovered from a solution by **distillation**. This is really evaporation followed by condensation. Fig 42.3 shows distillation apparatus being used to recover the solvent from a solution. The condenser efficiently condenses the steam. Cold water passes through the condenser to cool down the steam. Fig 42.4 shows how this process is used to obtain fresh water from salt water in hot countries.

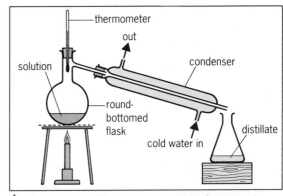

- thermometer
- out
- solution
- condenser
- round-bottomed flask
- cold water in
- distillate

▲ **Fig 42.3 Distillation – a means of separating a solvent from a solution**

Fig 42.4 A desalination plant at Lake Mead, Nevada, USA ▶

SEPARATING MIXTURES OF LIQUIDS

Immiscible liquids

Hexane and water do not mix well. They form two separate layers. The top liquid is almost completely hexane while the lower liquid is almost completely water. The two liquids are said to be **immiscible**. They can be separated using a tap funnel as in fig 42.5.

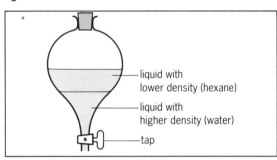

▲ **Fig 42.5 Separating two immiscible liquids using a tap funnel**

Miscible liquids

Ethanol and water mix completely and form a single liquid. They are called **miscible**. Miscible liquids are much more difficult than immiscible liquids to separate, but can be separated by **fractional distillation**.

Fig 42.6 shows how ethanol (boiling point 78 °C) and water (boiling point 100 °C) can be separated. The flask is heated slowly with receiver number 1 in place. The ethanol starts to boil first because it has a lower boiling point. Any water vapour which gets into the column at this stage condenses in the fractionating column and drops back into the flask.

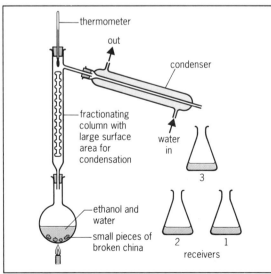

▲ **Fig 42.6 Fractional distillation – a means of separating two miscible liquids**

The temperature shown by the thermometer remains below 80 °C. The liquid collected in the first receiver is called the first **fraction**. The liquid distilling over between 80 °C and 95 °C is called the second fraction and is collected in receiver 2. The third fraction is collected above 95 °C in receiver 3.

Q2 What is the main chemical present in **a** fraction 1 **b** fraction 3?

Q3 Is it easier to separate substances by this method if the boiling points are close together or further apart?

CHROMATOGRAPHY

Chromatography is a relatively simple method used to separate mixtures of substances dissolved in a solvent. It can also be used to identify substances. The simplest form of chromatography is called **paper chromatography**.

Paper chromatography is often used to separate mixtures of inks or dyes. The dyes spread across a piece of filter paper at different rates. Some dyes stick to the paper more, while others dissolve better in the solvent.

Sample spots are put on the base line of a piece of filter paper and the paper is dried. It is then put into a tank with a lid (fig 42.7). At the bottom of the tank is a small amount of solvent. The solvent travels up the filter paper and the spots are separated.

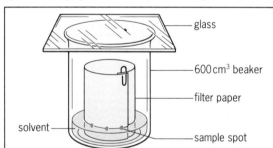

◄ **Fig 42.7 Chromatography - a means of separating mixtures of substances dissolved in a solvent**

When the solvent has nearly reached the top of the filter paper, the filter paper is removed and the position of the solvent marked. The paper is dried. Fig 42.8 shows a chromatogram produced from a food dye mixture, X, and five pure food dyes, labelled A–E.

Q4 Which food dyes are present in X?

Q5 What is a suitable method for separating

a bits of broken glass from a solution
b the coloured substances dissolved out of grass
c water from sea water
d oxygen and nitrogen from liquid air?

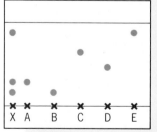

▲ **Fig 42.8 A sample chromatogram**

43 CHEMICAL FAMILIES

By the end of this section you should be able to

- recall that elements can be divided into chemical families
- understand the similarities and differences between elements in two such families – the alkali metals and the alkaline earth metals
- make predictions about another member of a chemical family.

From a study of the properties of the elements and their compounds, it is possible to identify elements with similar properties. In this way, elements can be put into chemical families.

THE ALKALI METALS

What are the alkali metals?

Although the alkali metal elements exist in large quantities in the Earth, they do not have many everyday uses because of their great reactivity. However, you will have seen the orange light which comes from modern street lights. This is 'sodium light' formed in the lamps which contain small amounts of sodium.

Fig 43.1 Sodium gives street lamps their orange light

The table below contains information about three elements in group I of the Periodic table. We call these elements the **alkali metals**. The alkali metals have low melting and boiling points, which decrease as atomic number increases. The pattern of densities is less easy to see, but all three metals are less dense than water.

Reactions of the alkali metals

The metals are all very reactive. They are stored under paraffin oil because they react with oxygen and water vapour. They quickly corrode in air. They burn in air or oxygen to form solid alkaline oxides, for example

$$\text{sodium} + \text{oxygen} \rightarrow \text{sodium oxide}$$
$$4Na(s) + O_2(g) \rightarrow 2Na_2O(s)$$

The alkali metals all react with cold water to produce an alkaline solution and hydrogen gas.

$$\text{lithium} + \text{water} \rightarrow \text{lithium hydroxide} + \text{hydrogen}$$
$$2Li(s) + 2H_2O(l) \rightarrow 2LiOH(aq) + H_2(g)$$

$$\text{sodium} + \text{water} \rightarrow \text{sodium hydroxide} + \text{hydrogen}$$
$$2Na(s) + 2H_2O(l) \rightarrow 2NaOH(aq) + H_2(g)$$

$$\text{potassium} + \text{water} \rightarrow \text{potassium hydroxide} + \text{hydrogen}$$
$$2K(s) + 2H_2O(l) \rightarrow 2KOH(aq) + H_2(g)$$

There are differences in the speeds of these reactions. Lithium is less reactive than sodium and sodium is less reactive than potassium. The reactions become more rapid and violent as we use metals lower down group I. This applies to all reactions, not only reactions with water.

Q1 Using the information in the Periodic table (see Data section, page 188) and the information given about lithium, sodium and potassium, *either* find out *or* predict the following information about the element rubidium

a the symbol for rubidium
b the group and period in which rubidium is placed in the Periodic table
c the melting point of rubidium
d the boiling point of rubidium
e the atomic number of rubidium
f the formula of rubidium oxide
g how rubidium reacts with cold water.

Do not use any other information in the Data section apart from the Periodic table. You can check some of your answers in the Data section. Which of your answers did you find out and which did you predict?

Alkali metal	Atomic number	Melting point (°C)	Boiling point (°C)	Density (g/cm³)
lithium	3	181	1331	0.54
sodium	11	98	890	0.97
potassium	19	63	766	0.86

Although there are few uses of alkali metals, there are many uses of alkali metal compounds (see page 170).

HISTORY OF THE ALKALI INDUSTRY

In the eighteenth century, the French chemist Nicholas Leblanc devised a method of producing alkali from salt in two stages.

In the first stage salt and sulphuric acid were roasted together to form crude sodium sulphate (called saltcake) and hydrogen chloride gas. In the second stage saltcake was heated in a furnace with coke and limestone. The product, 'blackash', contained a mixture of sodium carbonate, calcium sulphide, unburnt coke and other impurities. Sodium carbonate was then extracted with water and this solution was used to make soda (sodium bicarbonate) or to produce caustic soda (sodium hydroxide).

During the second half of the nineteenth century the towns of Widnes and Runcorn, on opposite sides of the River Mersey, grew greatly as the alkali industry expanded. Widnes alone had 24 alkali works in 1875. One million tonnes of coal were burned annually in Widnes factories. The waste from the factories, locally called 'galligu', was just heaped up.

In about 1860 better methods led to the closure of the Leblanc factories.

Q2 Use an atlas to draw a sketch map of the area around the River Mersey. Suggest why the industry developed here.

Q3 Imagine the conditions in one of these early factories. Workers would work 12-hour shifts. Write a paragraph describing the conditions in and around these factories.

THE ALKALINE EARTH METALS

Comparing properties

The elements in group II of the Periodic table are called **alkaline earth metals**. They are beryllium, magnesium, calcium, strontium, barium and radium.

Q4 Using the information about the elements on pages 186–7, make a table including the symbols, relative atomic masses, melting points, boiling points and densities of these elements.

You will not notice any particular trends in the melting points, boiling points and densities. You should note, however, that these elements generally have higher melting points, boiling points and densities than the alkali metals.

Activity

Compare the reactivities of three alkaline earth metals – magnesium, calcium and barium – with water. Any gas produced will be hydrogen. Try and establish fair conditions for your tests. Arrange the three metals in order of decreasing reactivity.

Q5 Which of the six alkaline earth metals would you expect to be most reactive?

Solubilities of alkaline earth metal compounds

The table below compares the solubilites in water of sulphates and hydroxides of alkaline earth metals. These are masses, in grams, of anhydrous materials dissolving in $1\,dm^3$ of water at 20°C.

Element	Sulphate	Hydroxide
beryllium	390	—
magnesium	330	0.009
calcium	2.1	1.6
strontium	0.13	8.0
barium	0.0024	39

Q6 Describe the trends in solubility of sulphates and hydroxides of the alkaline earth metals.

Q7 A patient suspected of having a stomach ulcer may have a barium meal followed by an X-ray. The barium compound in the barium meal shows up on the X-ray and any defect in the stomach lining can be seen, fig 43.2.

Barium compounds which are soluble in water are highly poisonous. Suggest a barium compound which is suitable for using in a barium meal.

Q8 A person who has swallowed barium chloride solution is given magnesium sulphate solution to swallow as an antidote. Write a symbolic equation for the reaction taking place.

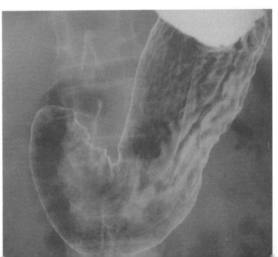

◀ **Fig 43.2 An X-ray of the stomach taken after a barium meal**

44 THE PERIODIC TABLE

By the end of this section you should be able to

- recall that the Periodic table consists of elements arranged in order of atomic number
- recall that elements in the same column or group have similar properties
- predict the properties of an element from its position in the Periodic table
- understand how the modern Periodic table has been developed.

The modern Periodic table which includes all of the known elements is shown on page 188. It is based upon the Periodic table first devised by the Russian chemist Dmitri Mendeleef in 1869.

The Periodic table can be represented in other ways. Fig 44.1 shows a spiral form of the Periodic table known as Crooke's spiral.

▼ **Fig 44.1 Crooke's spiral**

THE HISTORY OF THE PERIODIC TABLE

The age of discovery

At the beginning of the nineteenth century, a large number of elements were discovered.

At this time scientists were able, using long tedious experiments, to calculate relative atomic masses accurately. They called them atomic weights.

When a great deal of new information becomes available, there is a desire to catalogue and organise it. Today we would have the benefits of computers and could organise information like this on a database.

Q1 Find out how many new elements were discovered between 1800 and 1825 using the Data section, pages 186–7.

Groups of threes

Johann Dobereiner (1829) suggested that elements could be grouped in threes called **triads**. Each member of a triad has similar properties. Examples of triads are:

    lithium, sodium and potassium
    chlorine, bromine and iodine
    calcium, strontium and barium

Q2 Can you see any relationship between the relative atomic masses of the elements in each triad?

The law of octaves

John Alexander Newlands (1837–98) arranged the *known* elements in order of increasing atomic weight in 1863. He noticed that there was a similarity between each eighth element.

Li	Be	B	C	N	O	F
Na	Mg	Al	Si	P	S	Cl

Lithium is similar to sodium, beryllium is similar to magnesium, etc. Remember that the noble gases (helium, neon, etc.) had not been discovered at this time. Newlands saw a similarity to notes in music and called this the **law of octaves**. His work broke down because he did not leave appropriate gaps for undiscovered elements, and could not fit in the heavier elements. Newlands was a very respected scientist, but his work was ahead of its time. Fellow members of the Chemical Society were not impressed with Newlands' work.

The Periodic table

Dmitri Ivanovich Mendeleef (1834–1907), shown in fig 44.2, was responsible for devising the Periodic table in 1869.

▲ **Fig 44.2 Dmitri Mendeleef, who devised the Periodic table**

Like Newlands, he arranged elements in order of increasing atomic weight. However, he realised he should leave gaps for undiscovered elements.

Mendeleef was born in Siberia. He was the 14th and last child of the Director of the Gymnasium at Tobolsk. He was educated at St Petersburg, Paris and Heidelberg.

He was extremely hardworking in his post as Professor of Chemistry at St Petersburg University. He wrote over 300 books and papers. His work on the Periodic table was done in complete ignorance of the work of Newlands and others.

His Periodic table was shown in many different ways but essentially it is the same today.

Atomic volumes

In 1870 Lothar Meyer published values for the atomic volumes of the elements, that is, the volume (in cm^3) of 1 mole of atoms of each solid element. (The 'mole' is explained on page 160.) He then plotted the atomic volumes of the elements in a graph (fig 44.3). He noticed that the graph was not a simple straight line or simple curve, but a repeating pattern of peaks and troughs. Elements with similar properties were in similar places on the graph. Also, the number of elements in between peaks was not always the same.

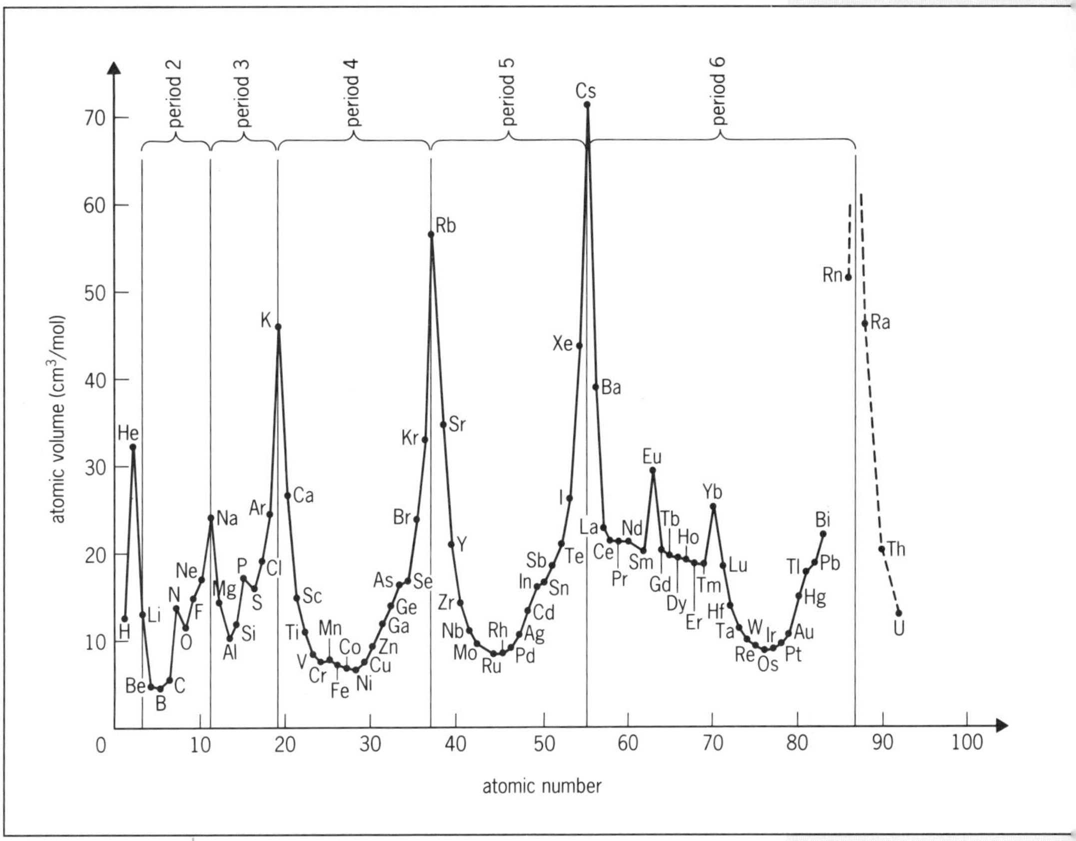

Fig 44.3 Graph of atomic volume against atomic number for the elements ▶

Q3 Look at the relative atomic masses of the elements (pages 186–7) and the atomic numbers of the elements. Are there any differences in the orders?

These differences were resolved following the work of Ernest Rutherford and Henry Moseley, who showed that atoms contained protons and electrons and so related atomic structure to the Periodic table. Neutrons were not discovered until much later.

Q4 Looking at Lothar Meyer's atomic volume graph (fig 44.3), which element is at the top of each major peak? In which group of the Periodic table are these elements placed?

Q5 Graphs like Lothar Meyer's, which repeat, are called **periodic** graphs. Plot graphs of

a melting point against atomic number
b boiling point against atomic number
c density against atomic number
d number of electrons in outer energy level against atomic number (see pages 126–7).

Are these periodic graphs?

Predictions

The following table compares Mendeleef's predictions about the undiscovered element he called ekasilicon, and the same element which was called germanium after its discovery in 1886.

Q6 What is your view about the accuracy of Mendeleef's predictions made nearly 20 years before the discovery of germanium?

Mendeleef's prediction	Property of germanium
light grey metal	dark grey metal
will form a white oxide (EsO$_2$) with a high melting point	forms a white oxide (GeO$_2$) with a high melting point
the chloride will have a boiling point less than 100°C and a density of about 1.9 g/cm^3	the chloride boils at 86.5°C and its density is 1.887 g/cm^3

GROUPS AND PERIODS

The Periodic table is an arrangement of elements in order of increasing **atomic number** in such a way that elements with similar properties are placed in the same vertical column or **group**. The horizontal rows are called **periods**.

The shaded elements in the Periodic table on page 188 make up the main block of elements. This consists of eight groups numbered I–VII and group 0 which was added later.
Elements in group I are called **alkali metals**.
Elements in group II are **alkaline earth metals**.
Elements in group VII are called **halogens**.
Elements in group 0 are called **noble gases**.
Elements between the two parts of the main block of the Periodic table are **transition metals**.

45 THE HALOGENS

By the end of this section you should be able to

- recall that the halogens are a family of reactive non-metallic elements
- understand some of the similarities and differences between the halogens.

PROPERTIES OF THE HALOGENS

The **halogens** are the elements in group VII of the Periodic table.

Q1 Use the information in the Data section on pages 186–7 to compile a table comparing the melting points and boiling points of the halogens – fluorine, chlorine, bromine and iodine. How do the melting and boiling points change with increasing atomic number?

REACTIONS OF THE HALOGENS

The halogens react to form solid compounds called **salts**. For example, sodium burns in chlorine to form sodium chloride.

sodium + chlorine → sodium chloride
$2Na(s) + Cl_2(g) \rightarrow 2NaCl(s)$

All halogens react with hydrogen, for example

hydrogen + chlorine → hydrogen chloride
$H_2(g) + Cl_2(g) \rightarrow 2HCl(g)$

hydrogen + bromine → hydrogen bromide
$H_2(g) + Br_2(g) \rightarrow 2HBr(g)$

hydrogen + iodine ⇌ hydrogen iodide
$H_2(g) + I_2(g) \rightleftharpoons 2HI(g)$

Reactivities of the halogens

There is a difference in the way that these elements react. A mixture of hydrogen and chlorine explodes in sunlight without heating. A mixture of hydrogen and iodine only reacts partially when heated with a catalyst. In all reactions chlorine is more reactive than bromine, and bromine is more reactive than iodine.

The differences in reactivity of the halogens can be seen in **displacement reactions**. The table below compares the reactions which take place when halogens in solution are added to solutions of potassium chloride, potassium bromide or potassium

Solution Halogen	Potassium chloride solution	Potassium bromide solution	Potassium iodide solution
Fluorine	✓	✓	✓
Chlorine	✗	✓	✓
Bromine	✗	✗	✓
Iodine	✗	✗	✗

iodide. A displacement reaction will take place if the halogen added is more reactive than the halogen present in the potassium compound.

Q2 Arrange the three halogens in order of reactivity, the most reactive halogen first.

DISCOVERY OF FLUORINE, CHLORINE, BROMINE AND IODINE

Chlorine, bromine and iodine

Chlorine, bromine and iodine were discovered within about 50 years of each other, at the end of the eighteenth and beginning of the nineteenth century. Carl Scheele, a Swedish chemist, discovered chlorine in 1774. Two French chemists were responsible for discovering bromine and iodine – Courtois discovered iodine in 1811 and Balard discovered bromine in 1824.

In each case a natural mineral containing chloride, bromide or iodide ions was treated with concentrated sulphuric acid and an oxidising agent, manganese(IV) oxide, for example

sodium chloride + concentrated sulphuric acid → hydrogen chloride + sodium hydrogensulphate
$NaCl + H_2SO_4 \rightarrow HCl + NaHSO_4$

hydrogen chloride + manganese(IV) oxide → chlorine + manganese(II) chloride + water
$4HCl + MnO_2 \rightarrow Cl_2 + MnCl_2 + 2H_2O$

Fig 45.1 ▶ Three of the halogens – a chlorine, b bromine and c iodine

Hydrogen fluoride

In 1810 André Ampere, the famous French physicist and mathematician, was the first to realise that hydrogen fluoride could be prepared by

122

treating minerals containing fluoride with concentrated sulphuric acid. He realised that hydrogen fluoride was closely related to hydrogen chloride. What he and many other scientists failed to do was to break up hydrogen fluoride and produce fluorine. Manganese(IV) oxide was not a strong enough oxidising agent, and another one strong enough could not be found.

Attempts to produce fluorine by electrolysis

In 1807, Sir Humphrey Davy had succeeded in extracting sodium and potassium by electrolysis of molten minerals. Following his success with reactive metals he attempted to isolate fluorine by electrolysis of molten fluoride minerals. He failed to do it, however, but damaged his health by inhaling hydrogen fluoride fumes. Attempts by the Belgian chemist Louyet (1818–50) and the French chemist Nicklés of Nancy (died 1869) to carry out similar experiments lead to deaths of both men due to poisoning by hydrogen fluoride fumes. Two Irish chemists, George and Thomas Knox, suffered serious injuries in a similar way in 1830.

All the attempts to produce fluorine by electrolysis of molten fluoride minerals seemed to be unsuccessful because any fluorine produced reacted with the electrodes or the container.

Edmond Fremy in 1856 claimed to have produced fluorine during the electrolysis of molten potassium fluoride using a platinum anode. However, at the temperature of 850 °C the anode was destroyed by the fluorine.

At the beginning of the nineteenth century Ampere had suggested electrolysis of anhydrous hydrogen fluoride using a carbon anode. Anhydrous hydrogen fluoride (which contains no water) was first produced in 1856 by Fremy and in 1860 by George Gore. It reacts with many materials including glass and was stored in platinum vessels.

However, anhydrous hydrogen fluoride contains no ions, being made up of covalent bonds. It does not, therefore, conduct electricity and cannot be split up by electrolysis.

Success

In 1884 Henri Moissan started seriously to try to make fluorine. His original experiments involved trying to decompose boron trifluoride, silicon tetrafluoride and arsenic trifluoride by heating to high temperatures. Having failed with these experiments, he attempted electrolysis but realised that only low-temperature electrolysis could be suitable.

He used arsenic trifluoride (a liquid at room temperature) and increased its conductivity by adding potassium fluoride. Electrolysis did produce fluorine but, to his surprise, this fluorine reacted with the arsenic trifluoride.

$$\text{arsenic trifluoride} + \text{fluorine} \rightarrow \text{arsenic pentafluoride}$$
$$AsF_3 + F_2 \rightarrow AsF_5$$

Moissan did not give up. He attempted the electrolysis of anhydrous hydrogen fluoride at −50 °C. Hydrogen was produced at the cathode

$$2H^+ + 2e^- \rightarrow H_2$$

A gas was produced at the anode which ignited silicon, phosphorus and mercury. He rightly concluded that this gas was fluorine.

$$2F^- \rightarrow F_2 + 2e^-$$

This experiment was carried out for the first time at midday on Saturday 26 June 1886. Moissan was obviously overjoyed to have succeeded where so many people had failed. He set up a demonstration of the apparatus for the French Academy of Science. He could not make the experiment work.

Only later did he find out that the anhydrous hydrogen fluoride he used originally was contaminated with potassium fluoride. Without potassium fluoride, electrolysis of anhydrous hydrogen fluoride is impossible, for the reason given earlier – the compound is not ionic. When he repeated his experiments with one part potassium fluoride to 12 parts anhydrous hydrogen fluoride, he was able to show how fluorine could be obtained.

Modern production of fluorine

Moissan's method of obtaining fluorine was the usual method until earlier this century. Nowadays, fluorine is widely available by electrolysis of an electrolyte containing 40% hydrogen fluoride at 85–105 °C using a carbon anode and steel cathode. It is interesting to note that the method used is one proposed by Ampere at the start of the nineteenth century.

Q3 Given that an aqueous solution of hydrogen fluoride contains H^+, OH^- and F^- ions, state the products of electrolysis formed at the anode and cathode and write ionic equations to show how these products are formed.

Q4 Fluorine is the most reactive element in the Periodic table. What evidence in the passage justifies this statement?

Q5 Find the element fluorine in the Periodic table on page 188. Using the information given write an account of the chemistry of fluorine.

46 ATOMIC STRUCTURE

By the end of this section you should be able to

- recall that atoms are composed of protons, neutrons and electrons and know the relative masses and charges of protons, neutrons and electrons
- state that the protons and neutrons are tightly packed in the nucleus with the electrons moving around the nucleus
- give the electronic arrangements of the first 18 elements
- explain the existence of isotopes as atoms of the same element containing different numbers of neutrons
- describe how atomic masses can be measured using a mass spectrometer.

^1_1H

^4_2He

^7_3Li

^9_4Be

$^{11}_5B$

$^{12}_6C$

$^{14}_7N$

$^{16}_8O$

$^{19}_9F$

$^{20}_{10}Ne$

$^{23}_{11}Na$

$^{24}_{12}Mg$

$^{27}_{13}Al$

$^{28}_{14}Si$

$^{31}_{15}P$

PARTICLES IN AN ATOM

All elements are made up of **atoms**, and these atoms are in turn made up of smaller particles called **protons** (p), **neutrons** (n) and **electrons** (e). The table below summarises the masses and charges of these three particles.

Particle	Approximate mass*	Charge
proton, p	1 u	+1
neutron, n	1 u	0
electron, e	negligible	−1

* u stands for **atomic mass unit** which is the unit we use for comparing the masses of particles and atoms.

Q1 Other subatomic particles are often mentioned, for example mesons. Find out what you can about these particles.

Charges in an atom

All atoms are neutral, that is, they have no overall charge. Therefore, all atoms must contain equal numbers of protons and electrons. If the numbers of protons and electrons are not the same, usually because electrons have been lost or gained, an **ion** is produced.

The number of neutrons is of less importance. It alters the mass of the atom but does not affect the charge.

Atomic number and mass number

The **atomic number** is the number of protons in an atom (equal also to the number of electrons). The **mass number** is the number of protons and neutrons in an atom.

A sulphur atom has a mass number of 32 and an atomic number of 16. It therefore contains 16 protons, 16 electrons and coincidentally 16 neutrons. A sulphur atom is written $^{32}_{16}S$.

Q2 Work out for the 15 elements in the margin the number of protons, neutrons and electrons in an atom.

ARRANGEMENT OF PARTICLES IN AN ATOM

The protons and neutrons in any atom are tightly packed together in the **nucleus** of the atom. The nucleus is positively charged. The electrons move around the nucleus.

The electrons move around in certain **energy levels**. Each energy level is able to hold a certain maximum number of electrons. Fig 46.1 shows a simple two-dimensional representation of an atom.

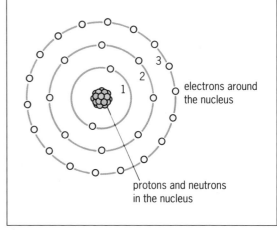

electrons around the nucleus

protons and neutrons in the nucleus

▲ **Fig 46.1 Two-dimensional representation of an atom**

The first energy level (labelled 1 in fig 46.1) can hold a maximum of two electrons. This energy level is filled first. The second energy level (labelled 2) can hold up to eight electrons. It is filled after the first energy level and before the third. There are further energy levels which hold larger numbers of electrons.

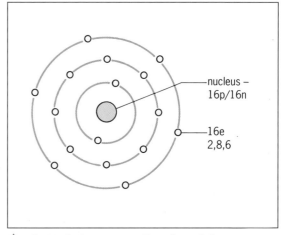

nucleus – 16p/16n

16e 2,8,6

▲ **Fig 46.2 Representation of a sulphur atom**

A sulphur atom (containing 16p, 16n, 16e) can be represented as in fig 46.2. The **electron arrangement** of a sulphur atom is written as 2, 8, 6.

Q3 Draw simple representations of

a a hydrogen atom   **b** a carbon atom
c a sodium atom   **d** a magnesium atom.

Give the electron arrangement in each case.

ISOTOPES

It is possible to have different atoms of the same element, containing different numbers of neutrons. These different atoms are called **isotopes**.

Chlorine, for example, has two isotopes: chlorine-35 and chlorine-37. Chlorine-35 (mass number 35, atomic number 17) contains 17 protons, 17 electrons and 18 neutrons. Chlorine-37 (mass number 37, atomic number 17) contains 17 protons,17 electrons and 20 neutrons. Both isotopes have identical electron arrangements and hence identical chemical properties. They will have different masses and, therefore, different physical properties. The chlorine produced in the laboratory is made up of 75% chlorine-35 and 25% chlorine-37. The weighted average mass is therefore 35.5. This average mass of the atoms of an element is called the **atomic mass**. Because of the existence of different isotopes, atomic masses are not all whole numbers.

The **relative atomic mass** (abbreviated to RAM or A_r) of an element is based on the average mass of all the atoms in the element (taking the isotope carbon-12 as standard).

Q4 The element europium contains equal quantities of two isotopes, europium-151 and europium-153. The atomic number of europium is 63.

a Calculate the numbers of protons, neutrons and electrons in each isotope.
b What will be the relative atomic mass of europium?

THE MASS SPECTROMETER

Because atoms are very small they are impossible to weigh individually. The mass of an atom can, however, be compared with the mass of a standard atom using a **mass spectrometer**. Fig 46.3 shows a simplified diagram of a mass spectrometer.

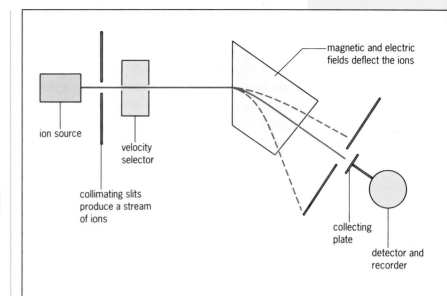

▲ Fig 46.3 A mass spectrometer

Atoms in a stream are stripped of their outer electrons to form positively charged ions. They are then passed through a strong magnetic field. Their pathway is bent by the magnetic field and from the extent of this bending in a known field, calculations can be made about the mass of the atoms. To understand this better, imagine an exposed motorway in a strong wind – the light vehicles are more affected by the wind than the heavy ones.

The standard atom used today for comparison is the carbon-12 atom, composed of 6 protons, 6 neutrons and 6 electrons.

▼ Fig 46.4 Mass spectrum for tetrachloromethane

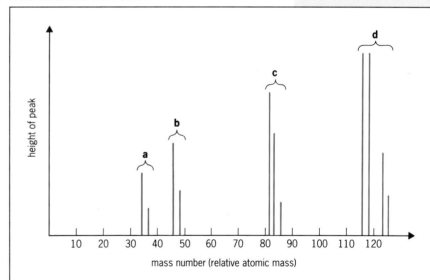

Q5 Fig 46.4 shows the results obtained with tetrachloromethane, CCl_4, in a mass spectrometer. Explain the existence of each line within the sets **a**, **b**, **c** and **d**.

Assume carbon has only one isotope, carbon-12, and chlorine has two isotopes, chlorine-35 and chlorine-37.

47 PATTERNS IN THE PERIODIC TABLE

By the end of this section you should be able to

- see patterns within the Periodic table
- relate changes in properties within the Periodic table to changes in electronic arrangement.

CHANGES IN THE PERIODIC TABLE

Chemical changes

In any period (horizontal row) there is a change in chemical properties across the period from left to right, from metal to non-metal. In any group (vertical column) there is an increase in the metallic properties down the group.

The dark stepped line in the Periodic table on page 188 divides the metals on the left-hand side from the non-metals on the right-hand side. Gases are near the top of the Periodic table on the right-hand side.

Electron arrangements

The position of an element in the Periodic table is related to the electron arrangement in atoms of the element. An element in period 3 will have electrons in three energy levels, for example the electron arrangement for sodium is 2, 8, 1.

There is also a relationship between the number of electrons in the *outer* energy level and the *group* in which the element is placed in the Periodic table, as the table below shows.

Element	Electron arrangement	Group in Periodic table
lithium	2, 1	I
beryllium	2, 2	II
boron	2, 3	III
carbon	2, 4	IV
nitrogen	2, 5	V
oxygen	2, 6	VI
fluorine	2, 7	VII
neon	2, 8	0
sodium	2, 8, 1	I
magnesium	2, 8, 2	II
aluminium	2, 8, 3	III
silicon	2, 8, 4	IV

You will notice, looking at the table, that the number of electrons in the outer energy level is the same as the number of the group in which the element is placed. Note, however, that elements in group 0 (called the noble gases) do not fit this pattern.

Q1 Use the Periodic table on page 188 to find the elements chlorine, sodium, magnesium and sulphur. The number of electrons in each atom is the same as the atomic number given in the Periodic table.

For each element, state in which group it is placed, and suggest the electron arrangement in each case.

Q2 For each of the following elements state how many electrons are in the outer energy level: barium, lead, selenium, thallium.

CHANGES ACROSS A PERIOD

The table on the next page gives information about the oxides and chlorides of the elements in the third period of the Periodic table.

Q3 Which oxide has the highest boiling point?

Q4 Which elements form oxides which react with water to give acidic solutions? In which groups are these elements placed?

Q5 Which elements form oxides which react with water to give alkaline solutions? In which groups are these elements placed?

Q6 Copy and complete the following statements by adding suitable words from the following list:

neutral   acidic   alkaline

Elements on the left-hand side of the Periodic table form oxides which are _____ .

Elements on the right-hand side of the Periodic table form oxides which are _____ .

Elements in the centre of the Periodic table form oxides which are _____ .

Q7 Compounds which react with water are **hydrolysed** by water.

Which elements form chlorides which are hydrolysed by water?

In which groups are these elements placed?

Q8 Elements in groups I and II form chlorides which have high melting points and boiling points and are soluble in water. True or false?

Compound	Formula	State	Melting point (°C)	Boiling point (°C)	Solubility in water	pH of solution
Oxides						
sodium oxide	Na_2O	s	sublimes		reacts	13
magnesium oxide	MgO	s	2800	3600	almost insoluble	11
aluminium oxide	Al_2O_3	s	2015	2980	insoluble	7
silicon(IV) oxide	SiO_2	s	1610	2230	insoluble	7
phosphorus(V) oxide	P_2O_5	s	sublimes		reacts	1
sulphur trioxide	SO_3	l	−17	43	reacts	1
chlorine monoxide	Cl_2O	g	−11	2	reacts	1
Chlorides						
sodium chloride	$NaCl$	s	808	1465	soluble	7
magnesium chloride	$MgCl_2$	s	714	1418	soluble	7
aluminium chloride	$AlCl_3$	s	sublimes		reacts	2
silicon(IV) chloride	$SiCl_4$	l	−70	58	reacts	2
phosphorus(V) chloride	PCl_5	g	−112	76	reacts	1
sulphur chloride	S_2Cl_2	l	−20	138	reacts	1

Q9 Compounds of hydrogen (called hydrides) with the elements in period 2 show similar patterns.
  a Write the formula of the hydride of each element in period 2.
  b Use reference books and/or a data book to find out information about these hydrides. In particular, you could find

  melting points
  boiling points
  reaction with water or solubility in water
  conductivity of the resulting solution
  pH of the resulting solution.

IONIC AND COVALENT BONDING

Ionic bonding and **covalent** bonding are two different methods of joining atoms together in compounds. There is more about ionic and covalent bonding in section 51. A compound containing ionic bonding has a high melting and boiling point and dissolves in water to form a solution which conducts electricity. A compound containing covalent bonding usually has a low melting and boiling point and does not conduct electricity.

Q10 What trends in bonding are seen in compounds across the third period of the Periodic table?

Are the same trends seen in other periods?

▲ **Fig 47.1 Salt is a typical ionic compound**

By the end of this section you should be able to

- recall that matter is composed of elements
- recall the names and symbols of the common elements
- understand that materials can be divided into metals and non-metals by considering the physical and chemical properties of the materials
- understand that considering chemical properties is a more reliable way of doing this
- understand that compounds are formed when elements combine
- understand that atoms of different elements combine together in fixed numbers
- recall the elements present in a particular compound
- name simple compounds.

ELEMENTS

All pure substances are made up from one or more of the 105 elements. These are joined together in different ways to give all of the substances in the world around us.

An **element** is a pure substance which cannot be split up into anything simpler by chemical reactions. Many of these elements are found in nature, but some are made in factories.

In the Periodic table on page 188 you will find the chemical symbols for all the elements.

Properties of elements

Most of the known elements are solids and metals. There are only two liquid elements at room temperature and atmospheric pressure – bromine is a liquid non-metal and mercury is a liquid metal.

Hydrogen, helium, nitrogen, oxygen, fluorine, neon, chlorine, argon, krypton, xenon and radon are the only elements that are gases at room temperature and atmospheric pressure.

Atoms

All elements are made up from tiny particles called **atoms**. These atoms are so small that they cannot be seen with a microscope. In fact, a 12g pile of carbon contains 6×10^{23} atoms.

Q1 Calculate the mass, in grams, of one carbon atom.

Mixtures

Elements can be mixed together to form a **mixture**. For example, iron and copper powders can be mixed together to form a mixture. The mixture can be separated with a magnet. If you look carefully at the mixture with a hand lens you will be able to see pieces of iron and copper. The mixture has all of the properties of both iron and copper.

METALS AND NON-METALS

Elements can be divided into **metals** and **non-metals**. The following table summarises the physical properties of metals and non-metals.

Metals	Non-metals
solid at room temperature	solid, liquid or gas at room temperature
shiny	dull
high density	low density
conducts heat and electricity	does not conduct heat or electricity
can be beaten into thin sheets (malleable) or drawn into fine wires (ductile)	easily broken (brittle)

Activity

You have been given five different materials E, F, G, H and I.
Using only the physical properties in the table above, classify them as metals or non-metals.

Chemical properties of metals and non-metals

You may not find classifying materials easy to do using physical properties alone. A better method of classifying a material as a metal or a non-metal is to use chemical properties. These are more reliable.

1 Add dilute hydrochloric acid to the material. If it reacts with the acid to form bubbles of colourless gas, test the gas with a lighted splint. If the gas burns with a pop the gas is hydrogen. Only metals will produce hydrogen with an acid, but beware, not *all* metals will produce hydrogen.

2 If a piece of material is burned in oxygen as in fig 48.1, an oxide will be produced. Test the oxide with universal indicator solution. If the oxide produced is neutral or alkaline (pH 7 or greater), the material is a metal. If the oxide is acidic (pH less than 7), the material is a non-metal.

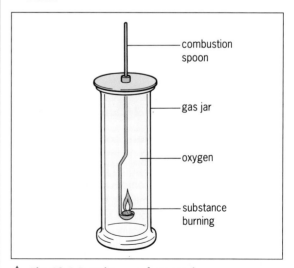

▲ **Fig 48.1 Burning a substance in oxygen**

Metalloids

The distinction between metals and non-metals is more reliable using chemical tests, but it is still not a clear distinction to make. It is rather like trying to classify tins of paint by colour as black or white when some of them are better described as grey.

There are some materials which have properties between metal and non-metal. Silicon is a good example. It is a grey, shiny solid with a comparatively low density. It is a semiconductor and is brittle. It does not react with dilute acids, and it burns to form an oxide with a pH of 7. Materials like this are called **metalloids**. They are used in transistors and microchips because of their semiconducting properties, fig 48.2.

▼ **Fig 48.2 A piece of silicon and a silicon 'chip', with a matchstick to show the scale**

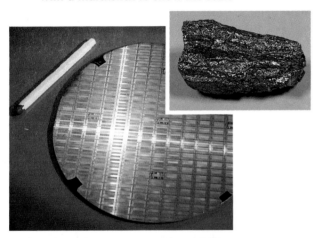

COMBINING ELEMENTS

Certain mixtures of elements react together or **combine** to form **compounds**.

For example, a mixture of hydrogen and oxygen explodes and forms droplets of water, fig 48.3.

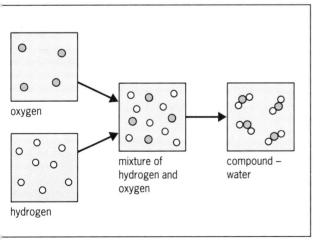

▲ **Fig 48.3 Forming water from hydrogen and oxygen**

Q2 What ratio of hydrogen and oxygen atoms combine to form water?

Forming a compound from its constituent elements is sometimes called **synthesis**. Iron(II) sulphide, the compound formed when the elements iron and sulphur combine, has entirely different properties from iron and sulphur. It is extremely difficult to get iron and sulphur back from iron(II) sulphide. The iron and sulphur atoms join together to form pairs of atoms called **molecules**, fig 48.4.

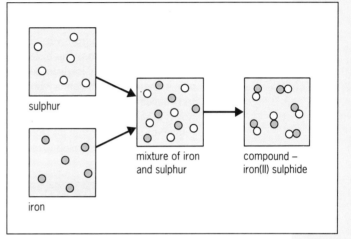

▲ **Fig 48.4 The synthesis of iron(II) sulphide**

Naming compounds

If a compound ends in -ide, the compound contains only two elements. For example,

> sodium chloride – sodium and chlorine
> copper(II) oxide – copper and oxygen

Hydroxides are an important exception to this rule. Sodium hydroxide is composed of *three* elements – sodium, oxygen and hydrogen.

If a compound ends in -ate, the compound contains oxygen. For example,

> calcium carbonate – calcium, carbon and oxygen
> copper(II) sulphate – copper, sulphur and oxygen

Q3 Name the elements combined in each of the following compounds.

  a calcium oxide
  b potassium chloride
  c sodium fluoride
  d lead(II) nitrate
  e potassium manganate(VII)
  f sodium hydrogencarbonate
  g potassium hydroxide
  h potassium chlorate
  i sodium iodide
  j sodium iodate

49 MATTER IS MADE UP OF PARTICLES

By the end of this section you should be able to

- recall that matter is composed of tiny particles called atoms
- understand evidence for the very small size of atoms
- understand the process of diffusion
- know that gases diffuse faster than liquids or solids and that small particles diffuse faster than large particles
- understand Brownian motion.

▲ Fig 49.1
John Dalton and his list of elements

ATOMS

If you were to stand in the middle of the desert you would see yellow-orange sand stretching in all directions. If you picked up the sand and looked closely you would know that what you can see is not a continuous mass but billions and billions of very tiny grains of sand. Together the grains of sand look like a solid mass.

In the same way, as we have seen, all matter is made up from very tiny particles called **atoms**. The history of the theory of atoms is given below. Later in the nineteenth century and in the twentieth century it became known to scientists that atoms themselves were all made up from even smaller particles called protons, electrons and neutrons.

HISTORY OF THE THEORY OF ATOMS

About 350BC in Ancient Greece, Democritus tried to explain why pieces of different materials of the same size had different masses. A piece of lead was much heavier than a piece of wood of the same size. In order to explain this he proposed that less dense substances had more 'open spaces' in them and that matter was not continuous but made up of 'pieces'. Building on the work of others, he described matter as being made up of 'atoms and open space'. Democritus was the first person to use the word 'atom', which means 'indivisible'.

However, the work of Democritus brought him into conflict with the most important thinker of the day, Aristotle. Aristotle supported the theory that all things were made up from four 'elements' – air, earth, fire and water, combined together in different proportions. Because of the power of Aristotle, the work of Democritus was discarded. Matter being composed of four elements was accepted throughout the Middle Ages and until only about 500 years ago. The idea of matter being made up from particles was revived by John Dalton.

The life of John Dalton

John Dalton (1766–1844) was the son of a poor Quaker handloom weaver who lived in Eaglesfield near Cockermouth in Cumberland.

He loved the countryside and especially the weather. He was very bright and went to the local Quaker school. He took over there as teacher when he was only 12 years old. As a Quaker Dalton was

unable to study at Oxford or Cambridge Universities where entry was restricted to members of the Church of England. When Dalton was 27, he decided teaching was getting in the way of his scientific studies. He resigned his teaching post in Manchester and joined the Manchester Literary and Philosophical Society and devoted much of the rest of his life to it.

Dalton's studies

From his early childhood he made a daily note of the weather and collected over 200000 observations on it.

Many of Dalton's experiments were rather inaccurate and it is his theoretical work that will be remembered, especially his work on the atomic theory. In 1808 Dalton proposed that matter was made up of tiny, indivisible particles called atoms, and that atoms of different materials were different. Atoms in a block of iron were different from atoms in a block of carbon. Atoms could be joined together in different ways to produce all the materials we know.

He realised that atoms of different elements would have different sizes and masses. Realising that the mass of an atom would be too small to weigh, he suggested the idea of relative masses. He also devised his own symbols for the elements.

What he could not work out was the number of atoms of each element which combine to form a compound. He assumed, for example, that the formula of water was HO and not H_2O. Dalton also studied colour-blindness, probably because he was a sufferer.

Q1 Scientists often study topics because they are particularly interested in them. Give three topics studied by Dalton because they interested him.

Q2 Dalton is particularly remembered because of his theoretical studies rather than his practical ones. Why was this so?

Q3 What could have been the effect on science if the work of Democritus had not been discarded so readily?

Find out about the life and work of Amadeus Avagadro. Do you see any similarities between his work and that of Democritus?

Q4 What lesson should we learn about scientific method from the story of Aristotle and Democritus?

Q5 Look at the list of elements and their symbols drawn up by Dalton in fig 49.1. Which of these do we know are not elements?

DIFFUSION

A single purple crystal of potassium manganate(VII) (potassium permanganate) can be dissolved in a beaker of water to give a pink solution. When this solution is diluted many times, the solution retains its pink colour.

A perfumed deodorant block is weighed and then passed round the class for everybody to smell. At the end of the exercise the block is weighed again. The weight is unchanged.

Q6 What can you conclude from these two pieces of evidence?

Particles and diffusion

The smell of the deodorant block will quickly spread around the room. This movement of particles is called **diffusion**. Fig 49.2 shows an experiment with the coloured liquid bromine, which quickly turns to a red gas which is much denser than air. You will notice that, despite the higher density of bromine, the mixture in both gas jars becomes the same.

The movement of the particles in the gas jars is random. The particles move to fill available spaces and there is no pattern to this movement.

Diffusion occurs rapidly in gases, and more slowly in liquids. This is because particles generally move much faster in a gas than in a liquid. Diffusion also occurs in solids but, because the movement of particles in a solid is very slow indeed, the diffusion is extremely slow.

Diffusion is an important biological process (see pages 8–9).

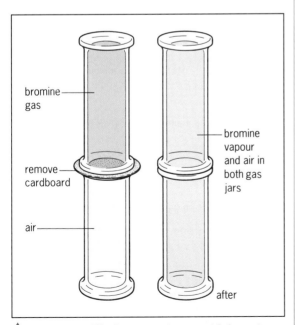

▲ **Fig 49.2 Diffusion experiment with bromine**

Diffusion and particle size

Fig 49.3 shows an experiment to compare the rate of movement of particles of ammonia and hydrogen chloride. Both are composed of tiny particles, but the ammonia particles are about half the mass and much smaller than the hydrogen chloride particles. When the two gases meet in the tube, a white solid called ammonium chloride is formed.

A long, dry glass tube is clamped horizontally and pads of cotton wool soaked in ammonia solution and hydrogen chloride solution are put into opposite ends of the tube at the same time. After about 5 minutes a white ring forms.

▼ **Fig 49.3 Diffusion and particle size**

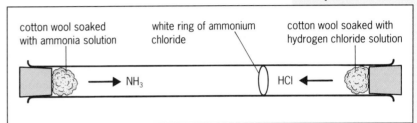

Q7 Describe the position of the ring in the tube.

Q8 What does the position of the ring tell you about the speed of movement of ammonia and hydrogen chloride particles?

Q9 Give two reasons why the ring takes so long to form.

Brownian motion

In 1827 Robert Brown, a biologist, was observing the movement of pollen grains on the surface of water under a microscope. To his surprise the pollen grains were not stationary, but were moving around in a zig-zag random way. He called this random motion **Brownian motion**. There are two points to remember about Brownian motion.

▼ **Fig 49.4 Brownian motion**

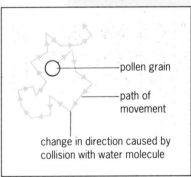

1 The movement of the pollen grains is caused by the impact of much smaller water particles which cannot be seen with the microscope. To move the pollen grains in this way the water particles must be moving very fast (see momentum, page 242).
2 The direction of movement of the pollen grains is random because the impacts of the water particles are random.

Brownian motion is summarised in fig 49.4. Brownian motion can also be seen in a smoke cell, where large particles in the smoke are moved by particles in the air and the same zig-zag motion can be seen.

50 STATES OF MATTER

SOLID, LIQUID AND GAS

There are different ways of grouping materials. One way is to divide them according to their **states**. Matter or materials can exist in three different forms or states – solid, liquid or gas. Water, for example, can exist in three forms.

ice – solid
water – liquid
steam (or water vapour) – gas

When liquid water is heated, it **boils** at 100 °C (the **boiling point** of water). At this temperature the liquid water turns to a gas (steam).

When steam is cooled down it turns back to water. You will have seen the water which forms on a cold window in a steamy kitchen. This change back from steam to liquid water is called **condensation.**

When water is cooled it **freezes** to form ice at 0 °C (the **freezing point** of water). At 0 °C, **melting** of ice also takes place. 0 °C is also the **melting point** of ice.

Steam (or water vapour) can turn directly into a solid. This happens inside a freezer. Solid ice forms inside the freezer when the steam in the air rapidly cools and forms solid ice. This is called **sublimation**. Solid carbon dioxide (sometimes called Drikold) turns straight to a gas, missing out the liquid stage. It is sometimes used to keep ice cream cold when there is no refrigerator.

▼ **Fig 50.1 Solid carbon dioxide is used for stage effects**

Q1 An ice-cream seller carries a wooden tray containing tubs of ice cream. Why is it better to use solid carbon dioxide rather than ice to keep it cold?

Q2 Solid carbon dioxide is used for stage effects. Look at the photograph in fig 50.1 and describe how it is used.

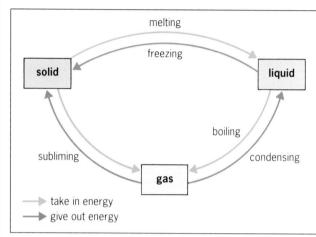

▲ **Fig 50.2 Changes of state**

Changes of state can be summarised as in fig 50.2. Similar changes of state take place in other substances. All substances can exist in the three states of matter depending upon conditions.

Properties of solids, liquids and gases

The typical properties of solids, liquids and gases are compared in the table below.

Property	Solid	Liquid	Gas
volume	definite	definite	fills the whole container
shape	definite	takes up shape of bottom of the container	takes up shape of whole container
density	high	medium	low
expansion on heating	low	medium	high
ease of compression	very low	low	high
movement of particles	very slow	medium	fast

Melting and boiling points

The following table compares the melting and boiling points of some substances you might meet in science.

Room temperature is usually taken to be 20 °C.

Substance	Melting point (°C)	Boiling point (°C)
oxygen	−219	−183
nitrogen	−214	−196
ethanol	−117	78
ammonia	−78	−33
mercury	−39	357
bromine	−7	58
sodium	78	890
iodine	114	183
sulphur	119	445
zinc	419	908
potassium chloride	776	1427
sodium chloride	801	1420
copper	1083	2582
iron	1539	2887

A substance will be a solid at room temperature if both the melting and boiling points of the substance are above 20 °C.

A substance will be a liquid at room temperature if the melting point is below 20 °C and the boiling point is above 20 °C.

A substance is a gas at room temperature if both the melting and boiling points are below 20 °C.

Q3 Which substance in the table has the lowest boiling point?

Q4 Which substances in the table are **a** solids **b** liquids **c** gases at room temperature?

Q5 In Siberia the winter temperature is −40 °C. Which substances in the table would be in a different state at this temperature than at normal room temperature?

Q6 Which substance in the table is liquid over the greatest range of temperature?

ARRANGEMENTS OF PARTICLES

Fig 50.3 shows a simple representation of particles in a solid, a liquid and a gas.

1 Particles are usually arranged regularly in solids but irregularly in liquids and gases.
2 Generally, particles are more closely packed in solids than in liquids and more closely packed in liquids than in gases.

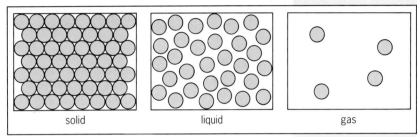

▲ **Fig 50.3 Arrangements of particles in solids, liquids and gases**

The diagrams cannot show how the particles are moving. In a solid the particles are not moving very much. It is rather like being in a very crowded room and trying to get to the door! In gases the particles are moving rapidly and in all directions. The particles in a gas collide frequently with each other and with the walls of the container. There is no pattern to the movement of particles in solids, liquids and gases. It is said to be **random** movement.

CHANGES OF STATE

Some solid crystals were heated in a test tube using a water bath until they melted. A thermometer was put into the liquid and the test tube removed from the water bath. The test tube and contents cooled. The temperature was recorded every half minute and the results are shown in fig 50.4.

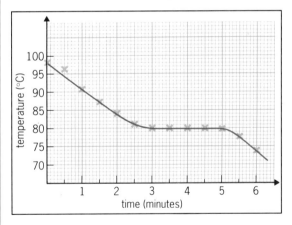

◀ **Fig 50.4 Cooling curve**

Q7 Draw a diagram of the apparatus used

a to heat the test tube to melt the crystals
b during the cooling of the liquid.

Q8 What was the temperature after 2 minutes?

Q9 Which result is likely to be inaccurate?

Q10 At which temperature did the liquid turn to a solid?

By the end of this section you should be able to

- recall that the term bonding is used to describe the joining together of particles
- explain bonding in metals
- explain ionic and covalent bonding
- recall that substances can exist as simple molecules or in giant structures (macromolecules)
- explain how the physical properties of a substance depend upon bonding and structure
- appreciate that for many uses, mixtures of metals (called alloys) are more suitable than pure metals
- give examples of common alloys and their uses
- give an example of a use where a pure metal is more suitable than an alloy.

BONDING

The forces holding atoms together are called **bonds**. In this section we shall consider the bonding in metals, and two types of bonding which occur in compounds – ionic bonding and covalent bonding.

When atoms are joined together they produce a **structure**. The properties of a substance will depend upon the bonding and the structure.

METALLIC BONDING

Most metals have high densities and this suggests that the particles or **ions** are closely packed together. Fig 51.1 shows the closest packing of ions in a layer. Any ion in the layer has six other ions around it, arranged in a regular hexagon. These close-packed layers can be arranged in two alternative ways. These are shown in fig 51.2. Some metals have one arrangement and some the other.

▼ **Fig 51.1 Ions in a layer of metal**

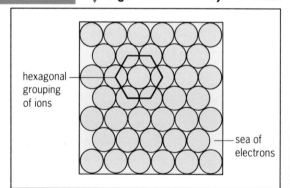

hexagonal grouping of ions

sea of electrons

Fig 51.2 Ways of stacking the layers in a metal

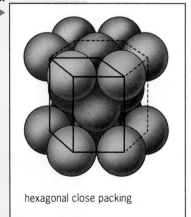

hexagonal close packing

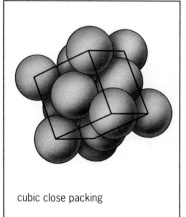

cubic close packing

Alkali metals such as sodium and potassium have a much lower density than other metals. This suggests that their ions are not so closely packed. Fig 51.3 shows the arrangement of ions in an alkali metal.

Fig 51.3 ▶ Arrangement of ions in an alkali metal

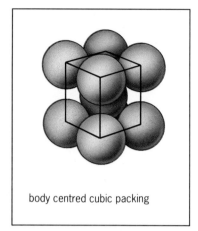

body centred cubic packing

IONIC BONDING

Ionic bonding occurs in compounds where a metal atom and a non-metal atom (or group of atoms) are joined together. Ionic bonding involves the complete transfer of one or more electrons, forming positive and negative ions. A good example of ionic bonding is sodium chloride.

A sodium atom has an electron arrangement of 2, 8, 1 (see page 126) and a chlorine atom has an electron arrangement of 2, 8, 7. A sodium atom has one more electron and a chlorine atom one less electron than a neon atom. Neon atoms are very stable and it is assumed that its electron arrangement (2, 8) is a stable one.

A sodium atom loses an electron to form a sodium ion.

$$Na \rightarrow Na^+ + e^-$$

A chlorine atom gains an electron to form a chloride ion.

$$Cl + e^- \rightarrow Cl^-$$

Both ions have an electron arrangement which is stable and they are held together by strong electrostatic forces. The strong bonds between the ions give compounds with ionic bonding high melting points.

Q1 Magnesium oxide, MgO, also has ionic bonding.

a Describe the changes which occur when magnesium oxide is formed from magnesium and oxygen atoms.

b The melting point of magnesium oxide is much higher than that of sodium chloride. How can this difference be explained?

COVALENT BONDING

Covalent bonding involves sharing of electrons. The atoms joined together are atoms of non-metals. An example of covalent bonding is the chlorine molecule (Cl_2).

A chlorine atom can be represented as:

$$\overset{\times\times}{\underset{\times\times}{\times}} Cl \times$$

where 'x' represents an electron in the outer (third) energy level. The electrons in the other energy levels are not involved.

A chlorine atom has one less electron than the noble gas argon. Argon has a stable electron arrangement of 2, 8, 8.

In a chlorine molecule, Cl_2, each chlorine atom gives a single electron to form an **electron pair**. This pair of electrons holds the two atoms together and can be represented by —.

The individual chlorine molecules are separate from one another.

Cl — Cl

Other examples of covalent bonding are shown below.

oxygen   nitrogen   water

methane   hydrogen   hydrogen chloride

In each example the covalent bonding leads to the formation of molecules, with atoms sharing electrons so that they both have a stable electron arrangement.

EFFECTS OF BONDING ON THE PROPERTIES OF SUBSTANCES

Properties of metallic substances

The layers in a metal structure can slide over one another, which explains why metals can be beaten into thin sheets or drawn into wires. Heat passes through a metal because the vibrations of one ion are easily passed on to adjacent ions.

In metals the ions are tightly packed together and held together by free electrons. Free electrons can move through the metal, which accounts for the good electrical conductivity of metals.

Properties of ionic substances

Substances with ionic bonding have high melting points and boiling points. Therefore they are usually solids at room temperature and pressure. The ions are usually held together in a **lattice**. Fig 51.4 shows a sodium chloride lattice.

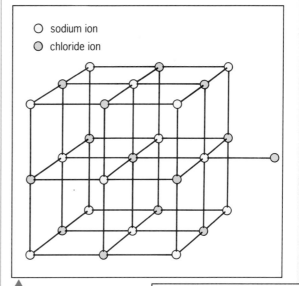

O sodium ion
● chloride ion

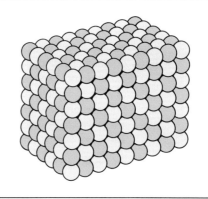

▲ **Fig 51.4 Two representations of a sodium chloride lattice** ▶

Q2 How many chloride ions surround each sodium ion in the lattice, and how many sodium ions surround each chloride ion?

This number is called the **coordination number**.

What is the coordination number of a metal ion in a close packed structure?

Substances with ionic bonding usually dissolve in water forming solutions which conduct electricity. Ionic substances do not dissolve in other solvents such as hexane or methylbenzene.

Property/behaviour	Iodine, I_2	Silicon(IV) oxide, SiO_2	Sodium chloride, NaCl
type of bonding	covalent	covalent	ionic
change on heating to 700 °C	melts, boils to form purple vapour	no change	no change
structure	molecular	giant structure of atoms	giant structure of ions

Properties of covalent substances

Substances with covalent bonding may be solids, liquids or gases. They are usually soluble in solvents such as hexane but insoluble in water. They do not conduct electricity under any circumstances. Some substances containing covalent bonding are solids. They usually contain large molecules called **macromolecules**. Poly(ethene) and starch are examples of macromolecules.

TYPES OF STRUCTURE

The three solids iodine, silicon(IV) oxide and sodium chloride have different structures and behave differently when heated. These changes are summarised in the table above.

Iodine is said to have a **molecular structure**. Although there are strong forces between the iodine atoms in an I_2 molecule, the forces between the molecules are weak. The solid structure breaks down on gentle heating. Sodium chloride and silicon(IV) oxide do not change even if heated to temperatures of 700 °C. In both cases the forces between the particles are very strong and not easily broken. These structures are called **giant structures**. There are two types of giant structure:

a made up of atoms, for example silicon(IV) oxide
b made up of ions, for example sodium chloride.

On melting, a giant structure of ions produces free ions which conduct electricity.

STRENGTHS OF MATERIALS

When choosing suitable materials, it is often wise to test the strength of possible materials. It is necessary to test samples that are the same size and shape and to test them in the same way. A fair test of strength will only be made if all these **variables** are kept the same.

Tensile strengths

The **tensile strength** of a material is the force which can be applied before the material breaks. The table (below left) compares the tensile strength and the amount that the material will stretch before breaking for six materials.

Q3 Name three materials in the table which do not stretch before breaking.

Q4 List the six materials in the table in increasing order of tensile strength.

Q5 Cast iron used to be used for metal drainpipes.

a Why is cast iron not a good material for this purpose?
b What are the advantages of poly(vinyl chloride) (PVC) which is more commonly used now?

HARDNESS OF MATERIALS

The Mohs scale

The **Mohs scale** of hardness was developed by Friedrich Mohs in 1812. It is used to compare the hardness of materials, especially rocks and minerals. It was devised by taking diamond (the hardest substance known) and giving it a value of 10. Other substances were put in order depending upon whether they scratch other substances. A substance with hardness 6 will scratch a substance with hardness 5, and will be scratched by a substance with hardness 7.

Material	Tensile strength (MN /m²)	Percentage stretching before breaking
copper	215	60
cast iron	200	0
steel	700	20
concrete	5	0
glass	130	0
poly(vinyl chloride)	600	80

Testing the hardness of minerals

A geologist working in the field is able to find the approximate hardness of minerals using the following tests.

The hardened steel blade of a penknife has a hardness of about 6. A 2p coin has a hardness of 3.5 and a fingernail a hardness of 2.

 Q6 What can you conclude about four minerals labelled A, B, C and D from the results in the table below?

Mineral	Mineral scratched by		
	Steel blade	2p coin	Fingernail
A	✓	✓	✓
B	✗	✗	✗
C	✓	✗	✗
D	✓	✓	✗

The Mohs scale of hardness is shown here:

Hardness	Material
10	diamond
9	corundum
8	topaz
7	quartz
6	feldspar
5	apatite
4	fluorite
3	calcite
2	gypsum
1	talc

 Q7 Match the minerals in the list below with A, B, C and D.

calcite   fluorite   quartz   talc

MAKING SYNTHETIC DIAMONDS, AND EVEN HARDER MATERIALS

Apart from jewellery, there is also a tremendous demand for diamonds for cutting tools. Diamonds were formed in the Earth by the action of heat and pressure on graphite.

Synthetic diamonds

Henri Moissan (who was later to discover the element fluorine, see page 123) claimed over a century ago to have produced diamonds by allowing molten iron, containing dissolved carbon, to solidify. The tremendous pressures created, he claimed, turned graphite into diamond. However, nobody was able to repeat his experiment successfully.

Only in the mid 1950s did modern engineering provide the way of producing synthetic diamonds. To do this the graphite has to be subjected simultaneously to a pressure of 100 000 atmospheres and a temperature of 3000 °C.

Harder than diamond

Materials harder than diamond are now possible. Boron nitride, a compound of the elements boron and nitrogen, has the same crystal structure as graphite. By treating this with high temperatures and pressures, scientists have been able to turn it into a diamond form called borazon, which is harder than diamond.

More recently, Japanese scientists have claimed to have produced an even harder substance. They subjected magnesium silicate (a compound of magnesium, silicon and oxygen) to a very high pressure and produced a material harder than diamond.

 Q8 How would you attempt to show that borazon is harder than diamond?

 Fig 51.5 Diamonds are used for drill bits as well as for jewellery

▶▶

ALLOYS

Pure metals are not widely used. Generally, pure metals are weak and soft. Mixing metals together produces a harder and stronger material. We can explain this in terms of the change of structure which occurs when metals are mixed or carbon is added to a metal such as iron. In fig 51.6 we can see that two different ions in the structure distort the regular arrangement in the layers and therefore prevent the layers sliding over one another as easily. Adding carbon to iron to make steel fills the gaps between the iron ions in the structure, again inhibiting the sliding of layers.

**Fig 51.6 ▶
Arrangements of
particles in alloys**

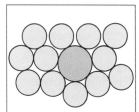 

alloy with metals having larger ions – the larger ions distort the structure and prevent the layers sliding

steel – carbon atoms in the gaps prevent layers sliding

Pure metals are used for conducting electricity because the pure metals copper and aluminium conduct electricity better than alloys.

Examples of alloys in use are shown below.

Steel, fig 51.7, is an alloy of iron and carbon. It is relatively cheap and can be rolled into sheets. It corrodes (rusts).

**Fig 51.7 Steel can ▶
be rolled into
sheets and
pressed to form
car panels**

Stainless steel, fig 51.8, is an alloy of iron and carbon with added chromium and nickel. It is shiny, hard and corrosion resistant. It is more expensive than steel.

▲ **Fig 51.8 Stainless steel is hard, shiny and resistant to corrosion**

Solder, fig 51.9, is an alloy of tin and lead. It has a lower melting point than tin or lead.

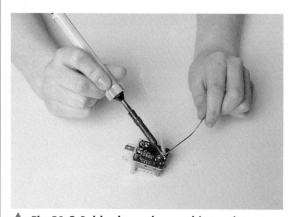

▲ **Fig 51.9 Solder has a low melting point**

Nichrome, fig 51.10, is an alloy of nickel and chromium. It has a high melting point and is a good conductor of electricity.

▲ **Fig 51.10 Nichrome has a high melting point and conducts electricity well**

Cupronickel, fig 51.11, is an alloy of copper and nickel. It is hard, corrosion resistant and relatively cheap.

▲ **Fig 51.11 Cupronickel is hard and resists corrosion – it is used for coins**

Duralumin, fig 51.12, is an alloy of aluminium and copper. It has a low density, is strong and resists corrosion.

▲ **Fig 51.12 Duralumin has a low density and is strong**

Brass, fig 51.13, is an alloy of copper and zinc. It is shiny and resists corrosion.

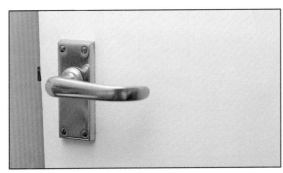

▲ **Fig 51.13 Brass is shiny and resists corrosion**

Bronze, fig 51.14, is an alloy of copper and tin. It resists corrosion and does not contract much when solidifying.

▲ **Fig 51.14 Bronze does not contract much when it solidifies so can be cast. Long exposure to the air causes the bronze to oxidise on the surface**

Properties of alloys

The properties of an alloy can depend upon

1 the composition of the alloy
2 the method of forming the alloy
3 heat treatment of the alloy.

These differences can be shown using steel as an example.

1 The table below compares the properties of three types of steel.
2 If steel is allowed to cool slowly during its formation, large crystals are produced. Rapid cooling leads to small crystals. The properties of the steel depend upon crystal size.
3 If a piece of steel is heated to 950 °C and allowed to cool, the properties of the steel depend upon the method of cooling. If the steel is cooled quickly by plunging into cold water (a process called **quenching**), the steel becomes brittle.

Type	Percentage of carbon	Examples of use
low-carbon steel	0.03–0.25	sheet metal for car bodies, steel containers
medium-carbon steel	0.25–0.50	machine parts, ship structures
high-carbon steel	0.85–1.20	springs, cutting tools, drills

52 RADIOACTIVITY

By the end of this section you should be able to

- recall the different types of radiation given out during radioactive decay and the properties of these radiations
- work out the half-life of a radioactive isotope from experimental results
- work out the changes which take place within an atom during alpha and beta decay
- explain the processes of fission and fusion.

WHAT IS RADIOACTIVITY?

Radioactivity (sometimes called **radioactive decay**) is the spontaneous break-up (decay) of the nuclei of atoms. Unlike chemical reactions, the rate of decay does not depend on factors such as temperature (see pages 154–7). Substances that decay in this way are called **radioactive**, and they give out **radiation**.

THE DISCOVERY OF RADIOACTIVITY

Uranium

Henri Becquerel was experimenting with the reactions of uranium compounds in 1896. He left one of these uranium compounds in a drawer close to a photographic plate wrapped in black paper. When the photographic plate was developed he found that it had been darkened, as if it had been exposed to light. This led Becquerel to carry out further experiments and show that the uranium compounds were giving out **radiation** which passed through the black paper and affected the photographic plate. This discovery of radioactivity was accidental, like many other important discoveries.

Radium and polonium

Marie Curie was one of Becquerel's assistants. She and her husband Pierre carried out experiments on impure uranium sulphide (called pitchblende). By careful extraction from a large quantity of pitchblende, she isolated two elements more radioactive than uranium, which she named radium and polonium. She also showed that all uranium compounds are radioactive.

TYPES OF RADIOACTIVE DECAY

Most atoms have stable nuclei which do not break up. However, the nuclei of some atoms can break up or decay. These atoms, for example uranium-235, often have a large number of protons and neutrons within the nucleus.

Q1 How many protons and neutrons are there in a uranium-235 atom?

Hydrogen-3 (sometimes called tritium) has unstable nuclei which undergo radioactive decay. A hydrogen-3 atom contains only one proton and two neutrons. This shows that radioactive decay can occur in lighter atoms, but in these atoms there is usually an excess of neutrons.

▲ **Fig 52.1 Marie Curie (1867–1934)**

Alpha, beta and gamma radiation

When radioactive atoms break up energy is given out and three types of radiation can be detected – alpha (α), beta (β) and gamma (γ). Alpha-rays and beta-rays are made up of particles. Gamma-rays are electromagnetic waves (see page 252) and have greater penetration than alpha- or beta-particles. The table summarises the nature and properties of these three types of radiation.

Type of radiation	Nature of radiation	Distance travelled in air	Effect of electric and magnetic fields
alpha	helium nuclei (2 protons and 2 neutrons)	a few centimetres	small deflection
beta	electrons	a few metres	large deflection
gamma	electromagnetic waves	several kilometres	no deflection

Fig 52.2 shows the relative penetrating powers of the three types of radiation.

Q2 Explain the type of packaging you would recommend for transporting
a a small amount of an alpha source
b a gamma source.

Q3 Explain the different deflections of the three types of radiation in electric and magnetic fields.

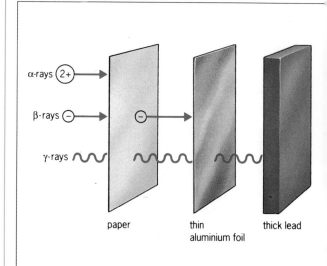

▲ **Fig 52.2 Relative penetrating powers of the three types of radiation**

WHAT HAPPENS WHEN AN ATOM DECAYS?

Alpha decay

When an atom of uranium-238 decays it gives out an alpha-particle. The product of the decay, called thorium, therefore contains two protons less and two neutrons less than uranium-238.

$$^{238}_{92}U \rightarrow {}^{4}_{2}He + {}^{234}_{90}Th$$

Note that in this equation the sum of the atomic numbers and the mass numbers is the same on both sides of the equation. The product thorium-234 contains two protons less than uranium and is therefore two places to the left of uranium in the Periodic table.

Beta decay

Thorium-234 itself undergoes radioactive decay. It decays by giving out beta-particles. A neutron in the nucleus is changed into a proton and an electron, and the electron is then given out as beta-radiation. The new atom, actinium, contains the same number of particles in the nucleus as the original atom (which means it has the same mass number). However, it contains one more proton than the original thorium atom and is therefore one place to the right of thorium in the Periodic table.

$$^{234}_{90}Th \rightarrow {}^{0}_{-1}e + {}^{234}_{89}Ac$$

Gamma decay

When gamma radiation is given out, protons and neutrons are rearranged but the element does not change.

 Copy and complete the following equations.

a $^{27}_{13}Al + {}^{1}_{1}H \rightarrow {}^{24}_{12}Mg + \underline{\quad}$

b $^{9}_{4}Be + {}^{4}_{2}He \rightarrow {}^{12}_{6}C + \underline{\quad}$

c $^{24}_{12}Mg + \underline{\quad} \rightarrow {}^{27}_{14}Si + {}^{1}_{0}n$

d $^{238}_{92}U + {}^{14}_{7}N \rightarrow {}^{248}_{99}Es + 4\underline{\quad}$

MEASURING RADIOACTIVITY

The Geiger counter

Radioactivity can be detected using a **Geiger counter**, which is a Geiger-Müller (GM) tube attached to a counter. Fig 52.3 shows a GM tube.

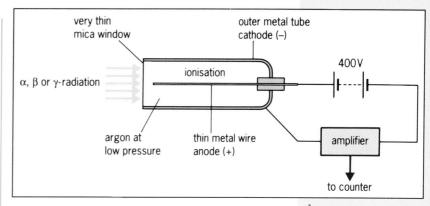

▲ Fig 52.3 A GM tube

The GM tube contains argon gas. When radiation enters the GM tube, it ionises the argon atoms.

The charged particles (argon ions and electrons) are attracted to the electrodes and a tiny current flows in the circuit. This current is then amplified.

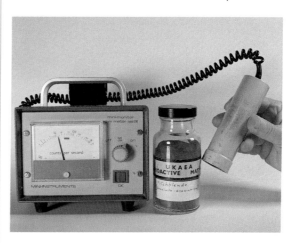

◀ Fig 52.4 A Geiger counter showing a reading of about 13 counts per second for this sample of pitchblende

Background radiation

Even when there is no radioactive source, a small amount of radioactivity will still be recorded. This natural radiation is called **background radiation**. Certain rocks, for example granite, contain radioactive thorium, uranium and potassium compounds. We are also exposed to radiation from the Sun and traces of radioactive gases (radon and thoron) in the air. Background radiation is usually low and causes no risk to health.

When making radioactivity measurements it is usual to find the background radiation first by finding the counts per minute without a radioactive sample. This is then subtracted from the readings taken with the sample present.

HALF-LIFE

The rate of decay of a radioactive isotope is shown by its **half-life**. This is the time taken for half of any given number of radioactive atoms to decay, or for the radioactive count to drop to half its original value.

Half-lives of radioactive isotopes can vary from a fraction of a second to millions of years. The longer the half-life, the slower the radioactive decay process.

Half-life of polonium-214 = 1.5×10^{-4}s
Half-life of radium-226 = 1620 years

Fig 52.5 shows the graph obtained during an experiment to measure the decay of a radioactive isotope. The time taken for the counts per minute to drop from 200 to 100 is 39 minutes.

Fig 52.5 Graph showing the decay of a radioactive isotope

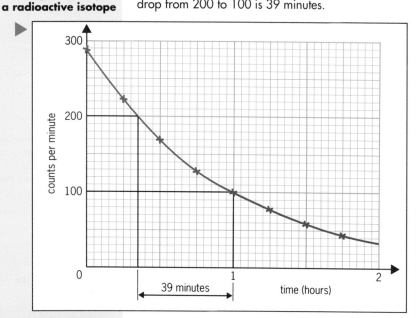

counts per minute

300

200

100

0

39 minutes

time (hours)

1

2

All results were corrected for background radiation, which was 10 counts per second.

a What reading was shown on the counter at 10 minutes, before correction for background radiation?
b Plot these results and draw a graph.
c Which result appears to be incorrect?
d What is the half-life of this isotope? Explain how you arrived at this answer.
e What would be the half-life of the same isotope at 30°C?

CARBON DATING

Radioactive decay of carbon-14 is used to date ancient objects. All living things contain a small fixed amount of carbon-14. When the organism dies the carbon-14 decays by beta decay (half-life 5736 years). By finding the level of carbon-14 remaining, a scientist can estimate the age of the object, fig 52.6.

NUCLEAR FISSION

Very heavy atoms, such as uranium, can decay by losing alpha- or beta-particles. Some of these heavy atoms can also become stable by **nuclear fission**. The process is summarised in fig 52.7.

Nuclear fission involves the bombardment of a nucleus with a neutron. The final products are two smaller nuclei, two or three separate neutrons and enormous amounts of energy. Nuclear fission was first shown by the German scientist Otto Hahn in 1936.

Natural uranium contains 0.7% uranium-235 and 99.3% uranium-238. Only the uranium-235 will undergo nuclear fission. Scientists soon realised that **enriched** uranium (uranium containing a larger proportion of uranium-235) could carry on undergoing fission. The neutrons released on the fission of one atom could split another uranium-235 nucleus. This could cause a **chain reaction**.

Q5 How long will it take for the counts per minute in fig 52.5 to drop from 100 to **a** 50 **b** 25?

Q6 Measurements were made with a Geiger counter at 20°C to find the half-life of a radioactive isotope X. Here are the results.

Time (minutes)	0	10	20	30	40	50	60	70
Count rate (counts /s)	650	520	416	333	300	213	170	136

▼ **Fig 52.7 Nuclear fission**

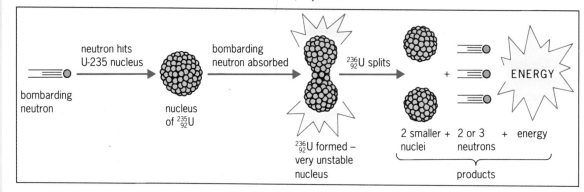

bombarding neutron

neutron hits U-235 nucleus

nucleus of $^{235}_{92}$U

bombarding neutron absorbed

$^{236}_{92}$U formed – very unstable nucleus

$^{236}_{92}$U splits

2 smaller nuclei + 2 or 3 neutrons + energy

ENERGY

products

▲ **Fig 52.6 The Turin shroud is about 500 years old, so could not have been used to cover the body of Jesus.**

142

Fig 52.8 shows a chain reaction for uranium-235. Each time fission occurs, more neutrons and more energy are released.

An uncontrolled chain reaction involving pure uranium-235 produces an atomic bomb, fig 52.9. All the neutrons produced are used to bombard other uranium nuclei. This produces vast amounts of energy and radiation.

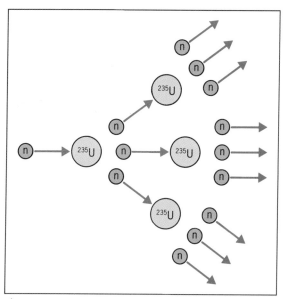

▲ **Fig 52.8 A nuclear chain reaction**

▼ **Fig 52.9 Explosion of an atomic bomb**

Nuclear reactors

If a nuclear chain reaction is controlled, an atomic or nuclear reactor can be set up. A mixture of 3% uranium-235 and 97% uranium-238 is used. The reaction is controlled so only one neutron from each fission goes on to produce further fission. The

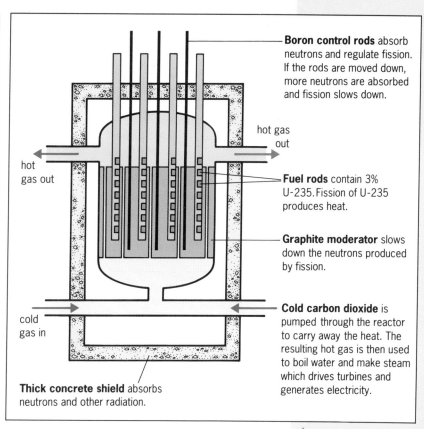

Boron control rods absorb neutrons and regulate fission. If the rods are moved down, more neutrons are absorbed and fission slows down.

hot gas out

Fuel rods contain 3% U-235. Fission of U-235 produces heat.

Graphite moderator slows down the neutrons produced by fission.

Cold carbon dioxide is pumped through the reactor to carry away the heat. The resulting hot gas is then used to boil water and make steam which drives turbines and generates electricity.

hot gas out

cold gas in

Thick concrete shield absorbs neutrons and other radiation.

▲ **Fig 52.10 A gas-cooled nuclear reactor**

heat produced is used to generate electricity. Fig 52.10 shows a simplified diagram of a gas-cooled nuclear reactor.

NUCLEAR FUSION

Nuclear fusion is the opposite of fission, and could be used to provide useful energy in the future. Fusion involves the joining of nuclei together. The energy from the Sun comes from the fusion of two heavy hydrogen (deuterium) nuclei within the Sun. This is shown in fig 52.11. This process liberates very large amounts of energy, even more energy than nuclear fission, and could provide a solution to the world's energy problems.

◄ **Fig 52.11 Nuclear fusion**

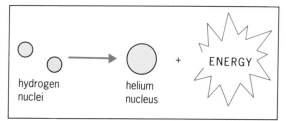

hydrogen nuclei   helium nucleus   +   ENERGY

Q7 Scientists in Britain and America have recently aroused great interest by claiming to have produced nuclear fusion at room temperature, called cold fusion. Find out what you can about this research.

EXPLAINING HOW MATERIALS BEHAVE

143

53 THE VOLUME OF A GAS

By the end of this section you should be able to

- understand how the volume of a gas changes with changes in temperature and pressure
- carry out simple calculations involving changes in the volume of a gas.

CHANGING THE VOLUME OF A GAS

The volume of a solid or liquid does not change appreciably when pressure is increased. An increase in temperature causes a solid to expand a little and a liquid to expand more. The expansion of a liquid on heating is the principle behind the simple mercury thermometer. A gas expands much more on heating than does a solid or liquid. This fact is used in a gas thermometer, shown in fig 53.1.

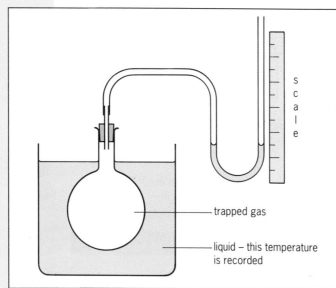

scale

trapped gas

liquid – this temperature is recorded

▲ **Fig 53.1 A gas thermometer**

The effect of changes in pressure and temperature on a fixed mass of gas is summarised by Boyle's law and Charles' law.

Boyle's law

Boyle's law says that the volume (V) of a fixed mass of gas is inversely proportional to the pressure (p), providing the temperature remains constant. That is,

$$pV = \text{constant}$$

Example

$100\,cm^3$ of air in a gas syringe is at a pressure of $100\,kPa$. The plunger of the syringe is pushed in until the volume of the air is $50\,cm^3$. The pressure of the air is now $200\,kPa$.

$$pV = \text{constant, so } p_1V_1 = p_2V_2$$
$$100\,cm^3 \times 100\,kPa = 50\,cm^3 \times 200\,kPa$$

Q1 Calculate the pressure of the air in the syringe if the volume of the gas is

a $20\,cm^3$
b $65\,cm^3$.

Q2 Calculate the volume of the air in the syringe when the pressure of the air is

a $10\,kPa$
b $37\,kPa$.

Charles' law

Charles' law says that the volume (V) of a fixed mass of gas is directly proportional to its absolute temperature (T) (that is its temperature on the kelvin scale), provided the pressure remains constant. That is,

$$V/T = \text{constant}$$

Note that the temperature must be in kelvins. To convert a temperature in degrees Celsius to kelvins you have to add 273.

$$0°C \text{ is the same as } 273\,K$$
$$100°C \text{ is the same as } (273 + 100)°C = 373\,K$$

Example

$100\,cm^3$ of gas at $27°C$ is heated to $127°C$ while the pressure is kept constant. Calculate the volume of the gas at $127°C$.

First, the temperatures must be converted to kelvins.

$$27°C = 300\,K$$
$$127°C = 400\,K$$

$$\text{At } 300\,K, \quad \frac{V_1}{T_1} = \frac{100}{300} = 0.33\,cm^3/K$$

$$\text{At } 400\,K, \quad \frac{V_2}{T_2} = \frac{V_2}{400\,K}$$

According to Charles' law, V/T is constant, so $V_1T_1 = V_2T_2$.

$$V_2 = 0.33 \times 400\,cm^3$$
$$= 132\,cm^3$$

Q3 Calculate the volume when $100\,cm^3$ of gas at $27°C$ and $100\,kPa$ is heated to $227°C$ at constant pressure.

Q4 A gas tank at a factory stores oxygen gas. The tank's volume can vary between $100\,m^3$ and $200\,m^3$.

a Assuming that the mass of oxygen in the tank and the pressure of the gas do not change, what would happen to the volume of the tank when the temperature fell overnight?

b If the volume of the tank was fixed at $100\,m^3$ and the temperature remained constant, how would the pressure change if the mass of oxygen gas was doubled?

THE GENERAL GAS EQUATION

Sometimes Boyle's law and Charles' law are combined to give the **general gas equation**. This enables changes of volume, pressure and temperature to be considered. The equation is

$$\frac{p_1 V_1}{T_1} = \frac{p_2 V_2}{T_2}$$

Example

Suppose a fixed mass of gas occupying $1000\,cm^3$ at $27\,°C$ is heated to $227\,°C$ and at the same time the pressure is changed from $100\,kPa$ to $200\,kPa$. The final volume of the gas V_2 can be calculated from

$$\frac{p_1 V_1}{T_1} = \frac{p_2 V_2}{T_2}$$

$$\frac{100 \times 1000}{300} = \frac{200 \times V_2}{500}$$

$$V_2 = \frac{100 \times 1000 \times 500}{300 \times 200}$$

$$= 833\,cm^3$$

 Q5 Calculate the volume when $10\,dm^3$ of gas at $27\,°C$ and 1 atmosphere pressure is heated to $473\,°C$ at 10 atmospheres pressure.

ROBERT BOYLE (1627–91)

Robert Boyle was an Irishman. He was the seventh son of the first Earl of Cork. He was educated by a private tutor in his father's castle in Lismore before being sent to school at Eton. He completed his education in France, Switzerland and Italy.

In 1645, aged 18, he moved to Dorset and began carrying out experiments. His experiments were different from those carried out by people before him. They were planned and logical, rather than the haphazard experiments of others.

In 1654 he moved to Oxford and in 1663, with friends, he formed the Royal Society to study and advance science. In 1670 he published his famous law – Boyle's law. However, this law was first worked out by Richard Towneley and Henry Power.

Boyle was also interested in disease, possibly because he suffered much ill health himself.

Boyle is often regarded as the father of chemistry.

 Q6 What special approach did Boyle bring to his scientific studies?

JACQUES CHARLES (1746–1823)

Jacques Alexandre Charles was born in Beaugency in France. He became a clerk in the Ministry of Finance in Paris. Later he became interested in science.

In 1782 Tiberius Cavello showed that hydrogen was less dense than air by making soap bubbles filled with hydrogen. These rose to the ceiling.

In August 1783 Charles released a small hydrogen-filled balloon. On 1 December 1783 Charles, accompanied by one of the Robert brothers, went up in a rubberised silk balloon filled with hydrogen. They reached a height of $700\,m$ and flew over $40\,km$.

In addition to studying the behaviour of gases, Charles produced a number of pieces of scientific equipment.

Q7 Hydrogen-filled balloons were a big step forward compared with balloons that had been used before. Find out what was used to fill earlier balloons.

Q8 Why was the silk in Charles' balloon rubberised?

Q9 In the development of the hydrogen-filled balloon, there were two steps before Charles could go up in his balloon. What were the two steps and why were they necessary?

Q10 Look at fig 53.2 which shows a famous hydrogen-filled balloon in the 1930s. Why were hydrogen-filled balloons not used again? What is used to fill modern airships?

▲ **Fig 53.2 The Hindenberg hydrogen-filled airship**

By the end of this section you should be able to

- recall that ionic compounds such as sodium chloride exist as a lattice of sodium and chloride ions
- understand that a lattice can be broken down by melting or dissolving in water
- understand the energy changes which occur when an ionic compound dissolves in water
- use data to work out whether dissolving an ionic compound in water is exothermic or endothermic
- understand some of the factors which affect the values of hydration and lattice energies.

BREAKING UP AN IONIC LATTICE

In fig 51.4 (page 135) there are two representations of a sodium chloride lattice. Strong electrostatic forces hold the sodium and chloride ions together.

The lattice can be broken down by melting or dissolving in water.

Breaking up the lattice by dissolving in water

Water molecules are covalent (page 135) but contain slight positive and negative charges.

$$\delta- \atop O$$
$$\delta+ \atop H \qquad H \atop \delta+$$

These charges are caused by a slight movement of the electrons in each O—H bond towards the oxygen atom.

Fig 54.1 shows how water molecules can break down an ionic lattice by pulling ions from the lattice. This process requires energy, that is, it is **endothermic** (see page 148).

When the ions are removed from the lattice, they are surrounded by water molecules. This process is called **hydration** of the ions. This process is **exothermic** – it gives out energy (see page 148). (If a solvent other than water is used, the arranging of the solvent molecules around the ions is called **solvation** rather than hydration.)

Boiling points of group VI hydrides

The table below shows the boiling points of the hydrides of the elements of group VI of the Periodic table.

Hydride	Boiling point (°C)
H_2O	100
H_2S	−61
H_2Se	−41
H_2Te	−21

The molecules have similar shapes but the partial charges that exist in water molecules are not present in hydrogen sulphide, hydrogen selenide and hydrogen telluride.

Q1 How can you explain the differences in boiling points of these hydrides?

ENERGY CHANGES ON DISSOLVING

Lattice energy

The **lattice energy** of sodium chloride is the energy required to turn 1 mole (see page 160) of sodium chloride into ions in the vapour state, that is

$$NaCl(s) \rightarrow Na^+(g) + Cl^-(g)$$

This process is endothermic. The energy required to do this is 771 kJ/mol.

Hydration energy

The **hydration energy** of an ion is the energy given out when 1 mole of ions in the vapour state is dissolved in a large quantity of water. The hydration energies for sodium and chloride ions are

$$Na^+(g) + aq \rightarrow Na^+(aq) \qquad -406\,kJ/mol$$
$$Cl^-(g) + aq \rightarrow Cl^-(aq) \qquad -364\,kJ/mol$$

'aq' in the equation stands for a large quantity of water.

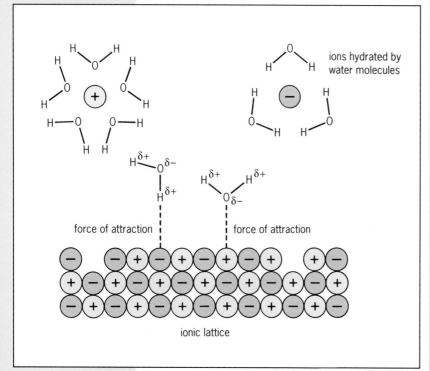

▲ **Fig 54.1 The negative ions are attracted to the hydrogen ends of the water molecules and the positive ions to the oxygen ends. The ions become hydrated or surrounded by water molecules**

Putting it together – energy of dissolving

Adding the three equations together gives an equation which summarises the process of dissolving sodium chloride in water, namely

$$NaCl(s) + aq \rightarrow Na^+(aq) + Cl^-(aq)$$

Adding the three energy values together gives the energy value for the whole dissolving process

$$+771 - 406 - 364 = +1 \text{ kJ/mol}$$

This confirms our experience when dissolving sodium chloride in water. The resulting solution does not feel noticeably warmer or colder than the water used.

If the sum of the hydration energies is much greater than the lattice energy, the resulting solution will rise in temperature on dissolving. Dissolving will be an **exothermic** change. If the lattice energy is much greater than the sum of the hydration energies, the lattice will not break up, so the solid will not dissolve. If the lattice energy is slightly greater than the sum of the hydration energies, the solid will dissolve but the temperature of the solution will fall. Dissolving will be an **endothermic** change.

CALCULATIONS

Hydration energies

The table below shows the hydration energies of some ions.

$$M^{z+}(g) + aq \rightarrow M^{z+}(aq)$$
$$\text{or} \quad X^{z-}(g) + aq \rightarrow X^{z-}(aq)$$

Cation	Hydration energy (kJ/mol)	Anion	Hydration energy (kJ/mol)
Li$^+$	–519	OH$^-$	–460
Na$^+$	–406	F$^-$	–506
K$^+$	–322	Cl$^-$	–364
Rb$^+$	–301	Br$^-$	–335
Cs$^+$	–276	I$^-$	–293
Mg^{2+}	–1920		
Ca^{2+}	–1650		
Ba^{2+}	–1360		
Al^{3+}	–4960		
NH$_4^+$	–260		

Q2 Estimate the hydration energy of the strontium ion, Sr^{2+}.

Q3 How do the hydration energies of the ions of the elements in group I of the Periodic table vary? Is this true in other groups? Suggest an explanation for this.

Q4 Explain why the hydration energy of the aluminium ion is much greater than that of the magnesium or sodium ion.

Lattice energies

The table below shows the lattice energies of some common compounds.

	Lattice energies (kJ/mol)			
	F	Cl	Br	I
Li	1022	846	800	744
Na	902	771	733	684
K	801	701	670	629
Rb	767	675	647	609
Cs	716	645	619	585

Q5 Explain why lithium fluoride is almost insoluble in water while lithium iodide is very soluble. How does the temperature of the solution change on dissolving lithium iodide in water?

Q6 Explain why lithium fluoride has a very high lattice energy.

55 ENERGY CHANGES IN CHEMICAL REACTIONS

By the end of this section you should be able to

- recall that energy changes accompany many chemical changes
- recall that a reaction which gives out heat is exothermic and one which takes in heat is endothermic
- understand that energy changes are due to breaking and forming of chemical bonds
- understand something of explosions which are very fast exothermic reactions.

ENERGY CHANGES

In a chemical reaction, an energy change can often be observed. Energy is either taken in or, more commonly, given out.

In a combustion reaction or in respiration (see page 6), energy is given out. A reaction which gives out energy is said to be **exothermic**.

The energy level diagram for an exothermic reaction is shown in fig 55.1. The products contain less energy than the reactants. The surplus energy is given out. The change in energy is represented by ΔH.

In photosynthesis (see page 4), energy is taken in from sunlight. A reaction which takes in energy is called an **endothermic reaction**. The energy level diagram for an endothermic reaction is shown in fig 55.2

▼ **Fig 55.1 Energy level diagram for an exothermic reaction**

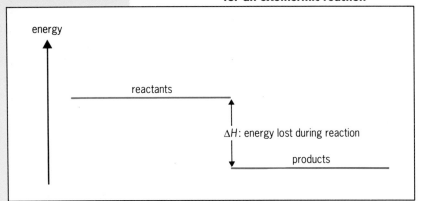

▲ **Fig 55.2 Energy level diagram for an endothermic reaction**

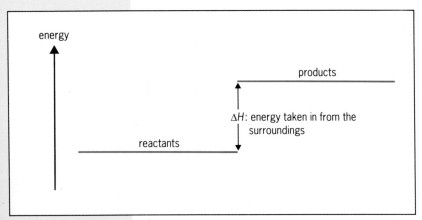

Where does this energy come from? During a reaction, chemical bonds may be made or broken. Energy is produced when bonds are made, and energy is required to break bonds.

If the energy produced when bonds are formed is greater than the energy required to break the necessary bonds, then the reaction will be exothermic. However, if the energy required to break the bonds is greater, the reaction is endothermic.

Q1 Hydrogen and chlorine react together to produce hydrogen chloride.

$$H_2(g) + Cl_2(g) \rightarrow 2HCl(g)$$

The energy required to break certain bonds is given below. (The **mole** is a measure of the amount of a substance, explained on page 160.)

H—H	+437 kJ/mole
Cl—Cl	+244 kJ/mole
H—Cl	+433 kJ/mole

The energy given out when a bond is formed is of the same magnitude as that needed to break the same bond but will be negative. For example,

to form H—Cl   −433 kJ/mole

Calculate the energy change when one mole of hydrogen molecules reacts with one mole of chlorine molecules.

Is the reaction exothermic or endothermic?

(Hint: If the overall energy change is negative, the reaction is exothermic.)

Q2 A similar reaction takes place when hydrogen and fluorine react.

$$H_2(g) + F_2(g) \rightarrow 2HF(g)$$

The energy required to break bonds is

F—F	+155 kJ/mole
H—F	+577 kJ/mole

Calculate the energy change when one mole of hydrogen molecules and one mole of fluorine molecules react.

Is the reaction exothermic or endothermic?

Q3 Hydrazine, H_2NNH_2, is used as a rocket fuel. It burns in oxygen to form nitrogen and water. Calculate the energy produced when 1 mole of hydrazine is burned.
(Bond energies in kJ/mole: N——N + 163
N—H + 388   O==O + 496
N≡≡N + 994   O—H + 463)

Activity

1 Sodium hydroxide and hydrochloric acid – a neutralisation reaction

Put about 5 cm depth of sodium hydroxide solution into one test tube and 5 cm depth of hydrochloric acid into another. Put thermometers into the test tubes. Read the temperatures and calculate the average temperature of the solutions.

Mix the two solutions, keeping a thermometer in the solution during mixing. Record the highest temperature.

a Is the reaction exothermic or endothermic?

b Draw an energy level diagram for the reaction.

2 A precipitation reaction

Carry out an identical experiment, replacing the sodium hydroxide and hydrochloric acid solutions with calcium nitrate solution and sodium carbonate solution.

a Write an equation for the reaction taking place.

b Is the reaction exothermic or endothermic?

c Draw an energy level diagram for the reaction.

3 A displacement reaction

Repeat the experiment again using copper(II) sulphate solution and zinc powder.

a Write a word equation for the reaction taking place.

b Is the reaction exothermic or endothermic?

c Draw an energy level diagram for the reaction taking place.

EXPLOSIVES

An **explosive** is a substance that gives off so much hot gas so quickly that it will burst open and even shatter anything around it. An **explosion** is a very strongly exothermic reaction that produces a large volume of gas.

The history of explosives

The oldest known explosive is **gunpowder**, a mixture of potassium nitrate (saltpetre), charcoal and sulphur. This was known to the ancient Chinese thousands of years ago. In Europe, however, it was first described by the English friar, Roger Bacon, in 1249. It was then 100 years before it was used to fire guns and revolutionise warfare, and 400 years before it was used for quarrying. When gunpowder burns it produces about 4000 times its own volume of gas.

A more powerful explosive, **guncotton**, was developed by Christian Schonbein in 1846. This was made by nitrating cotton fibre with concentrated nitric and sulphuric acids. Guncotton burns quietly but explodes violently when struck.

In 1847 Ascanio Sobrero produced **nitroglycerine** by nitrating glycerine in a similar way. Nitroglycerine produces 12000 times its own volume of gas on explosion. However, pure nitroglycerine is difficult to handle safely.

In 1866 the Swedish chemist Alfred Nobel found by accident that nitroglycerine could be stabilised by mixing it with a sandy earth material. The more stable mixture is called **dynamite**. With the vast fortune made from explosives, Nobel set up the Nobel prizes for achievement in various fields.

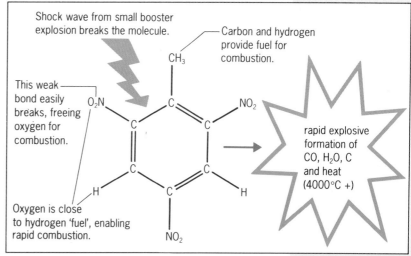

Shock wave from small booster explosion breaks the molecule.

Carbon and hydrogen provide fuel for combustion.

This weak bond easily breaks, freeing oxygen for combustion.

Oxygen is close to hydrogen 'fuel', enabling rapid combustion.

rapid explosive formation of CO, H_2O, C and heat (4000°C +)

▲ **Fig 55.3 The structure of TNT makes it a powerful explosive**

More modern explosives have included picric acid (used in the First World War) and trinitrotoluene (TNT). These explosives were again produced by nitrating carbon compounds with a mixture of concentrated sulphuric and nitric acids. TNT, unlike other explosives, can be melted and cast into shape. Fig 55.3 summarises the changes taking place when TNT explodes. The energy given out when new bonds are formed is much greater than the energy required to break the bonds. The TNT molecule is broken by an initial shock wave.

Explosive power

The **explosive power** of an explosive is calculated by multiplying the energy generated per gram and the volume of outrushing gas.

Q4 Calculate the explosive power for picric acid given that the energy generated is 3745 J/g and the volume of gas is 790 cm³/g.

56 TYPES OF REACTION

By the end of this section you should be able to

- define the processes of oxidation and reduction and understand that they are opposites
- understand that oxidation and reduction occur together in redox reactions
- understand the terms oxidising agent and reducing agent
- state examples of oxidation and reduction
- understand oxidation and reduction in terms of electron transfer
- state that rusting of iron is a corrosion process involving oxidation
- know that rusting takes place in iron or steel in the presence of water and oxygen
- appreciate that rusting is a serious economic problem
- describe methods used to reduce rusting of iron and steel
- understand the process of neutralisation and everyday uses of neutralisation
- know that some reactions do not completely convert the products into reactants, and that equilibrium can be set up
- understand the economic importance of equilibrium in industrial processes.

OXIDATION AND REDUCTION

Oxidation takes place when oxygen is added or hydrogen is removed during a chemical reaction. **Reduction** is the opposite of oxidation, so oxygen is removed or hydrogen is added.

magnesium + oxygen → magnesium oxide

$$2Mg(s) + O_2(g) \rightarrow 2MgO(s)$$

Magnesium is oxidised – oxygen is added.

ethene + hydrogen → ethane

$$C_2H_4(g) + H_2(g) \rightarrow C_2H_6(g)$$

Ethene is reduced – hydrogen is added.

Redox reactions

Oxidation and reduction always take place together. A reaction in which oxidation and reduction take place is called a **redox** reaction. For example, when lead(II) oxide is heated in a stream of dry hydrogen:

lead(II) oxide + hydrogen → lead + water

$$PbO(s) + H_2(g) \rightarrow Pb(s) + H_2O(l)$$

Lead(II) oxide is reduced to lead – oxygen is lost. Hydrogen is oxidised– oxygen is added. Hydrogen, which brings about the reduction of lead(II) oxide, is called the **reducing agent**. Lead(II) oxide, which brings about the oxidation of hydrogen, is called the **oxidising agent**.

Electron transfer

A more advanced definition of oxidation and reduction involves **electron transfer**. A process where electrons are lost, for example

$$Fe \rightarrow Fe^{3+} + 3e^-$$

is an oxidation process. In the reduction of ethene, hydrogen is oxidised.
A process where electrons are gained, for example

$$Cu^{2+} + 2e^- \rightarrow Cu$$

is a reduction process. In the oxidation of magnesium, oxygen is reduced.
Oxidation and reduction processes also occur in electrolysis (see page 162).

(see page 162)

Q1 For each of the following examples state whether the substance in bold type is oxidised or reduced.

a $2\mathbf{Ca} + O_2 \rightarrow 2CaO$
b $\mathbf{C} + O_2 \rightarrow CO_2$
c $\mathbf{Cr_2O_3} + 2Al \rightarrow 2Cr + Al_2O_3$
d $\mathbf{Fe^{3+}} + 3e^- \rightarrow Fe$
e $\mathbf{Fe_2O_3} + 3CO \rightarrow 2Fe + 3CO_2$
f $\mathbf{2Br^-} \rightarrow Br_2 + 2e^-$

Q2 Using the equations above, decide which of the following substances are acting as oxidising agents and which reducing agents.

oxygen   aluminium   carbon monoxide

CORROSION OF METALS

One of the disadvantages of some metals in use is their tendency to **corrode**, and the costs of preventing them corroding. When a metal corrodes it reacts with oxygen and water in the air. Corrosion is an oxidation process in which electrons are lost.

Rusting

Corrosion of iron and steel is usually called **rusting**. This can be summarised by the equation

$$Fe \rightarrow Fe^{3+} + 3e^-$$

It has been estimated that rusting costs at least £2 000 000 000 in Great Britain each year. Because of this, millions of pounds have been spent finding ways of reducing it.

Rust is a flaky red-brown solid which is largely hydrated iron(III) oxide. Rusting takes place when both water and oxygen (or air) are present. An electrolyte speeds up rusting greatly, which may be dissolved carbon dioxide or salt. This is why cars rust more quickly near the sea or during the winter when roads are regularly salted.

▲ **Fig 56.1 Salt on the roads makes cars rust more quickly**

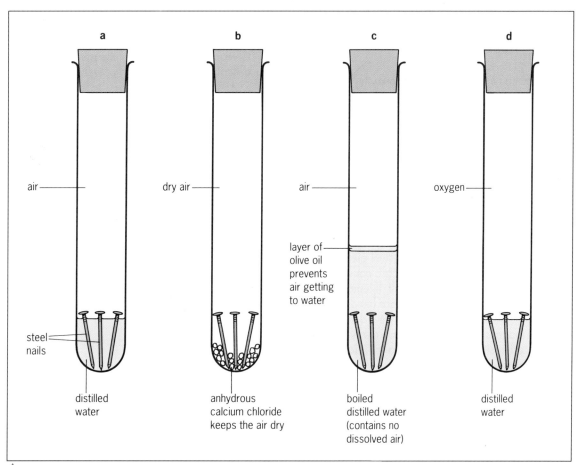

▲ **Fig 56.2 Investigating rusting**

Q3 Fig 56.2 shows apparatus set up to demonstrate the rusting of steel. In which tubes will rusting occur? Devise an experiment to show that carbon dioxide speeds up rusting.

Q4 Explain fully why a car exhaust system rusts more quickly than the body of the car.

The process of rusting

Rusting of iron involves various stages. There are two factors about the surface of the iron which help to start the process of rusting.

1 Impurities and mechanical strains cause imperfections in the iron. You may have noticed that rusting of nails takes place initially around the head and point, where the metal was strained during the manufacture.
2 A large amount of dissolved oxygen in contact with the surface will encourage rusting to start.

These factors cause some areas of the iron to become **anodic**. Here there is a lower oxygen content. Other areas become **cathodic**, where there is a higher oxygen concentration.

In an anodic area, iron atoms are oxidised by loss of electrons to a cathodic area. Iron(II) ions are formed which go into solution

$$Fe(s) \rightarrow Fe^{2+}(aq) + 2e^-$$

These ions are further oxidised by dissolved oxygen to form iron(III) ions

$$Fe^{2+}(aq) \rightarrow Fe^{3+}(aq) + e^-$$

In the cathodic areas, dissolved oxygen takes up the electrons coming in from the anodic areas. The oxygen is reduced in the presence of water to form hydroxide ions

$$\tfrac{1}{2}O_2(aq) + H_2O(l) + 2e^- \rightarrow 2OH^-(aq)$$

The iron(III) ions combine with the hydroxide ions to form iron(III) hydroxide, which then loses some of its water to the atmosphere

$$2Fe(OH)_3(s) \rightarrow Fe_2O_3.xH_2O(s) + (3-x)H_2O(l)$$

It can be seen, therefore, that both oxygen and water are required to produce the characteristic brown rust.

▶▶

SLOWING DOWN RUSTING

Coating

There are many ways of slowing down the rusting of iron and steel by preventing water and oxygen getting to the surface. These include **oiling or greasing, painting, coating with pitch** and **coating with plastic. Galvanising** involves coating the steel with a more reactive metal such as zinc, which reacts with the oxygen more readily than the steel and so protects the steel.

Sacrificial protection

Steel can be protected by being connected to a more reactive metal. For example, steel pier legs are very prone to rusting because they are constantly in contact with air, water and also salt. If lumps of magnesium metal (called anodes) are fixed onto the steel legs below the water line, the steel does not rust. The magnesium anodes corrode away but can be replaced easily. This is called **sacrificial protection**.

An alternative way of protecting pier legs, or a ship, involves using steel anodes connected to a d.c. generator. The pier legs are kept negative and the steel anodes positive. This prevents the pier rusting, while the anodes slowly rust away. The anodes could be scrap steel, or titanium coated with platinum, which do not corrode.

Pure iron and iron alloys

Very pure iron does not rust. The Delhi column in India, fig 56.3, is made of pure iron. It has shown no signs of rusting over many centuries.

Fig 56.3 The Delhi column (on the left) is made of pure iron and does not rust ▶

Steel can also be protected from rusting by mixing it with other metals to form **alloys** (see page 138).

Q5 Give examples of each of the methods described on this page in preventing rusting.

Q6 Why are pieces of household equipment often packed in cartons with a sachet of silica gel?

Q7 Most car bodies are attached to the negative terminal of the battery. Can you think of any advantages of doing this?

A rusting disaster

An American millionaire once asked a boatbuilder to produce the best yacht in the world. He was going to call it 'The Call of the Sea'. No money was to be spared. However, the boat never sailed because shortly after launching the body and bottom of the boat were found to have completely rusted.

▲ **Fig 56.4 The call of the sea**

The shipbuilders had decided to plate the bottom of the yacht with a nickel–copper alloy called German silver. It seemed a good idea because this alloy, though expensive, resists corrosion in sea water very well. However, because the alloy is not very strong, parts of the structure had to be made of steel. Rusting is an electrochemical process. In the same way as rusting is slowed down by contact with a more reactive metal, such as magnesium or zinc, it is speeded up by contact with a less reactive metal, such as copper.

NEUTRALISATION

When an alkali is added to an acid, the solution becomes less acidic. If exactly equivalent amounts of acid and alkali are mixed together a **neutral** solution is formed, that has neither acidic nor alkaline properties. This process is called **neutralisation**.

Sodium chloride (commonly called salt) is produced when sodium hydroxide (an alkali) neutralises hydrochloric acid.

sodium hydroxide + hydrochloric acid →
sodium chloride + water
$NaOH(aq) + HCl(aq) \rightarrow NaCl(aq) + H_2O(l)$

There are many everyday examples of neutralisation.

Indigestion remedies

Every adult can produce several hundred cubic centimetres of hydrochloric acid in the gastric juices in the stomach. This is used in the digestion of food (see page 14). Minor indigestion problems are caused by excess acid in the stomach. This can be corrected by taking antacids (alkalis) such as milk of magnesia (a suspension of magnesium hydroxide) or bicarbonate of soda (sodium hydrogencarbonate).

Setting of lime mortar

Lime mortar consists of a mixture of calcium hydroxide and water. The mortar hardens when it absorbs acidic gases such as carbon dioxide from the air. The calcium hydroxide is neutralised by the carbon dioxide and calcium carbonate is formed.

calcium hydroxide + carbon dioxide →
calcium carbonate + water
$Ca(OH)_2(aq) + CO_2(g) \rightarrow CaCO_3(s) + H_2O(l)$

Stings and bites

Insect bites and stings involve the injection of a small amount of acid or alkali into the skin. This causes irritation. Nettle stings, ant bites and bee stings involve the injection of an acid. The sting or bite should be treated with calamine lotion (a suspension of zinc carbonate) or bicarbonate of soda to neutralise the acidity and remove the irritation.

Acid rain

Many inland lakes in Scotland and Scandinavia are becoming increasingly acidic because of air pollution and acid rain (see page 93). Fish are dying and lakes are becoming totally lifeless. In an attempt to correct this, the land around the lakes is being treated with lime. When the lime is washed into the lakes it neutralises some of the acidity.

Liming the soil

Farmers have to control the pH of their soil. If the soil becomes too acidic, a good yield of crops cannot be obtained. Rain and artificial fertilisers tend to make the soil more acidic. The farmer can neutralise acidic soil by treating it with lime, fig 56.5.

▲ Fig 56.5 Lime is used to neutralise acidic soil

REVERSIBLE REACTIONS AND EQUILIBRIUM

In most reactions, the reactants are completely converted into products. However, in some reactions, as soon as some products start to form, a competing reaction takes place reforming the reactants.

For example, the manufacture of sulphuric acid by the Contact process involves the reaction of sulphur dioxide with oxygen to produce sulphur trioxide

$$2SO_2(g) + O_2(g) \rightleftharpoons 2SO_3(g)$$

The sign between the reactants and the products indicates the reaction is **reversible**.

Initially the reverse reaction is slow, but its speed increases as the concentration of the products (sulphur trioxide in this example) increases. Eventually a stage is reached where the rate of the forward reaction is the same as the rate of the reverse reaction. At this point both reactions are taking place but the concentrations of the reactants remain unchanged unless the reaction is disturbed in some way. This state is called **equilibrium**.

Equilibrium reactions in industry

In economic terms, it is important to realise that in this kind of situation it is not possible to convert 100% of the reactants into products. Conditions have to be devised to obtain the maximum conversion possible, within the limits of cost involved in the process. Examples of such reactions will be seen on pages 172–3.

57 RATES OF REACTION

By the end of this section you should be able to

- list the factors which affect the rate of a reaction
- give examples of experiments to show how altering these factors affects the rate of a reaction
- give everyday examples where rates of reaction are important.

FAST AND SLOW

A reaction which takes place quickly and is finished in a short time is called a **fast** reaction. It is said to have a high **rate of reaction**. An explosion (see page 149) is a very fast reaction which is often accompanied by an rapid expansion of gaseous products. It is difficult to study very fast reactions.

Other reactions are very **slow** (they have a low rate of reaction) and again it is very difficult to study slow reactions.

Various factors are important to the speed of a reaction. A reaction can be made to go faster by

1 increasing the surface area of a solid
2 increasing the concentration of reacting substances
3 increasing the temperature
4 using a catalyst.

We shall look at each of these in turn.

Answer these questions after carrying out the activity below.

Q1 Which of the reactions is faster? Sketch the graph you would expect if the same mass of *fine* powder had been used.

Q2 Copy and complete the following passage by inserting words from the list below.

  decreases   increases   remains unchanged

As the pieces of calcium carbonate get smaller, the surface area in contact with the acid _____. The time taken for the reaction to be completed _____ as the calcium carbonate is more finely divided. The rate of reaction, therefore, _____ as the surface area _____ .

INCREASING THE SURFACE AREA OF A SOLID

Activity

Equal masses of lumps of calcium carbonate and powdered calcium carbonate are reacted with separate samples of dilute hydrochloric acid.

calcium carbonate + hydrochloric acid →
  calcium chloride + water + carbon dioxide
$$CaCO_3(s) + 2HCl(aq) \rightarrow CaCl_2(aq) + H_2O(l) + CO_2(g)$$

The powdered calcium carbonate has a much larger surface area in contact with the acid than the lumps. All other factors are kept the same so that a comparison can be made.

1 Weigh accurately a lump of calcium carbonate with a mass between 0.35 g and 0.45 g. Weigh out the same amount of coarsely powdered calcium carbonate.
2 Set up the apparatus shown in fig 57.1. Check that the apparatus is airtight and that no gas can escape. Check that the syringe is showing zero.
3 Add 10 cm³ of dilute hydrochloric acid (2M) using a small measuring cylinder.
4 Drop in the lump of calcium carbonate, replace the bung and start timing.
5 Record the volume of gas collected in the syringe every 15 seconds. Continue for 5 minutes or until the reaction has stopped.

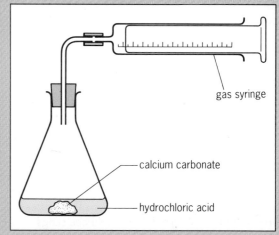

gas syringe

calcium carbonate

hydrochloric acid

▲ Fig 57.1 Following the progress of a reaction by measuring the gas given off

6 Wash out the flask thoroughly and shake it to remove as much surplus water as possible. Repeat the experiment with a fresh sample of dilute hydrochloric acid and the weighed sample of powdered calcium carbonate.
7 Record your results in a suitable table. Plot both your sets of results on the same axes and draw the two graphs. Label the graphs 'lump' and 'powder'.

The dangers of a large surface area

Small lumps of a chemical have a much larger surface area than a single lump of equal mass of the same chemical. Powders have a very large surface area.

Flour dust in a flour mill has to be carefully controlled. Mixtures of flour dust and air can explode.

Although lumps of coal do not react with oxygen in the air without heating, mixtures of coal dust and air can be explosive in coal mines. About 50 years ago 51 men were killed in such an explosion at Sneyd Colliery, Stoke-on-Trent. In a modern coal mine, careful control of ventilation ensures that dust and flammable gases do not build up underground.

Following a reaction by weighing

Fig 57.2 shows how the reaction of calcium carbonate and hydrochloric acid could be followed by weighing the flask and contents at regular intervals.

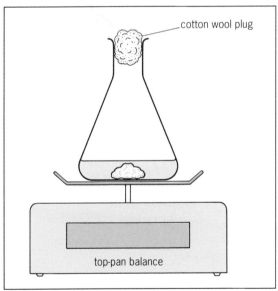
cotton wool plug

top-pan balance

▲ **Fig 57.2 Following the progress of a reaction by measuring mass**

Q3 Explain why the mass of flask and contents decreases during the reaction.

Q4 Why is the piece of cotton wool in the neck of the flask?

Q5 How would you know when the reaction had finished?

INCREASING THE CONCENTRATION OF REACTING SUBSTANCES

Activity

This experiment shows the effect of altering the concentration on the rate of the reaction between magnesium ribbon and dilute hydrochloric acid

magnesium + hydrochloric acid →
　　　　　　　　　　magnesium chloride + hydrogen
$Mg(s) + 2HCl(aq) → MgCl_2(aq) + H_2(g)$

In this experiment all possible variables will be kept unchanged except for the concentration of the acid.

1 Cut seven lengths of magnesium ribbon, each exactly 3 cm long. Each piece should then have the same mass. This is an alternative to weighing them.

2 For each experiment, use measuring cylinders to measure the volumes of 2M hydrochloric acid and water given in the table below into seven beakers. Stir the mixtures thoroughly.

3 Drop one piece of magnesium ribbon into each beaker and record the time taken for the magnesium to just disappear.

Copy and complete the table for your results.

Experiment	Volume of hydrochloric acid (cm³)	Volume of water (cm³)	Time (s)
1	50	0	
2	40	10	
3	35	15	
4	30	20	
5	25	25	
6	20	30	
7	15	35	

Plot a graph of the time taken in seconds (on the vertical axis) against the volume of acid used (on the horizontal axis).

Q6 What is the total volume of the solution used in each experiment?

Q7 In which experiment does the solution in the beaker contain the lowest concentration of hydrochloric acid?

Copy and complete the following passage by inserting words from the list below.

　decreases　increases　remains unchanged

As the concentration of hydrochloric acid in the beaker increases, the time taken for the magnesium to disappear _____

The rate of reaction _____ as the acid becomes more concentrated.

Concentration and pressure

Often, as in the experiment on page 155, doubling the concentration of one of the reacting substances will double the rate of reaction (that is, halve the time taken for the reaction).

In reactions involving gases, the concentration can be increased by increasing the pressure.

INCREASING THE TEMPERATURE

Activity

This experiment examines the effect of temperature on the rate of reaction between sodium thiosulphate solution and hydrochloric acid.
The equation for the reaction is

sodium thiosulphate + hydrochloric acid → sodium chloride + water + sulphur dioxide + sulphur

$$Na_2S_2O_3(aq) + 2HCl(aq) \rightarrow 2NaCl(aq) + H_2O(l) + SO_2(g) + S(s)$$

When colourless solutions of sodium thiosulphate and hydrochloric acid are mixed together, the solution is colourless. However, the solution starts to go cloudy as sulphur is produced. If you look at a cross on a piece of paper under the flask through the solution, eventually the cross disappears from view. The time is taken from the mixing of the solutions to the point at which the cross disappears.

1 Make a small cross in the centre of a piece of white paper.
2 Add $10\,cm^3$ of sodium thiosulphate to a conical flask and put a thermometer into the solution.
3 Heat the flask until the solution is just above 25°C.
4 Add $5\,cm^3$ of dilute hydrochloric acid to the flask, start the clock and note the temperature of the solution.
5 Swirl the flask above the cross and note the time taken until the cross just disappears.
6 Repeat the experiment four times at different temperatures between 25°C and 60°C.

Draw and complete a table for your results.

 What can you conclude from your results?

Time and rate

What is actually measured in this experiment is the time taken for the concentration of sulphur to develop enough to mask the cross. Since the rate of reaction can be expressed as

$$rate = \frac{concentration\ of\ product\ formed}{time\ taken}$$

the rate of reaction is proportional to the **reciprocal** of the time taken for the cross to disappear, that is, rate $\propto 1/t$.

The practical effects of heating

The rate of reaction increases with increase in temperature. As an approximate 'rule of thumb', a 10°C temperature rise approximately doubles the rate of reaction. This is often an understatement of the effect, depending on the reaction.

The rate of souring of milk or spoiling of food is reduced by cooling. A refrigerator or deep freezer cools the food down and the chemical reactions which lead to spoiling are greatly slowed down. Many of these reactions are oxidation reactions. However, although freezing food slows down the decaying process, it may also alter the texture of food.

 Explain why rusting occurs rapidly in tropical countries such as the Gambia, West Africa, where no salt is used on the roads.

USING A CATALYST

A **catalyst** is a substance which alters the rate of a chemical reaction without being used up. A catalyst is usually used to speed up reactions.

A common example of a reaction speeded up by using a catalyst is

hydrogen peroxide → water + oxygen

$$2H_2O_2(aq) \rightarrow 2H_2O(l) + O_2(g)$$

The catalyst in this case is manganese(IV) oxide.

Catalysts in industry

Examples of industrial catalysts include vanadium(V) oxide in the Contact process to produce sulphuric acid

sulphur dioxide + oxygen ⇌ sulphur trioxide

$$2SO_2(g) + O_2(g) \rightleftharpoons 2SO_3(g)$$

The Haber process (page 172) also uses an industrial catalyst.

Slowing a reaction down

Sometimes a catalyst is used to slow down a reaction. For example, additives are added to food to prevent it going bad. Fruit squashes may contain sulphur dioxide to slow down oxidation processes.

Some chemicals have substances added to slow down a reaction so that they can be transported and stored safely. These substances are called **inhibitors**. Hydrogen peroxide, for example, has phosphoric acid added as an inhibitor to slow down its decomposition.

Activity

This experiment investigates the effect of a catalyst on the decomposition of hydrogen peroxide.
1 Set up the apparatus in fig 57.3 and add 25 cm³ of hydrogen peroxide to the flask.
2 Note the volume of gas collected in the syringe over a period of 5 minutes.
3 Repeat the experiment with a fresh sample of hydrogen peroxide and add one spatula measure of manganese(IV) oxide to the flask. Push the bung tightly into the flask and note the volume of gas collected every 15 seconds.

Draw and complete a table of your results.

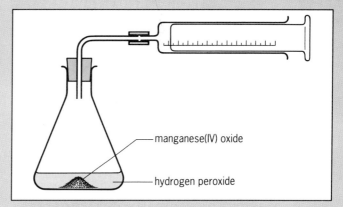

manganese(IV) oxide

hydrogen peroxide

Fig 57.3 The catalytic decomposition of hydrogen peroxide

 Q10 What can you conclude about the effect of manganese(IV) oxide on the reaction?

Q11 What would you need to do to check that manganese(IV) oxide is a catalyst for the reaction? (Hint: Look back to the definition of a catalyst.)

Enzymes

Many chemical reactions taking place in living things are controlled by biological catalysts called **enzymes**. Enzymes are special protein molecules. They have certain specific properties.
1 A particular enzyme will only catalyse certain reactions, not all reactions.
2 Enzymes only work over a limited range of temperature, for example enzymes which operate in the human body will work at temperatures around normal body temperature (37 °C).
3 They will only work within a limited range of temperature.

Examples of enzymes include amylase in saliva, which breaks down large starch molecules into smaller glucose molecules (see page 14). Enzymes in biological washing powders help remove stains in cool water, and enzymes in yeast convert sugar into ethanol during fermentation.

EXPLAINING THE CHANGES IN RATE OF REACTION

In general, reactions take place when particles of reacting substances (the reactants) collide with one another. Not every collision leads to a reaction. There needs to be a certain amount of energy in the colliding particles if the reaction is to take place. This amount of energy is called the **activation energy**.

1 Small particles of solid have a large surface area and so more collisions with an aqueous reactant are possible. Since there are more collisions, there will be more which have enough energy for reaction to take place, as fig 57.4 shows.
2 Increasing the concentration of a reactant increases the likelihood of collisions. Increasing the pressure of a gas has the same effect.
3 Increasing the temperature increases the kinetic energy of the particles. This increases the number of collisions per second and also the average energy of such collisions.
4 A catalyst can act by increasing the concentration of reactants near a surface, or by lowering the activation energy of a reaction.

Increased frequency of collisions, increased energy of collisions and lowering of activation energy will all have the effect of increasing the rate of reaction.

Fig 57.5 summarises the energy changes during a typical catalysed and uncatalysed reaction.

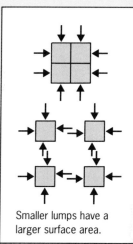

Smaller lumps have a larger surface area.

▲ **Fig 57.4 Surface area and the collision theory**

◀ **Fig 57.5 Energy level diagram for a catalysed and uncatalysed reaction**

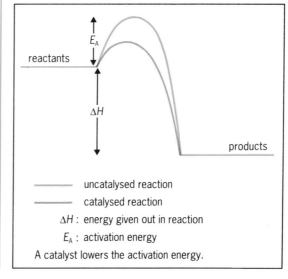

reactants

E_A

ΔH

products

—— uncatalysed reaction
—— catalysed reaction
ΔH : energy given out in reaction
E_A : activation energy

A catalyst lowers the activation energy.

58 CHEMICAL EQUATIONS

By the end of this section you should be able to
- write the formulae of simple compounds using a list of ions
- write word and symbolic equations.

WORDS AND SYMBOLS

A **chemical equation** is a summary of a chemical reaction. Word equations are often seen, for example

magnesium + sulphuric acid $\rightarrow$ magnesium sulphate + hydrogen

Symbolic equations are more useful and can be recognised by scientists throughout the world, no matter what language they speak. Symbolic equations also enable you to work out the quantities of the reacting substances and products and, with a little common sense, to predict reactions. An example of a symbolic equation is

$$Mg + H_2SO_4 \rightarrow MgSO_4 + H_2$$

WORKING OUT THE FORMULA OF A COMPOUND

From electrolysis calculations (page 165) it is possible to work out the charges on common ions. The table shows the formulae of some common ions.

Cations (positively charged)		Anions (negatively charged)	
sodium	Na^+	chloride	Cl^-
potassium	K^+	bromide	Br^-
ammonium	NH_4^+	iodide	I^-
silver	Ag^+	hydroxide	OH^-
copper	Cu^{2+}	nitrate	NO_3^-
lead	Pb^{2+}	hydrogencarbonate	HCO_3^-
magnesium	Mg^{2+}	sulphate	SO_4^{2-}
calcium	Ca^{2+}	carbonate	CO_3^{2-}
zinc	Zn^{2+}	oxide	O^{2-}
barium	Ba^{2+}	sulphide	S^{2-}
iron(II)	Fe^{2+}	phosphate	PO_4^{3-}
iron(III)	Fe^{3+}		
aluminium	Al^{3+}		

From these ions it is possible to work out the correct formula of a range of common compounds. For example, magnesium sulphate is composed of Mg^{2+} and SO_4^{2-} ions. The sum of the positive charges and negative charges is zero. The formula of magnesium sulphate is written as $MgSO_4$.

Sodium oxide contains Na^+ and O^{2-} ions. In order for the sum of positive and negative charges to equal zero, there must be twice the number of sodium ions as oxygen ions. The formula is written as Na_2O.

Other examples include

aluminium oxide	$Al^{3+}\ O^{2-}$	Al_2O_3
calcium hydroxide	$Ca^{2+}\ OH^-$	$Ca(OH)_2$
iron(III) chloride	$Fe^{3+}\ Cl^-$	$FeCl_3$

Q1 Write the correct formulae for the following compounds.

- **a** potassium chloride
- **b** potassium sulphate
- **c** potassium hydroxide
- **d** zinc oxide
- **e** zinc nitrate
- **f** zinc carbonate
- **g** zinc hydroxide
- **h** aluminium hydroxide
- **i** aluminium chloride
- **j** aluminium phosphate
- **k** sodium phosphate
- **l** calcium phosphate
- **m** ammonium chloride
- **n** ammonium sulphate
- **o** sodium carbonate
- **p** sodium hydrogencarbonate
- **q** calcium hydrogencarbonate
- **r** hydrochloric acid
- **s** sulphuric acid
- **t** nitric acid

(Note: All acids contain H^+ ions.)

Non-ionic compounds

Some compounds are not composed of ions and it easier at this stage to learn their formulae rather than trying to use rules to work them out.

H_2O water	CO_2 carbon dioxide
NH_3 ammonia	HCl hydrogen chloride
NO_2 nitrogen dioxide	SO_2 sulphur dioxide

Common gases, for example oxygen, hydrogen, nitrogen and chlorine, are composed of molecules of two atoms. They are written in symbols as O_2, H_2, N_2 and Cl_2.

State symbols

In chemical equations, letters are used in brackets after the formulae to show the state of the substance.

(s)	solid
(l)	liquid
(g)	gas
(aq)	in solution in water

CALCULATING THE FORMULA OF A COMPOUND BY EXPERIMENT

It is possible to work out the formula of a compound from the results of an experiment involving a series of weighings.

To find the formula of magnesium oxide, a weighed amount of magnesium ribbon is burnt in a crucible (fig 58.1). The lid is lifted from time to time to let air in. The escape of smoke should be avoided. Some sample results are given here.

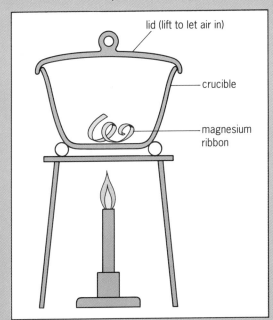

Fig 58.1 **Burning magnesium in a crucible**

a	mass of crucible and lid	25.15 g
b	mass of crucible, lid and magnesium	25.27 g
c	mass of magnesium (**b** − **a**)	0.12 g
d	mass of crucible, lid and magnesium oxide	25.35 g
e	mass of magnesium oxide (**d** − **a**)	0.20 g

From these results, 0.12 g of magnesium combines with (0.20−0.12) g of oxygen to form 0.20 g of magnesium oxide.

0.12 g of magnesium combines with 0.08 g of oxygen
24 g of magnesium would combine with 16 g of oxygen
1 mole of magnesium combines with 1 mole of oxygen (this is explained in the next section)
the formula of magnesium oxide is **MgO**

Q2 Copper forms two oxides. In one oxide, **A**, 0.80 g of copper oxide contain 0.64 g of copper. In the other oxide, **B**, 1.28 g of copper combine with 0.16 g of oxygen.

a Calculate the formulae of **A** and **B**. You will need to look up the relative atomic masses of copper and oxygen.

b How would you carry out the experiment to find these results?

THE STEPS IN WRITING A CHEMICAL EQUATION

1 Write the corresponding word equation. For example,

calcium carbonate + → calcium chloride + hydrochloric acid   water + carbon dioxide

2 Fill in the correct formulae.

$CaCO_3 + HCl \rightarrow CaCl_2 + H_2O + CO_2$

3 Balance the equation. In any chemical reaction no atoms can be created or destroyed. There must be the same number of atoms of each element before and after the reaction. This 'accounting' cannot be done by altering any formulae. Only the proportions of the reacting substances and products can be changed. Thus

$CaCO_3 + 2HCl \rightarrow CaCl_2 + H_2O + CO_2$

Finally, state symbols can be added if required.

$CaCO_3(s) + 2HCl(aq) \rightarrow CaCl_2(aq) + H_2O(l) + CO_2(g)$

Q3 Copy and complete the following word equations.

a magnesium + oxygen →
b copper(II) oxide + sulphuric acid →
c sodium hydroxide + hydrochloric acid →
d potassium carbonate + nitric acid →
e calcium hydroxide + carbon dioxide →

Q4 Some of the following symbolic equations are incorrect. Write out these symbolic equations, correcting any mistakes.

a $Al(s) + HCl(aq) \rightarrow AlCl_3(aq) + H(g)$
b $Mg(s) + 3CO_2(g) \rightarrow MgO_2(s) + C(s)$
c $Al(s) + O(g) \rightarrow Al_2O_3(s)$
d $NH_3(g) + CuO(s) \rightarrow N(g) + H_2O(l) + Cu(s)$
e $2Na(s) + O(g) \rightarrow Na_2O(s)$
f $CH_4(g) + O_2(g) \rightarrow CO_2(g) + H_2O(l)$
g $CH_4(g) + O_2(g) \rightarrow CO(g) + H_2O(l)$
h $NH_3(g) + O_2(g) \rightarrow NO(g) + H_2O(l)$

59 CALCULATIONS FROM EQUATIONS

By the end of this section you should be able to

- understand that, although atoms cannot be weighed individually, the masses of atoms can be compared
- understand the terms 'relative atomic mass' and 'the mole'
- carry out simple mole calculations
- carry out simple calculations using equations.

The following relative atomic masses may be needed throughout this section.

H = 1	C = 12	N = 14
O = 16	Na = 23	Mg = 24
Al = 27	P = 31	S = 32
Cl = 35.5	K = 39	Ca = 40
Fe = 56	Cu = 64	Br = 80
Ag = 108	Sn = 118	
Hg = 200	Pb = 207	

RELATIVE ATOMIC MASS

The atoms that make up all substances are very small and cannot be weighed individually. A hydrogen atom is the lightest atom. The **relative atomic mass** of an atom is the number of times heavier an atom of the element is than an atom of hydrogen. For example, Na = 23 (sometimes written as $A_r(Na) = 23$) tells us that a sodium atom is 23 times heavier than a hydrogen atom.

Q1 Copy and complete the following:

A copper atom is _____ times heavier than an oxygen atom and _____ as heavy as a sulphur atom. Five _____ atoms will have the same mass as one mercury (Hg) atom.

Ratios and numbers of atoms

One atom of carbon weighs 12 times as much as a hydrogen atom.
Two atoms of carbon weigh 12 times as much as two atoms of hydrogen.
1000 atoms of carbon weigh 12 times as much as 1000 atoms of hydrogen.
x atoms of carbon weigh 12 times as much as x atoms of hydrogen.
Carbon atoms always weigh 12 times as much as the same number of hydrogen atoms.

Relative atomic mass and the carbon-12 atom

Nowadays, in order to find relative atomic masses very accurately, one-twelfth of the mass of the carbon-12 atom is taken as a standard, rather than the hydrogen atom.

AVOGADRO'S NUMBER AND THE MOLE

Avogadro's number

We often use names to represent certain numbers. For example, a dozen is the name for 12, a score

for 20 and a gross for 144. Scientists use the name **Avogadro's number** to represent 600 000 000 000 000 000 000 000 or 6×10^{23}. The mass of 6×10^{23} hydrogen atoms is 1 g (that is, the same as the relative atomic mass but with units of grams).

Q2 What is the mass of

1 mole of carbon atoms
1 mole of hydrogen molecules (H_2)?

If we weigh out 6×10^{23} atoms of any element it will weigh the same as the relative atomic mass of the element in grams.

Avogadro's number is named after the famous Italian chemist Avogadro. It is a very large number. If the whole population of the world wished to count up to this number between them, and they worked at counting without any breaks at all, it would take six million years for them to finish counting.

The mole

The **mole** is defined as the amount of substance which contains as many elementary units as there are in 1 g of hydrogen (that is, 6×10^{23}). In this definition elementary units can be

- atoms, for example C, Ne
- molecules, for example CH_4, H_2O
- ions, for example Cu^{2+}, Ag^+
- specified formula units, for example NaCl, $CaCO_3$.

Here are some sample calculations to show how the mole is used.

1 mole of calcium atoms (Ca) has a mass of 40 g
1 mole of chlorine molecules (Cl_2) has a mass of 71 g
1 mole of chloride ions (Cl^-) has a mass of 35.5 g
1 mole of sodium chloride (NaCl) has a mass of (23 + 35.5 g), that is 58.5 g

Q3 Choose answers from the list below to answer the following questions.

4g 8g 12g 16g 20g 24g

What is the mass of

a 1 mole of oxygen atoms (O)
b 0.5 moles of calcium atoms (Ca)
c 1 mole of magnesium ions (Mg^{2+})
d 0.5 moles of magnesium oxide (MgO)
e 0.2 moles of calcium carbonate ($CaCO_3$)
f 0.25 moles of methane (CH_4)
g 0.1 moles of bromine molecules (Br_2)
h 0.25 moles of sulphur dioxide (SO_2)?

CALCULATIONS FROM SYMBOLIC EQUATIONS

Before attempting these calculations you need a balanced symbolic equation.

$$CaCO_3 + 2HCl \rightarrow CaCl_2 + H_2O + CO_2$$

Using relative atomic masses we can work out that
$$40 + 12 + (3 \times 16)g = 100\,g$$
of calcium carbonate react with
$$2 \times (1 + 35.5)g = 73\,g$$
of hydrochloric acid to produce
$$40 + (2 \times 35.5)g = 111\,g$$
of calcium chloride,
$$(2 \times 1) + 16\,g = 18\,g$$
of water and
$$12 + (2 \times 16)g = 44\,g$$
of carbon dioxide.

Note that the sum of the masses of the reacting substances (calcium carbonate and hydrochloric acid) equals the sum of the masses of the products (calcium chloride, water and carbon dioxide).

Example

Calculate the masses of calcium chloride and carbon dioxide formed when 10 g of calcium carbonate react with excess hydrochloric acid.

From the information above,

100 g of calcium carbonate produce 111 g of calcium chloride

1 g of calcium carbonate produces 111/100 g of calcium chloride

10 g of calcium carbonate produce 10 × 111/100 g = 11.1 g of calcium chloride

100 g of calcium carbonate produce 44 g of carbon dioxide

1 g of calcium carbonate produces 44/100 g of carbon dioxide

10 g of calcium carbonate produces 10 × 44/100 g of carbon dioxide

Magnesium and sulphuric acid

The following symbolic equation summarises the reaction between magnesium and sulphuric acid.

$$Mg(s) + H_2SO_4(aq) \rightarrow MgSO_4(aq) + H_2(g)$$

Q4 Copy and complete the following.

One mole of magnesium atoms react with _____ mole(s) of sulphuric acid to produce _____ mole(s) of magnesium sulphate and _____ mole(s) of hydrogen molecules.

24 g of magnesium react with _____ g of sulphuric acid to produce _____ g of magnesium sulphate and _____ g of hydrogen.

Q5 Calculate the mass of magnesium sulphate formed when 0.48 g of magnesium reacts with excess acid.

Q6 Calculate the mass of hydrogen formed when 0.48 g of magnesium reacts with excess acid.

Q7 One mole of molecules of any gas occupies $24\,000\,cm^3$ at room temperature. Calculate the *volume* of hydrogen produced when 0.48 g of hydrogen reacts with excess acid.

Copper(II) oxide and hydrochloric acid

The symbolic equation for the reaction of copper(II) oxide with dilute hydrochloric acid is

$$CuO(s) + 2HCl(aq) \rightarrow CuCl_2(aq) + H_2O(l)$$

Q8 Calculate the mass of copper(II) chloride formed from 4.0 g of copper(II) oxide.

Q9 Calculate the volume of hydrochloric acid (concentration $2\,mol/dm^3$) which reacts exactly with 4.0 g of copper(II) oxide.

Q10 A sample of impure copper ore (mass 1.00 g) contains copper(II) oxide. 0.64 g of copper was produced by reduction. Calculate the percentage of copper(II) oxide in the ore.

Calculations from equations are frequently used by a person in the chemical industry to work out the quantities of materials which react and the quantities of products which can be formed.

Q11 Suggest reasons why this information about masses of reactants and products is important.

Q12 Quicklime, CaO, can be produced by heating limestone, $CaCO_3$, to a high temperature.

a Write a symbolic equation for this reaction.
b Calculate the mass of 1 mole of calcium carbonate and the mass of 1 mole of calcium oxide.
c Calculate the mass of calcium carbonate which would produce 1 tonne of calcium oxide.

60 ELECTROLYSIS

By the end of this section you should be able to

- understand that certain substances called electrolytes may be split up by electricity when molten or dissolved in water during the process called electrolysis
- explain the processes of the moving of ions and discharging of ions which take place during electrolysis
- write ionic equations for reactions taking place when simple positive and negative ions are discharged
- predict the products discharged at the anode and cathode during the electrolysis of molten and simple aqueous solutions.

WHAT IS ELECTROLYSIS?

Substances which cannot be decomposed by heating may be decomposed with electricity. This process is called **electrolysis**. The substance being decomposed, called the **electrolyte**, must be molten or in solution.

Molten lead(II) bromide can be decomposed into lead and bromine by electrolysis using the apparatus in fig 60.1.

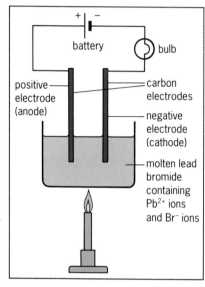

Fig 60.1 ▶ Electrolysis of molten lead(II) bromide

lead(II) bromide → lead + bromine

The metal (lead) is produced at the **cathode** (negative electrode) and the non-metal (bromine) is produced at the **anode** (positive electrode).

The equations for the reactions taking place are

cathode $Pb^{2+} + 2e^- \rightarrow Pb$
anode $2Br^- \rightarrow Br_2 + 2e^-$

Movement and discharge of ions

The electrolysis of lead(II) bromide can be explained in terms of movement and discharge of ions. In solid lead(II) bromide the ions are unable to move. When lead(II) bromide is melted (or dissolved in water) the structure breaks down and the ions are free to move or **migrate**. The ions move towards the electrode of opposite charge to the charge they carry.

The positively charged lead ions move to the cathode (the negative electrode) and the negatively charged bromide ions move to the anode (the positive electrode).

At the electrodes, electrons are transferred and **discharging** takes place. This is summarised in fig 60.2.

Q1 Explain the changes at the electrodes in the electrolysis of lead(II) bromide in terms of oxidation and reduction (see page 150).

Q2 A student carrying out the electrolysis of molten lead(II) bromide found that after a while the bulb started to glow more brightly. She left the apparatus to cool down with the electricity flowing. When the lead(II) bromide had solidified the bulb was still glowing brightly. Can you explain this?

Q3 Predict the products at the anode and cathode if molten sodium chloride, NaCl, is electrolysed.

ELECTROLYSIS OF AQUEOUS SOLUTIONS

When an aqueous solution is electrolysed, in addition to the ions from the dissolved compound there are also ions present from the water, namely H^+ and OH^- ions. There is now a choice of which ion can be discharged at each electrode.

The following rules about the formation products are useful

1 Metals or hydrogen are usually produced at the cathode. This is because they are formed by the discharge of positive ions (cations).
2 Hydrogen is discharged rather than a reactive metal, such as sodium or magnesium.
3 Hydroxide ions are usually discharged at the anode, producing oxygen

$$4OH^- \rightarrow 2H_2O + O_2$$

4 Other common products at the anode include the halogens (see page 122).

Q4 Find out what you can about the following industrial applications of electrolysis
  a electroplating
  b anodising.

Fig 60.2 Discharge of ions at the electrodes

▼

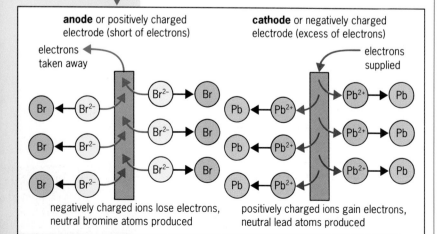

anode or positively charged electrode (short of electrons)

electrons taken away

negatively charged ions lose electrons, neutral bromine atoms produced

cathode or negatively charged electrode (excess of electrons)

electrons supplied

positively charged ions gain electrons, neutral lead atoms produced

Activity

In this experiment the effect of electricity on solid potassium iodide, molten potassium iodide and an aqueous solution of potassium iodide will be investigated.

1 Solid potassium iodide

Set up the apparatus as in fig 60.3. Check the circuit by joining points Y and Z with a piece of wire to check that the bulb lights up. Then remove the piece of wire.

Put 3 cm depth of potassium iodide crystals into the boiling tube. Wet a small strip of filter paper with starch solution and stick it to the inside of the boiling tube, near the mouth. Make a table to record whether the bulb lights and any change of colour in the filter paper.

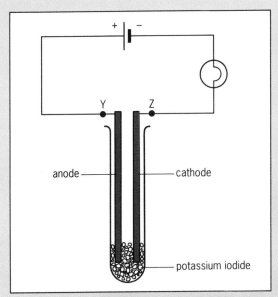

Fig 60.3 Electrolysis of potassium iodide

2 Molten potassium iodide

Heat the boiling tube strongly until the potassium iodide has melted. Record in your table whether the bulb lights and any change of colour of the filter paper soaked in starch solution.

Remove the Bunsen burner and leave the apparatus to cool.

3 Potassium iodide solution

Set up the electrolysis cell as in fig 60.4. Fill the cell with potassium iodide solution and place test tubes filled with potassium iodide solution over the electrodes.

If no bubbles form at the electrodes, check the connections on the circuit. If the solution starts to change colour, note where the colour change starts. Identify any gas produced and at which electrode it is produced.

Repeat the electrolysis of potassium iodide solution using a few drops of starch solution in the potassium iodide solution, and again using a few drops of universal indicator in the potassium iodide solution. Note any colour changes which take place around the electrodes.

Record your observations in your table.

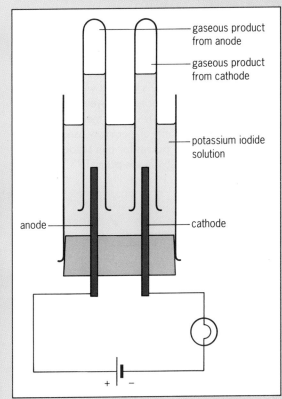

Fig 60.4 Electrolysis of potassium iodide solution

Q5 Which ions are present in molten potassium iodide?

Q6 During the electrolysis of molten potassium iodide, which ion is discharged at **a** the positive electrode **b** the negative electrode?

Q7 What are the products at the electrodes during the electrolysis of molten potassium iodide?

Q8 Which ions are present in an aqueous solution of potassium iodide?

Q9 During the electrolysis of potassium iodide solution, which ion is discharged at **a** the positive electrode **b** the negative electrode?

Q10 What are the products at the electrodes during the electrolysis of an aqueous solution of potassium iodide?

61 ELECTROLYSIS CALCULATIONS

By the end of this section you should be able to

- understand that the mass of a product is directly proportional to the quantity of electricity used
- understand that 1 mole of electrons passes when 96 500 coulombs of electricity have passed
- understand that the quantity of electricity required to deposit 1 mole of atoms depends upon the charge on the ion being discharged
- calculate the mass of product deposited by a given quantity of electricity
- work out the charge on an ion by calculation.

QUANTITY OF ELECTRICITY

Finding the mass of copper discharged

The mass of copper deposited on the cathode during the electrolysis of aqueous copper(II) sulphate solution can be found using the apparatus in fig 61.1. The reaction taking place at the cathode is

$$Cu^{2+}(aq) + 2e^- \rightarrow Cu(s)$$

The variable resistance or rheostat is used to adjust the current flowing in the circuit so that it remains constant throughout the experiment. The current flowing is measured on the ammeter, in the units amps (A).

The copper cathode is cleaned thoroughly before the experiment to ensure the deposited copper sticks to the surface, and is then weighed. At the end of each experiment the cathode is washed with distilled water, dried and weighed again. The quantity of electricity used is measured in coulombs. The quantity of electricity used when a current of one amp passes for one second is called **one coulomb**. ($Q = It$, see page 193.)

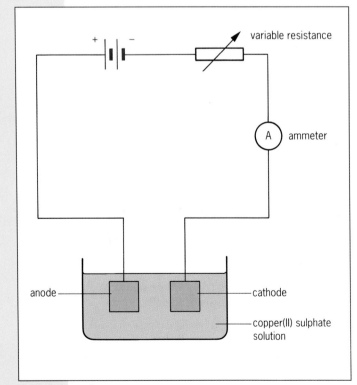

▲ **Fig 61.1 Quantitative electrolysis of copper(II) sulphate solution**

Q1 Calculate the quantity of electricity when

a 1A passes for 1 minute
b 2.5A passes for 1.5 hours
c 0.2A passes for 3 hours.

The experiment was carried out four times. The results are shown in the table.

Experiment	Current (A)	Time (s)	Mass of copper deposited
1	1	3000	1.0
2	2	3000	2.0
3	2	1500	1.0
4	1	1500	0.5

You will notice that the mass of the copper deposited depends upon the current and the time for which the current passes. In experiments 1 and 3, 3000 coulombs have passed. In experiment 2, 6000 coulombs have passed and twice the mass of copper is deposited. In experiment 4, 1500 coulombs have passed and only half the mass of copper is deposited.

The mass of product deposited is directly proportional to the quantity of electricity passed.

Q2 Calculate the mass of copper that would be deposited in other experiments where a current of

a 3A is passed for 1000 s
b 4A is passed for 750 s
c 0.5A is passed for 750 s.

Q3 From the results in the table, calculate the number of coulombs of electricity which would be required to deposit one mole of copper atoms (that is, 64g of copper).

THE QUANTITY OF ELECTRICITY REQUIRED TO DEPOSIT ONE MOLE OF ATOMS

The following table shows the quantity of electricity needed to produce one mole of atoms of different elements in different electrolysis experiments.

Ion being discharged	Product	Number of coulombs to deposit one mole of atoms
Na^+	Na	96 500
Ag^+	Ag	96 500
Cl^-	$\frac{1}{2}Cl_2$	96 500
Ca^{2+}	Ca	193 000
O^{2-}	$\frac{1}{2}O_2$	193 000
Al^{3+}	Al	289 500

If the ions being discharged at the cathode or anode have a single positive or negative charge, 96 500 coulombs are required per mole. If the ions have a double charge, twice the number of coulombs are required (that is, 193 000). If the ions have a triple charge, three times the number of coulombs are required (that is, 289 500).

Calculating the charge on an ion

When 96 500 coulombs of electricity have passed, one mole of electrons have passed through the wire. We can use this fact to calculate the charge on an ion – if it takes one mole of electrons to discharge one mole of ions, the charge on the ion must be +1, and so on.

Q4 A current of 1 A passed through a cell depositing nickel metal for 32 minutes. 0.59 g of nickel (A_r = 59) was deposited. Calculate the charge on the nickel ion.

Q5 A current was passed for some time through the circuit shown in fig 61.2. If 0.540 g of silver was deposited on the cathode of cell 1 and 0.130 g of chromium at the cathode of cell 3, calculate

  a the mass of copper deposited in cell 2
  b the charge on the chromium ion in cell 3.

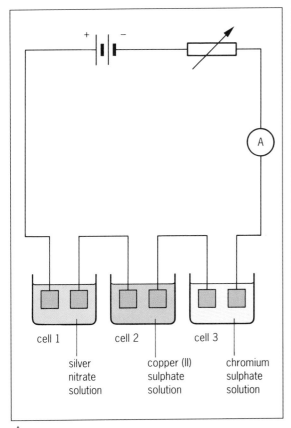
▲ **Fig 61.2**

Q6 A current of 5.0 A was passed for 10 minutes through a solution of a chromium compound. If 0.539 g of chromium was deposited, calculate the charge on the chromium ion.

Q7 The following results were obtained during the electrolysis of 500 cm³ of aqueous copper(II) sulphate using carbon electrodes.

Total mass of copper deposited on the cathode (g)	Number of coulombs passed
0.33	1000
1.00	3000
1.65	5000
2.30	7000
3.00	9000
3.00	11 000
3.00	13 000

  a Plot the total mass of copper deposited against the number of coulombs passed.
  b Explain the shape of your graph.
  c Calculate the concentration, in mol/dm³, of the original aqueous copper(II) sulphate.

MICHAEL FARADAY

Michael Faraday was born in London in 1791. His father was a blacksmith and Michael had little formal education. At the age of 13 he began working for a bookbinder. At first he only delivered messages. Later he learned how to bind books. From this came an interest in books and the information they contained.

One day a customer arranged for him to attend some scientific lectures at the Royal Institution. Michael was so influenced by the experience that he wrote to the Director of the Institution, Sir Humphrey Davy, and asked him for a job. Humphrey Davy, probably the most famous scientist of his day, was impressed with the sketches and notes that Michael had sent, and took him on. Michael, however, had to start at the bottom as 'bottle washer'. Through his efforts he worked his way up until finally he became the Director of the Royal Institution.

During his working life Michael Faraday laid the foundations for our understanding of electricity, including electrolysis. In 1821 he produced a simple electric motor and in 1831 a crude but effective dynamo, and also a transformer.

62 USEFUL MATERIALS FROM PETROLEUM

By the end of this section you should be able to

- describe how petroleum is refined by fractional distillation
- appreciate that the availability of different fractions from petroleum does not match demand
- understand the process of cracking and know that the products of cracking can be used to produce polymers.

PETROLEUM

Petroleum (sometimes called **crude oil**) is a raw material found in the Earth. It is a complicated mixture of **hydrocarbons**. Hydrocarbons are compounds containing only carbon and hydrogen.

History of the use of petroleum

Petroleum comes from the ground as a black treacle-like liquid. It has been known in this form for thousands of years.

It was called 'pitch' and used by the builders of ancient Babylon to make mortar to stick bricks together. Sir Walter Raleigh used pitch to make wooden ships watertight. Over 100 years ago, farmers in Texas used to burn the petroleum escaping from the earth because they did not know what to do with it.

REFINING PETROLEUM

When petroleum could be **refined** (the mixture split into different groups of hydrocarbons) it became valuable as a fuel and as a source of chemicals. Refining involves fractional distillation (see page 117).

Fig 62.1 ▶ Laboratory apparatus for the fractional distillation of petroleum

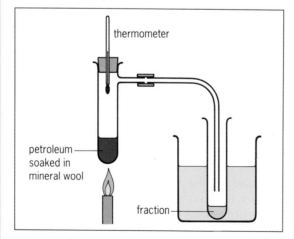

Fig 62.1 shows the apparatus which could be used to refine a small sample of petroleum in the laboratory. The test tube containing petroleum is slowly heated. Different fractions are collected over different temperature ranges. This process is a batch process – one batch of petroleum is refined, then another, etc. If repeated on a large scale in industry this would be slow and uneconomic. The industrial process used is continuous – petroleum is constantly fed into the plant.

Properties of the fractions of petroleum

The table summarises the properties of the different fractions obtained by fractional distillation of petroleum.

Fraction	Range of boiling point	Colour	Flamm-ability	Viscosity (ease of pouring)
first second third fourth	up to 70°C 70–120°C 120–170°C 170–222°C	increasing yellow colour ↓	decreasing flammability ↓	increasing viscosity ↓

Q1 How do the following properties change as the boiling point of the fractions increases?

a colour
b flammability
c viscosity

Refining petroleum on an industrial scale

Fig 62.2 shows the column used in industry for the fractional distillation of petroleum. All the petroleum is turned to a vapour before entering the column. As the vapour passes up the column the vapour cools. The lower the boiling point of the hydrocarbon, the further up the column the vapour reaches before it condenses. Low boiling point fractions, sometimes called light fractions, are therefore, piped off at the top of the column. These light fractions contain much smaller molecules than the other fractions. Bitumen contains extremely large, long-chain molecules. You will notice alongside the column the different uses of each fraction.

Supply and demand

The table below gives information about the composition of petroleum, and the demand for each fraction.

Fraction	Percentage of fraction obtained from refining	Approximate percentage demand
petroleum gases	2	2
petrol	6	22
naphtha	10	5
kerosine	12	8
gas oil	22	22
fuel oil	40	38
bitumen	8	3

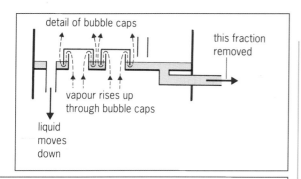

detail of bubble caps

this fraction removed

vapour rises up through bubble caps

liquid moves down

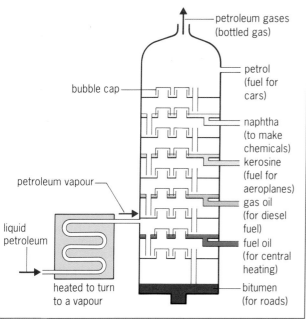

petroleum gases (bottled gas)

petrol (fuel for cars)

bubble cap

naphtha (to make chemicals)

kerosine (fuel for aeroplanes)

petroleum vapour

gas oil (for diesel fuel)

liquid petroleum

fuel oil (for central heating)

heated to turn to a vapour

bitumen (for roads)

▲ **Fig 62.2 Industrial fractional distillation of petroleum**

Q2 Identify the differences between the supply and demand of products from refining.

Q3 The waste gases can be liquefied and sold as liquefied petroleum gas, LPG. Suggest how they could be used within the refinery.

ALKANES AND ALKENES – FAMILIES OF HYDROCARBONS

Alkanes

Alkanes are a family of hydrocarbons present in petroleum. The table in the Data section (page 184) shows the first six members of the alkane family. All the alkanes are **saturated**, that is, all of the bonds are single covalent bonds.

Q4 Which alkanes in the table are liquid at room temperature?

Q5 Identify the alkane shown in fig 62.3.

Q6 Write the formula of the alkane containing

  a 8 carbon atoms **b** 12 carbon atoms
  c n carbon atoms.

Alkenes

Ethene is the simplest member of the **alkene** family, also present in petroleum. Alkenes are unsaturated hydrocarbons and contain a double bond between two carbon atoms. Fig 62.4 shows a model of ethene and its structural formula.

Q7 Write the molecular formula and structural formula of propene, which contains three carbon atoms.

Fig 62.4 Model and structural formula for ethene ▶

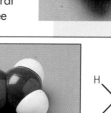

Alkenes undergo **addition reactions**. The table below summarises three common addition reactions of ethene.

▼ **Fig 62.3**

Ethene reacts with	Structure of product	Name of product
hydrogen	H—C—C—H (with H H above and H H below)	ethane
hydrogen bromide	H—C—C—Br (with H H above and H H below)	bromoethane
steam (in presence of a catalyst)	H—C—C—O—H (with H H above and H H below)	ethanol

CRACKING

Generally, more of the higher boiling point, long-chain hydrocarbons are produced from oil than there is demand for. If an oil company is to make a profit it needs to find ways of using all the products of petroleum.

An important process in the petroleum industry is **cracking**. This involves passing the vapour of long-chain hydrocarbons over a heated catalyst. The chains are then broken down to form smaller molecules.

A catalyst allows the reaction to take place at a lower temperature than would otherwise be possible.

Cracking the naphtha fraction

Naphtha contains a mixture of hydrocarbons containing between 5 and 7 carbon atoms and with a boiling point range of about 30–100 °C. This fraction is cracked in the presence of a suitable catalyst to form useful products such as ethene, C_2H_4, propene, C_3H_6, and butene, C_4H_8. These are used widely in the plastics industry.

63 POLYMERS

By the end of this section you should be able to

- recall that polymers are made by linking many monomer molecules
- recall that there are two types of polymerisation – addition and condensation polymerisation
- give examples of each type of polymer with structures and uses
- understand the terms thermosetting and thermoplastic
- understand the effects of cross-linking between chains.

USES OF POLYMERS

Many items which used to be made of metals are now made of plastic materials called **polymers**. Polymers are usually manufactured from petroleum products. A modern car, for example, contains many components made from polymers, fig 63.1.

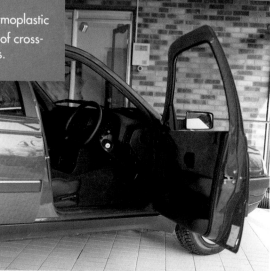

Fig 63.1 Polymers are used widely in modern cars

Q1 List as many components of the modern car as you can which are made from polymers. What are the advantages of polymers compared with traditional materials?

POLYMERISATION

Polymers are made up from very long chain molecules. These long chains are made up by joining together many small molecules called **monomers**. There can be between 1000 and 50000 monomer molecules linked together in a polymer chain. The equation below summarises the process of joining monomers, called **polymerisation**.

n monomer molecules linked in a chain

There are two types of polymerisation – **addition polymerisation** and **condensation polymerisation**.

ADDITION POLYMERISATION

An example of addition polymerisation is the formation of poly(ethene) from ethene. The ethene molecules link together to form long chains

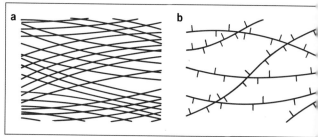

We write the polymer more simply as

$$\left[\begin{array}{cc} H & H \\ | & | \\ -C-C- \\ | & | \\ H & H \end{array}\right]_n$$

The chains produced will contain more than 1000 carbon atoms. There is no other product in this addition polymerisation reaction. The monomer in this example is ethene.

Different types of poly(ethene)

Different types of poly(ethene) can be made, depending upon the conditions used for polymerisation. These are summarised in the table in the Data section (page 184). Fig 63.2 shows the arrangement of the chains in low-density and high-density poly(ethene).

▲ **Fig 63.2**

Q2 Which form, **a** or **b**, has the chains more closely packed together?

Q3 Which form represents low-density poly(ethene) and which high-density poly(ethene)?

Q4 A polymer is said to be crystalline when the chains are regularly arranged. Which form is more crystalline?

Q5 Which form has the higher melting point?

Q6 The relative molecular mass of ethene is 28. The average relative molecular mass of poly(ethene) is about 140000. How many ethene molecules, on average, join together to make a molecule of poly(ethene)?

Uses of addition polymers

The table in the Data section (page 185) gives examples of some other addition polymers.

CONDENSATION POLYMERISATION

Condensation reactions

A **condensation reaction** is a reaction between two molecules to form a larger molecule and leave a small molecule such as water, H_2O, hydrogen chloride, HCl, etc.

For example, the reaction between an organic acid and an alcohol produces an ester and water

ethanoic acid + ethanol $\rightleftharpoons$ ethyl ethanoate + water

$$CH_3-\overset{\displaystyle O}{\underset{\displaystyle O-H}{C}} + C_2H_5OH \rightleftharpoons CH_3-\overset{\displaystyle O}{\underset{\displaystyle O-C_2H_5}{C}} + H_2O$$

This could be represented in a simplified form by

$$\bullet-\overset{\displaystyle O}{\underset{\displaystyle O-H}{C}} + \blacksquare-O-H \rightleftharpoons \bullet-\overset{\displaystyle O}{\underset{\displaystyle O-\blacksquare}{C}} + H_2O$$

Here the symbols $\bullet$ and $\blacksquare$ are used to represent the hydrocarbon parts of the molecules not involved in the reaction. It can clearly be seen that the reaction involves the —COOH group in the acid and the —OH group in the alcohol.
Another condensation reaction is

acid chloride + amine $\rightarrow$ amide + hydrogen chloride

$$\bullet-\overset{\displaystyle O}{\underset{\displaystyle Cl}{C}} + H_2N-\blacksquare \rightarrow \bullet-\overset{\displaystyle O}{\underset{\displaystyle NH-\blacksquare}{C}} + HCl$$

Condensation polymers

Condensation polymers are formed when a series of condensation reactions takes place. The monomer molecules must contain two 'active' groups, for example acid and alcohol groups

$$\bullet-\overset{\displaystyle O}{\underset{\displaystyle O-H}{C}} + \blacksquare-O-H \rightleftharpoons \bullet-\overset{\displaystyle O}{\underset{\displaystyle O-\blacksquare}{C}} + H_2O$$

A series of reactions between acids and alcohols produces

$$\cdots-\bullet-\overset{O}{\underset{O-\blacksquare-O}{C}}\overset{O}{\underset{}{C}}-\bullet-\overset{O}{\underset{O-\blacksquare-O}{C}}\overset{O}{\underset{}{C}}-\bullet-\overset{O}{\underset{O-\blacksquare-O}{C}}\cdots$$

The resulting polymer, formed by a series of ester-forming reactions eliminating a water molecule each time, is a condensation polymer. It is called polyester. Terylene is a trade name for polyester.

A series of reactions between acid chlorides and amines produces another type of condensation polymer

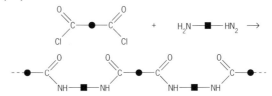

This polymer is called polyamide or nylon.

THERMOSETTING AND THERMOPLASTIC POLYMERS

Polymers or plastics can be classified as either **thermosetting** or **thermoplastic**, according to how they change on heating.

Thermoplastics

Thermoplastics become soft and mouldable on heating without undergoing significant chemical change. On cooling they harden again. This melting and hardening can be repeated over and over again.

Thermosetting plastics

Thermosetting plastics or thermosets are resistant to high temperatures and cannot be melted. They decompose before they melt and, therefore, cannot be softened and re-moulded. They are insoluble and swell only slightly in most organic solvents. At normal temperatures they are usually hard and brittle.

Structure of thermoplastics and thermosets

Fig 63.3 shows the arrangement of chains in a thermosetting and a thermoplastic polymer. The cross-linking between chains in a thermosetting

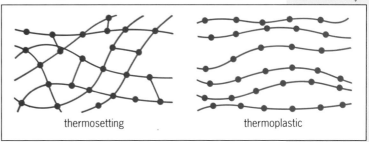

thermosetting   thermoplastic

polymer make melting difficult. A thermoplastic polymer can be made harder by forming cross-links. Rubber, for example, is an addition polymer which can be hardened by vulcanisation. This involves mixing sulphur with the rubber which forms cross-links.

Fig 63.3 Arrangements of chains in thermosetting and thermoplastic polymers ▼

64 THE CHLOR-ALKALI INDUSTRY

By the end of this section you should be able to

- understand how salt can be mined by solution mining
- recall the products of the electrolysis of brine
- compare the mercury and diaphragm cell methods
- understand the Solvay process
- appreciate the conditions in factories producing alkali.

The important chlor-alkali industry was built up close to the underground salt deposits in north Cheshire. Much of the industry relies on the electrolysis of salt and salt solution (called brine).

MINING UNDERGROUND SALT DEPOSITS

Most salt is mined by solution mining (fig 64.1). A hole is drilled down to the salt deposits, and water is pumped down. The water dissolves the salt and the solution is pumped to the surface.

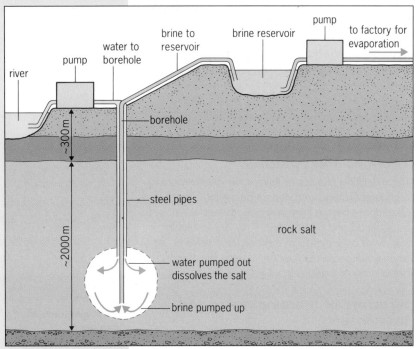

▲ **Fig 64.1 Solution mining of salt**

Q1 Use the Data section on page 184 to justify the use of cold water rather than hot water for solution mining.

Underground salt mining has caused considerable subsidence in the local area (fig 64.2).

Fig 64.2 Subsidence of an office in Northwich, Cheshire, about 1900 ▶

SPLITTING UP THE SODIUM CHLORIDE

Sodium chloride is used as table salt, to salt the roads in winter and in other ways. But its main use is as a source of sodium hydroxide and chlorine.

Electrolysis of molten sodium chloride

Electrolysis of molten sodium chloride produces sodium and chlorine. Calcium chloride is added to the sodium chloride to lower its melting point. The chlorine is produced at the anode and the sodium is produced at the cathode.

anode $\quad 2Cl^- \rightarrow Cl_2 + 2e^-$
cathode $\quad Na^+ + e^- \rightarrow Na$

The products must be kept separate or they recombine.

Electrolysis of sodium chloride solution (brine)

Q2 List the four ions present in an aqueous solution of sodium chloride.

There are two ways of carrying out this electrolysis – the **mercury cell** and the **diaphragm cell**. We shall look at each in turn.

The mercury cell

The mercury cell (fig 64.3) has a titanium anode and a moving mercury cathode. Chlorine is produced at the anode

$$2Cl^- \rightarrow Cl_2 + 2e^-$$

Sodium is produced at the cathode, and immediately forms an **amalgam** (an alloy of sodium and mercury) which does not react with the brine

$$Na^+ + e^- \rightarrow Na \quad Na + Hg \rightarrow Na/Hg$$

The mercury amalgam is run out of the cell into a container where it reacts with distilled water to produce sodium hydroxide solution and hydrogen. The expensive mercury is entirely recovered and can be re-used.

$$2Na/Hg + 2H_2O \rightarrow 2NaOH + H_2 + 2Hg$$

▼ **Fig 64.3 The mercury cell**

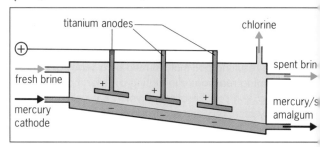

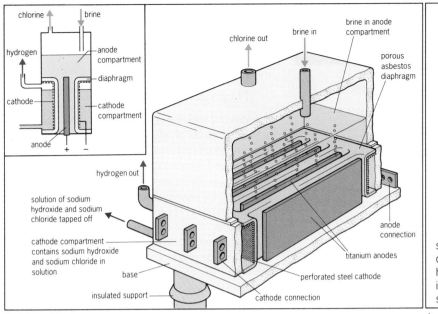

▲ Fig 64.4 The diaphragm cell

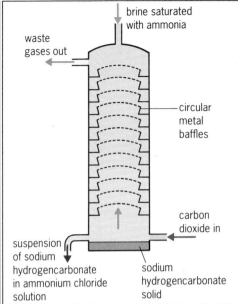

▲ Fig 64.5 The Solvay tower

The diaphragm cell

In the diaphragm cell (fig 64.4) the electrolysis of brine uses a steel cathode and a titanium anode. The anode and cathode compartments are separated by a porous diaphragm which allows the solution to pass through slowly.

Q3 Why are the anodes in the mercury cell and the diaphragm cell made of titanium rather than steel?

Q4 Why can the cathode in the diaphragm cell be made of steel?

Q5 In the diaphragm cell the brine moves through the diaphragm from the anode compartment to the cathode compartment. Why does it move in this direction rather than the reverse?

In the anode compartment of the diaphragm cell, over half of the chloride ions are converted into chlorine gas. In the cathode, hydrogen gas is produced

$$2H^+ + 2e^- \rightarrow H_2$$

The solution leaving the cell contains about 10% sodium hydroxide and 15% sodium chloride. On partial evaporation sodium chloride crystallises out. The sodium hydroxide produced by this method contains sodium chloride.

Q6 Compare the advantages and disadvantages of producing sodium hydroxide in the mercury cell and the diaphragm cell.

Q7 Much of the sodium hydroxide produced is used as a cheap alkali and impurities in the alkali are not important. Which process would you recommend to produce this sodium hydroxide?

The Solvay process

The **Solvay process** also splits the sodium and chlorine in brine, but does not use electrolysis. It produces sodium hydrogencarbonate and sodium carbonate.

Brine saturated with ammonia falls through a tower (fig 64.5) and carbon dioxide is passed into the bottom of the tower.

Q8 Suggest a reason for having metal baffles in the tower.

The following reaction takes place.

$$NaCl + NH_3 + CO_2 + H_2O \rightarrow NaHCO_3 + NH_4Cl$$

The sodium hydrogencarbonate precipitates out and sodium carbonate can be produced by heating it.

Considerable heat is given out during the reaction and the tower has to be water cooled to obtain sodium hydrogencarbonate crystals of a suitable size to filter out of the ammonium chloride solution.

The ammonia can be regenerated by heating the ammonium chloride with an alkali, for example

$$2NH_4Cl + Ca(OH)_2 \rightarrow CaCl_2 + 2NH_3 + 2H_2O$$

Limestone is the source of the calcium hydroxide and carbon dioxide used.

Q9 Name the raw materials in the Solvay process. Which product is of little economic importance?

Q10 Describe how calcium hydroxide and carbon dioxide could be produced from limestone.

Q11 Sodium carbonate is formed by heating sodium hydrogencarbonate. Write a symbolic equation for this reaction.

Q12 Summarise the Solvay process in a flow diagram showing the reactants and products.

AMMONIA

By the end of this section you should be able to

- recall that ammonia is synthesised by the Haber process and understand the science behind the process
- understand that much of the ammonia is converted into nitric acid
- understand the importance of fertilisers in growing sufficient food for a growing world population.

The Haber process

In Great Britain each year we produce approximately 2 million tonnes of ammonia by the **Haber process**. This process is summarised in fig 65.1.

Most of the ammonia is turned into fertilisers, but some is also used for synthetic fibres, dyestuffs, polymers (such as polyurethanes) and explosives.

Hydrogen is produced for the Haber process by passing methane or naphtha, mixed with steam, over a heated nickel catalyst at pressures up to 30 atmospheres. The products are carbon oxides and hydrogen. The gases produced are mixed with steam and passed over a heated catalyst to produce carbon dioxide and hydrogen. The carbon dioxide is dissolved in water under pressure and then recovered for the production of urea.

Nitrogen is produced by fractional distillation of liquid air.

▼ **Fig 65.1 The Haber process**

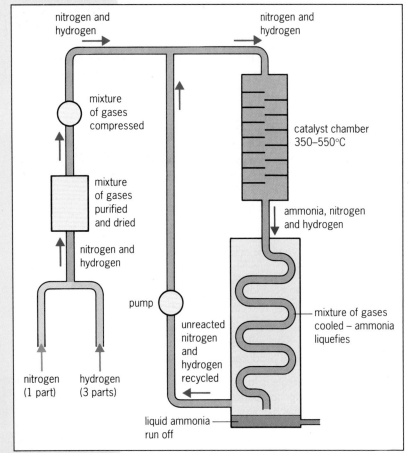

nitrogen and hydrogen

nitrogen and hydrogen

mixture of gases compressed

mixture of gases purified and dried

nitrogen and hydrogen

pump

nitrogen (1 part)

hydrogen (3 parts)

catalyst chamber 350–550°C

ammonia, nitrogen and hydrogen

mixture of gases cooled – ammonia liquefies

unreacted nitrogen and hydrogen recycled

liquid ammonia run off

An equilibrium reaction

The equation for the Haber process is

$$N_2(g) + 3H_2(g) \rightleftharpoons 2NH_3(g)$$

The forward reaction is exothermic. In the Haber process, 2 moles of ammonia are formed from 4 moles of reacting gases (a mixture of 1 mole of nitrogen and 3 moles of hydrogen). One mole of any gas occupies the same volume, so if the pressure is increased, the equilibrium moves to the right to give a smaller volume and produce more ammonia. This is an example of controlling an equilibrium to produce as much of the product as possible. More ammonia would also be produced if the temperature was decreased. Theoretically, high pressures and low temperatures would give the best yield of ammonia but the following factors also have to be considered.

1 Does the best equilibrium position have to be reached if unreacted gases can be recycled?
2 Equipment becomes increasingly expensive as pressure increases.
3 At low temperatures reactions are very slow. Even using a catalyst to speed up the reaction may not make the process fast enough to be economic.
4 At low temperatures catalyst life and activity is prolonged.

In practice a compromise is made and usual conditions are

pressure	200 atmospheres
temperature	380–450°C
catalyst	finely divided iron containing promoters to stop the catalyst being poisoned

The conversion under these conditions is about 15% and the equilibrium position is never reached.

Siting a plant

Large ammonia plants are more economic than smaller plants providing the plant is built with well-tried technology. When siting a new plant it should be close to sources of

- energy, whether coal, oil or natural gas
- water, which is required in large quantities for the process
- transport, by road, river, sea or rail.

In Great Britain plants are sited at Billingham (close to supplies of North Sea oil and gas), Ince Marsh in Cheshire (close to oil refineries), Avonmouth and Immingham. Ammonia is a profitable use of natural gas and refinery gases and so oil producers often build ammonia plants to increase the value of their products.

Q1 Typically only 10% of the nitrogen and hydrogen are converted to ammonia in the Haber process. What happens to the unreacted nitrogen and hydrogen?

Demand for fertilisers

World artificial fertiliser demand has increased in the past 50 years in response to growing world population (see page 98–9). Between 1945 and 1985 the quantities of nitrogen, phosphorus and potassium, the three elements required in largest quantities by plants, grew as follows

Year	Millions of tonnes of		
	Nitrogen	Phosphorus	Potassium
1945	2	3	1.5
1985	70	34	26

The chemical industry has expanded to meet these demands.

What are fertilisers?

Fertilisers provide nitrogen, phosphorus or potassium to enable plants to grow, flower and fruit. Nitrogen is taken into a plant in solution in the form of nitrates (see page 111) and helps to build up the leaves and stems of the plant. Phosphorus is required to build up a healthy root system. Potassium is needed for forming flowers and seeds.

Compound fertilisers contain a mixture of nitrogen, phosphorus and potassium in various different proportions. A typical compound fertiliser may contain, for example, 15%N, 7%P and 17%K. These **NPK values** are printed on the fertiliser bags.

Fertilisers may be solids, usually in a granular form for easy distribution on the land, or in liquid form, in which the nutrients are usually less concentrated.

The manufacture of fertilisers

The basic raw materials used in the manufacture of fertilisers are air as a source of nitrogen, phosphate rock as a source of phosphorus (see page 112) and sylvinite as a source of potassium. Various processes have to be carried out before these raw materials can be converted into a fertiliser. The sylvinite (a mixture of potassium chloride, sodium chloride and clay) can be used unchanged, but nitrogen has to be converted into ammonia and nitric acid before it can be used in a fertiliser.

Ammonia is produced by the Haber process. Ammonia is then converted to nitric acid by catalytic oxidation in a three-stage process.

1 $4NH_3(g) + 5O_2(g) \rightarrow 4NO(g) + 6H_2O(g)$
2 $2NO(g) + O_2(g) \rightarrow 2NO_2(g)$
3 $3NO_2(g) + H_2O(l) \rightarrow 2HNO_3(aq) + NO(g)$

The first stage is catalysed by a platinum/rhodium alloy. It is a very fast, exothermic reaction and up to 98% of the reactants are converted. Stage 2 occurs as the gases cool and stage 3 takes place in water.

Phosphate rock largely contains calcium phosphate which is insoluble. Before converting it into a fertiliser it has to be treated with sulphuric acid to make the dihydrogenphosphate salt, which is soluble and can be absorbed by plants.

Fertiliser production involves an integrated series of processes. These are summarised in fig 65.2.

▼ **Fig 65.2 Integrated processes to produce fertilisers. The masses given are the masses of material used or produced per day**

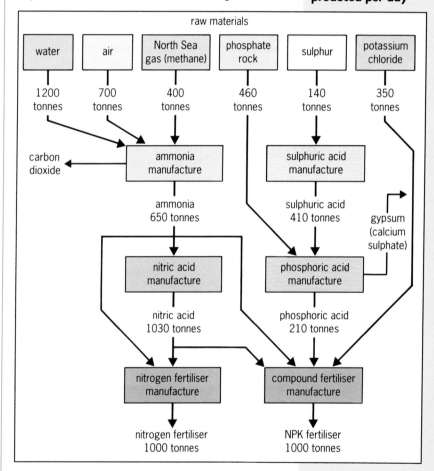

Q2 In some countries in Africa, farmers cannot afford fertilisers. They often clear an area of ground for crop production and use it for three years of growing. It then begins to be depleted of nutrients, and they leave it and clear a fresh area.
Explain the problems caused by this form of agriculture.

Q3 Fertilisers help farmers produce sufficient food to feed the population of the world. Write an essay of 400 words about other ways of ensuring that there is enough of the right kinds of food for everybody.

CHEMICAL CHANGES

173

66 WEATHER PATTERNS

By the end of this section you should be able to

- recognise symbols seen on weather maps
- understand that weather systems are driven by energy transfer processes.

METEOROLOGY

Our weather is largely determined by climatic conditions and movements of air in the **troposphere**, a layer of the atmosphere (see page 176). A study of the weather is called **meteorology**.

Convection currents

The surface of the Earth is heated by the absorption of solar radiation. The air immediately above the Earth is heated and the air expands. This air becomes less dense as its particles move apart. This causes the warm air to rise, and as it rises it cools and sinks back to the Earth. Cold air moves in to replace rising warm air. These **convection currents** are summarised in fig 66.1.

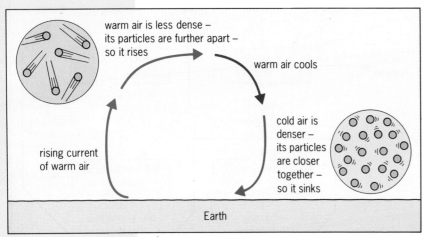

warm air is less dense –
its particles are further apart –
so it rises

warm air cools

rising current of warm air

cold air is denser – its particles are closer together – so it sinks

Earth

▲ **Fig 66.1 Convection currents**

WEATHER MAPS

Forecasting the weather

Fig 66.2 shows a typical weather map used to show the weather over the British Isles. The map forecasts the weather conditions for the next day. It is made by feeding many weather measurements into a computer, and the computer predicts the changes which are likely, based upon previous similar situations. However, these predictions are not always correct. Often the predicted changes do take place, but they take place either faster or slower than expected.

The weather readings that are fed into the computer come from weather stations on the ground and at sea, from weather balloons and from satellites.

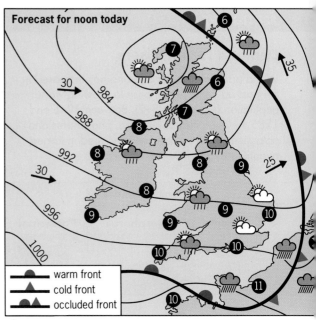

Forecast for noon today

- ━━◖━━ warm front
- ━━▲━━ cold front
- ━━◖▲━━ occluded front

▲ **Fig 66.2 A typical weather forecast map**

Isobars and atmospheric pressure

Isobars are lines which are drawn to join up places with the same atmospheric pressure at sea level. In fig 66.2 isobars are shown at 980, 984, 992, 996 and 1000 millibars. Atmospheric pressure usually varies from about 975 to about 1030 millibars. It is measured on a barometer.

Areas of low pressure are called **cyclones** or depressions. They are shown by LOW on a weather map. High pressure areas are called **anticyclones** and are marked HIGH.

Wind direction

Winds are movements of air from areas of high pressure to areas of low pressure.

The wind direction is shown by arrows on the weather map. The wind does not blow directly from high-pressure to low-pressure areas because of the interference of the rotation of the Earth. In the northern hemisphere the winds are deflected to the right of their intended direction and in the southern hemisphere to the left. This is called the **Coriolis effect**.

In the northern hemisphere the wind travels clockwise around a HIGH and anticlockwise around a LOW (fig 66.3). The air moves in the opposite directions in the southern hemisphere.

The Buys-Ballot law is useful for deciding where HIGH and LOW areas are. If you have your back to the wind in the northern hemisphere, there will be a LOW on your left and a HIGH on your right.

Wind direction is shown by a weather vane.

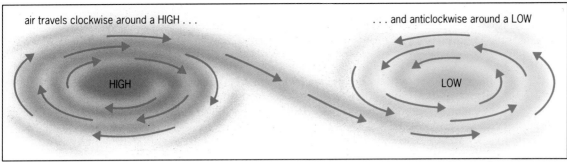

▲ **Fig 66.3 Winds around high-pressure and low-pressure areas in the northern hemisphere**

Weather fronts

A **front** is the boundary between two masses of moving air with different temperatures and humidities. There are three types of front, shown in fig 66.4.

When warm air moves above a block of cold air, a warm front is formed. When cold air moves under a block of warm air, a cold front is set up.

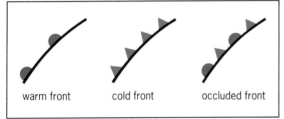

▲ **Fig 66.4 Weather fronts**

Fig 66.5 shows the weather changes which occur when cold and warm fronts pass.

As a **warm front** passes, there will be increasing wind speed and more cloud, light rain and a fall in air pressure. Heavy rain, very strong wind and a drop in temperature accompany the passing of a **cold front**.

The fronts move because of winds. If a cold front catches up with a warm front, it undercuts the warm air and lifts it off the ground. The front is then called an **occluded front**. This extra push can produce huge clouds and very heavy rain.

Temperature

Temperatures are shown in circles on a weather map in degrees Celsius.

Fig 66.5 Weather changes associated with cold and warm fronts ▼

Q1 Fig 66.6 shows the weather over the British Isles at noon on a day in February.

◄ **Fig 66.6**

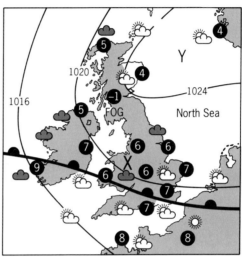

a i What is the temperature and atmospheric pressure at **X**?
  ii What is the meteorological term for an area such as **Y**?
  iii Estimate the wind direction and strength at **X**. Give reasons for your estimates.
b i What type of front is shown on the map?
  ii Describe and explain what is happening at this front.
  iii Describe the likely weather conditions at **X**.
c What sources of information does a meteorologist use to produce a weather map, and how is this information processed?
    (MEG Science B 1761/3 June 1992 Q4)

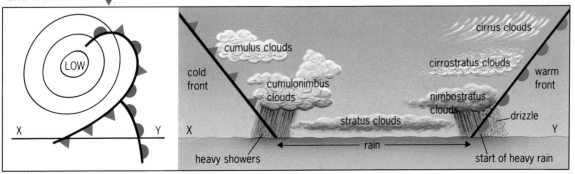

By the end of this section you should be able to

- understand that the atmosphere of the Earth is in layers
- recall the approximate composition of the atmosphere
- understand why the composition of the atmosphere remains approximately constant
- explain the greenhouse effect
- understand the effects that the destruction of the ozone layer could have.

There is a layer of gases around the Earth about 960 km thick called the Earth's **atmosphere**. It is divided into layers according to temperature, although there are no solid boundaries separating these layers. The layers are shown in the table.

Distance from the Earth (km)	Name of layer	Temperature of layer (°C)	Description of layer
0–20	troposphere	down to –50	layer where weather patterns take place
20–50	stratosphere	as high as 0	air is still – contains the **ozone layer** which absorbs harmful radiation
50–80	mesosphere	down to –100	
80–450	thermosphere	up to 2000	heated because it absorbs harmful solar radiation
450–900	exosphere		contains few gases
900–960	magnetosphere		contains charged particles

COMPOSITION OF THE ATMOSPHERE

The Earth's atmosphere is made up of a mixture of gases. Its composition can vary but typical figures are given below.

nitrogen	78%
oxygen	21%
carbon dioxide	0.03%
argon	0.9%
helium	0.0005%
neon	0.002%
krypton	0.0001%
xenon	0.000 001%

The Earth is the only planet in the Solar System to contain water vapour in its atmosphere. The amounts of water in the atmosphere vary.

Finding the percentage of oxygen in the atmosphere

The apparatus in fig 67.1 can be used to find the percentage of oxygen in a sample of air. 100 cm³ of air are trapped in one of the syringes. The air is passed backwards and forwards over heated copper in a hard glass tube. The oxygen in the air is removed by the copper, which forms black copper(II) oxide.

$$2Cu(s) + O_2(g) \rightarrow 2CuO(s)$$

After cooling, the volume of the air remaining can be measured.

A constant composition

The composition of the atmosphere remains approximately constant because of competing processes taking place. Combustion of fuels (coal, oil, wood) use up oxygen and produce carbon dioxide. Respiration in all living organisms also uses up oxygen and produces carbon dioxide. However, to compensate for these processes, green plants use up carbon dioxide from the atmosphere and release oxygen into the atmosphere during photosynthesis. Green algae in the oceans also photosynthesise.

Q1 There is considerable evidence that carbon dioxide levels in the atmosphere have increased by 25% in this century. What factors may have contributed to this change?

Originally the Earth's atmosphere probably contained much more carbon dioxide and little or no oxygen. The oxygen was provided by photosynthesis.

Fig 67.1 Finding the percentage of oxygen in the air ▶

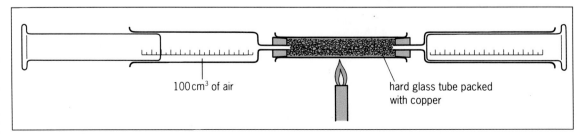

100 cm³ of air

hard glass tube packed with copper

UPSETTING THE BALANCE

The greenhouse effect

Apart from disturbing the oxygen–carbon dioxide balance in the atmosphere, one of the problems caused by burning fuels is the **greenhouse effect**. This is shown in fig 67.2. Solar energy from the Sun passes through the carbon dioxide in the atmosphere and heats up the Earth. The heated Earth then gives out radiation which is of a shorter wavelength. This radiation does not pass through the carbon dioxide in the atmosphere. The result is that the temperature of the Earth rises, which may affect climatic and weather conditions on the Earth. It has been estimated that average temperatures could increase by up to 4°C in the next 50 years. Without the greenhouse effect the Earth would be so cold it would be uninhabitable. The danger is that an increase in the greenhouse effect will cause the problem to spiral. As the Earth warms more evaporation will take place. This may reduce the amount of energy penetrating the atmosphere but it will also increase the greenhouse effect because water vapour is a greenhouse gas. The subsequent melting of the snow and ice will cause even more of the Sun's energy to be absorbed.

Destruction of the ozone layer

There is considerable evidence that the ozone layer within the stratosphere is being broken down. Evidence of holes in this layer have been detected, especially over the North and South Poles, and these holes are getting larger. The ozone layer prevents much of the lethal ultraviolet radiation from reaching the Earth's surface. If this radiation reaches the surface of the Earth without being absorbed in the atmosphere there will be a large increase in the incidence of skin cancer. The breakdown of the ozone layer has been caused by the use of chlorofluorocarbons (CFCs) in refrigerants and aerosols. CFCs are being replaced by alternatives which do not affect the ozone layer.

▼ **Fig 67.3 The ozone layer protects us from ultraviolet radiation**

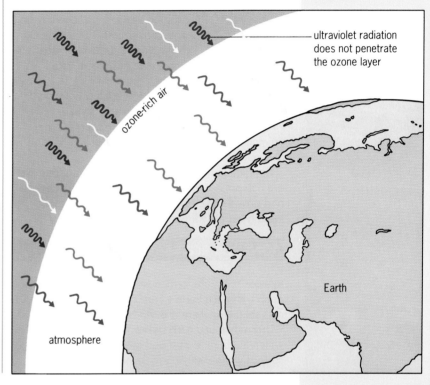

ultraviolet radiation does not penetrate the ozone layer

ozone-rich air

Earth

atmosphere

◀ **Fig 67.2 The greenhouse effect**

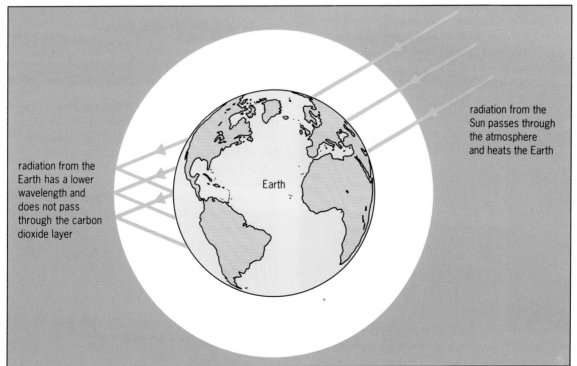

radiation from the Earth has a lower wavelength and does not pass through the carbon dioxide layer

Earth

radiation from the Sun passes through the atmosphere and heats the Earth

68 ROCKS

By the end of this section you should be able to

- distinguish igneous, sedimentary and metamorphic rocks and give examples of each
- explain the rock cycle
- explain the processes which cause weathering of rocks.

Rocks can be classified as **sedimentary rocks, igneous rocks** and **metamorphic rocks**.

SEDIMENTARY ROCKS

Sedimentary rocks are formed from **sediments**. These are fragments of other rocks and minerals or the remains of dead plants and animals. They can be transported, often in the sea or in a river bed. The sediments are then buried and compressed to form a hard rock. This process occurs over millions of years.

Limestone and sandstone are examples of sedimentary rocks. Limestone is composed of the remains of once-living organisms. In some limestones it is possible to see the remains of the animals. Sandstone was formed by grains of sand becoming cemented together.

Conglomerate is formed when pebbles and gravel are compressed to form a rock in which the pebbles and gravel can clearly be seen. Fig 68.1 shows these types of sedimentary rocks.

IGNEOUS ROCKS

Igneous rocks are formed when molten magma from deep within the Earth's crust and upper mantle cools and solidifies. There are two types of igneous rocks – **intrusive** and **extrusive**. Intrusive rocks solidify within the Earth's crust and are only found at the surface when overlying rocks have been eroded away. Extrusive rocks are formed when the magma crystallises on the surface of the Earth.

Crystals can be seen in igneous rocks and the size of the crystals depends upon the rate of cooling. Large crystals are formed when the crystallisation occurs slowly.

Granite is an example of an intrusive igneous rock and basalt is an extrusive igneous rock, shown in fig 68.2.

▲ **Fig 68.1 Conglomerate, limestone and sandstone**

▲ **Fig 68.2 Granite and basalt are igneous rocks**

 Q1 Some samples of igneous rock contain many tiny bubbles throughout the rock. How do you think these are formed?

METAMORPHIC ROCKS

Metamorphic rocks get their name from the Greek words 'meta' and 'morphe' which mean change of form. Both sedimentary and igneous rocks can be changed by heat and/or pressure in the Earth. These conditions can occur during mountain-building processes when plates move together (see page 182), by squeezing and folding of rocks or from the heat from cooling igneous rocks.

The metamorphic rock has a different structure from the original rock. Slate is formed when clay and mud are subjected to pressure. Marble is formed from limestone.

Metamorphic rocks rarely contain fossils because they are broken down when the rock is reformed. Metamorphic rocks often have a banded or striped appearance, as fig 68.3 shows.

▲ **Fig 68.3 Garnet mica schist, a metamorphic rock**

THE ROCK CYCLE

Rocks are continually being broken down and new rocks are being formed. These processes are summarised in the rock cycle, fig 68.4. The cycle has no starting point and has been going on for millions of years.

The processes taking place within the Earth, such as mountain-building and metamorphism, are driven by the Earth's internal heat. Processes taking place at the surface are powered by the Sun's energy.

Q2 Copy fig 68.5 and complete it by replacing the labels 1–7 with words from the following list. You can use the labels more than once.

erosion   heat and pressure   cooling
compacting   melting

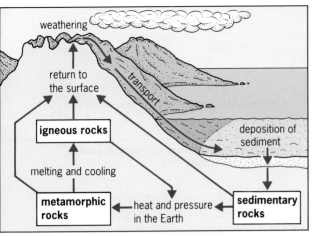

▲ **Fig 68.4 The rock cycle**

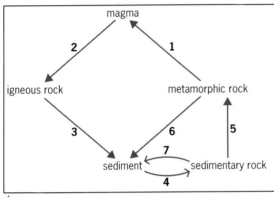

▲ **Fig 68.5**

Weathering

All rocks on the Earth's surface are broken down by **weathering** or **erosion**. This is mainly a chemical process aided by the presence of water. Rocks also break down by mechanical processes involving rain, alternate freezing and thawing (see below), the abrasive action of sediments, etc.

When water freezes it expands. If water is trapped inside crevices in a rock, and freezes and thaws repeatedly, coarse fragments will break off the rock. This process will cause a tough rock like granite to be broken up.

Winds bearing sediments can grind down rocks. The Sphinx in Egypt shows signs of erosion by wind, fig 68.6.

▼ **Fig 68.6 The Sphinx**

Q3 Explain why many pieces of rock found on a beach are smooth, without sharp edges.

Weathering of rocks is speeded up by atmospheric pollution. Pollution usually makes rainwater more acidic. Limestone is particularly affected by acidity in rainwater, fig 68.7.

ROCKS IN USE

Natural rock obtained from quarries is usually expensive. Cheaper alternatives to natural rock are frequently used as building materials. Bricks are made by baking clay, which artificially converts clay into a metamorphic rock.

Concrete also uses natural stone. Crushed rock fragments and sand are mixed with cement. The cement is made by heating limestone powder with clay. The concrete is poured into moulds to make railways sleepers, beams, etc. Concrete is not a strong material. A downward force on a concrete beam will cause it to break. Steel reinforcing rods transfer the force sideways and make the beam stronger, fig 68.8.

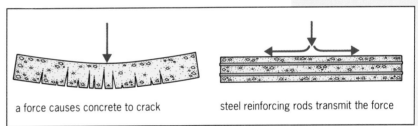

a force causes concrete to crack   steel reinforcing rods transmit the force

▲ **Fig 68.8 Reinforcing concrete beams**

Rocks are generally hard because they have stable giant structures, usually based upon silicates and aluminium oxide structures.

Q4 Fig 68.9 shows water running into the sea. At points A, B, C and D different sedimentary rocks are formed. The four rocks are

conglomerate   limestone   sandstone
shale

Which rock is formed at A, B, C and D? Explain the reasons for your answers.

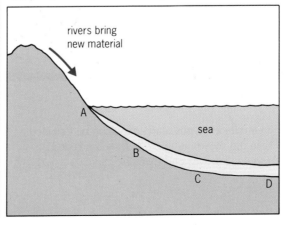

rivers bring
new material

sea

▲ **Fig 68.7 Limestone is particularly affected by acid rain**

◄ **Fig 68.9**

69 STRUCTURE OF THE EARTH

By the end of this section you should be able to

- describe the structure of the Earth and understand some of the evidence for this structure
- understand that the movement of plates over the surface of the Earth explains some of the observed changes.

The Earth consists of three parts – the **core**, the **mantle** and the **crust**. These are shown in fig 69.1.

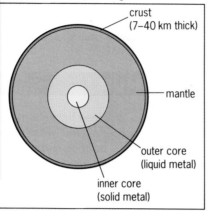

▲ **Fig 69.1 The structure of the Earth**

crust (7–40 km thick)

mantle

outer core (liquid metal)

inner core (solid metal)

EVIDENCE FOR THE STRUCTURE OF THE EARTH

The deepest hole drilled into the Earth is about 13 km deep. This hole was drilled in Russia and took more than 10 years to drill. Even this hole did not pass through the crust of the Earth. Evidence for the structure of the Earth comes from other studies.

Seismography

One important way of studying the structure of the Earth is to study the passage of sound waves from volcanic eruptions through the Earth. Vibrations can be detected using **seismometers**, fig 69.2, and a trace is produced on a rotating drum.

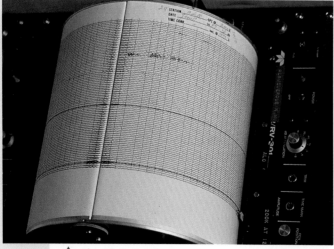

▲ **Fig 69.2 A seismometer**

Three different types of vibration can be detected. These are shown in fig 69.3. They are called P-waves, S-waves and L-waves.

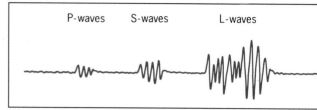

P-waves   S-waves   L-waves

▲ **Fig 69.3 Seismogram showing P-waves, S-waves and L-waves**

P-waves are compression waves that travel through the Earth. The rock is compressed and then stretched. The particles vibrate in the same direction as the direction of travel of the wave. P-waves are **longitudinal** waves. This means that P-waves travel quickly and are the first to arrive at the seismometer. P-waves travel through solids and liquids. Fig 69.4 shows a simulation of a P-wave with a slinky spring.

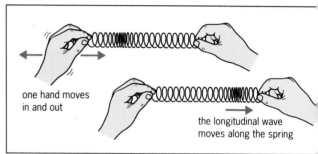

one hand moves in and out

the longitudinal wave moves along the spring

▲ **Fig 69.4 Simulation of a P-wave with a slinky spring**

S-waves also travel through the Earth but they differ from P-waves because they are **transverse** waves. In S-waves the particles vibrate from side to side, at right angles to the direction of wave travel. S-waves travel more slowly than P-waves. S-waves can only travel through solids. Fig 69.5 shows a simulation of an S-wave.

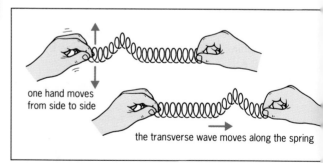

one hand moves from side to side

the transverse wave moves along the spring

▲ **Fig 69.5 Simulation of an S-wave with a slinky spring**

L-waves are the slowest moving waves and are most important in the surface layers of the Earth. They travel very slowly with a rolling motion. They can cause a great deal of damage to buildings.

Fig 69.6
Seismograms
after an
earthquake ▶

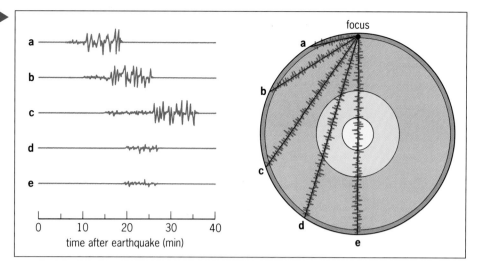

Fig 69.6 shows five seismograms labelled **a–e** obtained after an earthquake. The straight-line distances through the Earth from the focus to the points **a–e** are given below.

focus to **a**	3375 km
focus to **b**	6424 km
focus to **c**	10 126 km
focus to **d**	12 086 km
focus to **e**	12 740 km

Q1 What differences are there between the seismograms at **a**, **b** and **c** and the seismograms at **d** and **e**? What does this suggest to you about the structure of the Earth?

Q2 Look again at the seismograms at **d** and **e**. What do you notice about the arrival times for these two waves? How can you explain this?

PLATE TECTONICS

Alfred Wegener's theory of plate tectonics

Alfred Wegener, a German scientist, first proposed the theory of plate tectonics in 1912. He had noticed that the east coast of South America could fit into the west coast of Africa. Also, there were very similar fossils in South America and Africa which suggested that the continents were once joined. There was evidence also that a major ice sheet once covered southern Africa, southern Australia and India, suggesting they too were once joined.

Wegener proposed that all of the continents (Europe, Africa, America, Asia and Australasia) were once joined in a supercontinent, which he called the Pangaea. This is shown in fig 69.7.

◀ **Fig 69.7 Pangaea**

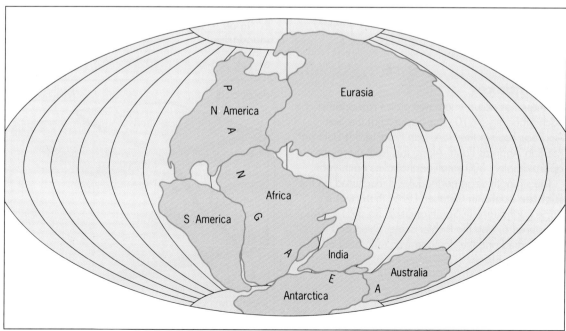

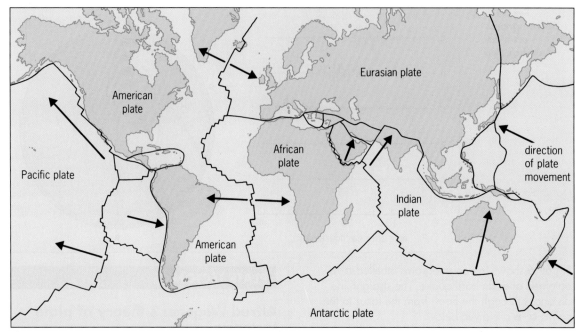

▲ **Fig 69.8 The plates of the Earth**

Plates of the Earth

Since the time when the continents were joined, about 200 million years ago, the continents have been moving apart because they are part of giant **tectonic plates** which float on the liquid mantle of the Earth. This movement is very slow, perhaps only 1 or 2 centimetres per year. Fig 69.8 show the plates and the direction in which they are moving.

Mountain ranges such as the Himalayas and the Andes are formed when two plates are moving towards one another and the land is pushed upwards. One of the plates moves over the other, fig 69.9. The plate underneath is pushed down into the magma. Here these rocks are melted and can be recycled.

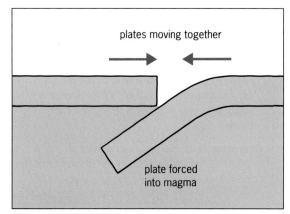

▲ **Fig 69.9 Rocks are recycled at plate boundaries**

Earthquakes

Earthquakes occur where two plates rub against each other, fig 69.10. This happens at the San Andreas Fault in the USA. San Francisco is built on the San Andreas Fault. Along this fault there are approximately 300 small earthquakes each year.

The strength of an earthquake is measured on the **Richter scale**. In October 1989, there was a large earthquake in San Francisco, fig 69.11. This registered 6.9 on the Richter scale. Over 270 people died and the damage was estimated at about £2.5 billion.

Fig 69.10 Earthquakes happen when plates rub together ▶

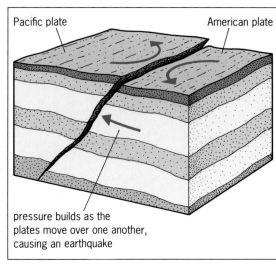

182

▲ **Fig 69.11 Effects of the earthquake in San Francisco, 1989**

Q3 Fig 69.12 shows the distribution of earthquakes around the Earth. What is significant about this distribution?

Q4 The Earth's surface is the top of a solid crust which is made up of slabs called plates. These plates move slowly; over millions of years the plates under the continents have moved great distances, changing the map of the world as they go. The crust under the continents is about 35 km thick and has an average density of about $2.7 \, g/dm^3$. The crust under the ocean floor is much thinner and has an average density of about $3.3 \, g/cm^3$. The material underneath the crust has an average density of about $4.5 \, g/cm^3$.

a Continental plates often collide with ocean floor plates. Describe what is likely to happen when a continental plate meets an ocean floor plate moving in the opposite direction. Explain your answer. A diagram could aid your explanation.

b Explain how earthquakes can occur where two plates meet.

c Two plates meet at the San Andreas Fault. The large earthquake there in 1989 caused destruction and loss of life at nearby San Francisco. One way in which engineers have been trying to prevent this was to pump water into the fault. Explain why this might prevent a major earthquake occuring.

d What evidence suggests that there may be molten material underneath the Earth's crust?

e The map in fig 69.13 represents South America and Africa. Fossils of the same species of a particular reptile are found on both continents. How does the theory of 'plate tectonics' explain this?

(MEG Science B 1761/3 June 1992 Q5)

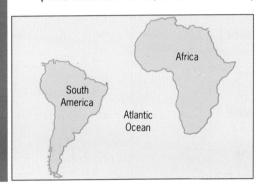

◀ **Fig 69.13**

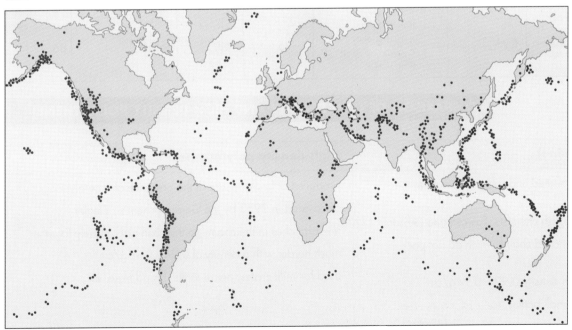

◀ **Fig 69.12 Distribution of earthquakes**

SOLUBILITIES OF COMMON SALTS IN WATER AT DIFFERENT TEMPERATURES

The table shows the number of grams of salt dissolving in 100g of water at different temperatures to produce saturated solutions.

Salt	Formula	Temperature (°C)						
		0	10	20	40	60	80	100
ammonium chloride	NH_4Cl	29.4	33.3	37.2	45.8	55.2	65.6	77.3
copper(II) sulphate	$CuSO_4.5H_2O$	14.3	17.4	20.7	28.5	40.0	55.0	75.4
potassium chloride	KCl	28.1	31.2	34.2	40.0	45.8	51.3	56.3
potassium bromide	KBr	53.5	59.5	65.2	75.5	85.5	95.0	104
potassium nitrate	KNO_3	13.3	20.9	31.6	63.9	110	169	246
sodium chloride	$NaCl$	35.7	35.8	36.0	36.6	37.3	38.4	39.8

THE FIRST SIX MEMBERS OF THE ALKANE FAMILY

Alkane	Molecular formula	Structural formula	Melting point (°C)	Boiling point (°C)	State at room temperature and pressure	Mass of one mole (g)
methane	CH_4		−182	−161	gas	16
ethane	C_2H_6		−183	−89	gas	30
propane	C_3H_8		−188	−42	gas	44
butane	C_4H_{10}		−138	0	gas	58
pentane	C_5H_{12}		−130	36	liquid	72
hexane	C_6H_{14}		−95	68	liquid	86

COMPARISON OF LOW-DENSITY AND HIGH-DENSITY POLY(ETHENE)

Low-density poly(ethene)	High-density poly(ethene)
produced when ethene is heated under high pressure in the presence of a catalyst Discovered in 1933 by English chemists, Fawcett and Gibson made up of extremely branched chains which do not pack closely together relatively soft polymer with density 0.92 – 0.94 g/cm³ used for packaging film, small bottles, etc.	produced at low pressure in the presence of a catalyst discovered in 1953 by the German chemist, Ziegler few branches in the chains so they can pack closely together much harder with a density of 0.94 – 0.96 g/cm³ used for milk crates, petrol tanks, bread trays, etc.

Monomer	Polymer	Uses
H H \ / C = C / \ H Cl chloroethene, also called vinyl chloride	$\left[\begin{array}{cc} H & H \\ \| & \| \\ C & C \\ \| & \| \\ H & Cl \end{array}\right]_n$ poly(chloroethene) or poly(vinylchloride) (PVC)	waste pipes, electrical wire insulation
C_6H_5 H \ / C = C / \ H H styrene	$\left[\begin{array}{cc} C_6H_5 & H \\ \| & \| \\ C & C \\ \| & \| \\ H & H \end{array}\right]_n$ poly(styrene)	flowerpots, ceiling tiles
H CH_3 \ / C = C / \ H $COOCH_3$ methyl methacrylate	$\left[\begin{array}{cc} H & CH_3 \\ \| & \| \\ C & C \\ \| & \| \\ H & COOCH_3 \end{array}\right]_n$ Perspex	plastic windscreens

Atomic number	Element	Symbol	Approximate relative atomic mass	Melting point (°C)	Boiling point (°C)	Density (g/cm³)	Date of discovery
1	hydrogen	H	1	−259	−253	0.00008	1766
2	helium	He	4	−270	−269	0.00017	1868
3	lithium	Li	7	180	1330	0.53	1817
4	beryllium	Be	9	1280	2700	1.9	1827
5	boron	B	11	2000	3000	2.3	1808
6	carbon	C	12		4200	2.2	*
7	nitrogen	N	14	−210	−196	0.00117	1772
8	oxygen	O	16	−219	−183	0.00132	1774
9	fluorine	F	19	−220	−188	0.0016	1886
10	neon	Ne	20	−249	−246	0.0008	1898
11	sodium	Na	23	98	890	0.97	1807
12	magnesium	Mg	24	650	1110	1.7	1808
13	aluminium	Al	27	660	2060	2.7	1825
14	silicon	Si	28	1410	2700	2.4	1823
15	phosphorus	P	31	44	280	1.8	1669
16	sulphur	S	32	119	445	2.1	*
17	chlorine	Cl	35.5	−101	−35	0.003	1774
18	argon	Ar	40	−189	−189	0.0017	1894
19	potassium	K	39	64	760	0.86	1807
20	calcium	Ca	40	850	1440	1.6	1808
21	scandium	Sc	45	1400	2500	3.1	1879
22	titanium	Ti	48	1670	3300	4.5	1789
23	vanadium	V	51	1900	3400	6.0	1801
24	chromium	Cr	52	1900	2500	7.2	1797
25	manganese	Mn	55	1250	2000	7.4	1774
26	iron	Fe	56	1540	3000	7.9	*
27	cobalt	Co	59	1490	2900	8.9	1735
28	nickel	Ni	59	1450	2800	8.9	1751
29	copper	Cu	63.5	1080	2500	9.0	*
30	zinc	Zn	65.5	419	910	7.1	17th century
31	gallium	Ga	70	30	2200	5.9	1875
32	germanium	Ge	72.5	950	2800	5.4	1886
33	arsenic	As	75		615	5.7	13th century
34	selenium	Se	79	217	690	4.8	1817
35	bromine	Br	80	−7	58	3.1	1826
36	krypton	Kr	84	−157	−153	0.0035	1898
37	rubidium	Rb	85.5	39	700	1.5	1861
38	strontium	Sr	88	770	1380	2.6	1808
39	yttrium	Y	89	1500	3000	4.5	1794
40	zirconium	Zr	91	1900	4000	6.5	1789
41	niobium	Nb	93	2500	4800	8.5	1801
42	molybdenum	Mo	96	2620	5000	10.2	1782
43	technetium	Tc	99	2200	4600	11.5	1937
44	ruthenium	Ru	101	2500	4000	12.2	1845
45	rhodium	Rh	103	1960	3700	12.4	1803
46	palladium	Pd	106	1550	3000	12.0	1803
47	silver	Ag	108	961	2200	10.5	*
48	cadmium	Cd	112	320	765	8.7	1817
49	indium	In	115	156	2000	7.3	1861
50	tin	Sn	119	232	2600	7.3	*
51	antimony	Sb	122	630	1400	6.6	*
52	tellurium	Te	128	450	990	6.2	1782
53	iodine	I	127	114	183	4.9	1811

*known for thousands of years

Atomic number	Element	Symbol	Approximate relative atomic mass	Melting point (°C)	Boiling point (°C)	Density (g/cm³)	Date of discovery
54	xenon	Xe	131	−112	−108	0.005	1898
55	caesium	Cs	133	29	680	1.9	1861
56	barium	Ba	137	710	1600	3.5	1805
57	lanthanum	La	139	920	3500	6.2	1839
58	cerium	Ce	140	800	3000	6.7	1803
59	praseodymium	Pr	141	935	3100	6.8	1885
60	neodymium	Nd	144	1020	3100	7.0	1885
61	promethium	Pm	147	1030	2700		1945
62	samarium	Sm	150	1080	1600	7.6	1879
63	europium	Eu	152	830	1430	5.3	1901
64	gadolinium	Gd	157	1320	3000	7.9	1886
65	terbium	Tb	159	1400	2600	8.3	1843
66	dysprosium	Dy	162.5	1500	2400	8.5	1886
67	holmium	Ho	165	1500	2500	8.8	1879
68	erbium	Er	167	1500	2700	9.0	1843
69	thulium	Tm	169	1550	2000	9.3	1879
70	ytterbium	Yb	173	824	1500	7.0	1878
71	lutetium	Lu	175	1700	3330	9.9	1907
72	hafnium	Hf	179	2000	5000	13.1	1923
73	tantalum	Ta	181	3000	5400	16.6	1802
74	tungsten	W	184	3400	6000	19.3	1789
75	rhenium	Re	186	3200	5630	21.0	1925
76	osmium	Os	190	2700	5000	22.6	1804
77	iridium	Ir	192	2440	5300	22.5	1804
78	platinum	Pt	195	1770	4000	21.4	1735
79	gold	Au	197	1060	2700	19.3	*
80	mercury	Hg	200	−39	357	13.6	*
81	thallium	Tl	204	300	1460	11.8	1861
82	lead	Pb	207	327	1744	11.3	*
83	bismuth	Bi	209	270	1560	9.8	16th century
84	polonium	Po	210	254	1000	9.3	1898
85	astatine	At	210	302			1940
86	radon	Rn	222	−71	−62	0.009	1900
87	francium	Fr	223	30	650		1936
88	radium	Ra	226	700	1500	5.0	1898
89	actinium	Ac	227	1050	3000		1899
90	thorium	Th	232	1700	4000	11.6	1929
91	protactinium	Pa	231	1200	4000	15.4	1917
92	uranium	U	238	1130	3800	19.0	1789
93	neptunium	Np	237	640		19.5	1940
94	plutonium	Pu	242	640	3200	19.6	1940
95	americium	Am	243	1200	2600	11.7	1944
96	curium	Cm	247				1944
97	berkelium	Bk	247				1949
98	californium	Cf	251				1950
99	einsteinium	Es	254				1952
100	fermium	Fm	253				1953
101	mendelevium	Md	256				1955
102	nobelium	No	254				1958
103	lawrencium	Lw	257				1961
104	kurchatovium or unnilquadrium	Ku or Unq					1969
105	hahnium or unnilpentium	Une					1970

*known for thousands of years

THE PERIODIC TABLE OF THE ELEMENTS

Group

I	II											III	IV	V	VI	VII	0
						1 **H** Hydrogen 1											4 **He** Helium 2
7 **Li** Lithium 3	9 **Be** Beryllium 4											11 **B** Boron 5	12 **C** Carbon 6	14 **N** Nitrogen 7	16 **O** Oxygen 8	19 **F** Fluorine 9	20 **Ne** Neon 10
23 **Na** Sodium 11	24 **Mg** Magnesium 12											27 **Al** Aluminium 13	28 **Si** Silicon 14	31 **P** Phosphorus 15	32 **S** Sulphur 16	35.5 **Cl** Chlorine 17	40 **Ar** Argon 18
39 **K** Potassium 19	40 **Ca** Calcium 20	45 **Sc** Scandium 21	48 **Ti** Titanium 22	51 **V** Vanadium 23	52 **Cr** Chromium 24	55 **Mn** Manganese 25	56 **Fe** Iron 26	59 **Co** Cobalt 27	59 **Ni** Nickel 28	64 **Cu** Copper 29	65 **Zn** Zinc 30	70 **Ga** Gallium 31	73 **Ge** Germanium 32	75 **As** Arsenic 33	79 **Se** Selenium 34	80 **Br** Bromine 35	84 **Kr** Krypton 36
85 **Rb** Rubidium 37	88 **Sr** Strontium 38	89 **Y** Yttrium 39	91 **Zr** Zirconium 40	93 **Nb** Niobium 41	96 **Mo** Molybdenum 42	**Tc** Technetium 43	101 **Ru** Ruthenium 44	103 **Rh** Rhodium 45	106 **Pd** Palladium 46	108 **Ag** Silver 47	112 **Cd** Cadmium 48	115 **In** Indium 49	119 **Sn** Tin 50	122 **Sb** Antimony 51	128 **Te** Tellurium 52	127 **I** Iodine 53	131 **Xe** Xenon 54
133 **Cs** Caesium 55	137 **Ba** Barium 56	139 **La** * Lanthanum 57	178 **Hf** Hafnium 72	181 **Ta** Tantalum 73	184 **W** Tungsten 74	186 **Re** Rhenium 75	190 **Os** Osmium 76	192 **Ir** Iridium 77	195 **Pt** Platinum 78	197 **Au** Gold 79	201 **Hg** Mercury 80	204 **Tl** Thallium 81	207 **Pb** Lead 82	209 **Bi** Bismuth 83	**Po** Polonium 84	**At** Astatine 85	**Rn** Radon 86
Fr Francium 87	226 **Ra** Radium 88	227 **Ac** + Actinium 89	**Unq** Unnilquadrium 104	**Unp** Unnilpentium 105	**Unh** Unnilhexium 106	**Uns** Unnilseptium 107	**Uno** Unniloctium 108	**Une** Unnilenium 109									

* 58 – 71 Lanthanum series

140 **Ce** Cerium 58	141 **Pr** Praseodymium 59	144 **Nd** Neodymium 60	**Pm** Promethium 61	150 **Sm** Samarium 62	152 **Eu** Europium 63	157 **Gd** Gadolinium 64	159 **Tb** Terbium 65	162 **Dy** Dysprosium 66	165 **Ho** Holmium 67	167 **Er** Erbium 68	169 **Tm** Thulium 69	173 **Yb** Ytterbium 70	175 **Lu** Lutetium 71

+ 90 – 103 Actinium series

232 **Th** Thorium 90	**Pa** Protactinium 91	238 **U** Uranium 92	**Np** Neptunium 93	**Pu** Plutonium 94	**Am** Americium 95	**Cm** Curium 96	**Bk** Berkelium 97	**Cf** Californium 98	**Es** Einsteinium 99	**Fm** Fermium 100	**Md** Mendelevium 101	**No** Nobelium 102	**Lr** Lawrencium 103

Key

a
X
b

a = relative atomic mass
X = atomic symbol
b = atomic number

PHYSICAL PROCESSES

71 ELECTRIC CHARGE

▲ Fig 71.1 Lightning is the result of a build-up of static charge

ELECTROSTATICS

Electric charge is a property of two of the particles in atoms – the proton and the electron. These particles have opposite types of charge. The charge on the proton is called positive and that on the electron is called negative.

Atoms are not hard, rigid particles. The outermost electrons can be removed. The friction forces which act when things rub together can remove these electrons.

Atoms which have lost electrons are **positive ions**. They contain more positive than negative charge. **Negative ions** consist of either free electrons or atoms which have gained electrons.

Static electricity

The Greeks discovered that when amber, a fossil resin which they called elektron, was rubbed it attracted dust and small pieces of paper. The amber becomes negatively charged – it takes electrons from the rubbing material, fig 71.2. These electrons stay on the amber – they are **static**.

Fig 71.2 Amber takes electrons from the rubbing material and becomes negatively charged ▶

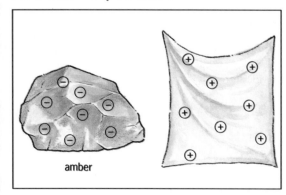

amber

Induced charge

The build-up of negative charge on the amber affects the distribution of charge in anything nearby that is not a good electrical insulator. Most materials allow some movement of charged particles, fig 71.3.

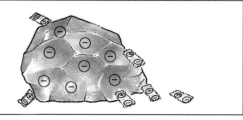

▲ Fig 71.3 Charged amber can induce charges on pieces of paper

Positive ions which are free to move are attracted to the part of the paper nearer to the amber, and free negative ions move away from the negatively charged amber. If only electrons are free to move, they move away from the amber leaving a positively charged area. This movement of charge is called **induction**.

Q1 Acetate is a clear plastic which becomes positively charged when rubbed with a duster.

 a In terms of electron movement, explain how the acetate becomes charged.
 b The charged acetate attracts small pieces of paper. Draw a diagram to show the charge distribution on some pieces of paper near a charged piece of acetate.

SOME EFFECTS AND USES OF ELECTROSTATICS

Spraying

Induction is used for efficient crop spraying and paint spraying, fig 71.4. The drops are charged electrically as they leave the spray. They induce an opposite charge on the surfaces of the plants. The drops are then attracted to all parts of the plant.

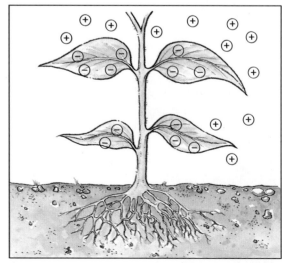

▲ Fig 71.4 The positive spray induces a negative charge on the leaves. More negative charges are attracted into the plant through the roots

Charging up

Anyone who has walked across a nylon carpet awaits a shock when they touch an earthed metal object such as a radiator or the fastening screws of a light switch. As the feet rub against the carpet, electrons rub off onto the carpet, leaving the person positively charged.

When the person becomes connected to earth by a good conductor, a pulse of negative charge passes from the Earth, attracted by the positive charge. As this charge passes through the body, the person feels a shock. If enough charge has built up on the body, it may not be necessary to touch the metal to get a shock – a **spark** can move through the air between the metal and the person.

What is a spark?

The large potential difference between the finger and the earthed screw causes the air to ionise, which means that the atoms split into positive and negative ions. These ions then conduct the charge between the finger and the screw. When the air is ionised and conducts electricity in this way, sparks result. Sparks are useful for lighting the gas on a hob, but they can also be dangerous.

Q2 Explain what happens to the ions in air when a spark passes between the finger of a positively charged person and an earthed metal screw.

Aircraft become charged through friction with the air when flying. When an aeroplane lands, it discharges through the tyres, which are made of conducting material. Charge also builds up when aircraft are being refuelled, due to friction between the fuel and the nozzle. A spark under these conditions could be hazardous, so the metal body of the aircraft is connected to earth during refuelling. This prevents any build-up of charge.

The van de Graaff generator

In a **van de Graaff generator**, fig 71.5, charge is built up on a well-insulated metal dome. A school laboratory model can generate a potential difference of several hundred kilovolts, enough to cause quite a big spark when it ionises the air.

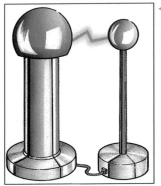

Fig 71.5 A spark flies when the air is ionised and completes the circuit

A dramatic effect is seen when a van de Graaff generator is used to charge a person, fig 71.6.

Larger van de Graaff generators are used to test electrical insulators and to produce large potential differences, of several million volts, for accelerating atomic particles in research on the structure of the nucleus.

Fig 71.6 The charge concentrates where there is the greatest curvature – the hair

Lightning

Lightning is probably the most spectacular display of the effects of a large build-up of charge.

Lightning is not fully understood, but a **charge separation** arises from convection currents within the cloud itself, fig 71.7. The charge at the bottom of the cloud induces an opposite charge in the earth beneath, and lightning is a massive spark between the two.

Fig 71.7 Charge separation in the cloud induces a positive charge in the copper

A **lightning conductor** prevents lightning from striking a building. The lightning conductor is a copper strip, pointed at the top and embedded in the earth at the bottom.

The negative charge at the base of the cloud repels free electrons in the copper to earth, leaving an intense region of positive charge at the tip of the lightning conductor. This creates a large electric force which ionises the air. The positive ions are repelled from the lightning conductor and attracted to the base of the cloud, discharging it.

Q3 Lightning conductors are made from copper.
a Explain why copper is used rather than iron, which is cheaper.
b Explain why the copper strip is pointed at the top.

72 CURRENT AND CHARGE

By the end of this section you should be able to

- describe how charge passes through metals and non-metallic conductors
- perform calculations involving current and charge.

ELECTRIC CURRENT

An **electric current** is a movement of charged particles. The following examples describe some of the ways in which charged particles can move.

Current in gases

Gas molecules can be split into positive and negative ions by using a large electric force to pull off some of the outer electrons. When this happens we say that the gas molecules have been **ionised**.

The electric current in neon lights and fluorescent tubes is due to these ions being accelerated towards the **electrodes**, charged plates at the ends of the tube, fig 72.1. As the ions move towards the electrodes they collide with other atoms and ionise them.

Light or other electromagnetic radiation (see page 252) is given out whenever one of the positive ions captures an electron. The mercury vapour in a fluorescent tube gives out mainly ultraviolet radiation, which is changed into light by the fluorescent coating on the inside of the glass tube.

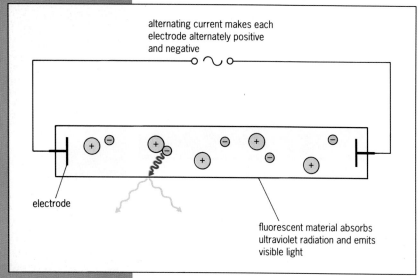

alternating current makes each electrode alternately positive and negative

electrode

fluorescent material absorbs ultraviolet radiation and emits visible light

▲ **Fig 72.1 The movement of ions in the gas of a fluorescent tube**

Current in liquids

An **electrolyte** (a conducting liquid) contains positive and negative ions. The ions are atoms or molecules which have lost or gained electrons. Electrodes in the electrolyte are connected to a cell and ions move towards the electrodes and are discharged (see page 162).

Current in metals

We picture an atom as being a positive nucleus of protons and neutrons which is surrounded by negatively charged electrons. In a neutral atom the positive charge of the protons is balanced by the negative charge of the electrons.

In metals, one or two of the outermost electrons have sufficient energy to move away from the pull of the nucleus and become 'free'. These 'free' electrons move within the metal in a way which is similar to the movement of molecules in a gas. They move in a rapid unordered motion, changing direction when they collide with the positive ions, fig 72.2.

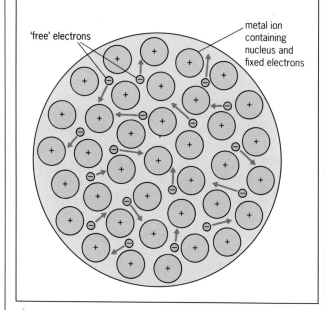

'free' electrons

metal ion containing nucleus and fixed electrons

▲ **Fig 72.2 Free electrons can move within the metal structure**

When a cell or battery of cells is connected to a metal, these 'free' electrons drift at low speeds away from the negative and towards the positive terminal. The cell pushes out electrons from its negative terminal and takes them in at the positive terminal.

Current in a vacuum

When metals are heated, some of the free electrons can gain enough kinetic energy to escape from the metal surface. This is called **thermionic emission** and it produces the electron beams used in television tubes and X-ray tubes, fig 72.3. The electrons are focused into a beam and accelerated to high speeds. The tubes are evacuated so that the beam is not scattered by air molecules.

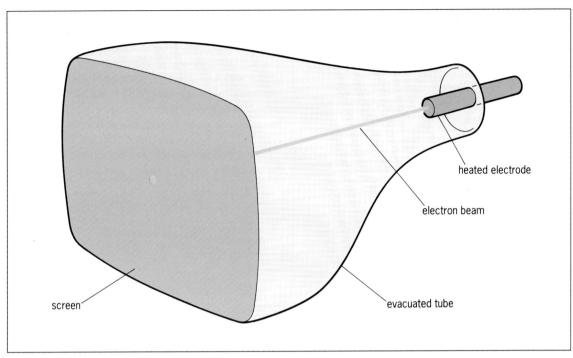

▲ **Fig 72.3 The television tube**

MEASURING CHARGE AND CURRENT

Electric charge is measured in units called **coulombs**. One coulomb is the amount of charge which flows when a current of one ampere passes for one second.

The smallest unit of charge

Robert Millikan was a scientist who realised that quantities of charge can only exist in whole-number multiples of the smallest unit. The smallest unit is the amount of charge on one electron or proton. In the same way, the amount of money which you can have in your pocket must be a multiple of 1p.

Millikan spent years measuring quantities of charge to find the size of this smallest unit, and so find the amount of charge carried by an electron or a proton. The amount is 1.6×10^{-19}C. The number of electrons which you must isolate in order to have one coulomb of charge is 6.25×10^{18}.

Measuring current

The size of an electric current in amperes, or amps for short, is equal to the rate of flow of charge in coulombs per second. The following equation shows this.

$$\text{current (A)} = \frac{\text{charge (C)}}{\text{time (s)}}$$

In symbols $I = \dfrac{Q}{t}$

Q1 1C of charge flows through a 60W mains lamp in 4s. Calculate the current.

Q2 The amount of charge which flows through a 60W car headlamp in 1 minute is 300C. Calculate the current.

Q3 An electric shower carries a current of 7A. How much charge flows through the heater in 5 minutes?

Q4 It takes 14 hours to recharge a set of nickel-cadmium cells. The current is 140mA (0.14A). How much charge flows through the cells in this time ?

Q5 A 1.5V cell can deliver a current of 0.15A to a cycle lamp. How long does it take for the cell to push out 100C of charge? What happens to this charge?

Energy carriers

The answer to question 5 is that after going through the lamp the charge returns to the cell. Lamps, motors and other electrical devices do not 'use up' electric charge or current; the current passing into a lamp is equal to the current coming out.

The movement of charge in a circuit enables the electrical energy to be transferred from the energy source to the devices which then transfer that energy into other forms.

By the end of this section you should be able to

■ calculate the cost of the electrical energy used at home

■ measure the energy and power transferred in a circuit.

MEASURING ENERGY

The kilowatt hour

Electricity companies charge for the energy which is transferred to our houses by the electric current. If you look at an electricity meter you will see the letters 'kWh', under the numbers. This stands for kilowatt hours, the units of energy used by electricity companies.

Fig 73.1 ▶ Electricity companies measure electrical energy in kilowatt hours

A kilowatt hour is the amount of energy converted by a 1 kW appliance in 1 hour. The energy transferred from the mains supply by an appliance is calculated using the formula

energy (kW h) = power (kW) × time (h)
In symbols $E = Pt$

Q1 Use the formula above to calculate the energy converted in the following examples.

  a A 2 kW convector heater used for 3 hours

  b A 2.4 kW kettle which takes 5 minutes to boil some water

  c A 60 W lamp left on from 10 p.m. to 7 a.m.

  d A 7 kW shower used for 8 minutes

  e A 2.5 kW immersion heater switched on for 8 hours

  f It is unlikely that the immersion heater in **e** will actually use this amount of energy. Explain why.

Q2 Find out the current price of 1 kW h of energy and calculate the cost of each example in question 1.

Q3 Monitor your electricity meter readings for a week by taking a reading at the same time each day. Make a bar chart of the results. Try to account for the energy consumption.

The joule

The kilowatt hour is a convenient unit of energy for electricity companies, but it is too large to use in school laboratory work. A **joulemeter** works in a similar way to a domestic electricity meter, but it measures the energy supplied in **joules**. The joule is the unit of energy normally used in scientific work. The joule is a much smaller unit of energy than the kilowatt hour – there are 3 600 000 J in 1 kW h.

Fig 73.2 shows a joulemeter being used to measure the amount of energy needed to make a cup of tea.

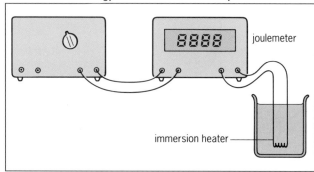

joulemeter

immersion heater

▲ **Fig 73.2 How much energy does it take to make a cup of tea?**

TRANSFERRING ENERGY

An electric circuit transfers energy from the source (the battery or power supply) to an appliance. At home the appliance could be, for example, a kettle, a vacuum cleaner or a cooker. In school laboratory work it is convenient to use lamps or small heaters to make circuits to experiment with.

Potential difference

Voltmeters measure the energy which is transferred in a circuit by measuring the energy gains and losses between two points in the circuit, fig 73.3.

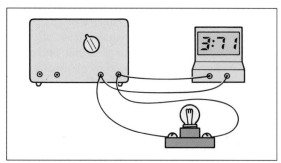

▲ **Fig 73.3 The voltmeter measures the energy difference across the power supply**

The voltmeter measures the energy gained by the charge from the power supply. The reading '3.71 V' means that 3.71 J of energy are taken from the supply by each coulomb of charge passing round the circuit. Fig 73.4 shows how much of this energy reaches the lamp.

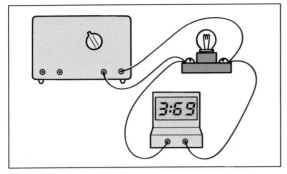

▲ **Fig 73.4 The voltmeter measures the energy difference across the bulb**

The reading is almost the same as before in fig 73.3, showing that most of the energy from the supply is being delivered to the lamp.

The connecting wires in circuits should be fairly thick. If they are too thin they absorb a significant amount of energy from the charge, which could lead to overheating.

The energy transfer to or from a coulomb of charge passing between two points in a circuit is called the **potential difference** (p.d.) or **voltage**.

CALCULATING ELECTRICAL ENERGY TRANSFER

The energy delivered to a circuit component can be calculated using ammeter and voltmeter readings, as shown in fig 73.5.

Q4 Work out how much energy is delivered each second in the circuit in fig 73.5.

Q5 Calculate the energy delivered each second in the circuits in fig 73.6.

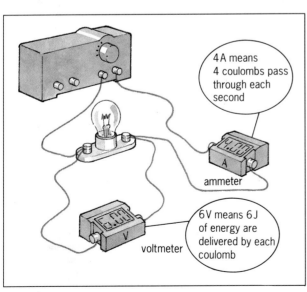

4A means 4 coulombs pass through each second

ammeter

6V means 6J of energy are delivered by each coulomb

voltmeter

▲ **Fig 73.5 Transfer of electrical energy**

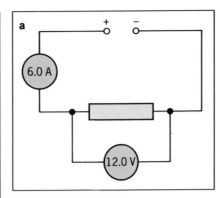

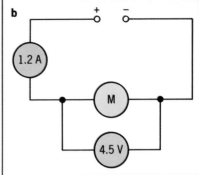

Fig 73.6

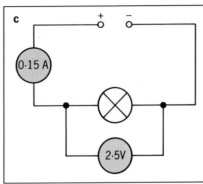

Electrical power

You have been calculating the energy delivered each second by multiplying the current in a component by the potential difference across it. The energy delivered each second is also known as the **power**. The equation for electrical power is

power (W) = current (A) × p.d. (V)
In symbols $P = IV$

The power is the energy transferred per second. To calculate the total energy transfer over a period of time, the power is multiplied by the time in seconds.

energy (J) = current (A) × p.d. (V) × time (s)
$$E = IVt$$
or $E = Pt$

Q6 Calculate the power of a 2.5V torch lamp carrying a current of 0.15A. How much energy is transferred in the lamp in 5 minutes?

Q7 Copy and complete the following table.

Device	Current (A)	p.d. (V)	Power (W)
iron	6	240	
headlamp		12	60
reading lamp		240	60
loudspeaker	0.3		1.5

COMPARING CONDUCTORS

By the end of this section you should be able to
- understand resistance and the factors which affect it
- measure the resistance of a conductor
- use the resistance equation.

Activity

1 Set up the circuit in fig 74.1 using samples of wire.
2 Place one of the wire samples in the gap and adjust the variable resistor until the current is 1.0 A. Note the reading on the voltmeter.
3 Repeat this for the other wire samples and record your results in a suitable table.

The sample which requires the smallest potential difference to pass a current of 1.0 A is the best **conductor**.

4 Make a list of the samples in order of electrical conductivity, starting with the best conductor.
5 Now write out the list in reverse order, so that the poorest conductor is at the beginning.

The poorest conductor has the greatest amount of **resistance** to the electric current.

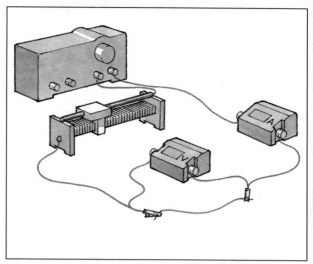

▲ Fig 74.1

Q1 To help you understand how resistance is measured, copy and complete the following table.

	Potential difference (V)	Current (A)	Number of volts of p.d. for each amp of current (V/A)
a	12	3	12 ÷ 3 = 4
b	12	6	
c	240	12	
d	15	0.5	
e	6	1.5	
f	2.5	0.15	

Resistance

Of the examples in question 1, **d** has the greatest **resistance** because it needs the greatest potential difference to pass 1A of current in it. Resistance is calculated as 'the number of volts per amp'. The unit of resistance is the **ohm** (Ω).

The equation for resistance is

resistance (Ω) = p.d. (V) ÷ current (A)

In symbols $R = V / I$

Q2 Copy and complete the following table using the resistance equation.

	Potential difference (V)	Current (A)	Resistance (Ω)
a	240	0.25	
b	12	4	
c	15	90	
d	3		6
e		2.5	12
f	25		15
g		0.2	4.7

INVESTIGATING THE RESISTANCE OF A METAL WIRE

Activity

Use the circuit in fig 74.2 to investigate the resistance of a piece of wire.

Measure the potential difference for a range of current values up to 1 A. Record your results in a table similar to that in question 2. Then plot your results on a graph of potential difference against current.

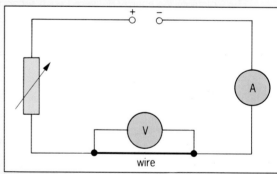

▲ Fig 74.2

Resistance and temperature

The resistance of a metal wire which stays at the same temperature has a constant value. The wire in your experiment may have become warm, but it should not have had a significant effect on the resistance. The slope of the graph of potential difference against current is a good indicator of the resistance – when the resistance increases, the graph becomes steeper.

INVESTIGATING THE RESISTANCE OF A FILAMENT LAMP

Activity

The wire in a filament lamp gets very hot – over 2000 °C. In this investigation you will measure the resistance as the filament heats up. If you use a circuit similar to fig 74.2 you will need to start with a low setting on the power pack to get a small potential difference across the lamp, gradually moving to a higher setting. The potential divider circuit in fig 74.3 allows you to vary the potential difference over the whole range without having to alter the power pack setting. As before, tabulate your results and plot a graph of potential difference against current. Look at the pattern in the change in resistance in your table and compare it with the slope of the graph.

Fig 74.3 ▶

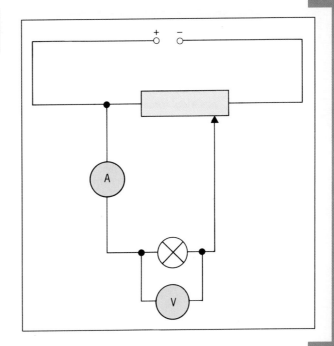

INVESTIGATING RESISTANCE AND AREA OF CROSS-SECTION

Activity

How does the resistance of a conductor depend on its cross-sectional area? You should be able to make a prediction, based on your understanding of charge flow in a circuit. Plan an investigation, using either conducting putty or resistance wire, to test your hypothesis.

USEFUL RESISTORS

Strain guages

A **strain gauge**, fig 74.4, is a piece of resistance wire which can be used to measure forces.

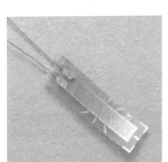

◀ **Fig 74.4 The strain guage is bonded to the material being tested. As it is stretched the wire becomes longer and thinner**

 Q3 What effect do the changes on stretching have on the resistance of the strain gauge?

Strain gauges can be built into structures such as bridges so that their resistance and so the forces in the bridge can be monitored by a computer.

Q4 What other physical changes could affect the resistance of a strain gauge?

Thermistors

A **thermistor**, fig 74.5, is made from semiconducting material. The resistance of a semiconductor is midway between that of a conductor and an insulator.

◀ **Fig 74.5 Thermistors**

Activity

Design and plan an experiment to investigate how the resistance of a thermistor changes with temperature between 0 °C and 100 °C. You need to pay due regard to safety. Carry out the experiment when your teacher has approved your plan.

The resistance of a thermistor changes greatly for small changes in temperature, much more than that of metallic conductors. Their uses range from temperature sensors in incubators to detectors of radiation from distant stars in infra-red telescopes.

75 MAGNETIC FORCES

By the end of this section you should be able to

- describe the magnetic effect of an electric current
- describe the operation of a relay.

ELECTRIC CURRENT AND MAGNETIC FIELD

You have seen how a build-up of electric charge can cause large electrical forces, such as in lightning. Electric currents also cause **magnetic forces**. Wherever there is an electric current, there is a magnetic field around it. This is called **electromagnetism**. There is no obvious effect if you put a magnetic material near a lamp, because the forces due to the current in the wires and the filament are very weak. The following experiments show magnetic forces due to electric currents. You will need to concentrate on careful observation when carrying them out.

DEMONSTRATING ELECTROMAGNETISM

Activity

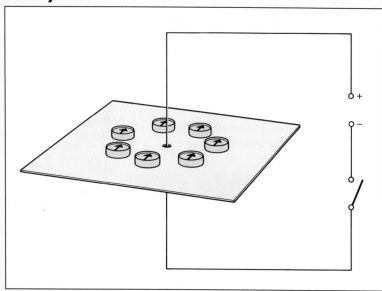

▲ **Fig 75.1**

Fig 75.1 shows an experiment to investigate the magnetic field around a wire.

Q1 Explain why all the compasses point the same way.

Q2 Describe what happens when the current is

- **a** switched on
- **b** switched off
- **c** reversed.

Q3 Draw and describe the pattern which is seen when the compasses are replaced by a sprinkling of iron filings.

Activity

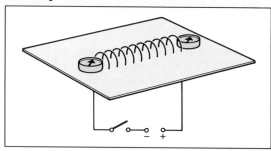

▲ **Fig 75.2**

The experiment in fig 75.2 is to investigate the magnetic field around the coil. It works best if the coil is placed so that it lies east–west.

Q4 Describe the effect on the compasses when the current is switched on and off.

MAKING AN ELECTROMAGNET

The experiments in figs 75.1 and 75.2 show that the magnetic forces due to electric currents are very weak. However, there is a simple way to make them stronger.

Activity

Place an iron nail in the centre of the coil of wire in fig 75.2. A coil with an iron core is called an **electromagnet**.

You should now find that, with the current switched on, the electromagnet is strong enough to pick up small objects made of magnetic materials. If you put the electromagnet flat on a piece of paper you will be able to see the shape of the magnetic field using iron filings. Do not take a small compass close to the electromagnet as it may destroy or reverse its magnetism.

Investigation

Think of the factors which could determine the pulling force of an electromagnet. Make a prediction about the effect of these factors. Design and carry out an investigation to test your hypothesis.

HOW AN ELECTROMAGNET WORKS

An electromagnet consists of a coil of wire around an iron core. When the current in the coil is switched on, the iron quickly becomes magnetised. The magnetic field of the iron is very strong. The iron loses its magnetism when the current is switched off.

USES OF ELECTROMAGNETS

Electromagnets have many uses. They are used to store information as magnetic regions on tape or disc, to control the water valves in automatic washing machines, to lift and sort metals, and all electric motors use electromagnets.

Cassette head

▲ **Fig 75.3 These devices all use an electromagnet**

Relays

A **relay**, fig 75.4, is a switch operated by an electromagnet. It is useful where remote switching is required.

▲ **Fig 75.4 A relay**

The coil only needs a small current to operate it, but the contacts can be used to switch much larger currents. The control circuit that switches the relay on and off can therefore carry a much smaller current than that needed to operate a device. Fig 75.4 shows a type of relay which is used to operate a rear window heater in a car.

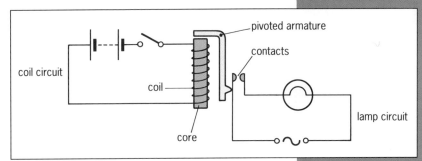

▲ **Fig 75.5**

Q5 Fig 75.5 shows a battery-operated relay being used to switch on a mains lamp. Write out the statements **a–f** so that they give a correct description of what happens when the current to the relay coil is switched on.

  a The relay contacts are pushed together.
  b Current passes through the lamp.
  c Current passes in the relay coil.
  d A magnetic field is produced in the the coil.
  e The core is magnetised.
  f The pivoted armature is attracted to the coil.

Q6 Write out a description of what happens when the current to the relay coil is switched off.

Advantages of relays

One advantage of using a relay is that the wires to the switch only have to carry a small current, so thin wires can be used. Relays are also used to operate starter motors in cars, fig 75.6. These motors need very large currents, in excess of 100 A. Without a relay, very thick cables would need to go to the ignition switch.

◀ **Fig 75.6 Using a relay in a car starter motor circuit**

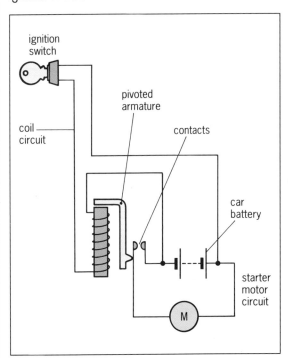

76 ELECTRO-MAGNETIC DEVICES

By the end of this section you should be able to

■ describe the use of electromagnetism in motors and loudspeakers.

A simple electromagnet made by winding a coil around an iron core can pull magnetic materials towards it, but it cannot push or turn things round. The interaction of two magnetic fields is needed to produce the turning forces in an electric motor and the forces which cause the vibration of a loudspeaker. One magnetic field comes from an electromagnet, the other from a fixed permanent magnet or another electromagnet.

THE CATAPULT FORCE

Activity

Fig 76.1 shows how to investigate the force on a current-carrying wire placed in a magnetic field.

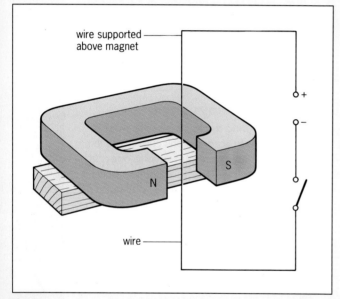

▲ **Fig 76.1**

Q1 Describe the effect on the force of

a increasing the current
b reversing the current, or magnetic field, or both.

Q2 Draw a diagram which shows the relative directions of the current, the magnetic field and the force on the wire.

THE ELECTRIC MOTOR

Electric motors use magnetic forces to produce a rotation. Fig 76.2 shows a simple d.c. motor which uses a permanent magnet.

Q3 Explain how the forces on the coil of wire cause it to rotate.

Practical motors

If you make a motor like that shown in fig 76.2 you will find that it cannot exert a very large force. In addition, the turning force is at its greatest when the coil is horizontal, and there is no turning force at all when the coil is vertical.

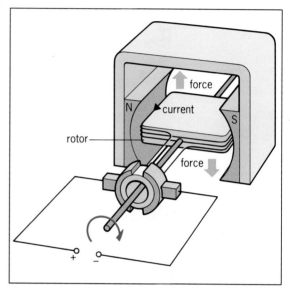

▲ **Fig 76.2 An electric motor. Relative to the magnetic field, the currents in the opposite sides of the coil are in opposite directions, so opposite sides of the coil move in opposite directions**

▲ **Fig 76.3 The motor of a washing machine has several coils of wire on the armature**

Practical motors such as that in fig 76.3 get over this by having several coils of wire on the armature. At any one time there is a coil in a position to give the maximum turning force. The fixed magnets (not shown) are also electromagnets, and iron cores are used to give a greater magnetic field.

Motors designed for domestic use also have to operate from alternating current. Alternating current motors cannot produce the large forces needed to accelerate very massive objects such as trains, so direct current motors are used, fig 76.4.

Fig 76.4 The windings on a motor from a train carry large currents, so the wires have to be very thick

LOUDSPEAKERS

Fig 76.5 Loudspeakers operate on the same principle as motors – a current at right angles to a magnetic field causes a force which is perpendicular to both the field and the current

How a loudspeaker works

The permanent magnet used in a loudspeaker is a cylindrical shape, with one pole in the centre and the other on the outside. Fig 76.6 shows the magnetic field.

The coil which carries the alternating curent from the amplifier is placed between the poles of the magnet, fixed to the back of a paper cone, fig 76.7.

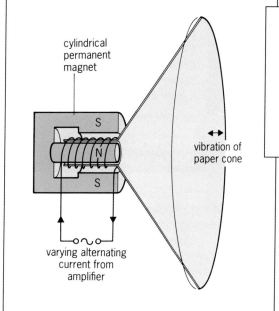

cylindrical permanent magnet

vibration of paper cone

varying alternating current from amplifier

Fig 76.6 A loudspeaker magnet

Fig 76.7 The construction of a loudspeaker

With the current in the direction shown in the diagram, the coil and cone are pushed out. When the current reverses, so does the direction of the movement. The reproduction of very high frequency sounds can require the coil to push the paper cone in and out 20 000 times each second, so the whole assembly needs to be very light in weight.

RECORDING ON TAPE

Electromagnets are used to record information on magnetic tape. The tape is coated with a powdered magnetic material which becomes magnetised as it passes a gap in the core of the electromagnet, fig 76.8.

Fig 76.8 The construction of a recording head

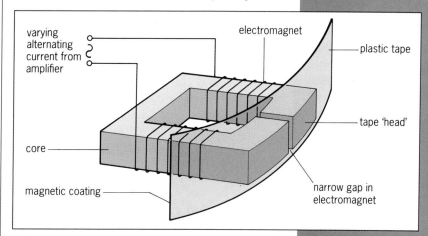

varying alternating current from amplifier

electromagnet

plastic tape

tape 'head'

core

narrow gap in electromagnet

magnetic coating

Very high frequency alternating current passes in the coil, causing a magnetic field in the core which alternates at the same frequency as the current. The part of the tape which is in the gap completes the core of the electromagnet, and the magnetic field passes through the magnetic coating of the tape.

By the end of this section you should be able to

- understand the process of electromagnetic induction
- describe how a dynamo generates electricity.

In 1831, Michael Faraday (see page 165) discovered that magnetism can be used to produce electricity. The electricity supply industry relies on this **electromagnetic induction** to generate electricity and to transmit it to all parts of the country.

DEMONSTRATING ELECTROMAGNETIC INDUCTION

The following experiments show the principles of the **generator** which produces electricity and the **transformer** which enables it to be transmitted over large distances with low energy losses. The experiments require very careful observation.

Activity

Set up the circuit shown in fig 77.1.

Q1 Watch carefully and describe what happens when

- **a** the magnet is moved slowly into the coil
- **b** the magnet is held steady inside the coil
- **c** the magnet is withdrawn slowly from the coil
- **d** the magnet is moved quickly in and out of the coil.

It is not essential to move the magnet; you can produce the same effect by standing the magnet upright and moving the coil.

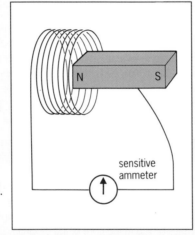

▲ **Fig 77.1**

You will have seen that the ammeter registered very small **induced currents** when the magnet was moving relative to the coil, fig 77.2.

Fig 77.2 Moving the magnet induces a current ▶

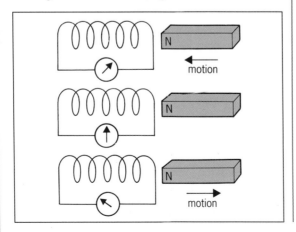

HOW DOES ELECTROMAGNETIC INDUCTION HAPPEN?

Electromagnetic induction occurs when the magnetic field around a conductor changes, and there are several ways in which this change can take place. You have seen two – by moving the magnet near the conductor or moving the conductor near the magnet.

You should have noticed that if you moved the magnet faster the meter needle showed a larger deflection. Another way of increasing the size of the induced current is to use more turns of wire on the coil.

Induced potential difference

Electromagnetic induction can be summarised by saying that a potential difference is created (**induced**) in a conductor when the magnetic field around it changes. If there is a complete circuit, then the induced potential difference causes a current to pass in the conductor. The size of the induced potential difference depends on how quickly the magnetic field is changing.

GENERATING ELECTRICITY

A bicycle dynamo

A **bicycle dynamo** generates electric current to light a lamp. It consists of a magnet which rotates next to a coil of wire. The induced potential difference is made as large as possible by winding the coil on soft iron. As the magnet rotates, the magnetic field around the coil is changing all the time, causing a continuous potential difference to be induced, fig 77.3.

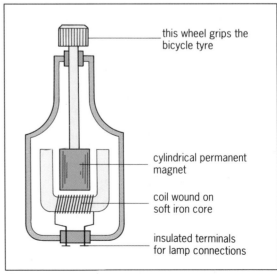

this wheel grips the bicycle tyre

cylindrical permanent magnet

coil wound on soft iron core

insulated terminals for lamp connections

▲ **Fig 77.3 A bicycle dynamo**

Activity

Use a cathode ray oscilloscope (CRO) to show how the potential difference from the dynamo changes with time, fig 77.4.

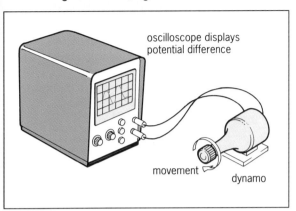

oscilloscope displays
potential difference

movement

dynamo

▲ **Fig 77.4**

It is not easy to study the trace on the CRO because it is only there while you are turning the dynamo. Use a computer to record the output potential difference from the dynamo over a period of 5 s and display the results as a graph.

Changing speed

The trace in fig 77.5 was obtained by turning the handle slowly at first and then speeding up.

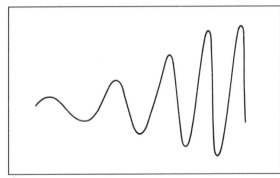

▲ **Fig 77.5 Sample trace**

 As the dynamo is turned faster, what two changes occur to the output potential difference? Explain these changes.

Generators

Generators at power stations are larger versions of bicycle dynamos, fig 77.6. An electromagnet spins inside three large coils. This causes an alternating potential difference to be induced in each coil, at a frequency of 50 Hz.

A CRO picture of the way in which the mains potential difference changes with time shows a much smoother trace than that from the bicycle dynamo, fig 77.7.

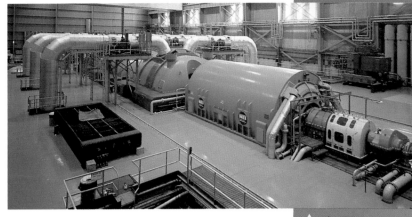

▲ **Fig 77.6
A generator in a power station**

p.d.

0.01   0.02   time(s)

◀ **Fig 77.7 One cycle of a mains waveform**

INDUCTION MELTING

Large quantities of metal are melted in foundries. The molten metal is poured into moulds to make metal objects. To melt the solid metal, it is placed in a heat-resistant container called a crucible. This is then placed inside a coil which carries a high-frequency current, fig 77.8.

The rapidly changing magnetic field causes a potential difference to be induced in the metal. This in turn causes a large current because of the low resistance. The induced current heats the metal and eventually melts it.

◀ **Fig 77.8 An induction furnace**

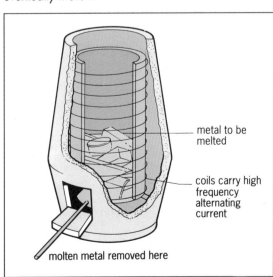

metal to be melted

coils carry high frequency alternating current

molten metal removed here

78 TRANSFORMERS

By the end of this section you should be able to
- describe the construction and operation of a transformer
- explain how transformers increase the efficiency of power transmission.

When electricity has been generated at a power station, the potential difference is increased before it is transmitted. This is done using a **transformer**. The next experiments will help you to understand what a transformer does and how it works.

MORE INDUCTION EXPERIMENTS

Activity

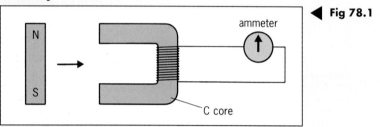
◀ **Fig 78.1**

Fig 78.1 shows the apparatus to investigate the size of an induced current.

Q1 Describe your observations of the ammeter reading when the magnet is moved towards and away from the coil. You should try moving the magnet both quickly and slowly.

Moving the magnet towards the coil makes the magnetic field around the coil stronger. The magnetic field becomes weaker as the magnet is moved away.

Q2 Describe how you can use the magnet and coil to generate an alternating current. What affects the size and frequency of the alternating current which you generate?

Now use an electromagnet instead of the permanent magnet. To make the electromagnet, wind a coil on another C core and use a 1.5V cell as a power supply. Clip the two C cores together as in fig 78.2.

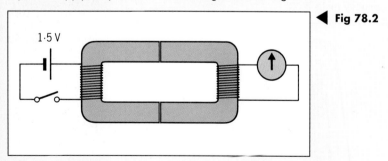
◀ **Fig 78.2**

Q3 Describe what happens to the meter needle when the current is

a switched on **b** left on **c** switched off.

Summarise your findings. Use the idea of changing magnetic fields to explain your observations.

MAKING A TRANSFORMER

Changing the magnetic field continuously

Connecting and disconnecting the cell in the last experiment has a similar effect to moving the magnet to and fro. This reinforces what you have seen earlier – that electromagnetic induction occurs when the magnetic field around a conductor changes. The magnetic field can be made to change continuously if the 1.5V cell is replaced with an alternating current source.

Activity

Use a 2V a.c. source for the electromagnet instead of the cell in fig 78.2. The ammeter which you used before will not be able to respond quickly enough to the change in direction of the induced current. Use a lamp or an a.c. voltmeter instead.

How a transformer works

You should notice that the lamp stays lit or the voltmeter gives a steady reading. The magnetic field due to the electromagnet is changing all the time, inducing an alternating current in the other coil. The device you have made is a **transformer**. It transfers electrical energy from one coil to another through a changing magnetic field.

TRANSFORMER EXPERIMENTS

To find out what a transformer does, experiment with different numbers of turns on the two coils.

The coil which is connected to the supply is called the **primary coil**. The one connected to the lamp or voltmeter is called the **secondary coil**, fig 78.3.

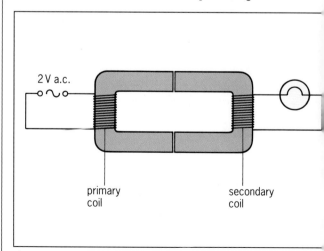

▲ **Fig 78.3 The two coils of a transformer**

Activity

Copy the table below.

Number of turns on primary coil	Number of turns on secondary coil	Brightness of lamp or voltmeter reading
20	20	
20	10	
20	30	
30	10	
30	20	
30	30	
30	50	

Carry out the experiment, completing the table as you go along. Write a summary of your results.

Step-up and step-down transformers

Transformers change the size of an alternating voltage. Whether a transformer makes the voltage bigger (**step-up**) or smaller (**step-down**) does not depend on the actual numbers of turns used on the coils, but on their ratio.

Q4 Use the results of your experiments to describe the difference in construction of a step-up and step-down transformer.

Q5 Make a list of things which use transformers. Find out which are step-up transformers and which are step-down.

THE TRANSFORMER EQUATION

A transformer which has twice as many turns of wire on the secondary coil as there are on the primary has an output voltage which is twice as big as the input voltage. The **turns ratio** is the same as the **voltage ratio**. This can be written as a formula

$$\frac{\text{number of turns on primary coil}}{\text{number of turns on secondary coil}} = \frac{\text{primary voltage}}{\text{secondary voltage}}$$

You will not need to use the formula if you can work with ratios.

Q6 Copy and complete the following table using ratios or the formula.

	Number of turns on primary coil	Number of turns on secondary coil	Primary voltage (V)	Secondary voltage (V)
a	100	200	6	
b		50	240	12
c	1500	6000		4800
d	2000		240	3
e		12000	1500	120 000
f		50	240	0.6
g	600	24 000	50	
h	150	1050		35

TRANSFORMERS AND EFFICIENCY

Power in and power out

Transformers provide a very efficient way of changing the size of an alternating voltage. As with any device which converts energy, there is some energy loss. Some of the energy input is changed to heat energy in the windings and in the iron core. Because this is a relatively small amount, it is normally assumed that the electrical power output is equal to the power input. The power is the voltage multiplied by the current, page 195.

Step-up transformers give an increase in voltage, but they do not give energy for nothing! Assuming the transformer is 100% efficient,

$$\frac{\text{primary voltage} \times}{\text{primary current}} = \frac{\text{secondary voltage}}{\times \text{ secondary current}}$$

A step-up transformer which doubles the input voltage also halves the input current. The relationship between the numbers of turns and the currents can be written as a formula

$$\frac{\text{number of turns on primary coil}}{\text{number of turns on secondary coil}} = \frac{\text{secondary current}}{\text{primary current}}$$

Like the formula for voltages, this can be cumbersome to use. You may find it easier to work with ratios.

By the end of this section you should be able to

- appreciate the need to reduce energy losses in the transmission of electrical energy and how this is achieved
- describe how transformers are used in the distribution of electricity
- discuss the economic and environmental issues associated with electricity supply.

GENERATING AND DISTRIBUTING ELECTRICITY

The National Grid network links the whole country. Power is fed into it from power stations and taken from it wherever it is needed. Most of the energy is produced by burning coal, and there are also significant contributions from oil and nuclear energy. Small amounts are generated from the energy in moving water and wind.

Power into the grid

The generators in power stations produce electricity at 25 kV (see page 225). Each generator has three large coils which are fixed, fig 79.1. A direct current electromagnet rotates inside these coils, completing 50 revolutions of the magnetic field each second. This causes an alternating current at a frequency of 50 Hz to be induced in each of the coils.

Fig 79.1 An alternating current is induced in the coils of a generator ▼

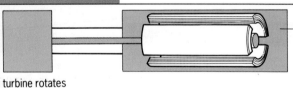

turbine rotates due to heat from fuel

the generator contains three sets of fixed coils. An electromagnet is turned inside the coils by the action of the turbine, and a current is induced in the coils.

Increasing the voltage

Electrical energy from the generators passes to transformers which are used to increase the voltage before the energy goes into the grid. The following experiment shows why.

Activity

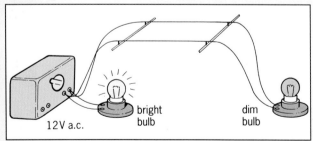

12 V a.c.   bright bulb   dim bulb

▲ **Fig 79.2**

Leave the power line in fig 79.2 running for a few minutes. Switch it off and feel the transmission wires.

Q1 Has energy been wasted? How can you tell?

When the energy is transmitted at a low voltage there are large energy losses in the cables.

How much power is lost?

The rate at which electrical energy is converted to heat in a resistor, such as a wire, is calculated from the formula

power = current × potential difference

Power transmission wires are like the connecting wires in a circuit. They carry the energy from the source to the consumer. The main difference is that they are a lot longer, and so the potential difference between the ends of each transmission wire cannot be ignored, fig 79.3.

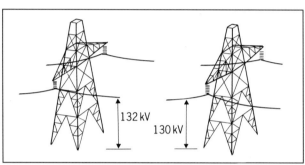

132 kV   130 kV

▲ **Fig 79.3 Energy losses in the transmission wires have caused a 2 kV drop in potential difference**

It is difficult to measure the potential difference loss as the power is transmitted, so to calculate power losses it is easier to use an alternative form of the power equation:

$$\text{power} = (\text{current})^2 \times \text{resistance}$$
In symbols $P = I^2 R$

This equation is easily derived by combining the equations $P = IV$ and $V = IR$.

Q2 A 100 MW (1×10^8 W) generator produces electrical energy at a potential difference of 25 kV (2.5×10^4 V).

- **a** Use the equation $P = IV$ to calculate the current which is generated.
- **b** If the power is transmitted at this potential difference through wires with a resistance of 2 Ω, use the equation $P = I^2R$ to calculate the power changed to heat in the wires.
- **c** The same power is stepped up to 400 kV before being transmitted. Calculate the current in the transmission wires.
- **d** Calculate the power loss when the power is transmitted at the higher potential difference and lower current.

The answers to question 2 show that there are large savings to be made in transmitting power at high voltage and low current. Because the power loss depends on (current)², reducing the current by a factor of 10 reduces the waste by a factor of 100.

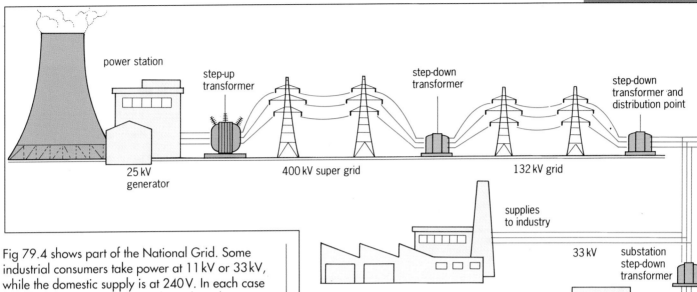

power station

step-up transformer

step-down transformer

step-down transformer and distribution point

25 kV generator

400 kV super grid

132 kV grid

supplies to industry

33 kV

substation step-down transformer

supply to domestic users

11 kV

substation step-down transformer

240 V

▲ **Fig 79.4 The National Grid**

Fig 79.4 shows part of the National Grid. Some industrial consumers take power at 11 kV or 33 kV, while the domestic supply is at 240 V. In each case transformers are used to step down the voltage . Between the transmission lines and our homes there are several step-down transformers.

Q3 Describe the use of transformers in the distribution of electricity and explain why they are necessary.

Q4 Explain why alternating current has to be used for transmitting electrical energy over long distances.

Saving energy, smaller cables

At high voltage the same power is transmitted using a current of hundreds of amps instead of thousands. This enables both the energy loss and the size of the cables required to be minimised.

▲ **Fig 79.5 Is overhead better than underground?**

OVERHEAD AND UNDERGROUND

Electricity pylons do not add to the beauty of the town or country landscape. However, there are two reasons why the electricity supply industry prefers using overhead cables and pylons to burying the cables underground.

Electrical insulation

Cables carrying very high potential difference need very good insulation. Several metres of air form a good electrical insulator.

Cooling

As you have seen, using a high voltage and low current reduces the energy losses, but the transmission wires do still get hot. The air surrounding the overhead wires acts as a coolant. It carries the heat energy away through convection currents (see page 218). When cables are buried underground, the electrical insulator used is also a very good heat insulator, so an alternative method has to be found to stop the cables from overheating.

Q5 Find out how underground cables in the National Grid are insulated and cooled.

ELECTRICITY AND MAGNETISM

207

By the end of this section you should be able to

- understand the principles of domestic wiring
- describe and explain the safety features which are necessary when using mains electricity.

DOMESTIC WIRING

Homes are wired using a number of parallel circuits, so each socket be can used independently of the rest. The circuits are connected to the main supply in the fuse box or consumer unit. Modern installations use circuit breakers instead of rewirable fuses.

Q1 Find out the advantages of circuit breakers over fuses.

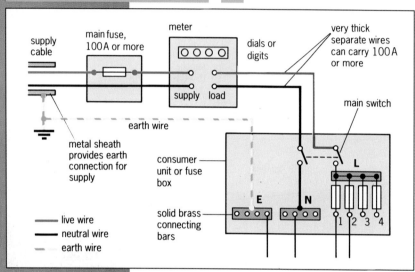

▲ **Fig 80.1 The electricity supply to your home**

Fig 80.1 shows how all the neutral and earth wires are connected together in the consumer unit. Each live wire is connected to the supply through a fuse or circuit breaker. This cuts off the electricity supply if the circuit is overloaded. Too much current could cause the cables to overheat and start a fire.

Radial and ring circuits

Fixed high-power appliances such as cookers, showers and immersion heaters should each have their own cable and fuse, fig 80.2. These are **radial circuits**.

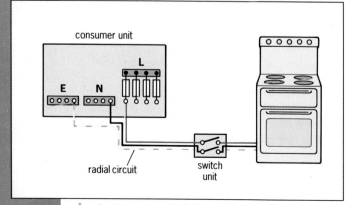

▲ **Fig 80.2 A radial circuit for a cooker**

Sockets are wired using a **ring main**. Each socket on the ring main is connected to the consumer unit by two sets of conductors. The ring main enables thinner cables to be used as there are two paths for the current to take from the consumer unit to each socket, fig 80.3.

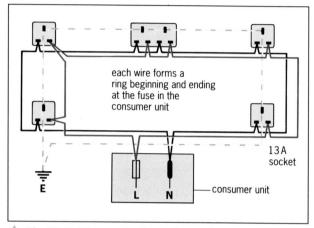

▲ **Fig 80.3 Ring main circuit for sockets**

Lighting circuit

The current in the **lighting circuit** is small, since lights are low power devices, so it is not necessary to have two current paths. Fig 80.4 shows how the switch for each light fitting is placed in the live connection.

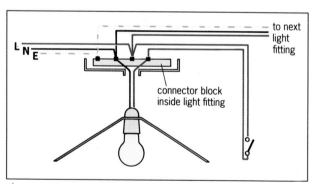

▲ **Fig 80.4 Lighting circuit**

Q2 If the switch were placed in the neutral wire it would still turn the light on and off. Under what circumstances could this be dangerous?

FUSES

The fuses in the consumer unit are normally 30 A for a radial or a ring main circuit and 5 A for a lighting circuit. These fuses are there to protect the fixed wiring cables. Each appliance connected to the ring main should also have its own fuse fitted in the plug, which allows sufficient current to pass in normal operation but cuts off the supply if a fault occurs to cause a larger current than normal.

Fuse ratings

Plug fuses are commonly available as 3A or 13A but other **ratings** are stocked by specialist electrical shops, fig 80.5.

Fig 80.5 Fuses are available in various ratings and types

Every electrical appliance has a label giving details of the electrical supply it is designed to operate from, and the power rating. Here is a label on an iron.

> ### 240 V   50 Hz a.c.
> ### 1400 W

To decide on the correct size of fuse to fit, first calculate the current using the power equation

$$P = IV$$

Rearrange to give	$I = P/V$
Put in the figures	$= 1400 \text{ W}/240 \text{ V}$
	$= 5.8 \text{ A}$

If the choice of fuse is between 3 A and 13 A, then a 13A fuse should be fitted.

Q3 Choose from a 1 A, 3 A, 5 A, 10 A or 13 A fuse the one which should be fitted to

a a bedside light with a 240 V, 60 W lamp
b a 12 V, 18 W lamp in a caravan
c a 240 V, 1200 W microwave cooker
d a 240 V, 450 W food mixer
e a 240 V, 2.5 kW kettle.

EARTHING

The National Grid cables which you see supported by pylons are all live wires. The earth is the return conductor from the transformer substations to the power stations, fig 80.6. Soil may not be a very good conducting material, but there is plenty of it so it provides a cheap very low resistance connector.

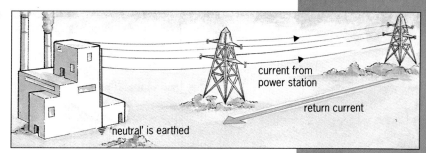

current from power station

return current

'neutral' is earthed

Fig 80.6 Earthing of the National Grid

Electric shocks

If you touch a live conductor, there is a complete circuit through you to earth. The amount of current which passes through you depends on how well you are connected to the earth. If you are inside in dry conditions you may get a severe shock, but it is unlikely that enough current will pass through you to kill you.

To prevent such shocks, all metal-cased appliances should be **earthed**. This is done by connecting the earth wire in the flex to the metal casing. If a fault develops which causes the case to become live, the earth wire provides a low-resistance path to earth, fig 80.7. A large current passes from live to earth and causes the fuse to blow. If there is no earth connection, then a person who touches the faulty appliance experiences a shock.

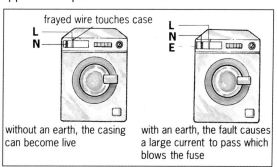

frayed wire touches case

without an earth, the casing can become live

with an earth, the fault causes a large current to pass which blows the fuse

Fig 80.7 Earthing of a metal cased appliance

Circuit breakers

The earth wire and fuse may not provide sufficient protection if an appliance develops a fault while it is being used. It might take a second for fuse wire to become hot enough to melt; it takes a fraction of a second for an electric current to kill a person. When you are outside there is normally a very good contact between you and the earth, so the resistance is much less than when you are inside.

A **residual current circuit breaker** (RCCB) should always be used to protect against electrocution when using an outdoor appliance. One common type plugs into a normal socket, fig 80.8. The RCCB cuts off the supply if there is a difference between the live and neutral currents, as happens if some currents passes to earth through a person. RCCBs operate very quickly, so that they cut off the supply before the person is killed.

Fig 80.8 A residual current circuit breaker compares the current in the live and neutral wires

By the end of this section you should be able to

- describe how a transistor can be used as a switch
- understand how potential dividers can provide varying voltages which depend on environmental factors
- recognise the important parts of an electronic system.

THE TRANSISTOR

The microelectronics revolution started in the 1950s with the invention of the transistor. Modern microchips contain thousands of transistors and other components on a single piece of silicon, fig 81.1.

▼ **Fig 81.1 Part of an integrated circuit or microchip**

What is a transistor?

A **transistor**, fig 81.2, is a three-terminal switch. The current which passes from the **collector** to the **emitter** is controlled at the **base**.

Activity

Fig 81.3 shows a circuit for investigating the conditions necessary for the transistor to be switched on. The voltmeter measures the potential difference between the base and the emitter, often abbreviated to V_{be}.

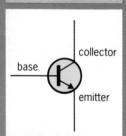

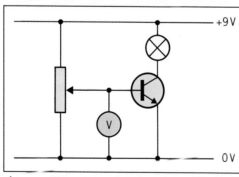

▲ **Fig 81.3**

Q1 What is the value of V_{be} when the transistor starts to conduct?

Q2 What is the value of V_{be} when the transistor is fully conducting?

base
collector
emitter

▲ **Fig 81.2
Transistor and circuit symbol**

THE POTENTIAL DIVIDER

A **potential divider** provides a way of obtaining any desired fraction of the supply potential difference. It consists of two resistors in series. The resistors can have fixed values or one or both can be variable.

Activity

Fig 81.4 shows several potential divider circuits which can be investigated.

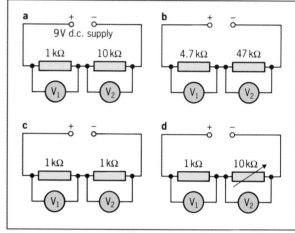

▲ **Fig 81.4**

Q3 Design a circuit consisting of two fixed resistors which splits a potential difference of 9V into 8.4V and 0.6V.

Potential divider circuits

Thermistors, light dependent resistors and moisture sensors can all be built into potential divider circuits. These then provide potential differences which vary with the physical conditions.

Activity

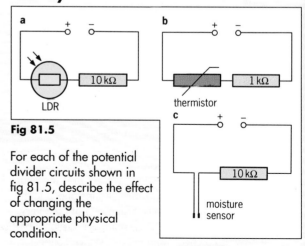

Fig 81.5

For each of the potential divider circuits shown in fig 81.5, describe the effect of changing the appropriate physical condition.

AUTOMATIC SWITCHING

On in the dark

Fig 81.6 shows a circuit which causes a transistor to be switched on in the dark and off when it is light.

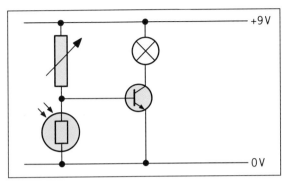

▲ **Fig 81.6 A light-sensitive circuit**

The variable resistor allows the base–emitter potential difference to be adjusted to about 0.5 V when the light dependent resistor (LDR) is illuminated by daylight. As the light level falls, the resistance of the LDR rises and so its share of the potential difference goes up. When the potential difference across the LDR reaches 0.6 V, the transistor starts to conduct.

Q4 Describe and explain what happens when the light level is increased.

Off in the dark

If the positions of the variable resistor and the LDR are reversed, the circuit is switched on in the light and off in the dark.

Q5 Describe some uses of the light dependent transistor switching circuit.

Q6 Design and test circuits which switch on a transistor in the following conditions

  a warm **b** cold **c** wet **d** dry.

  In each case, explain how environmental changes cause the transistor to become switched on.

BUILDING A SYSTEM

Sensors and switches

The circuits which you have studied so far consist of a **sensor** which gives a variable potential difference according to the environmental conditions, and a **switch** which operates according to a simple decision rule – if the potential difference is above a certain threshold value then it is on, below it the switch remains off.

Completing the system

The next stage is to make the switch operate another device, making a complete system.

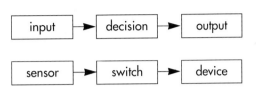

One example of such a system is a burglar alarm, which is activated when a light beam shining on an LDR is interrupted. The output is an alarm bell ringing.

Feedback control

Other systems have **feedback**, where the output also affects the input. An incubator is an example of an electronics system which uses feedback to control the temperature of the incubator.

Relays in systems

Transistors can only conduct small currents. The current needed to power a motor, a heater or a powerful lamp is too big to be passed through a transistor. When a transistor needs to switch a high-current device, a relay is used. This also allows the transistor to switch mains appliances, even though the transistor itself operates from a low voltage direct current.

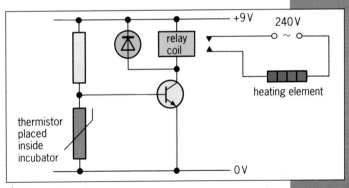

▲ **Fig 81.8**

Q7 Explain how the circuit in fig 81.8 uses feedback to keep the temperature of an incubator constant.

Q8 Design a circuit which uses feedback to maintain a constant level of water in a lavatory cistern. Assume that you have a water valve similar to that used in an automatic washing machine, that can be switched on and off.

▲ **Fig 81.7 This light incorporates an LDR that only allows the light to be switched on at night**

ELECTRICITY AND MAGNETISM

211

You have already seen how a number of electronic components can be built up into a system to solve a problem. This section introduces some new components which will allow you to address a wider range of problems.

DIODES

Diodes allow current to pass in one direction only. The circuit symbol for a diode includes an arrow head to show which way the current can pass.

Activity

Use the potential divider circuit in fig 82.1 to investigate the range of values of potential difference for which the diode conducts.

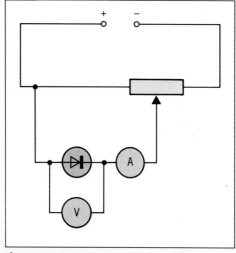

▲ **Fig 82.1**

Changing a.c. to d.c.

Diodes are important in **rectification**, that is, changing alternating current into direct current. Low voltage power packs such as those used to operate a keyboard or computer contain diodes as well as a transformer, fig 82.2.

Light emitting diodes

Light emitting diodes (LEDs) are useful indicators in electronic circuits, fig 82.3. They need less current than a filament lamp and they have a longer operational life. They are also available in several colours – red, green and yellow are common.

▲ **Fig 82.2 A power pack provides a low voltage direct current from the mains**

▲ **Fig 82.3 LEDs are used as indicators**

CAPACITORS

Capacitors store small quantities of electric charge. As more charge is put on a capacitor, the potential difference across it rises.

Activity

Fig 82.4 shows how the potential difference across a capacitor can be monitored.

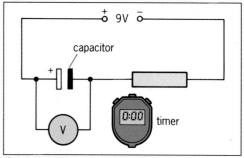

▲ **Fig 82.4**

Measure the time it takes for the potential difference across the capacitor to reach 6 V. Note that you will need to discharge the capacitor by connecting the two terminals together before each experiment.
Do the experiment for different combinations of capacitor and resistor.

Q1 What pattern do you notice in your results?

Capacitance

The ability of a capacitor to store charge is called its **capacitance**. This is usually measured in μF (microfarads). A 1 μF capacitor stores 1 μC (1×10^{-6} C) of charge for each volt of potential difference.

When a capacitor is connected to a battery through a fixed resistor, as in fig 82.4, the charge on the capacitor and its potential difference build up over a period of time. The larger the capacitance of the capacitor and the larger the value of the resistor, the longer it takes to reach a certain potential difference.

TIME DELAY SWITCHES

Fig 82.5 shows a circuit using a capacitor–resistor combination to switch a transistor on or off after a time delay. The push switch is for resetting the circuit by discharging the capacitor.

Activity

Investigate the effect of changing the values of the resistor and capacitor in the circuit in fig 82.5.

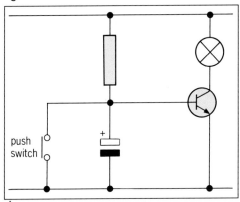

▲ **Fig 82.5**

Q2 Describe some uses for circuits such as that in fig 82.5.

OUTPUT DEVICES

Electronic systems can incorporate any electrically operated device as the output. Fig 82.6 shows some output devices which you may have available in school.

▲ **Fig 82.6 Motor, latch and relay**

Using a latch

A **latch** is useful when designing systems such as burglar alarms. An alarm which operates when a light beam is broken would only ring for a fraction of a second.

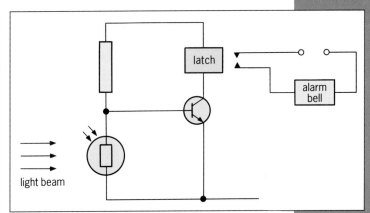

▲ **Fig 82.7 Burglar alarm circuit using a latch**

When the transistor in fig 82.7 is switched on, it operates the latch. The latch switches the current to the bell on and keeps this current switched on even if the transistor is switched off again.

Q3 Design electronic systems which
  a unlock a door at daybreak and lock it again at night
  b use a motor to open a garage door when the driver flashes the headlights
  c operate a fan in a greenhouse if the temperature gets too great
  d water the plants in a greenhouse when they are too dry.

LOGIC GATES

Logic gates are circuits made from several transistors and other components which are designed to do a specific task. You should be familiar with the use of AND, OR and NOT gates and their truth tables, fig 82.8.

Logic gates can only handle very small currents, enough to light up an LED but not enough to activate a relay. A 'high' output from a logic gate can be used to switch a transistor which in turn can operate a relay coil. When drawing block diagrams the transistor is usually omitted.

Q4 In fig 82.9 the input from the temperature sensor is 1 when the temperature rises above 20°C and that from the light sensor is 1 when it is illuminated.

Describe the conditions necessary for the relay to be switched on. Identify suitable applications for this electronic system.

AND

Input A	Input B	Output
0	0	0
1	0	0
0	1	0
1	1	1

OR

Input A	Input B	Output
0	0	0
1	0	1
0	1	1
1	1	1

NOT

Input	Output
0	1
1	0

▲ **Fig 82.8**

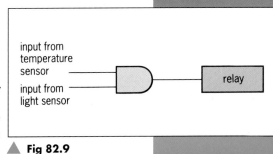

▲ **Fig 82.9**

83 MICRO-ELECTRONICS

By the end of this section you should be able to

- interpret the truth tables for NAND and NOR gates
- describe the behaviour and some of the uses of astable and bistable circuits.

NAND AND NOR GATES

The AND, OR and NOT logic gates have a limited number of applications. This section introduces you to the two logic gates which are the most widely used in modern microelectronics circuits.

Q1 Copy and complete the truth tables for the two logic gate combinations shown in fig 83.1.

Fig 83.1 ▶

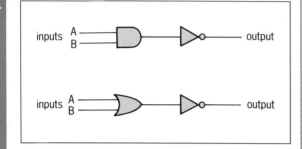

AND + NOT

Input A	Input B	Output from NOT
0	0	
1	0	
0	1	
1	1	

OR + NOT

Input A	Input B	Output from NOT
0	0	
1	0	
0	1	
1	1	

Combining gates

The AND and NOT gates are combined in this way to give the NAND gate. NAND stands for NOT AND, and its output is the inverse of that of the AND gate.

Similarly, the NOR gate is an OR gate followed by a NOT; its output is the inverse of an OR gate.

Fig 83.2 ▶

Input A	Input B	Output
0	0	1
1	0	1
0	1	1
1	1	0

Input A	Input B	Output
0	0	1
1	0	0
0	1	0
1	1	0

Using NAND and NOR gates

NAND and NOR are very versatile logic gates. They are used to make timers, clocks, counters and memories in computer systems.

It is possible to make any other logic gate from a combination of NAND and NOR gates.

Q2 If the inputs to a NAND or a NOR gate are connected together, there are only two possible input states, 1 or 0. To which logic gate are the combinations in fig 83.3 equivalent?

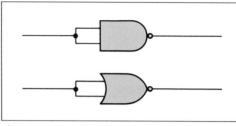

▲ **Fig 83.3**

Q3 a Make an AND gate from two NAND gates.
b Make an OR gate from two NOR gates.

THE BISTABLE CIRCUIT

Flip-flops

The output from a logic gate can have two possible states, 1 or 0. A **bistable circuit** is sometimes called a **flip-flop**. It can be flipped from one state to the other by applying a pulse. It then stays in that state (it is stable) until another pulse is applied to make it flop back again.

Fig 83.4 shows a simple bistable circuit made from two NAND gates.

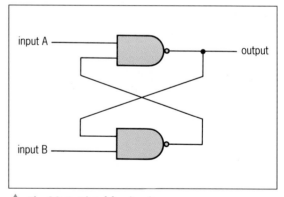

▲ **Fig 83.4 Bistable circuit**

Notice how feedback from the output of each gate is used to determine the input to the other gate. This can make it difficult to predict what the output state will be.

Activity

To investigate the circuit in fig 83.4, start with both inputs at 1. It is not possible to predict the output when this is done. The output can be made to toggle between its stable states by applying a 0 pulse to each input in turn.

Using bistable circuits

Useful bistable circuits use more than two logic gates. Fig 83.5 shows one practical bistable unit.

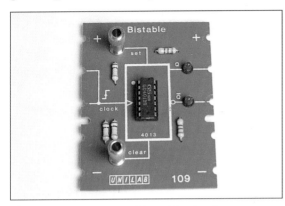

▲ **Fig 83.5 A practical bistable circuit**

When a pulse is applied to the input, the value of that pulse, 0 or 1, appears at the output and stays there when the pulse has been removed. This is a **memory circuit** – it remembers the last **binary digit**, or **bit**, which appeared at the input.

Four of these memory circuits, as in fig 83.6, are needed to be able to store a 4-bit binary number. A 4-bit binary number can be used to represent a decimal number between 0 and 15.

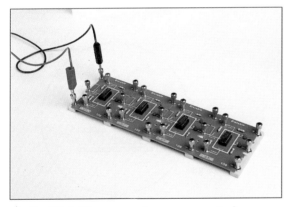

▲ **Fig 83.6 Binary numbers represented on a bistable circuit**

Using memory circuits

When you type information into a computer each letter or space that you type is stored as a binary number.

The **ASCII character set** is an international standard code which has 256 possible binary numbers.

Q4 How many binary digits are needed to represent each character in the ASCII code ?

Q5 How many flip-flops would you need to store the number of letters in this sentence?

THE ASTABLE CIRCUIT

▲ **Fig 83.7 Disco lights use astable circuits**

The prefix 'a' means 'not'. The **astable circuit** does not have a stable state – it repeatedly flips and flops from one state to the other.

Activity

Fig 83.8 shows how an astable can be made from two NAND gates, a capacitor and a resistor.

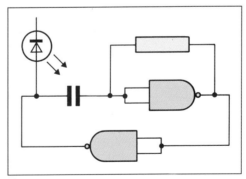

▲ **Fig 83.8**

Investigate the effect of changing the values of the resistor and capacitor on the pulsing rate of the astable circuit.

Using astable circuits

Astables can be used to provide colourful displays of flashing lights. They also form the basis of the clocks which control the operations inside a computer.

84 ELECTRON BEAMS

By the end of this section you should be able to
- describe thermionic emission
- explain how electron beams can be deflected
- understand how X-rays are produced.

THERMIONIC EMISSION

Producing electron beams

In a metal, positive ions are surrounded by free-moving electrons, page 192. There are strong attractive forces between the positive ions and the free electrons which prevent the electrons from becoming totally free and leaving the metal.

When metals are heated both the positive ions and the free electrons gain kinetic energy, and in some metals the free electrons gain enough kinetic energy to escape from the metal surface. This is called **thermionic emission**. It is used to produce the electron beams in cathode ray oscilloscopes and television tubes.

The Maltese cross tube

The **Maltese cross tube** consists of an electron gun, a Maltese cross and a fluorescent screen, fig 84.1.

Fig 84.1 The Maltese cross tube ▼

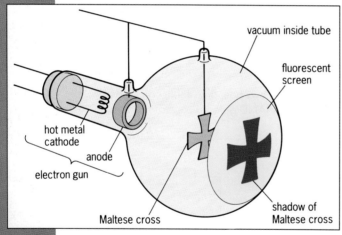

When the low voltage supply to the cathode is switched on, the cathode becomes hot enough to give out light and a shadow of the cross is seen on the screen. The cathode is also giving out electrons, but these remain near the cathode.

When a sufficiently high positive voltage is applied to the anode, this exerts an attractive force on the electrons and accelerates them away from the cathode. The anode is designed so that the electrons pass through it, rather than just moving to it. The electrons pass through the tube and cause the screen to fluoresce where they strike it.

The cathode ray oscilloscope

The tube in a cathode ray oscilloscope or CRO works on this principle, but it uses a sharply focused beam so that only a small part of the screen fluoresces at any instant, fig 84.2.

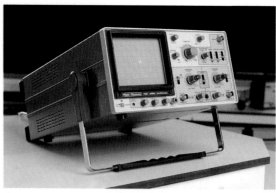

▲ Fig 84.2 Cathode ray oscilloscope

Q1 Describe the energy change which takes place when electrons hit a fluorescent screen.

Q2 The Maltese cross and CRO tubes are evacuated. Explain what would happen to the electron beam if air was present in the tube.

DEFLECTING THE BEAM

Deflection by electric force

Electrons and other charged particles are affected by electric forces. Fig 84.3 shows a deflection tube in which an electric force is applied to the electron beam.

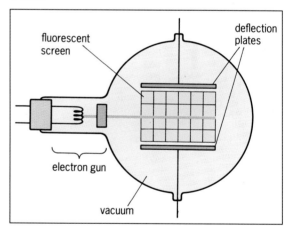

▲ Fig 84.3 A deflection tube

Q3 If the upper plate in the deflection tube is made positive, and the lower plate negative, which way will the electrons be deflected? Explain your answer.

Deflection by magnetic force

A beam of moving electrons is an electric current, so it should also be possible to deflect the beam using magnets. Fig 84.4 shows how this can be done with a permanent magnet and an electromagnet.

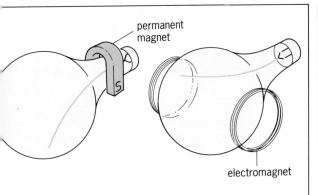

permanent
magnet

electromagnet

▲ **Fig 84.4 Electric current in the coils produces a magnetic field in a horizontal direction at right angles to the electron beam**

ELECTRON BEAMS IN A TELEVISION TUBE

Three electron guns

Colour televisions use three electron guns, each one aligned at a different fluorescent material, fig 84.5.

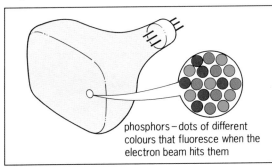

phosphors – dots of different colours that fluoresce when the electron beam hits them

▲ **Fig 84.5 The three electron guns in a colour television tube**

Persistence of vision

The beams scan the screen 25 times a second. In each scan the beams cross the screen horizontally 625 times to make a complete 'picture', fig 84.6. There are never more than three coloured dots on the screen at any one instant, though your eyes and brain see the complete screen lit up at once. The relative brightnesses of the three dots are continually adjusted to give the different colours.

The rapid movement of the electron beams is achieved using electromagnetic deflection. You can see the coils which form the electromagnet at the back of the tube in fig 84.6.

Fig 84.6 Your eyes and brain cannot resolve the scans individually, but see a complete picture ▶

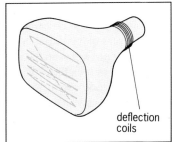

deflection coils

X-RAYS

You can see that light is given out from a television screen. The television screen also gives out invisible rays called X-rays which are harmful to the body.

The discovery of X-rays

X-rays were discovered by accident by Wilhelm Röntgen in 1895. He was doing some work which involved accelerating electrons inside a glass tube. While working in a darkened room he noticed that something from his experiment was causing fluorescence elsewhere in the room. He also discovered that these invisible rays affect photographic film just like light does, but pass through many things which light will not pass through. He was able to take a shadow photograph of the bones in his hand like the one in fig 84.7.

Q4 Explain why the bones appear as white on fig 84.7 and the flesh does not show clearly.

Producing X-rays

We now know that X-rays are short wavelength electromagnetic radiation (see page 252) with wavelengths up to 1×10^{-7}m. They are produced whenever fast-moving electrons are brought to a sudden halt.

In a modern X-ray tube, fig 84.8, electrons are produced by thermionic emission and accelerated through a potential difference of up to 40 MV. They strike a tungsten anode where the X-rays are produced. The efficiency of an X-ray tube is only about 1%, the rest of the energy heats up the anode. Some tubes use a rotating anode, others have a fixed anode with oil passing through it. The X-ray tube is shielded with lead apart from the small window where the X-rays emerge.

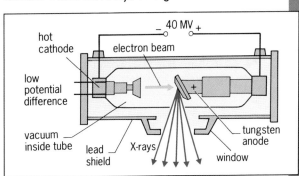

− 40 MV +

hot cathode

electron beam

low potential difference

vacuum inside tube

lead shield

X-rays

tungsten anode

window

Q5 Find out what property of tungsten makes it a suitable target for the electrons.

Q6 What is the purpose of the oil in a tube with a fixed target? Why is it not necessary when the target rotates?

Some of the uses of X-rays are described on page 255.

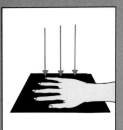

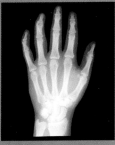

▲ **Fig 84.7 X-rays turn photographic paper black when they strike it**

◀ **Fig 84.8 An X-ray tube**

ELECTRICITY AND MAGNETISM

217

By the end of this section you should be able to

▸ describe the ways in which thermal energy can be transferred.

Hot things cool down, and cold things warm up. There is a constant interchange of thermal energy between every object and its surroundings. This section looks at the mechanisms by which this transfer takes place.

Q1 Draw a diagram to show the convection currents in a refrigerator.

Q2 Explain why water in a saucepan can be boiled without stirring but thick soup needs to be stirred.

Q3 When water is cooled it contracts until the temperature drops to 4°C. Further cooling causes the water to expand. Explain what happens to the water in a garden pond when the air temperature on a cold night drops from 10°C to −2°C.

MOVING FLUIDS

Cold air is denser than warm air

If you open the door of a fridge or freezer, you can feel the cold air falling out over your feet. The molecules in the cold air are, on average, closer together than those in the warmer air of the room, so cold air is denser than warm air, fig 85.1

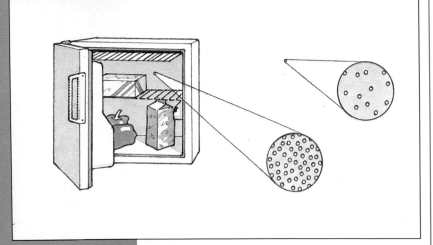

▼ **Fig 85.1 The air molecules in the refrigerator are less widely spaced than those in the room**

Convection currents

Convection currents are set up when parts of a fluid which are warmer or colder than their surroundings rise or fall because of the difference in density.

Fig 85.2 shows how a dye can be used to see convection currents in water.

▸ **Fig 85.2 Demonstrating convection currents**

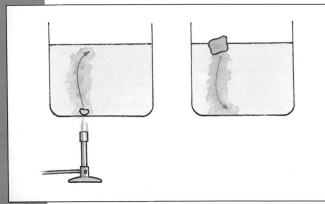

TRANSFERRING ENERGY IN A SOLID

Conduction

Convection involves the movement of molecules and so it cannot occur in a solid, where the particles vibrate about fixed positions. When part of a solid is warmed, the energy of these vibrations increases and some energy is passed on to neighbouring particles, fig 85.3.

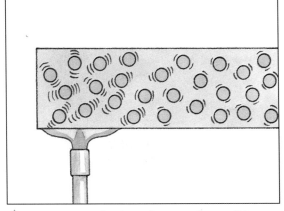

▲ **Fig 85.3 Conduction of energy in a solid**

Energy transfer by this process of **conduction** is comparatively slow.

Q4 How does the average spacing of molecules in a gas compare with that of particles in a solid? Use the difference in particle spacing to explain why gases are very poor conductors of thermal energy compared with solids.

Comparing rates of conduction in solids

Fig 85.4 shows how rates of conduction in different solid materials can be compared.

The results of this experiment show that there is a vast difference between the rates of conduction in metals and non-metals. It is no coincidence that metals are good conductors of thermal energy as well as good conductors of electricity.

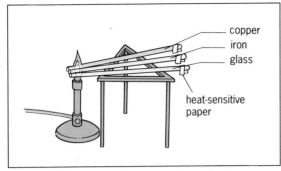

▲ **Fig 85.4 Comparing rates of conduction**

How do metals conduct energy?

Unlike non-metals, metals do have particles which are free to move about – the free electrons which are responsible for electrical conduction. These electrons move relatively large distances, typically about 20 atomic diameters, between collisions and so the energy can be transferred much more rapidly than in non-metals. Heating one end of a metal bar increases the kinetic energy of the free electrons as well as that of the metal ions. The energy is spread very rapidly to all parts of the bar by the diffusion of the electrons.

Q5 Copper is a better conductor of thermal energy than iron or steel. Suggest why the hot water pipes in a central heating system are made from copper but the radiators are made from steel.

ENERGY THROUGH A VACUUM

Radiation

Conduction and convection are mechanisms which transfer energy through materials. Infra-red radiation is part of the electromagnetic spectrum (see page 252) – it travels in a vacuum with no loss of energy, and is only partially absorbed when travelling in air. This energy transfer is called **radiation**.

Emission and absorption

Everything emits and absorbs infra-red radiation. The rate of emission and absorption of infra-red by an object depends on the temperature of the object and the nature of its surface. Fig 85.6 shows how a computer with two temperature probes can be used to compare emission and absorption by different surfaces. The radiant heater can be replaced by a hot plate with different surfaces for comparison.

The experiment shows that black surfaces are better at both emitting and absorbing infra-red radiation than silvered surfaces are.

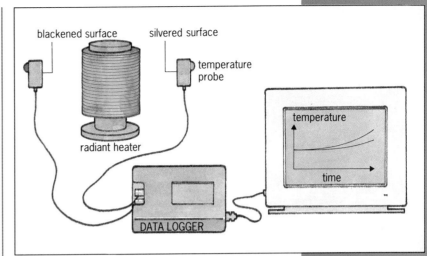

▲ **Fig 85.5 Emission and absorption of infra-red radiation by different surfaces**

Q6 'Aluminium foil reflects heat.' To what extent is this true? What advice would you give to a cook who wraps meat in aluminium foil before placing it in the oven?

EVAPORATION

Removing energy

Refrigerators and freezers use evaporation and condensation to remove the energy which enters by conduction through the walls. When a liquid evaporates it removes energy from its surroundings, causing them to cool. You can demonstrate this effect by putting a drop of a volatile liquid such as meths or white spirit on the back of your hand – you can feel the cooling of your hand as the liquid evaporates.

How a refrigerator works

In refrigeration a volatile liquid is squirted from a narrow tube to a much wider one, causing it to vaporise. This is where the cooling takes place. On the outside of the refrigerator the vapour is compressed and it condenses, heating up in the process, fig 85.6. Energy is removed from the liquid to cool it down before it is vaporised again.

Q7 Explain how the pipes at the back of a refrigerator are designed to maximise the energy transfer from the warm liquid into the room.

Fig 85.6 How a refrigerator works ▼

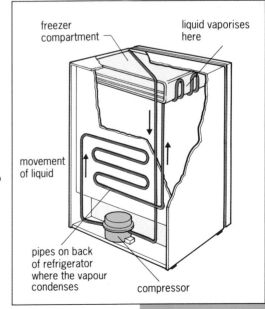

By the end of this section you should be able to

- understand how the rate of energy transfer can be controlled
- describe how energy is transferred between people and their environment.

In Britain we are concerned with keeping warm for most of the year, so we insulate the buildings we live and work in as well as our bodies. Cost-effective insulation requires knowledge of the ways in which we lose thermal energy and the relative quantities involved.

INSULATING BUILDINGS

Radiation and temperature difference

When the temperature difference between an object and its surroundings is relatively small, energy losses due to infra-red radiation are insignificant. This is because energy transfer by radiation is a two-way process – objects absorb energy radiated by their surroundings as well as emitting energy so if the temperature difference is small the net losses are also small.

A hot jacket potato taken from an oven into a cool room is much warmer than its surroundings and a significant amount of energy is lost due to radiation. Wrapping it in aluminium foil is very effective insulation, even though the aluminium is a good conductor, because the foil does not emit much infra-red radiation, fig 86.1.

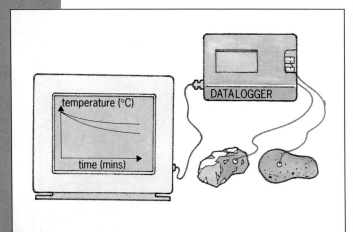

▲ **Fig 86.1 Aluminium foil does not emit much infra-red radiation**

Energy loss from buildings

Energy loss from buildings is mainly through a combination of conduction through solids and convection currents through air. Fig 86.2 shows the relative amounts of energy lost in different ways from an uninsulated house.

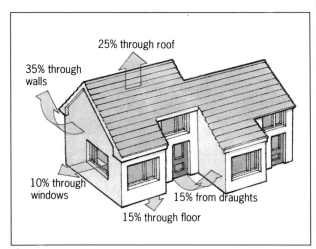

25% through roof
35% through walls
10% through windows
15% from draughts
15% through floor

▲ **Fig 86.2 Routes of energy loss from a house**

Insulation

Cavity wall insulation reduces energy loss by preventing convection currents in the cavity. Energy is still lost through conduction, but the trapped air in the insulation material is a poor conductor.

Loft insulation works on a similar principle – air is used as the insulator, trapped in the fibres of mineral wool to stop convection currents, fig 86.3.

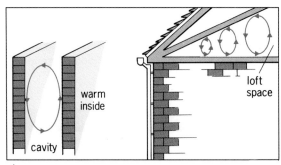

warm inside
cavity
loft space

▲ **Fig 86.3 Insulation prevents these convection currents**

Double glazing also uses trapped air as an insulator. A narrow air gap of a few millimetres is more effective than a gap of several centimetres as convection currents cannot flow in the narrow gap.

U-values

The insulation properties of construction materials are described by **U-values**. The U-value is the energy flow per second through each square metre per degree temperature difference between the inside and outside. Some typical U-values are shown in the table on the next page.

Q1 Estimate the rate of energy loss through a 5 m × 2.5 m uninsulated outside wall on a cold winter night. You will need to make estimates of the inside and outside temperatures.

Material	U-value (W/m²°C)
uninsulated cavity wall	0.8
foam insulated cavity wall	0.4
single glazed window	5.5
double glazed window	3
uninsulated loft	1.6
insulated loft	0.4

Q2 Find out the prices of cavity wall insulation, loft insulation and double glazing. Which method of home insulation is the most cost effective? Which is the least cost effective? Give reasons for your answers.

THE VACUUM FLASK

The vacuum flask, fig 86.4, is designed to minimise the energy transfer between its contents and the outside of the vessel.

Q3 Important features of the design of the vacuum flask are

a the double silvered walls
b the vacuum between the walls
c the hollow plastic stopper.

Explain how these design features enable energy transfer due to conduction, convection and radiation to be kept to a minimum.

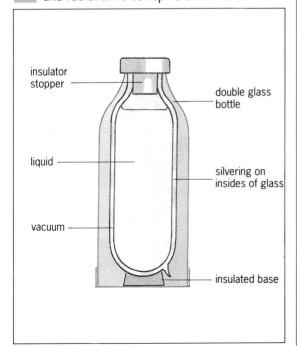

▲ **Fig 86.4 The vacuum flask cuts down energy loss by conduction, convection and radiation**

HEATING BUILDINGS

Convector and radiant heaters
Fig 86.5 shows two types of electrical heater.

▲ **Fig 86.5 Convector heater and radiant heater** ▶

The convector heater warms the air in a room. The radiant heater warms the objects in a room – very little of the infra-red radiation is absorbed by the air.

Q4 Explain one disadvantage of each type of heater.

Keeping ourselves warm
Our bodies lose energy in a variety of ways. To maintain a constant temperature we must lose thermal energy at the same rate as our bodies generate it. Much of this energy is lost through evaporation, the rest by radiation and convection, fig 86.6.

The loss of energy through convection currents can be controlled by the amount of clothing which we wear and how loose it is. If these factors are kept the same the energy loss through convection depends on the temperature of the air around us. If the air is too warm then we sweat more to lose energy by evaporation. If it is too cold we lose thermal energy at too great a rate and we feel cold and shiver.

Our comfort does not depend only on the air temperature. If two rooms have the same air temperature, one can feel colder than the other if the air is warm but the walls are cold, so that we receive much less radiation than we emit.

▲ **Fig 86.6 The convection currents around the body**

◀ **Fig 86.7 Modern gas fires emit energy by both radiation and convection**

By the end of this section you should be able to

- calculate the energy transfer when an object is heated or cooled
- answer some of the following questions:

How much energy does it take to heat a bathful of water, a room full of air, a hot-water central heating system? Why are the red-hot sparks from a sparkler harmless, while boiling water, which is much cooler, can cause a severe burn? How do heating engineers know which size radiator to fit in each room of a house?

STORING ENERGY

Some forms of energy can be very difficult to store for future use. During our normal daily lives we 'waste' a lot of energy which we can never recover. A car moving at 60 m.p.h. has a lot of kinetic energy – about 500 000 J. When the car brakes and comes to a stop, all this energy is wasted.

Q1 Describe in detail what happens to the kinetic energy of a car when it is slowing down.

Gravitational potential energy

Electricity generating companies have surplus capacity at night when demand is low, so they store electrical energy as gravitational potential energy, fig 87.1.

▼ **Fig 87.1 Storing electrical energy as gravitational potential energy at a pumped-storage station**

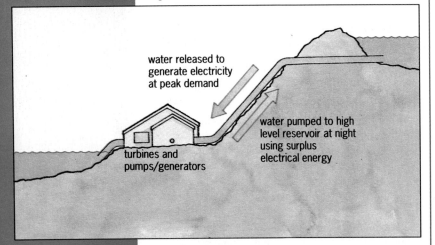

water released to generate electricity at peak demand

water pumped to high level reservoir at night using surplus electrical energy

turbines and pumps/generators

Chemical energy

Batteries can also be used to store energy as chemical energy, but their use is limited because of their weight. Electric motors are ideal for the stop – start journey of a milk float, but they need to be recharged overnight and they have a limited range.

Thermal energy

Electrical energy bought at night, when it is cheaper if you have a 'white meter' fitted, can be stored at home as thermal energy in a hot-water tank or a storage heater.

▲ **Fig 87.2 Electric cars have a limited range**

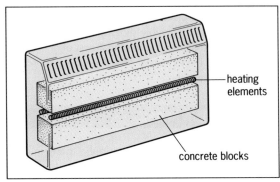

heating elements

concrete blocks

▲ **Fig 87.3 A storage heater absorbs energy at night and releases it during the day**

A storage heater consists of blocks of concrete and electrical heating elements, fig 87.3. Thermal energy is absorbed by the concrete at night and released during the day.

Q2 Storage heaters are cheap to install compared with other types of central heating but they are not a very popular form of central heating. Describe some of the disadvantages of using storage heaters.

One disadvantage of storage heaters is that they can be bulky. To keep the size down, the concrete which is used to store the thermal energy must store the required amount of energy in as little space as possible. The factors which determine the energy stored are

- the density of the concrete
- the temperature it can be heated to
- the specific heat capacity of the concrete.

The **specific heat capacity** of a material is the energy required to change the temperature of 1 kg by 1 °C.

CALCULATING THE ENERGY STORED

Specific heat capacity calculations

The specific heat capacity of concrete is 900 J/kg °C. This means that for each kilogram of concrete, 900 J of thermal energy are absorbed when it heats up by 1 °C, and 900 J are given out when it cools down by 1 °C.

How much energy is stored by 8 kg of concrete when it is heated from 20 °C to 60 °C?

To heat 1 kg of concrete by 1 °C needs 900 J
so heating 8 kg by 1 °C needs 8 × 900 J
and to heat 8 kg by 40 °C requires
40 × 8 × 900 J
which is equal to 288 000 J of energy.

This calculation can be summarised by the equation

energy change = mass × specific heat capacity × temperature change or

In symbols $E = m c \, \Delta T$

Activity

Fig 87.4 shows how specific heat capacity can be measured. Energy losses to the surroundings are always a problem when measuring thermal energy transfer. In planning your experiment you should think of ways in which these energy losses can be minimised.

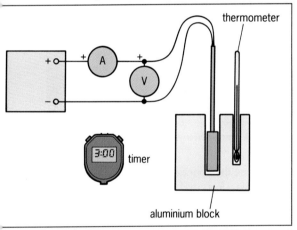

▲ **Fig 87.4**

The table shows the specific heat capacities of some common materials.

Material	Specific heat capacity (J/kg°C)
water	4200
glass	700
air	1100
copper	380
aluminium	880
sand	800
iron	450

Use the data in the table to answer the following questions.

Q3 A storage heater contains 50 kg of concrete.

  a How much energy is absorbed by the concrete when it is heated from 20 °C to 300 °C?
  b If the concrete is heated by a 2.5 kW element, how long should it take to absorb this quantity of energy?
  c Explain why it would actually take longer than the time you calculated in **b**.

Q4 Calculate the energy required to heat

  a 140 kg of water in a hot water tank from 10 °C to 60 °C
  b the 25 kg copper tank from 10 °C to 60 °C
  c the air in a classroom from 5 °C to 19 °C. You will need to estimate the volume of air in the room. The density of air is 1.1 kg/m³.

Q5 Compare the energy released by 1 mg of iron cooling from 1000 °C to 20 °C with that released by 0.1 kg of water cooling from 100 °C to 20 °C.

Q6 Compare the specific heat capacities of sand and water. Does this explain why the sand on a beach warms up more quickly than the sea? What other factors need to be considered?

THE ELECTRIC SHOWER

Most electric showers have a fixed-power heater, either 7 kW or 8.4 kW. The temperature is controlled by regulating the rate at which water flows through the shower, fig 87.5.

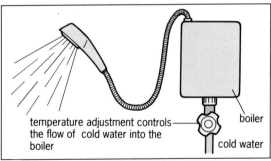

temperature adjustment controls the flow of cold water into the boiler

boiler

cold water

▲ **Fig 87.5 The temperature of the water from an electric shower is controlled by adjusting the flow of water through the boiler**

Q7 Water enters the shower at 10 °C and leaves it at 50 °C.

  a Calculate the mass of water heated per second if the power output is 7 kW.
  b Compare the amount of hot water used during a 5-minute shower with that used in a bath.

88 ENERGY FOR LIVING

By the end of this section you should be able to

- identify patterns in the distribution and use of energy resources
- describe the principles of electricity generation from fossil fuels.

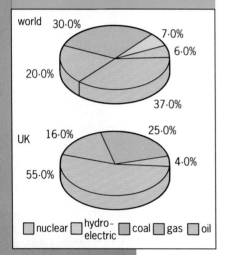

▲ **Fig 88.1 Primary energy use in the world and in the UK**

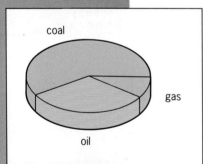

▲ **Fig 88.2 World fossil fuel resources**

ENERGY RESOURCES

Worldwide use of energy resources

The pie charts in fig 88.1 compare the use of energy resources in the UK with that worldwide. Although some hydroelectric power is used in the UK, it is not a large enough proportion to show on the pie chart.

Q1 Explain why the UK and other industrialised nations are more dependent on the use of oil than thirld-world countries.

Q2 The UK is both an importer and an exporter of energy resources. Suggest why oil is both imported and exported.

Q3 Draw a pie chart which shows a possible distribution of energy use for the UK in the year 2100. Explain why the pattern will have changed.

World fossil fuel resources

The total world fossil fuel resources are estimated to be 1×10^{23} J, although estimates are constantly being revised. The distribution is shown in fig 88.2.

Q4 Explain why oil is currently the world's major fuel supply, though coal is the most abundant fuel.

Q5 What events could cause the amount and proportions of known fuel resources to change in the future?

There is a large variation in the use of energy sources worldwide, the energy consumed per person in the USA being twice that of the other industrialised nations.

CHANGING PATTERNS OF ENERGY USE

Use of energy

Parents will tell you that life in the 1990s is very different from that in the 1960s. Fig 88.3 compares the proportions of energy used by different sectors in the UK in 1960 and in 1989.

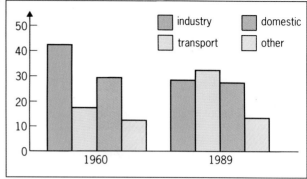

▲ **Fig 88.3 Proportions of energy used**

Q6 Identify the trends shown in the chart. What explanations can you give for these trends?

Types of fuel

The type of fuel we use has also changed dramatically, as Fig 88.4 shows.

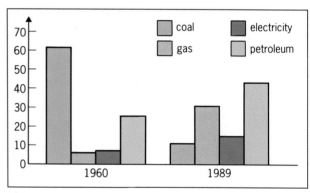

▲ **Fig 88.4 Proportions of fuels used by consumers**

Q7 Describe the changes which have taken place between 1960 and 1989. How do changes in lifestyle account for the changes in fuel used?

ELECTRICITY FROM FOSSIL FUELS

Fig 88.5 shows the proportions of electrical energy generated from the various energy sources in the UK in 1989. It does not include the small amount generated from burning natural gas.

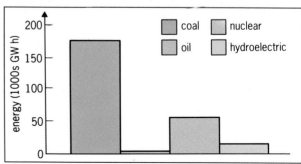

▲ **Fig 88.5 Electricity generated in 1989**

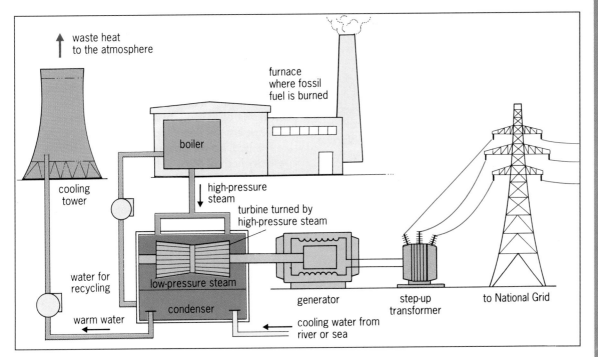

- waste heat to the atmosphere
- cooling tower
- water for recycling
- warm water
- furnace where fossil fuel is burned
- boiler
- high-pressure steam
- turbine turned by high-pressure steam
- low-pressure steam
- condenser
- cooling water from river or sea
- generator
- step-up transformer
- to National Grid

As a nation, we rely on fossil fuels for the generation of electricity. This is likely to remain the case in the forseeable future, although the balance is shifting away from coal as more gas-burning stations are built in the 1990s. Alternative energy sources will have to be found as fossil fuel reserves become exhausted. Nuclear power does not seem to have a long-term future unless ways can be found of harnessing fusion reactions, see page 143.

How is electrical energy generated from fossil fuels?

Power stations which burn fossil fuels use the energy from the fuel to produce high-pressure steam. The burning fuel heats water in the boiler.
The high-pressure steam drives the blades in the turbines, fig 88.6, losing energy as it does so. It leaves the turbines at a lower temperature and pressure. It is then condensed to water and returned to the boiler for recirculation. This is where most of the energy wastage takes place in the power station – the energy extracted from the condensing steam goes straight into the environment as thermal energy.

Q8 Draw an energy flow diagram which shows how energy is transformed from chemical energy in the fuel into electrical energy.

Q9 Modern power stations have an efficiency approaching 50%. Identify the main sources of energy waste in a power station. Why is the efficiency so low?

Waste products from power stations

Thermal energy is not the only waste product from a power station. The burning of fossil fuels also produces carbon dioxide, which is a greenhouse gas, see page 177. The burning of coal produces sulphur dioxide, which causes acid rain, and ash.

Sulphur dioxide emissions can be reduced by passing the waste gases through a slurry of lime and water. This produces calcium sulphate, which is used to make plaster.

Electrostatic precipitators reduce the ash emissions from coal-fired power stations. A high voltage is applied between a central electrode and the walls of the chimney. The strong electric field which is created ionises the air molecules, and the resulting ions are accelerated towards the electrodes. The negative ions (electrons) become attached to the dust particles, which are then attracted towards the metal plates which form the positive electrodes, fig 88.7.

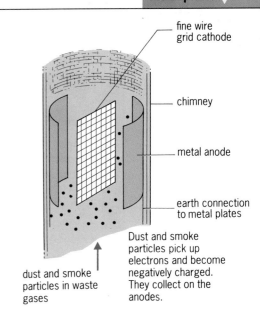

- fine wire grid cathode
- chimney
- metal anode
- earth connection to metal plates
- dust and smoke particles in waste gases
- Dust and smoke particles pick up electrons and become negatively charged. They collect on the anodes.

By the end of this section you should be able to

- evaluate the use of renewable energy sources
- explain how the energy from a renewable source can be transferred to a usable output.

WATER POWER

Hydroelectric power

Hydroelectric power is an important source of energy in Scotland, fig 89.1, and it is also used to recover energy stored as gravitational potential energy in pumped storage schemes, see page 222. In a hydroelectric power station the turbines are turned by moving water as it falls downhill. One advantage of hydroelectric power using natural streams and rivers is that it is a renewable resource. It does not use up any of the Earth's fuel reserves, but instead takes advantage of the water cycle process.

▲ **Fig 89.1 Sloy power station, Loch Lomond. The four turbines can generate 130 MW and the power station can regulate the level of water to prevent flooding**

Q1 The Sun is the ultimate energy source for hydroelectric power. Draw an energy flow diagram to show what happens to the energy between arriving at the Earth and becoming electrical energy.

Q2 Pumped storage systems can change gravitational potential energy to electrical energy with an efficiency of about 50%. 2×10^5 kg of water pass through the turbines each second after dropping from a height of 220 m. Gravitational potential energy = mgh, see page 229.

Calculate the gravitational potential energy lost each second, and the power output of the generator.

Q3 Capital costs, running costs and social and environmental implications are all important when evaluating an energy source. What are the advantages and disadvantages of hydroelectric power?

Tidal power

Water power from the sea can also be used to generate electricity. Energy from the tides has been used in Britain for hundreds of years to drive mills – the tide never fails, unlike the wind! It has been suggested that the Severn Estuary would be suitable for a tide-operated power station, though no scheme has yet been approved.

The tidal power station built on the La Rance estuary near St Malo in France has been operating since 1966. Fig 89.2 shows how the turbines are turned by the incoming tide. Electricity is generated at low tides by releasing the water from the dam.

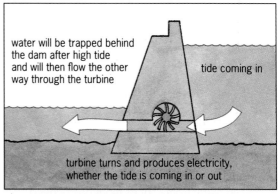

water will be trapped behind the dam after high tide and will then flow the other way through the turbine

tide coming in

turbine turns and produces electricity, whether the tide is coming in or out

▲ **Fig 89.2 Turbines in a dam at a tidal power station generate electricity both as the tide comes in and as it goes out**

Q4 Why do you think that some river estuaries are more suitable than others for tidal power stations?

Q5 One disadvantage of tidal power stations is that they cannot generate electricity at a constant rate. Explain why the amount of electricity generated varies during the tidal cycle.

Wave power

Wave power could be an important energy source of the future if it can be successfully harnessed. Although the waves around Britain's coastline have a great deal of energy, attempts to extract this energy have proved costly and largely unsuccessful.

One of the more successful devices which have been invented to extract energy from the waves is shown in fig 89.3.

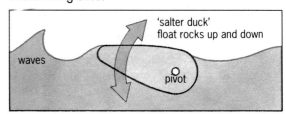

'salter duck' float rocks up and down

waves

pivot

▲ **Fig 89.3 As the waves pass, the duck rocks. This rolling motion is used to generate electricity inside the duck**

POWER FROM THE SUN

Over the past 200 years, fossil fuels have been used at an increasing rate. Projections of how long the known reserves will last vary. Gas and oil will take us well into the next century, and coal should last until the year 2200, but we cannot wait until then before we find alternative energy supplies. Apart from the fossil fuels running out, we have to consider the environmental effects of burning fossil fuels.

As long as there is life on Earth the Sun will be shining, so all energy sources which rely on the Sun can be considered as renewable.

Wind turbines

Wind-operated turbines, fig 89.4, can be used in windy areas such as exposed coastlines and moors where the wind almost never stops blowing. The wind is caused by the effect of the Sun on the atmosphere, see pages 174–5.

Fig 89.4 Ten wind turbines at Delabole in Cornwall together generate 4 MW of electricity

Large numbers of wind turbines are needed to generate the same amount of electricity as a coal- or gas-fired station.

Q6 Describe the environmental advantages and disadvantages of a wind-powered electricity station.

Solar cells

Solar cells which produce electricity from solar energy, fig 89.5, are currently very expensive and inefficient. Although they provide useful power sources for satellites, calculators and remote telephone kiosks, power generation on a large scale is not economically viable.

Solar heating

Solar heating of domestic water supplies is not very reliable in Britain where there is no guarantee of sunshine at any time of year. In the more southern parts of Europe solar heating is used to provide plentiful supplies of hot water, page 257.

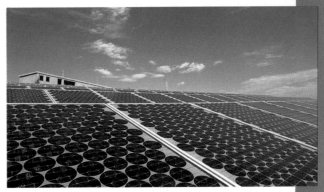

Fig 89.5 Silicon cells produce only a small voltage and current, even in bright sunlight. A large area of cells is needed to generate a significant amount of electrical power at this solar power station in Italy

Q7 A house in a remote area obtains all its energy for heating, cooking and lighting from the wind and the Sun.

  a What features need to be incorporated into the design of the house to capture the maximum amount of energy?

  b Describe the ways in which the energy can gathered and stored.

  c What difficulties might there be in using the stored energy?

GEOTHERMAL ENERGY

The Earth's core is very hot and is a vast untapped energy resource. Some places are fortunate in having hot water springs, or hot water held in porous rocks near the surface. This hot water is not hot enough for generating electricity, but it is used for heating houses – the only energy cost is in pumping it to where it is needed.

In certain parts of the UK there are hot rocks sufficiently close to the surface to make energy extraction from them a viable proposition, fig 89.6. This energy can be used for heating greenhouses to grow winter salad crops as well as for heating in houses, hospitals and industry.

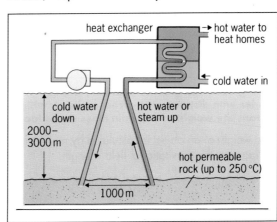

Fig 89.6 Cold water is pumped down one pipe. This forces hot water to the surface through the return pipe

90 FORCES AT WORK

By the end of this section you should be able to

- understand that weight is a gravitational force
- calculate the work done when a force causes movement
- describe the energy changes when a force does work
- calculate changes in gravitational potential energy.

GRAVITATIONAL FORCES

Gravitational forces are universal. Everything pulls everything else towards it. You do not notice the force of attraction between yourself and this book because the force is very small, much smaller than the frictional forces which are acting to oppose motion.

The Earth's pull

Very massive objects like the Earth and the other planets can pull things towards them with large forces. **Weight** is the force which pulls us and other things towards the Earth, fig 90.1.

Fig 90.1 ▶ **Weight is a force which pulls things towards the Earth**

weight of satellite

weight of apple

Gravitational field strength

Close to the surface of the Earth, the size of the gravitational pull or **gravitational field strength** is approximately 10 N on each kilogram of mass, so a 60 kg person weighs 600 N. The gravitational field strength g at any place in the Universe is the gravitational force acting per kilogram mass, fig 90.2.

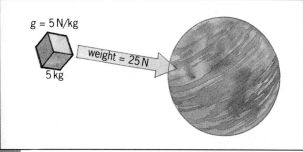

$g = 5$ N/kg

weight = 25 N

5 kg

▲ **Fig 90.2 The gravitational field strength varies with distance away from a planet, which means the weight of a certain mass varies too**

The weight of an object is calculated by multiplying its mass by the gravitational field strength.

weight = mass × gravitational field strength
$$w = mg$$

There are slight variations in the value of g at different places on Earth, but on the surface of the Earth it is usually taken as 10 N/kg.

The Moon's gravitational field strength at its surface is about 1.5 N/kg. When astronauts landed on the Moon they found that they could jump much higher than they could on the Earth.

Q1 Calculate the weight of an 80 kg astronaut on the Earth and on the Moon.

Q2 In terms of upward and downward forces, explain why it is possible to jump higher on the Moon than on the Earth.

WORK

What is work?

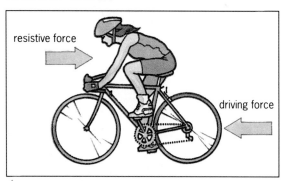

resistive force

driving force

▲ **Fig 90.3 This cyclist is doing work against the resistive forces of air resistance and friction**

Work is done when a force moves in the direction in which it is acting. In fig 90.3, the driving force is moving in its direction of action, so work is being done. The driving force acts against the resistive force of the air resistance and friction. To move at a steady speed along a level road, the driving force equals the resistive force. So the cyclist has to keep pedalling to provide the energy to do this work.

Q3 List six examples of forces which do work and six examples of forces which are not working.

How much work?

The amount of work which a force does is calculated using the formula

work done = force × distance moved in its own direction
$$W = fd$$

So pushing a pram with a force of 30 N for 250 m requires 30 N × 250 m = 7500 J of work.

Q4 Calculate the amount of work done when a force of 150 N propels a cycle for 40 m on a level road.

Work and energy

Notice that work is measured in the same units as energy. Doing 6000 J of work requires 6000 J of energy input. This energy comes from the cyclist, but where does it go to? The cyclist is travelling at a constant speed, so there is no increase in kinetic energy. All the energy ends up as heat, in the air, the tyres and the road surface. Because the energy has been spread around, it can never be recovered – it is **dissipated**.

Uphill work

When the cyclist goes uphill, a bigger driving force is needed because as well as doing work against resistive forces, the cyclist and his machine have to be lifted up. Work is done against their weight. Fig 90.4 shows the forces now acting.

When cycling up a $12\frac{1}{2}$% hill the cyclist in question 4 travels 1 m vertically for every 8 m travelled horizontally. To cycle at the same speed as before, the driving force has to be increased to 250 N.

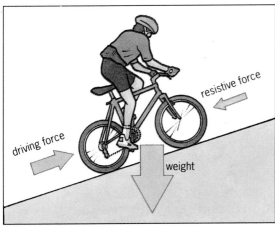

▲ **Fig 90.4** This cyclist is doing work against the resistive forces, and also against his weight as he is moving it upwards, against the direction in which it acts

Q5 How much work is done by the driving force when the cycle travels 40 m up the hill?

GRAVITATIONAL POTENTIAL ENERGY

The answer to question 5 also gives the amount of energy input from the cyclist. Of this energy, 6000 J has been spread out as heat energy as before, and the rest is stored in the cycle and cyclist. Because of their increased height the cyclist and machine have **gravitational potential energy**, or g.p.e., fig 90.5. This energy could be converted into kinetic energy and heat energy if the cyclist freewheeled back down the hill.

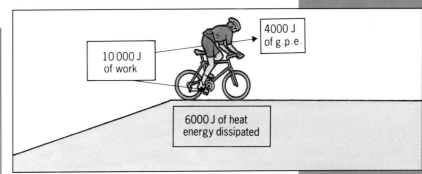

Measuring potential energy

The amount of gravitational potential energy gained or lost when an object changes height can be calculated from the formula for work:

$$\text{work done} = \text{force} \times \text{distance moved in its own direction}$$

Remember that the work which is done is equal to the amount of energy which is transformed. Fig 90.6 shows a rock being lifted.

The upward force has to be just big enough to counteract the weight, so the work done in lifting the rock is equal to weight × the change in height. Weight is mass × gravitational field strength, so the work done is *mgh*, where *h* is the height the rock is lifted. *mgh* also gives the amount of gravitational potential energy which the rock loses when it falls through the same distance.

$$\text{change in g.p.e.} = mgh.$$

Note that it is the *vertical* change in height which is used in the formula *mgh*. A cyclist who travels 40 m up a $12\frac{1}{2}$% incline moves a vertical distance of 5 m and gains the same amount of gravitational potential energy as someone of equal mass who travels 5 m vertically in a lift.

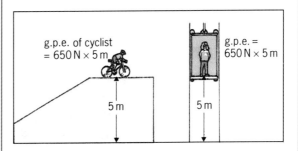

Q6 Calculate the quantity of g.p.e. gained by the cycle and cyclist, of total mass 80 kg, when they travel through a vertical distance of 5 m.

Q7 Minibuses for disabled people are often fitted with a lift to enable a wheelchair-bound person to board the minibus. If the weight of the wheelchair and person is 930 N and the height of the lift is 0.8 m, find the gain in gravitational potential energy of a person and wheelchair being lifted onto the minibus.

▲ **Fig 90.5 The energy used to do work in cycling up the hill is converted to gravitational potential energy and heat energy**

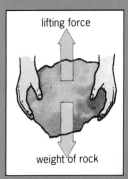

▲ **Fig 90.6 The forces on a rock being lifted**

◄ **Fig 90.7 The gain in g.p.e. depends only on the vertical distance travelled, not the horizontal distance**

By the end of this section you should be able to

- calculate the kinetic energy of a moving object
- understand the relationship between power, work and time
- use data to calculate the power and efficiency of machines.

KINETIC ENERGY

Fig 91.1 These objects all have kinetic energy

Movement requires energy. An object that is moving has **kinetic energy**. The energy to make something move comes from g.p.e. or from chemical energy in the form of food or fuel.

Calculating kinetic energy

The formula for calculating the kinetic energy of a moving object is

$$\text{kinetic energy} = \tfrac{1}{2} \times \text{mass} \times (\text{speed})^2$$
$$KE = \tfrac{1}{2}mv^2$$

For example, the kinetic energy of a 5000 kg bus travelling at 12 m/s is equal to $\tfrac{1}{2} \times 5000 \times (12)^2 = 360\,000$ J.

Q1 Calculate the kinetic energy of an 800 kg car travelling at 15 m/s.

Q2 The car engine provides energy at a rate of 15 000 J/s. How long does it take to reach a speed of 15 m/s?

Q3 The answer to question 2 is impractical. Think of three reasons why it takes longer than this time.

Q4 An electric train has a mass of 400 tonnes. (1 tonne = 1000 kg) What is the minimum energy required to increase its speed from rest to 15 m/s in 20 s?

POWER

A 1600 W hair dryer is more powerful than a 1000 W one. You would expect to be able to dry your hair faster with the 1600 W dryer.

Fig 91.2 The 1600 W hair dryer is more powerful than the 1000 W hair dryer

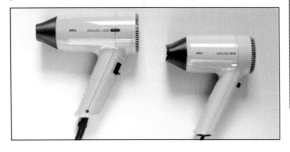

A Jaguar car is more powerful than a Mini – it can carry four people to the top of a hill in a shorter time. But if 60 people are to be taken on the same journey, a bus can do the work faster than either of the cars, fig 91.3, so is more powerful.

▲ **Fig 91.3 The Jaguar is more powerful than the Mini, but the bus is most powerful**

Calculating power

Power means the rate of working, or how much work is done each second:

$$\text{power} = \frac{\text{work done (or energy changed)}}{\text{time taken}}$$

A sprinter who does 50 000 J of work in 12 s has a power output of 50 000 J / 12 s = 4167 W. The watt (W) is the unit of power, 1 W = 1 J/s, see also page 194.

Q5 A shopper does 20 000 J of work pushing a supermarket trolley. He spends 15 minutes doing the shopping. What was his average power output? Explain why this is an *average* power.

Q6 A crane does 45 000 J of work as it lifts a 500 kg load in 30 s. What is the power output of the crane and how far did it lift the load?

Q7 A car is towing a caravan at a speed of 25 m/s. The pulling force is 1200 N. How much engine power is being used to tow the caravan?

How powerful are you?

The power of a person can be found by timing how long it takes to do a measured amount of work. Fig 91.4 shows one way of doing this. Work is done in lifting the weight of the body up the stairs.

stopwatch

▲ **Fig 91.4 Finding how powerful you are**

Activity

Think of other ways in which the amount of work done by a person can be measured. Carry out experiments to compare the power output of a person doing different jobs.

The human body can produce a large power output, several kilowatts, for a short space of time.

▲ **Fig 91.5 An exercise bicycle tells you how much power you are generating**

Q8 Estimate the power output of a weightlifter in making a lift.

Q9 List sports which require a short burst of power. Make a separate list of those which need power over a sustained period.

Q10 What do you think are the factors which limit the output power available to a marathon runner?

Power ratings

Domestic and industrial tools and appliances all have a **power rating**.

> Vacuum cleaner
> 240 V   40–60 Hz
> 1600 W
> Made in the UK

This rating gives the input power. Not all of this power will be output in the desired form. A 650W microwave cooker takes in electrical energy at the rate of 650J/s, but this does not all appear as energy in the microwaves.

Calculating efficiency

The **efficiency** of a machine as an energy conversion device is the fraction of the energy which is converted into the desirable form

$$\text{efficiency} = \frac{\text{useful energy or power output}}{\text{total energy or power input}}$$

Q11 Calculate the efficiency of a 650 W microwave cooker which produces 400 W of microwave energy.

Q12 Tungsten filament lamps are some of the least efficient devices available, with an efficiency of about 0.05, or 5%. Find out why they are popular when other forms of lighting are more efficient.

Q13 The power of a car engine is usually between 30 and 100 kW. This is the maximum power output from the engine, available to drive the car.
Explain why the input power to the engine is greater than the output.

Q14 A diesel engine used for lifting rocks has a power output of 50 kW. How long would it take it to lift a 2500 kg rock through a height of 18 m?

Activity

Lifts use electric motors to change electrical energy into gravitational potential energy. Devise and carry out an experiment to measure the power of an electric motor. You could extend this to measure the efficiency of an electric motor. Factors which affect the efficiency of an electric motor would be a suitable topic for an investigation.

92 FORCE AND ROTATION

By the end of this section you should be able to

- understand and calculate the turning effect of a force
- describe examples of turning forces being used to amplify force and distance
- explain how the position of the centre of mass affects the stability of an object.

TURNING FORCES

Riding a bike, flexing your arm and opening a door are all examples of everyday movements which use forces to turn things round. Try closing a door by pushing it near to the hinge and you realise that it is much more difficult than using the handle, fig 92.1.

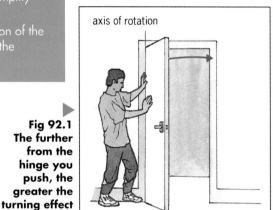

axis of rotation

▶ **Fig 92.1 The further from the hinge you push, the greater the turning effect of your force**

How effective a force is at causing rotation depends on where it acts. A force which is applied close to the pivot or axis of rotation produces a smaller turning effect than one which is applied further away.

The moment of a force

The turning effect of a force is called its **moment** and is measured in newton metres, N m. It is calculated using the formula

moment = size of force × perpendicular distance to pivot

Fig 92.2 shows what is meant by perpendicular distance.

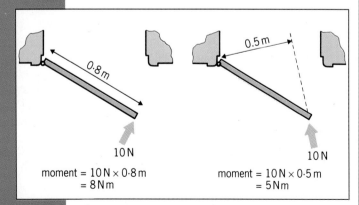

moment = 10 N × 0·8 m
= 8 N m

moment = 10 N × 0·5 m
= 5 N m

▲ **Fig 92.2 In the right-hand diagram, the 10 N force is less effective in closing the door because the perpendicular distance from the axis of rotation is smaller**

Torque

A torque wrench, fig 92.3, is an instrument used by mechanics to measure the moment of the force used to tighten bolts. **Torque** is another word which means 'the turning effect of a force', or moment.

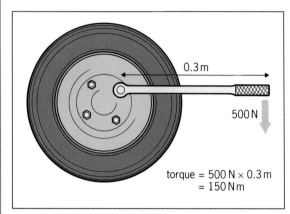

0.3 m

500 N

torque = 500 N × 0.3 m
= 150 N m

▲ **Fig 92.3 Torque means turning effect or moment**

Q1 The correct torque for a wheel bolt is about 100 N m. How much force would be required to produce this torque using a spanner which has a handle 0.2 m long?

Turning forces in cycling

Two of the turning forces involved in cycling are shown in fig 92.4.

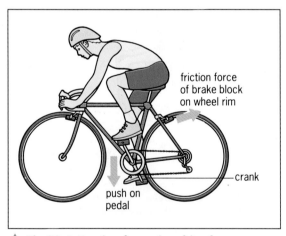

friction force of brake block on wheel rim

crank

push on pedal

▲ **Fig 92.4 Turning forces in a bicycle**

Q2 The cyclist turns the crank. Whereabouts is the pedal when the maximum moment is achieved?

The turning effect of the friction force of the brakes is in the opposite direction to the rotation of the wheel, slowing the bike down.

LEVERS

Balanced systems

Levers are examples of systems where there are two turning forces acting in opposition. Fig 92.5 shows the forces acting on a fishing rod.

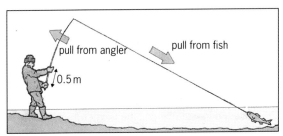

▲ **Fig 92.5 If the rod is not moving, the system is balanced**

The force from the angler has an anticlockwise turning effect which is opposed by that of the fish. For the system to be **balanced** each force must have the same moment, but they act in opposite directions. The system moves out of balance when one force has a bigger moment than that of the other force.

 If the pulling force in the fishing line is 15N and the rod 3m long, what size force does the angler need to use to balance this?

STATICS

Maintaining balance

Turning forces are present even in **static** structures such as bridges and tower cranes. These have to be designed to ensure that the system never goes out of balance. The tower crane shown in fig 92.6 uses a **counterbalance** weight to stop it from toppling when it is lifting a load.

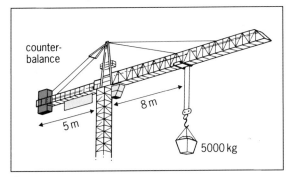

▲ **Fig 92.6 The counterbalance prevents the crane from falling over**

Q4 Calculate the weight of the counterbalance needed for its moment to equal the moment of the load.

Q5 So that the crane can remain balanced when lifting different loads, the counterbalance can be moved towards or away from the tower. Explain how this helps to keep the crane balanced.

Stability and centre of mass

Some things, such as ten-pin bowling pins, are designed so that they can be knocked over easily. Traffic cones should be difficult to knock over. One important design feature is the position of the **centre of mass**. The centre of mass of a golf ball is in the middle, as is that of a polo mint! If one end of a dumb-bell is heavier than the other then the centre of mass is nearer to the heavy end, as fig 92.7 shows.

The centre of mass of any object is the point where the downward force of the weight can be balanced by a single upward force. An object's weight is always drawn as a force acting from the centre of mass. The traffic cone's centre of mass is lower down than that of the bowling pin because it has a greater proportion of its mass at the bottom. Fig 92.8 shows what happens when they are made to lean by the same amount.

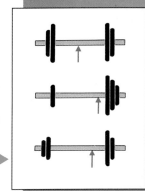

Fig 92.7 The centre of mass is the point where all the mass of the object seems to act, and where the object can be balanced ▶

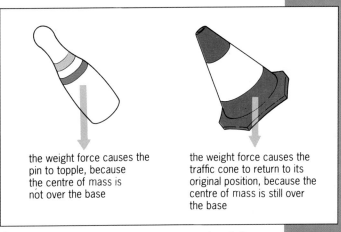

the weight force causes the pin to topple, because the centre of mass is not over the base

the weight force causes the traffic cone to return to its original position, because the centre of mass is still over the base

▲ **Fig 92.8 Some objects are designed to fall over, and others are designed to be stable**

In each case the weight has a moment, but they produce rotation in different directions. The diagrams also give a clue to another important design feature which determines the stability of an object.

Q6 What is the other important design feature? How could you demonstrate this to a friend?

Q7 Can you explain why the leaning tower of Pisa is in danger of toppling over?

By the end of this section you should be able to

- calculate acceleration from given data
- describe what happens to the kinetic energy of a vehicle when it stops
- understand the factors which affect stopping distance.

ACCELERATION

0–60 times

Car advertisements often boast about the short length of time it takes for a particular model to reach a certain speed, fig 93.1.

However, it is not realistic to compare all accelerations by the time it takes to reach 60 m.p.h. – many objects do not move this quickly.

▼ **Fig 93.1 The Mitsubishi 3000GT accelerates from 0–60 m.p.h. in 5.6 seconds**

Calculating acceleration

For something moving in a straight line the acceleration is the increase in speed each second

$$\text{acceleration} = \frac{\text{increase in speed}}{\text{time taken}}$$

For the car in the advertisement the acceleration would be

60 m.p.h. ÷ 5.6 s = 10.7 m.p.h. per second

This means that, on average, the car's speed increased by 10.7 m.p.h. each second. It is likely that the acceleration was greater than this in the early stages, becoming less as the car went faster and the resistive forces increased.

The following example uses the units for speed which we normally use in science, metres and seconds.

Find the acceleration of a bus which speeds up from 2 m/s to 15 m/s in 17 s.
Using the formula above, we find that

acceleration = 13 m/s ÷ 17 s
= 0.76 m/s each second

The average increase in speed of the bus is 0.76 m/s each second. The accepted shorthand way of writing 'm/s each second' is m/s^2 or m s^{-2}.

Q1 Work out the following accelerations.
- **a** A sprinter accelerates from rest to 8.9 m/s in 1.7 s.
- **b** An aircraft accelerates from 10 m/s to 60 m/s in 4 s.
- **c** A milk float reduces its speed from 2.7 m/s to 0.4 m/s in 3.5 s.

The last example shows an object slowing down. This is a **negative acceleration** or **deceleration**.

Going flat out

It is much easier to accelerate a bicycle from 0 m/s to 1 m/s than from 7 m/s to 8 m/s. The reason is because the faster you go, the bigger the resistive forces become, fig 93.2. This is true for all motion on Earth. Spacecraft do not have the same problem, because there are no resistive forces.

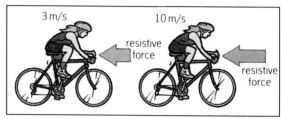

▲ **Fig 93.2 The faster you go, the greater the resistive forces**

Fig 92.3 shows how the speed of a cyclist changes as she accelerates from rest.

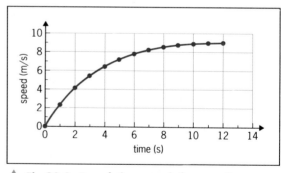

▲ **Fig 93.3 Speed–time graph for a cyclist**

As she goes faster, the resistive forces increase and this reduces the acceleration. At the greatest possible speed, the **terminal velocity**, the forwards force and the resistive force are equal.

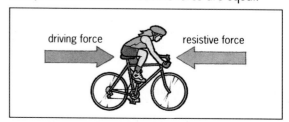

▲ **Fig 93.4 At terminal velocity, the resistive force equals the driving force so there is no more acceleration**

Measuring acceleration

Acceleration of model cars is easy to measure if you have access to light-sensitive switches and a computer, fig 93.5.

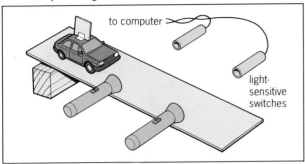

▲ **Fig 93.5 Measuring acceleration**

The car is fitted with a piece of card of known length. 10 cm is often a suitable length to use. The computer records the times for which each light beam is broken, and the time it takes to travel from one beam to the next. Here are some sample data.

length of card = 10.0 cm
time for which first beam is broken = 0.24 s
time for which second beam is broken = 0.07 s
time to travel from first beam
to second beam = 1.3 s

Q2 Use the data to calculate

a the speed of the car as it passed through the first beam

b the speed of the car as it passed through the second beam

c the acceleration of the car between the two beams.

BRAKING AND KINETIC ENERGY

All moving objects have kinetic energy. When a car stops, this energy has to go somewhere. Car brakes apply a friction force acting in the opposite direction to the motion of the wheel, fig 93.6.

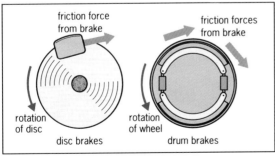

▲ **Fig 93.6 Brakes oppose the motion of the wheel**

During braking the high-friction material of the disc or drum becomes very hot. The kinetic energy of the car is converted into heat energy in the brakes.

Q3 Use the kinetic energy formula, page 230, to calculate the kinetic energy of a 900 kg car moving at 30 m/s and at 60 m/s.

Stopping distances

A car moving at 60 m/s has four times as much kinetic energy as one travelling at 30 m/s. Many motorists do not realise how this affects the distance travelled by a car during braking.

Q4 The shortest braking distance for a car travelling at 15 m/s is 15 m. The braking force on an 800 kg car needs to do 90 000 J of work in order to change 90 000 J of kinetic energy into heat energy. Use the formula for work, page 228, to calculate the braking force needed to do this.

Q5 The same braking force is used to stop the same car from a speed of 30 m/s. What is the shortest braking distance at this speed?

Q6 What advice would you give to a driver who says that 'at 30 m/s I need to leave twice as much distance between myself and the car in front as I do at 15 m/s'?

Braking distance and thinking distance

Your calculations have shown that the braking distance quadruples if the speed is doubled. The braking distance at 45 m/s is nine times that at 15 m/s.

The total stopping distance of a vehicle is the sum of the 'thinking distance' and the braking distance, fig 93.7. The 'thinking distance' is the distance which the car travels while the driver reacts to the need to brake.

▼ **Fig 93.7 The stopping distance is the sum of the thinking distance and the braking distance**

	thinking distance	braking distance
30 m.p.h.	thinking distance = 10 m	braking distance = 15 m
45 m.p.h.	thinking distance = 15 m	braking distance = 35 m
60 m.p.h.	thinking distance = 20 m	braking distance = 60 m

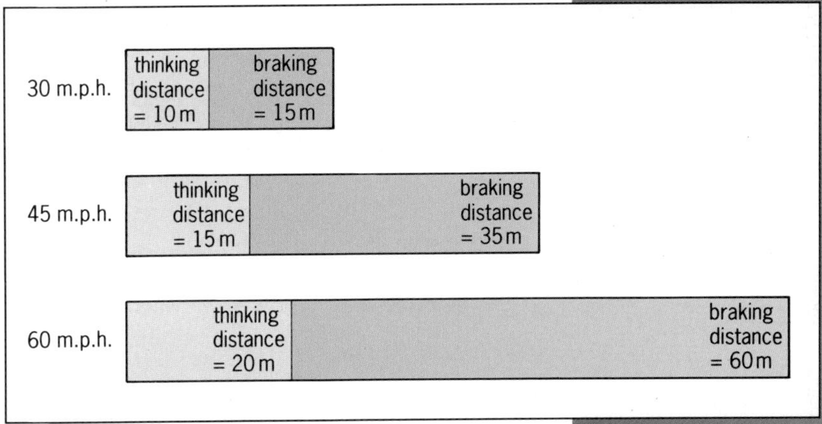

Q7 Explain why the 'thinking distance' at 60 m.p.h. is twice that at 30 m.p.h.

Q8 What other factors affect 'thinking distance' and 'braking distance'?

By the end of this section you should be able to

- understand how the acceleration of an object depends on its mass and the resultant force
- describe free-fall motion
- appreciate that an object moving at terminal velocity is subject to equal forces acting in opposite directions.

NEWTON'S DISCOVERIES

Our present-day understanding of how forces can change the motion of an object is due to Isaac Newton's discoveries made over 300 years ago. Newton realised that it is necessary to consider the sum or **resultant** of all the forces which are acting on the object. Forces have direction, so they can add together to make smaller forces as well as bigger ones, fig 94.1.

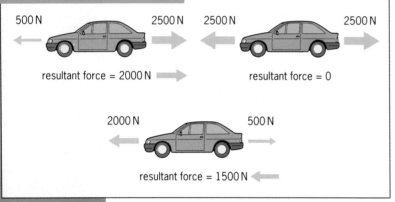

Fig 94.1 The resultant force is the sum of the forces acting

Newton's first law

Newton's first law of motion describes what happens when the sum of all the forces acting is zero. There is no acceleration so an object either stays stationary or carries on moving in a straight line at a constant speed, fig 94.2.

Fig 94.2 A car travelling in a straight line at a constant speed has equal sized forwards and backwards forces acting on it

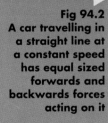 **Q1** Why does a bike slow down when you stop pedalling?

Newton's second law

Newton's second law of motion describes how acceleration depends on the size of the resultant force and the mass of the object being accelerated. Fig 94.3 shows apparatus which can be used to investigate these factors.

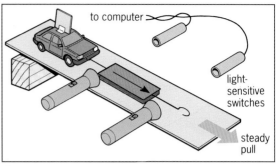

▲ **Fig 94.3 Investigating Newton's second law of motion**

To achieve reliable results it is a good idea to tilt the track a little so that the slope causes the car to speed up at the same rate as the friction forces slow it down. This is called **compensating for friction**.

Unbalanced forces

Any unbalanced force causes an acceleration. An electron in a television tube, page 193, is subject to a very small unbalanced force, about 1×10^{-15} N. This causes it to accelerate to a speed of 1×10^{7} m/s in a tiny fraction of a second.

For a train to accelerate from rest to a speed of 60 m/s in 2 minutes needs an unbalanced force of at least 250 000 N, fig 94.4.

▲ **Fig 94.4 A large unbalanced force is needed to accelerate a train**

Newton realised that it is not just the size of the unbalanced force which determines how quickly something speeds up, but the mass of the object is also important, fig 94.5.

▲ **Fig 94.5 A large mass needs a greater force to accelerate it than a smaller mass**

He concluded that if the same size force is used to pull a 2 kg object and a 4 kg object, the one with twice the mass has half the acceleration. This is an example of **inverse proportion**.

Calculating force, mass and acceleration

Newton's findings are summarised in the formula

force = mass × acceleration
$$F = ma$$

Q2 Calculate the force needed to accelerate a 40 000 kg lorry at 1.5 m/s².

Q3 Use the data given earlier to calculate the mass of the train.

Q4 An empty bus has a mass of approximately 10 000 kg. Enough passengers to fill the bus would have a mass of 7000 kg. If a braking force of 5000 N is used, what deceleration would this cause to an empty bus and to a full bus? What extra care should the driver of a full bus take to ensure the safety of the passengers?

FREE FALL

Theories about falling

Prior to Newton's discoveries, Galilei Galileo in AD1600 had put forward the idea that all falling objects have the same acceleration, provided that air resistance does not have a significant effect.

For 2000 years before this people had believed Aristotle, a Greek philosopher, who stated that the heavier an object is, the faster it falls. This is so easily disproved that it seems incredible to us now that it was accepted for so long.

Galileo probably did not put his idea to the test, but he based his argument on things falling from the top of the leaning tower of Pisa.

Had Galileo lived after Newton's discoveries, he might have said 'A heavy object has a bigger force pulling it down than something which is light, but it also has more mass, so it needs more force to give it the same acceleration'.

Free-fall acceleration and gravitational field strength

Precise measurements of the acceleration of freely falling objects give a value of 9.8 m/s², but for most purposes we use the value of 10 m/s².

Q5 A 5 kg mass is falling with an acceleration of 10 m/s². Calculate the size of the force which is causing this acceleration.

The answer to question 5 shows that a 5 kg mass has a downward force, or weight, of 50 N. This is equivalent to saying that the Earth pulls each kilogram of mass with a force of 10 N.

Comparing the two equations

force = mass × acceleration

and   weight = mass × gravitational field strength (see page 228)

shows that **free-fall acceleration** and **gravitational field strength** are the same thing.

Q6 A freely falling object accelerates from 0 m/s to 10 m/s during the first second after it has been released. Its average speed during this time is 5 m/s and so the distance travelled (average speed × time) is 5 m. Calculate the total distance travelled after 2 s, 3 s, 4 s, ... You should be able to see a clear pattern and be able to predict the total distance travelled after any time interval.

Free fall and terminal velocity

The Earth's pull causes unrestrained objects to fall towards it with an acceleration of 10 m/s². This means that a sky-diver who free-falls for 30 s should have a speed of 300 m/s! In fact the speed after 30 s is the same as that after 20 s, about 60 m/s. This is because the air resistance has a significant effect at such speeds, and the sky-diver quickly reaches terminal velocity, with equal forces acting in opposite directions, fig 94.6.

air resistance

weight

▲ **Fig 94.6 The air resistance equals the weight, so the velocity of fall is constant – terminal velocity has been reached**

95 FORCES AND SHAPE

By the end of this section you should be able to

- apply Hooke's law to elastic materials
- understand and apply the limit of proportionality
- use the quantitative relationships between kinetic and potential energy.

Activity

Fig 95.1 shows how you can investigate the range of forces for which materials are elastic.

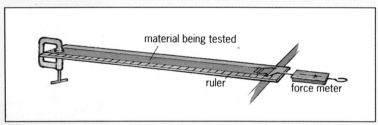

material being tested

ruler

force meter

▲ **Fig 95.1**

You can also take measurements of the extension caused by different forces. Suitable materials to test include nylon, string, copper wire and rubber.

Hooke's law

The graphs in fig 95.2 show how the extension of samples of rubber and steel changes as the stretching force is increased. Note that the scales on the two graphs are not the same – the forces used to stretch steel were much bigger and the extensions produced were smaller.

Fig 95.2 ▶
How rubber and steel stretch as the force increases

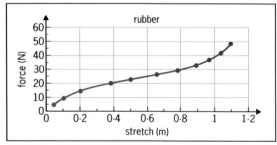

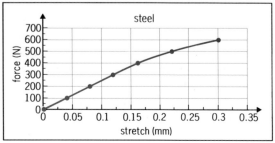

STRETCHABILITY AND ELASTICITY

A material is **elastic** if it returns to its original shape after it has been stretched, compressed or twisted. Steel and rubber are both elastic materials. No material is completely elastic – a big enough force will cause any material to break or be permanently deformed. Plasticine and putty are not elastic – they can easily be reshaped.

The first part of the graph for steel is a straight line – doubling the force also causes the extension to double. Another way of saying this is 'the extension is proportional to the force'. This statement is known as **Hooke's law**. All metals follow Hooke's law for small extensions.

The end of the straight line is called the **limit of proportionality**. Hooke's law cannot be used to predict the extension when the force goes beyond this limit. The limit of proportionality is usually considered to be the safe elastic limit. This limit is very important for engineers who design structures. They must make sure that the materials are never exposed to forces bigger than the elastic limit, or the structure could be permanently reshaped or break.

Rubber does not follow Hooke's law. If you experiment with rubber you will also find that as the stretching force is removed the force–extension curve is not the same as when the force is being increased. The result of this is that not all of the potential energy, or **strain energy**, of the stretched rubber is released again when the force is removed from the rubber. Some remains as heat energy in the rubber. Car tyres, which are subjected to repeated stretching and compression as they rotate, can get very hot, fig 95.3.

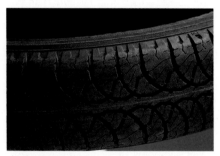

▲ **Fig 95.3 Car tyres can get hot**

Q1 The table shows results obtained by a student who was investigating the stretchiness of a spring.

Load (N)	5	10	15	20	25	30	35
Extension (cm)	0.9	1.6	2.4	3.1	4.4	6.7	10.2

- **a** Plot a graph of force against extension for the spring.
- **b** Estimate the force at which the spring reaches its limit of proportionality.
- **c** For what range of forces could a manufacturer of spring balances use this spring?
- **d** Explain why, when using Hooke's law, it is important to know the limit of proportionality.

BUILDING BRIDGES

The Bridge over the River Kwai is a famous film about a railway bridge built by prisoners of war in Thailand, fig 95.4.

▲ **Fig 95.4 The bridge over the River Kwai**

Wood was used to build the bridge because it was a readily available raw material. The weight of a train on a wooden bridge compresses the structure. Wood is a poor material to use to withstand compression forces, as large forces can cause it to collapse.

Compression and tension

A modern suspension bridge, fig 95.5, uses a combination of **compression** and **tension** forces. The steel cables which hold the road are in tension. Traffic using the bridge causes them to stretch as the tension force increases to support the increased weight. The tension forces in the cables push down on the towers at each end of the bridge. Steel rods are used to reinforce the concrete towers. These steel rods are being compressed. Steel is very good at resisting compressive forces – it needs a very large force to produce a tiny compression in steel.

We do not see the towers of a suspension bridge bobbing up and down as heavy traffic goes over the bridge, because the amount of movement is very small. This movement is continually monitored by strain gauges (see page 197) placed at various points in the structure. The resistance of a strain gauge changes when the tension or compression force changes, and these changes in resistance are monitored by computer, so that engineers can check that the forces are within the safe limits.

▲ **Fig 95.5 The Golden Gate bridge, San Francisco**

ELASTIC MATERIALS AND SAFETY

Climbing rope is designed to be stretchy. Fig 95.6 shows what should happen if a climber falls.

rope is slack at first

rope becomes taut …

… and stretches to absorb the climber's kinetic energy

The climber loses gravitational potential energy and gains kinetic energy as he falls. When the rope becomes taut this energy has to be absorbed as strain energy in the rope. Too stiff a rope would only stretch a small amount, exerting a large force on the climber and possibly even cutting him in half.

Q2
a Calculate the gravitational potential energy lost by a 75 kg climber who falls a distance of 15 m.

b Calculate the speed of the climber after falling 15 m.

c The rope stretches and brings the climber to rest after 0.8 s. Calculate the average force needed to do this.

d Explain why the tension force in the rope when the climber is halted is greater than the force which you have just calculated. (Hint: there are two reasons.)

e In what way is the action of a climbing rope similar to that of a car seat belt?

Q3 Fig 95.7 shows a high-jumper. To clear the 2.3 m high bar he must raise his centre of mass by 0.9 m. His mass is 65 kg.

▼ **Fig 95.7**

a Calculate the gain in potential energy at the top of the jump.

b What is his minimum take-off speed if he is to clear the bar?

c Explain why his actual speed at take-off is greater than this.

d Describe the motion of the high-jumper in the time between landing on the mat and finally coming to rest. Link this motion with the energy changes taking place.

e Explain how the jump of a pole-vaulter differs from that of a high-jumper.

96 FORCES IN LIQUIDS

By the end of this section you should be able to
- describe the action of a hydraulic system
- calculate the pressures and forces in a hydraulic system.

PRESSURE IN LIQUIDS

Fig 96.1 This vehicle uses hydraulics to transmit forces from the controls to the bucket

Machines which produce large forces, such as presses for car body panels and earth-moving machinery, fig 96.1, have their moving parts driven by liquids. Liquids can transmit a pressure around bends and they provide a convenient way of amplifying forces, allowing very big forces to be developed from much smaller ones. Using liquids in this way is a branch of science called **hydraulics**.

Solids, liquids and gases

The difference in the arrangements of particles in gases and liquids is shown in fig 96.2.

▼ **Fig 96.2 The particles are closer together in a liquid than in a gas**

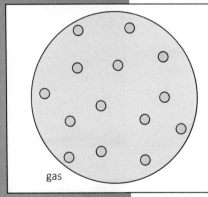
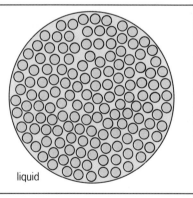

gas   liquid

Gases are mainly free space so they can be compressed relatively easily. However, compressing a gas increases its pressure. If you block the exit hole of a bicycle pump and push the handle in, you can feel the gas pushing back. Let go of the handle and it springs out. If you try to compress a liquid you are immediately forcing the molecules into each other, creating large repulsive forces. The result is a very big pressure increase for a tiny reduction in volume.

Solids exert pressure due to their weight, so a solid object only exerts a pressure on its base. Liquids and gases exert pressure due to molecular motion, and that pressure pushes upwards and sideways as well as down. A demonstration of this is shown in fig 96.3. You can do this easily at home – preferably outside.

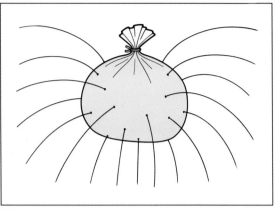

▲ **Fig 96.3 Liquids exert pressure in all directions**

Activity

Using two syringes and a piece of plastic pipe you can show that pressure can be passed through a liquid around corners and circles, and even if a knot is tied in the pipe, as long as the flow of liquid is not restricted, fig 96.4.

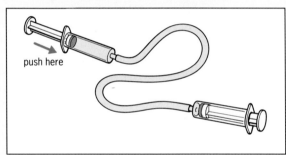

push here

▲ **Fig 96.4**

Force amplification can be shown using two unequal-sized syringes, fig 96.5.

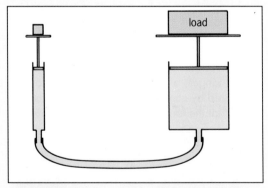

load

▲ **Fig 96.5**

Add weights to the small syringe to lift the load on the larger one.

Q1 Describe how you could compare the energy input and energy output of this force amplifier.

240

Transmitting pressure

Liquids can be made to amplify force in this way because they transmit pressure, not force. By making the liquid pressure act over different sized areas, the force can be made bigger or smaller. This is shown in fig 96.6.

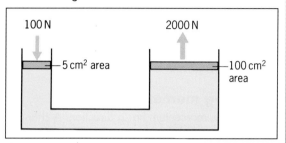

▲ **Fig 96.6 Liquids transmit pressure, so the force can be increased by using a piston of greater area**

A force of 100N pushing on an area of 5cm^2 in the smaller tube produces a pressure of 20N/cm^2. This pressure acts in all directions all the way through the liquid. The pressure of 20N/cm^2 acting upwards on the 100cm^2 platform in the larger tube exerts a force of 2000N on it. Hydraulic ramps used to lift cars in garages work in this way, fig 96.7.

Fig 96.7 ▶
Hydraulic ramp

Q2 Refer to fig 96.6. How much movement of the 100N force is required to move the 2000N force by 1cm? What assumptions have you made in working this out? Think carefully about what happens when the 100N push is applied.

BRAKES

The most common use of hydraulic transmission is in car braking systems like the one shown in fig 96.8.

The driver pushes on the 'master' cylinder piston. The pressure is transmitted in the brake fluid to each 'slave' cylinder, which then operates the brake shoes or discs. One advantage of using hydraulics is that the same pressure is applied to each brake cylinder, producing even and smooth braking. If the car designer wants a bigger braking force at the front than the back, this is easily achieved by using 'slave' cylinders with larger area pistons on the front brakes.

Q3 Fig 96.9 shows part of a car braking system.

▼ Fig 96.9

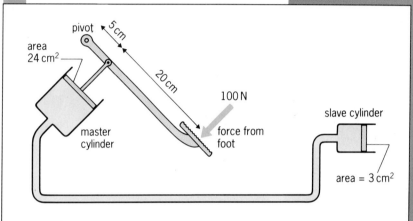

a Calculate the force exerted on the master cylinder.
b Calculate the pressure which is transmitted through the brake fluid.
c Calculate the force which is exerted at the slave cylinder.
d If the piston on the brake cylinder moves 1.5mm, calculate how far the master cylinder piston and the driver's foot move.
e Why is it important that brake fluid does not contain air bubbles?

◀ Fig 96.8
The pressure on the master cylinder is transmitted to the front and rear slave cylinders

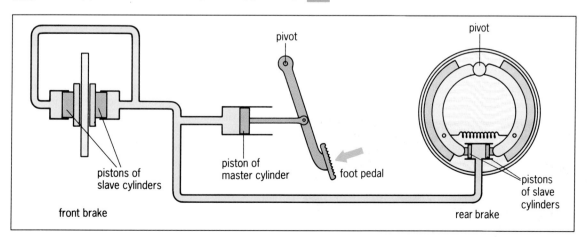

97 FORCE AND MOMENTUM

By the end of this section you should be able to

- understand momentum and its conservation
- describe how a force can change the momentum of an object.

MOMENTUM AND MOTION

All moving things have **momentum**. Imagine a rifle bullet, a golf ball and a bus each hitting a brick wall. The one which would do most damage to the wall is the one with the greatest momentum.

The idea of momentum is useful when thinking about the effect forces have in starting things moving, stopping things and causing changes in direction, fig 97.1.

Fig 97.1 We use momentum to explain changes like these

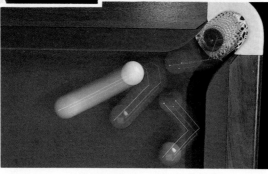

What is momentum?

To understand momentum you first need to know the difference between **speed** and **velocity**. Speed only measures how fast something is travelling but velocity describes both speed and direction. To an aircraft pilot or ship's captain the direction of travel is very important.

The momentum of an object is given by

$$\text{momentum} = \text{mass} \times \text{velocity}$$

A bowl used in tenpin bowling is intended to knock the pins over, fig 97.2.

Fig 97.2 ▶ Ten-pin bowling bowls have a large mass so when rolled at speed they have a large momentum

The more momentum the bowl has, the better it can do this. A 6 kg bowl projected at a speed of 8 m/s has momentum 6 kg × 8 m/s = 48 kg m/s or 48 Ns. (Ns is an alternative unit for momentum.)

Q1 Calculate the momentum of each of the following.

  a a 10 000 kg bus travelling at 20 m/s
  b a 45 g (0.045 kg) golf ball travelling at 80 m/s
  c a 10 g bullet travelling at 500 m/s

Changing momentum

Like velocity, momentum has a direction. A change in the mass, speed or direction of motion is a change in momentum.

In order to change the momentum of an object a force is required.

Q2 Study the examples in fig 97.3 and identify the direction of the force which is causing the momentum to change.

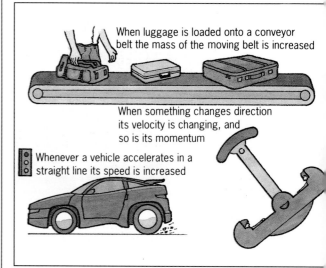

When luggage is loaded onto a conveyor belt the mass of the moving belt is increased

When something changes direction its velocity is changing, and so is its momentum

Whenever a vehicle accelerates in a straight line its speed is increased

▲ **Fig 97.3**

MOMENTUM AND COLLISIONS

Conservation of momentum

When two objects collide they each have the same change in momentum, but the changes are in opposite directions, so the total amount of momentum stays the same. This is known as the **principle of conservation of momentum** – it applies to collisions where no other forces are acting. It is important when using this principle to take movement in one direction as being positive, and to give a negative value to movement in the opposite direction.

In a road accident, an 800 kg car travelling at 40 m/s collides head-on with a 1200 kg van moving at 30 m/s. The two vehicles stick together. What is the velocity after the impact?

The initial momentum of the car
= 800 kg × 40 m/s
= 32 000 kg m/s
The initial momentum of the van
= 1200 kg × −30 m/s
= −36 000 kg m/s
The total momentum before the collision
= −4000 kg m/s

This is also equal to the combined momentum after the collision. The total mass is 2000 kg, so the velocity is −2 m/s. This means that the car and the van move together at a speed of 2 m/s in the direction in which the van was travelling before the collision.

Q3 A 40 kg railway truck moving at 8 m/s collides with a 30 kg truck which is stationary. Calculate the velocity with which the trucks move together.

Q4 Snooker balls have a mass of 0.6 kg. A white ball travelling at 16 m/s hits a stationary red ball and rebounds at 12 m/s. Calculate the velocity of the red ball.

Q5 A 1000 kg car travelling at 12 m/s collides head-on with a 700 kg car moving in the opposite direction. Both cars stop. Calculate the velocity of the 700 kg car before the collision.

EXPLOSIONS

Conservation of momentum also applies to explosions. You may have seen on television that when a weapon fires a bullet or a shell, the weapon moves backwards. This is known as **recoil**. When a cannon is fired, it gains the same amount of momentum as the shell, but in the opposite direction, so that the combined momentum of cannon and shell remains zero. The same effect can be felt when using a 'trigger-action' hosepipe.

Q6 Two ice-skaters stand together on the ice. A 70 kg man pushes his daughter, who has a mass of 30 kg. The man moves backwards at 1.5 m/s. Calculate the speed of his daughter.

Q7 Radium-226 decays to radon-222 by emitting an alpha particle, page 141. The alpha particle is emitted at a high velocity. Describe what happens to the radon-222.

EFFECTS OF CHANGING MOMENTUM

When a force changes the momentum of an object, the result depends on the size of the force and the length of time it acts.

Tennis players and cricketers try to move the racket or bat so that it is pushing on the ball for as long a time as possible to get a big momentum change.

Young children soon learn that a solid ball has more momentum than a soft one. Stopping a hard ball hurts less if a small force is used over a longer period of time.

Calculating momentum change

The change in momentum caused by a force is calculated from the equation

change in momentum = force × time for which the force acts

This is not a new equation, just a different way of writing $F = ma$.

A 1000 kg car travelling at 30 m/s has momentum 30 000 kg m/s. In a collision such a car could be stopped in 0.2 s or less. This requires a force of 150 000 N. **Crumple zones** extend the time it takes for the car to stop, so reducing the force of the impact, fig 97.4.

▲ **Fig 97.4 Crumple zones protect passengers by absorbing the kinetic energy of the car. What other safety feature does the picture show?**

Q8 a Calculate the momentum of the driver, mass 80 kg, of a car travelling at 30 m/s.
b Calculate the force needed to stop the driver in 0.1 s.
c Calculate the force needed to stop the driver in 1.5 s.
d Explain why seat belts need to be stretchy, but not too stretchy.

By the end of this section you should be able to

- describe how sound waveforms can be examined
- appreciate that different musical instruments have their own characteristic waveforms
- explain the meaning of frequency and how it can be measured from an oscilloscope.

MUSIC AND NOISE

Q1 Make a list of 20 different things which produce sound. Put an 'M' beside those which make music and an 'N' beside those which make noise.

Activity

Fig 98.1 shows how to use a microphone and an oscilloscope to look at pictures of the sounds made by different things. Sounds do not last for very long, so if a data logger is used to record the sound the patterns can be studied later.

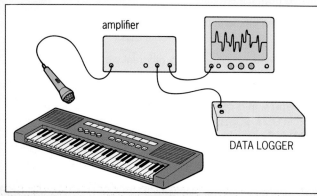

amplifier

DATA LOGGER

▲ **Fig 98.1**

Q2 Sketch the patterns produced by the following.
a someone playing a recorder
b a keyboard synthesising different instruments
c a recording of playground or traffic noise
These sketches are easier to do if you have a computer printout of the patterns.

Unlike the sound patterns from musical instruments, noise is irregular. There is no repetition in the sound pattern for noise.

FREQUENCY

The sound patterns from musical instruments are **regular**. The same waveform is repeated over and over again. The number of complete cycles of the wave which occur each second is called the **frequency**, measured in hertz (Hz). It is the frequency of a sound wave which determines the pitch of the note.

Measuring frequency

Fig 98.2 shows the oscilloscope traces of a low-pitched and a higher pitched note produced by a signal generator.

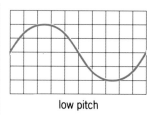
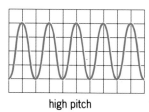

low pitch   high pitch

▲ **Fig 98.2 The frequency of a note determines its pitch**

In this example the oscilloscope time base, which controls the horizontal speed of the electron beam, was set to 1 ms/cm. This means that it took the beam 10 ms or 0.01 s to do one sweep of the screen.

Q3 By counting the number of cycles of each wave shown on the screen, calculate the frequencies of both waves.

Often there will not be a whole number of waves on the screen, in which case the time interval for one cycle can be measured and the frequency calculated using the relationship

frequency (Hz) = 1 ÷ time for one cycle (s)

Q4 Calculate the frequencies of the waves shown in fig 98.3.

a
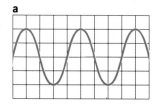

b
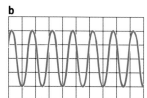

c
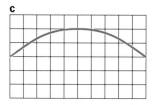

▲ **Fig 98.3**

MUSICAL INSTRUMENTS

A keyboard which can mimic other instruments produces a different waveform for each instrument. The recorder waveform is a very simple one. Waveforms produced by other instruments are more complex.

The diagrams in fig 98.4 show the oscilloscope traces obtained from three instruments playing the

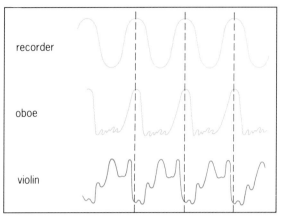

recorder

oboe

violin

▲ **Fig 98.4 The shape of the waveform gives the note its distinctive sound or quality**

same note. The more complex waveform of the oboe is due to the presence of a number of higher frequencies combined with the frequency of the note being played. The number of higher frequencies present, and the amount of energy they carry, gives each type of instrument its own individual sound.

REFLECTIONS OF SOUND

▲ **Fig 98.5 Bats use the echoes of very high-pitched sounds to find their way around**

Snooker players use the 'angle of incidence = angle of reflection' rule when playing shots which involve bouncing a ball off a cushion. To the snooker ball, the cushion presents a smooth surface. If the snooker ball were much smaller, or the surface irregularities of the cushion were much bigger, the direction of the reflection would not be so predictable. This is the case with sound waves.

Absorbing sound

Like the kinetic energy of a snooker ball, sound waves are transient. After a few reflections all the energy has been absorbed. Inside a large hall a sound can often be heard for several seconds after it has been made. Designers of concert halls use sound-absorbing materials to control the length of time for which a sound persists, known as the **reverberation time**. Rooms used for the testing of loudspeakers have the walls covered in wedge-shaped blocks, like those shown in fig 98.6.

Q5 Explain how the the wedges prevent sound from being reflected from the wall.

Q6 Explain why double glazing is effective at reducing the noise entering a building.

Q7 Explain why sounds are very different in an empty room compared with one which is furnished.

NOISE POLLUTION

Measuring sound levels

Noise levels are measured on the **decibel scale**, fig 98.7. This is not a linear scale – each increase of 10 dB corresponds to a doubling in the loudness of the sound.

Preventing noise

Sound levels in excess of 120 dB can cause discomfort and pain, and continued exposure to loud sounds causes damage to the ear and loss of hearing.

It is not only loud noises which are a nuisance. Relatively quiet sounds can carry a long way in buildings which have long corridors.

Q8 Discuss ways in which noise can be prevented from
   a entering a building
   b leaving a building
   c travelling within a building.

You should consider the cost as well as the effectiveness of different measures.

▲ **Fig 98.6 Measuring the noise generated by an aircraft propellor. The walls of the room produce no echoes**

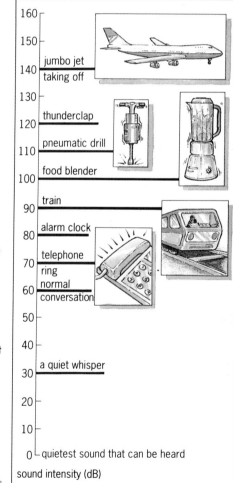

Fig 98.7 The decibel scale ▶

160
150
140 jumbo jet taking off
130
120 thunderclap
110 pneumatic drill
100 food blender
90 train
80 alarm clock
70 telephone ring
60 normal conversation
50
40
30 a quiet whisper
20
10
0 quietest sound that can be heard

sound intensity (dB)

99 SOUNDS DIFFERENT

By the end of this section you should be able to

- describe how sound travels
- solve problems using the wave speed equation
- understand how the terms wavelength and amplitude apply to sound waves.

Activity

Many of the sounds which we hear every day come from loudspeakers. Fig 99.1 shows how a loudspeaker and a candle can be used to study the effect of the loudspeaker cone on the surrounding air.

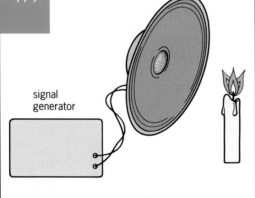

signal generator

▲ **Fig 99.1**

With the signal generator set to a low frequency such as 1 Hz, the in-and-out movement of the cone can be seen clearly. The candle flame shows how the air in front of the loudspeaker is also moving to and fro.

Longitudinal waves

This type of wave is a **longitudinal wave**. Each part of the spring moves to and fro parallel to the direction in which the wave is travelling, passing on the energy to the next part.

Q1 Use the slinky model to explain how sound travels in a solid.

Like the waveforms which you looked at using the oscilloscope, a continuous wave on a slinky is a repetition of the same movement, in this case a compression followed by a rarefaction, over and over again, fig 99.3.

Notice how turning up the output voltage of the signal generator causes a bigger movement of the paper cone and the candle flame. The maximum displacement is called the **amplitude** of the sound wave. It is the amplitude that determines the loudness of the sound.

Increasing the frequency of the signal generator output causes more oscillations of the loudspeaker cone each second. As you can hear, this gives a higher pitched sound.

Modelling sound waves

A slinky spring can be used to show how sound travels in the air. If one end of the spring is pushed in, a **compression** travels along the length of the spring. To make a model of a sound wave travelling, the end of the spring should be alternately pushed and pulled. A piece of tape stuck onto part of the spring allows you to study its motion.

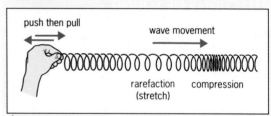

push then pull | wave movement

rarefaction (stretch) | compression

▲ **Fig 99.2**

Sound waves

Like the slinky, air is elastic. Sound is transmitted from a loudspeaker to your ear by longitudinal vibrations of the air molecules. Each air molecule moves in the same way as the coils of the slinky, to and fro parallel to the direction in which the sound wave is travelling, fig 99.4.

molecular spacing in still air

spacing due to sound wave passing

representation of sound wave

▲ **Fig 99.4 Air molecules in a sound wave oscillate like the coils of a slinky**

▼ **Fig 99.3 A continuous wave is a series of compressions and rarefactions**

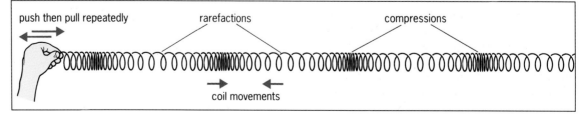

push then pull repeatedly | rarefactions | compressions

coil movements

246

WAVE MEASUREMENTS

Activity

Use the slinky to see the effect of increasing the number of oscillations made each second. If the slinky is pushed in and out more rapidly the compressions and rarefactions are closer together, as fig 99.5 shows.

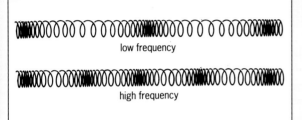

low frequency

high frequency

▲ **Fig 99.5**

Wavelength

One compression and one rarefaction is a complete cycle or **wavelength** of the wave. To go through one cycle means that you end up at the point where you started. A continuous wave is made up of repetitions of this cycle. All the distances marked on fig 99.6 represent one complete wavelength.

▲ **Fig 99.6 The wavelength can be measured from any point on the wave to the next identical point**

> **Q2** Measure the marked distances in fig 99.6. What do you notice about them?

The wavelength is the length of one complete cycle of a wave. This length can be measured from the middle of one compression to the middle of the next, or between any two points if the length between them takes in exactly one compression and one rarefaction. The symbol used for wavelength is the Greek letter λ, pronounced lamda.

Frequency

The wavelength of a wave on a slinky depends on how rapidly the end of the slinky is pushed in and out, or the **frequency** of the wave. If the end of the slinky is pushed in and out at a higher frequency, the compressions and rarefactions become closer together and the wavelength has decreased.

Every tuning fork has a number stamped on it. Fig 99.7 shows a tuning fork which produces the note known as 'middle C'. In one second each prong of the fork does 256 complete cycles of oscillation.

A piano tuner sounds the tuning fork and the piano key together. If a wow-ow-ow sound is heard then the note is out of tune and the tension of the string is adjusted until this disappears.

Speed

A high frequency sound has a short wavelength and a low frequency sound has a long wavelength. Both these measurements are related to the **speed** with which the wave travels. To understand this relationship, imagine that you are watching a very long train. The train is a repetition of the same thing over and over again, in this case a carriage, fig 99.8.

▲ **Fig 99.7 A middle C tuning fork has a frequency of 256 Hz**

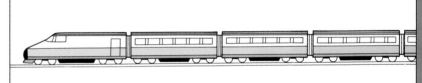

> **Q3** If the carriage length is 20 m and the frequency is 3 carriages per second, how fast is the train travelling?

> **Q4** A goods train has carriages which are 12 m long and it is travelling at the same speed as the train in question 3. How many carriages go past each second?

The equation which relates the speed of a wave to its wavelength and frequency is the same for all waves. You may have discovered by answering the last two questions that

wave speed = frequency × wavelength
$$v = f\lambda$$

> **Q5** Copy the following table and use the equation to fill in the blanks.

Wave speed (m/s)	Frequency (Hz)	Wavelength (m)
	22	1.5
	320	0.5
500		2.5
330	15	
25	1.25	
1500		0.75

▲ **Fig 99.8 Each carriage corresponds to one cycle of a wave and the frequency is the number of carriages which go past in one second. The wavelength is the length of each carriage**

VIBRATIONS

By the end of this section you should be able to

- understand how resonance occurs
- explain advantages and disadvantages of resonance in sound and mechanical systems.

All sound is produced by something vibrating. Many musical instruments produce a note by making a string or an air column vibrate.

Q1 Name three stringed instruments and three instruments which use air columns. Answer the following questions for each instrument.

a How is the string or air column made to vibrate?

b How does the player change the note being played?

c Is the instrument particularly suitable for playing high or low notes?

Q2 Name three instruments which do not use a string or an air column.

a For each instrument, find out what vibrates and how it is made to vibrate.

b Do these instruments allow the note to be changed?

Natural frequency

All objects have a **natural frequency** of vibration. A ruler vibrates at its natural frequency if one end is fixed and the other end is displaced and then released, fig 100.1.

Q3 How is the natural frequency of vibration of a ruler changed?

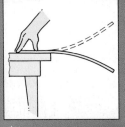

▲ **Fig 100.1 A ruler has a natural frequency of vibration**

Activity

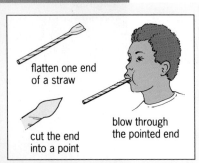

flatten one end of a straw

cut the end into a point

blow through the pointed end

▲ **Fig 100.2**

Try the experiment in fig 100.2 with a drinking straw. When you blow through the straw the air column inside the straw vibrates and you can hear the note which it produces. The length of the air column can be made smaller by cutting bits off the end of the straw. This changes the natural frequency of vibration of the air column, giving a higher pitched note.

Fig 100.3 shows the pipes of a church organ.

Q4 Explain why there are so many pipes of different sizes.

Q5 Small animals such as rats make high frequency sounds which are above the range of human hearing. Suggest an explanation for this.

◄ **Fig 100.3 Organ pipes at a church in Oxford**

Low frequencies

Vibrations with a frequency less than 20 Hz are not detected as sound by human ears, but the ears of some animals and birds can detect these low frequencies.

Activity

Fig 100.4 shows a method of studying low frequency vibrations.

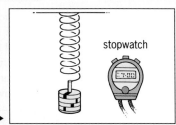

stopwatch

Fig 100.4 ▶

Investigate how the natural frequency of the spring depends on

a how far the mass is pulled down to start with (the displacement) and

b what mass is placed on the spring.

Damping

Cars and other motor vehicles use springs to cushion the blow when they go over a bump in the road, fig 100.5.

▲ **Fig 100.5 The springs help keep the car level as it goes over bumps and dips in the road**

The car would bounce up and down on the springs if shock absorbers were not also fitted. The job of the shock absorbers is to return the car to its normal position without vibration. This is called **damping**.

Car mechanics can tell the condition of a car's shock absorbers by pushing down at one corner and then releasing the car. Describe what should happen and what would happen if the shock absorbers were faulty.

RESONANCE

A swing is an everyday example of something which vibrates at its natural frequency. The electronic circuits which tune in a radio or television use electrical oscillations at the natural frequency of the circuit. Studying an object such as a swing can help us to understand oscillations which we cannot actually see.

Activity

Hold the brick next to your nose and let it go. Keep your head still while the brick swings away from you ... and back towards you ... and doesn't reach your nose.

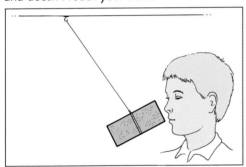

▲ **Fig 100.6**

Losing energy

When an object such as the brick or a guitar string is made to vibrate the amplitude of the vibrations gradually decreases as energy is lost to the surroundings. The same thing happens when a swing is given a single push.

Q7 Where does the energy go to in the case of the swing?

Replacing the energy

To make the swing go higher it needs to be pushed at regular intervals. Each push has to occur when the swing has completed exactly one oscillation.

Once the swing has reached the required height the pushes are needed to keep it swinging at that height. Each push of the swing replaces the energy it loses while completing one oscillation. This is an example of **resonance** – the swing is kept vibrating by pushing it at a frequency which is the same as its natural frequency of vibration, or **resonant frequency**.

Activity

Fig 100.7 shows how the resonance of a piano string can be studied. Adjust the frequency of the signal generator until the string resonates. You will see the large amplitude vibrations at this frequency.

A piano string has several resonant frequencies. Compare the notes at the resonant frequencies with the note at the natural frequency of vibration, produced by plucking the string in the middle.

Fig 100.7 ▶

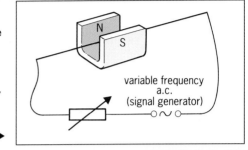

variable frequency a.c. (signal generator)

Using resonance

The resonance of a crystal of quartz is used in clocks and watches. The resonant frequency of the quartz depends on the size of the crystal used but it is about 1 MHz (1×10^6 Hz). There is very little change in the resonant frequency when the temperature changes, so quartz crystals should maintain accurate time-keeping all year round.

Resonance has to be allowed for in large structures, as civil engineers found out in 1939 when the Tacoma Narrows bridge collapsed, fig 100.8.

◀ **Fig 100.8 The collapse of the Tacoma Narrows bridge, Washington State, USA**

Wind caused the large amplitude vibrations which led to the collapse of the bridge. Modern suspension bridges have shock absorbers which prevent this happening.

◀ **Fig 100.9 Shock absorbers prevent resonance being set up**

By the end of this section you should be able to

- describe the use of echoes for measuring distances and locating minerals
- understand how ultrasound can be used to examine body tissue
- describe the effects of the diffraction of sound waves.

ECHO SOUNDING

Echo sounding is used for many purposes, from detecting long-lost ships on the sea bed to routine antenatal scans to monitor the development of a fetus. These and other applications rely on the partial reflection which takes place whenever waves pass from one material into another.

Measuring distance

The principle of echo sounding is to send out a pulse or short burst of waves and measure the time which elapses between sending out the pulse and detecting the reflection, fig 101.1.

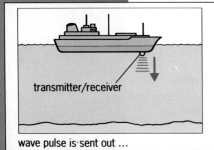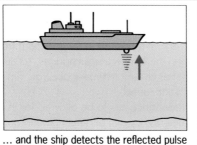

wave pulse is sent out ...   ... and the ship detects the reflected pulse

▲ **Fig 101.1 Echo sounding is used to measure distances**

Q1 Use the following data to calculate the distance travelled by the wave pulse.

    time between emitting pulse and receiving reflection = 0.60 s
    speed of sound in water = 1500 m/s

The distance which you calculated in question 1 is the total distance travelled by the wave pulse. The depth of the water is half of this distance.

Sonar

Ships use **sonar** (**so**und **n**avigation **a**nd **r**anging) to find the position of shoals of fish, shipwrecks and submarines. A pulse of ultrasonic (very high frequency, well above the limit of human hearing) waves is sent out and reflections take place from solid objects. The distance of the object from the ship is determined from the time delay between the pulse being emitted and the reflection being received.

Q2 Ultrasound waves are reflected by a shoal of fish. Calculate the time taken for the ultrasound to travel from the ship to the fish and back again if the depth of the shoal is 50 m. The speed of sound in water is 1500 m/s.

The relatively slow speed of sound in water can be a drawback when a ship is trying to determine the position of a submarine which may be several kilometres away.

Q3 Calculate the time delay between an ultrasound pulse being emitted from a ship and the reflection being received from a submarine which is 5 km away. If the submarine is travelling at 12 m/s, how far does it travel in the interval while the reflected pulse travels back to the ship?

LOOKING UNDER THE SURFACE

Seismic surveying

Reflections of a sound pulse can reveal more information than just how far away something is. The amount of energy which is reflected depends on the change of speed as the wave crosses the boundary between two materials, and this in turn depends on the density of the materials. The bigger the change of speed, the more energy is reflected. When geologists undertake a seismic survey a large shock wave is sent into the ground and the reflections are monitored over the surrounding area, fig 101.2.

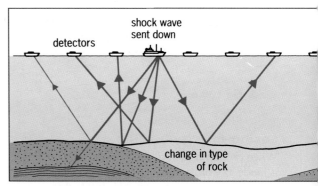

▲ **Fig 101.2 Sound pulses are reflected to build up a seismic survey picture**

The amplitude of the reflections indicates the density of the material. More energy is reflected when there is a large change in density than for a small change. This is a useful technique for finding valuable mineral deposits.

Antenatal scanning

Ultrasound waves are used for antenatal scanning. They are produced by the resonance of a small crystal. The waves are sent out in bursts at regular intervals and detected by the same crystal which produces them.

A layer of gel is first placed over the mother's skin – without this most of the energy would be reflected at the air–skin boundary due to the large change in density. Some reflection then occurs at each boundary between different types of tissue. A computer uses these reflections to build up a picture on a television screen, fig 101.3.

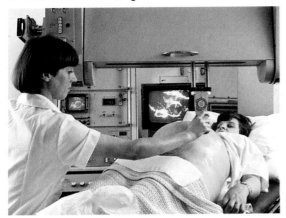

▲ **Fig 101.3 An ultrasound scan shows boundaries between tissues of different densities**

The mother can see the picture of her child-to-be in the womb. These pictures can also reveal the sex of the fetus, but many parents still prefer to wait until the child is born before they know this.

Q4 Explain why ultrasound scans are used in preference to X-rays for antenatal scanning.

Ultrasound scans have many other applications in medicine. They can be used to detect tumours in the brain and other organs and check the operation of the heart.

Q5 Fig 101.4 shows how a pulse of ultrasound can be used to detect a tumour which is 7.0 cm below the surface of the skin.

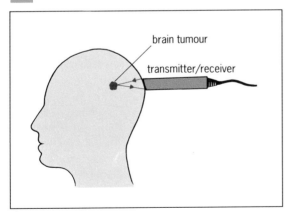

brain tumour

transmitter/receiver

▲ **Fig 101.4**

For best results the wavelength used should be about 1/200 times the depth of the tumour.

a Calculate the most suitable wavelength.
b The speed of sound in body tissues is about 1.5×10^3 m/s. What frequency should be used?

SPREADING SOUND

When sound passes through an opening such as a doorway, it spreads out. This spreading out effect is called **diffraction**. The diffraction of water waves can be seen using a ripple tank.

The photographs in fig 101.5 show that the amount of spreading depends on the size of the opening compared with the wavelength of the waves. The maximum amount of spreading occurs when the gap size is equal to the wavelength. When the gap is much bigger than the wavelength there is very little spreading of the waves.

Q6 The speed of sound in air is 330 m/s. Calculate the wavelength of middle C ($f = 256$ Hz), and compare this to the width of a doorway.

Q7 A note of frequency 15000 Hz is very high-pitched. How well would the sound spread out after passing through an open window?

Q8 Diffraction is very important in the design of loudspeakers. Explain why loudspeakers which reproduce high-pitched sounds are much smaller than those used for low-pitched sounds.

▼ **Fig 101.5 The degree of diffraction depends on the size of the gap**

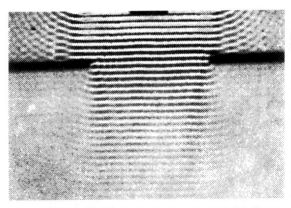

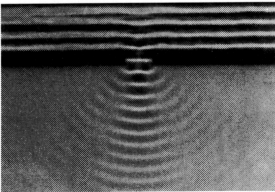

By the end of this section you should be able to

- appreciate that light is a small part of the electromagnetic spectrum
- understand that the colour of an object depends on the frequencies of light which it reflects
- understand the differences between sound waves and electromagnetic waves
- name the different parts of the electromagnetic spectrum.

LIGHT AND THE SPECTRUM

Isaac Newton realised that white light contains all the colours of the spectrum. Prior to Newton's discovery it was thought that coloured objects add the colouring to white light, like adding a pigment to white paint, fig 102.1.

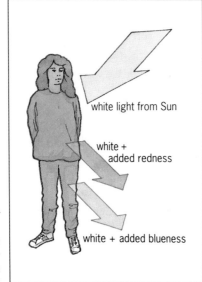

Fig 102.1 Ideas about colour before Newton

white light from Sun

white + added redness

white + added blueness

Producing a spectrum

Fig 102.2 shows how a triangular prism can be used to produce a spectrum from a single ray of white light.

Fig 102.2 White light is a mixture of different coloured lights

Splitting white light into a spectrum is a way of spreading out the mixture of colours in order of wavelength. Fig 102.3 shows the range of wavelengths in the visible spectrum.

Seeing colours

The colour which is registered by our eyes is determined by the frequency of the radiation rather than the wavelength. We shall see on page 263 that blue light of a given frequency changes its wavelength when passing through different materials, but this does not affect the colour which our eyes see.

Having established that white light contains all the colours, Newton was able to explain that a red object looks red because it only reflects the longer wavelengths in the visible spectrum. Leaves look green because green light is reflected by the leaves, the other wavelengths are absorbed, fig 102.4.

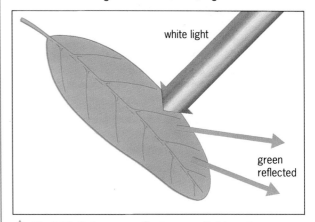

white light

green reflected

Fig 102.4 Leaves reflect green light and absorb other colours

THE ELECTROMAGNETIC SPECTRUM

The visible spectrum is just a tiny part of a family of waves which all have the same nature but cover a vast range of wavelengths. They are called **electromagnetic radiation** because of the way in which the energy travels.

Using electromagnetic radiation

Electromagnetic radiation is essential to our everyday lives. We use it for seeing, cooking, heating our houses, long-distance communication and diagnosing and treating illness. When using electromagnetic radiation we have to be aware of its dangers. It can give us skin cancer, cause leukaemia and even kill us. Like sound, electromagnetic radiation travels as a wave motion, but there are some important differences. Sound and other mechanical waves need a material to

Fig 102.3 The visible spectrum

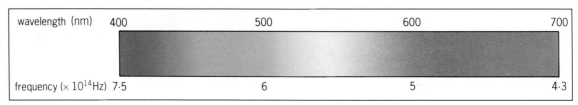

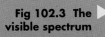

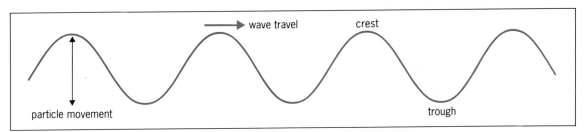

**Fig 102.5 A
tranverse wave**

travel in. The energy is transmitted as kinetic energy of the vibrating particles. The energy of an electromagnetic wave is in electric and magnetic fields. These pass easily through a vacuum.

Although they are different types of wave, sound and electromagnetic radiation have certain things in common. They are both **reflected** at a boundary between two materials. They are both **refracted**, that is they change speed and wavelength when they pass from one material to another.

Transverse waves

Electromagnetic radiation travels as a **transverse wave**. This means that the oscillations are at right angles to the direction in which the wave is travelling. A slinky spring or rope can be used to show a model of a transverse wave, fig 102.5. One cycle of a transverse wave consists of a wave crest and a trough.

All electromagnetic waves travel at the same speed in a vacuum, 3×10^8 m/s (300 000 000 m/s). They travel slower and with a range of speeds in other

substances. The range of wavelength is from approximately 1×10^{-16} m to 1×10^5 m, but there is no definite beginning or end. Fig 102.6 shows the names given to different parts of the spectrum. There are no strict dividing lines between the types of radiation. The name given to a particular radiation depends on its origin as well as its wavelength.

Q1 Copy the table and use the wave speed equation $v = f\lambda$ to complete the blanks. The data refers to electromagnetic waves travelling in a vacuum with a speed of 3×10^8 m/s.

	Wave	Frequency (Hz)	Wavelength (m)
a	radio		247
b	X-ray		5×10^{-10}
c	microwave	5×10^9	
d	red light	5×10^{14}	
e	gamma		2×10^{-12}
f	infra-red		1.5×10^{-6}
g	ultraviolet	3×10^{15}	

**Fig 102.6 The
electromagnetic
spectrum**

frequency (Hz)	10^{24}	10^{21}	10^{18}	10^{15}	10^{12}	10^9	10^6
wavelength (m)	10^{-15}	10^{-12}	10^{-9}	10^{-6}	10^{-3}	1	10^3

gamma-rays (γ-rays)

radio waves

X-rays

microwaves

ultraviolet   infra-red

By the end of this section you should be able to

- describe some uses of gamma-rays and X-rays
- appreciate the possible dangers of very short wavelength electromagnetic radiation.

USING GAMMA-RAYS

Of all the family of electromagnetic waves, **gamma-rays** have the shortest wavelength and highest frequency. Their high penetration makes them useful as tracers for medical and engineering purposes. When choosing a radioisotope for a particular purpose, both the half-life of the radioisotope (see page 142) and the energy of the gamma-rays have to be considered. The shortest wavelength gamma-rays have the highest energy.

Tracers in medicine

Technetium-99 is a radioactive isotope which is used as a tracer in medicine. It emits low energy gamma-rays and has a half-life of 6 hours.

Q1 Explain why these two properties make technetium-99 particularly suitable as a tracer to be used inside the body.

The technetium-99 is chemically attached to another substance before being injected into the blood. The substance used depends on which part of the body is being studied. To get a picture of a patient's bone structure, phosphates are used because these chemicals are directed by the body into the bones. The technetium-99 is attached to red blood cells to study a patient's heart and blood circulation. After allowing sufficient time for the radioactive material to reach its target, a **gamma camera** is used to detect the radiation from the patient's body, fig 103.1.

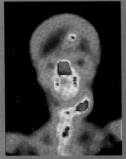

**Fig 103.1
The gamma camera is used to detect cancers. The red areas on the scan show bone cancer**

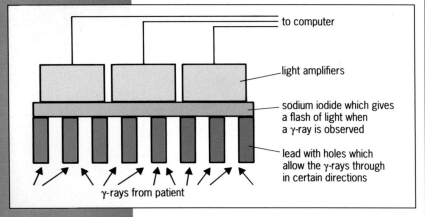

to computer

light amplifiers

sodium iodide which gives a flash of light when a γ-ray is observed

lead with holes which allow the γ-rays through in certain directions

γ-rays from patient

Treatment of cancer

High energy gamma-rays are used in the treatment of cancer to kill cancerous cells. The isotope used is cobalt-60 which has a half-life of 5 years. In order to target the cancer which is being treated, the patient is subjected to beams of gamma-rays from different directions, fig 103.2.

this area receives the greatest intensity of radiation

▲ Fig 103.2 The body tissues receive a lower dose than the area being treated, where the beams intersect

The beams intersect at the area being treated. This ensures that the cancer receives a large dose of gamma-rays while the other body tissues which the beam passes through are not over-exposed to the gamma-radiation.

Q2 What safety precautions should the operators of gamma-ray medical equipment observe?

Sterilising medical equipment

The ability of gamma-rays to kill cells and bacteria enables them to be used to sterilise medical equipment such as syringes and scalpels. The equipment is sealed into a plastic package before being subjected to a large dose of gamma radiation.

Q3 Explain why irradiated syringes present no radiation hazard to the users. What advantage does this method of sterilisation have over heat treatment?

Irradiating food

Food can also be irradiated to increase its shelf life, fig 103.3.

▲ Fig 103.3 Food is irradiated with gamma-rays

The gamma-radiation kills bacteria which would cause the food to decay, and prevents the sprouting of foods such as potatoes. However, the chemical changes caused by irradiation can give some foods an unpleasant taste and so it is not widely used as a method of food preservation.

USING X-RAYS

Diagnosis

In medicine, **X-rays** are used both for diagnosis and for treatment. Dentists use small X-ray machines for examining the bone which supports the teeth and hospitals use X-rays to examine bones for fractures. Fig 103.4 is an X-ray photograph showing the bone in a broken leg.

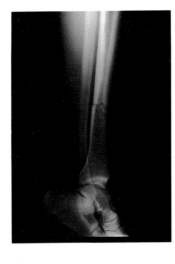

Fig 103.4 X-rays are used for diagnosis – bones show up clearly on an X-ray picture

When an X-ray photograph is taken, the film detects the radiation which passes through the body, unlike a normal photograph which detects the light reflected from objects. Fig 103.5 shows a chest X-ray machine in use. The person is placed between the film and the X-ray tube.

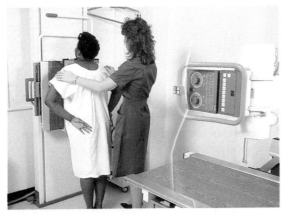

▲ **Fig 103.5 A chest X-ray is used to diagnose tuberculosis**

Chest X-rays are used to check for tuberculosis. The diseased lung tissue absorbs more of the X-rays than healthy tissue and so it shows up as white on the film.

Dangers of X-rays

X-rays can also have harmful effects, and this is why their use in diagnosis has been replaced where possible by ultrasound scanning, see pages 250–51. X-rays can create hydrogen peroxide from water in the body and this can damage essential enzymes and chromosomes, see pages 70–71.

Treatment of cancer

X-rays can be used in the same way as gamma-rays for medical treatment such as killing cancer growths, fig 103.6. As with gamma-rays, it is important to reduce the risk of damaging other cells. One way of reducing the exposure of the normal cells to X-rays is to direct the beam at the cancer cells from several different angles. Very short wavelength X-rays are used because these have the highest energy and cause the greatest amount of damage to cells.

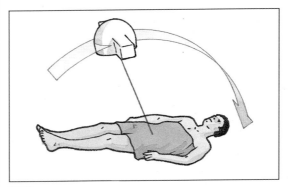

Q4 Imagine yourself as
a someone who is suffering fom cancer
b a pregnant woman looking forward to the birth of her child.
How important would possible side-effects from X-rays be to you in each case?

COMPARING X-RAYS AND GAMMA-RAYS

X-rays and gamma-rays differ in their origin. X-rays come from X-ray machines and gamma-rays come from an unstable nucleus. Apart from this they are similar, so it is not surprising that they have the same uses. Both are used for checking welds in pipework and pressure vessels, for example. A source of gamma-rays has the advantage of being small, portable and manoeuvreable, though a major disadvantage is storing it safely. X-ray machines require a power supply and are not readily portable, but their main advantage is that when switched off they are not hazardous.

◄ **Fig 103.6 The X-ray beam is rotated around the patient, always pointing at the tumour being treated, to protect the other body tissues from too high a dose**

104 EITHER SIDE OF LIGHT

By the end of this section you should be able to

- appreciate the properties and dangers of ultraviolet radiation
- describe the origins and some uses of infra-red radiation.

▲ **Fig 104.1 Welders protect their eyes from ultraviolet radiation**

Ultraviolet radiation

Ultraviolet radiation is the name given to the part of the electromagnetic spectrum which has a wavelength which is shorter than that of light but longer than that of X-rays. Ultraviolet radiation is given out by the Sun and other very hot objects as well as by some gases when they conduct electricity. It is responsible for suntans and skin cancers and can be used to treat some skin disorders.

Welders need to protect their eyes from the damaging effect of the ultraviolet radiation given out from the sparks, fig 104.1.

Fortunately most of the ultraviolet radiation which reaches the Earth from the Sun does not penetrate the atmosphere—it is absorbed by the ozone layer, page 177.

Q1 Why do you think skin cancer is more common in people living near the equator?

Q2 What steps have been taken in recent years to try to conserve the ozone layer?

Q3 Explain how sun protection lotions work.

Q4 You cannot get a suntan by sunbathing in a greenhouse. What does this tell you about the ability of ultraviolet radiation to penetrate glass?

Fluorescence

Like X-rays and gamma-rays, ultraviolet radiation causes some materials to **fluoresce**. When a material fluoresces it absorbs high energy radiation and gives out light, which has a lower energy. Manufacturers of washing powders add fluorescent dyes to them. The washed clothes absorb ultraviolet radiation from the Sun and give out more light than they would without the fluorescent dye, making them look whiter.

Fluorescent lights produce ultraviolet radiation by passing an electric current through mercury vapour. The outside of the tube is coated with a material which absorbs the ultraviolet radiation and emits the energy as light, fig 104.2.

Fig 104.2 The coating absorbs the ultraviolet radiation and emits light

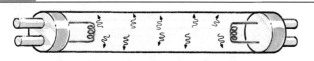

Q5 Sunbeds use mercury vapour lamps without the fluorescent coating. Explain why the fluorescent coating is not used. What safety advice would you give to a person using a sunbed?

Infra-red radiation

Infra-red radiation is given off by everything. It is sometimes called 'radiant heat' or 'heat radiation' because it has a warming effect when it is absorbed. Hot objects emit more infra-red radiation than cold ones, and the radiation which they emit includes shorter wavelengths, fig 104.3.

▲ **Fig 104.3 Hot objects emit more infra-red radiation of shorter wavelengths than cold objects**

Activity

Fig 104.4 shows experiments to investigate how the amount of infra-red radiation which objects emit and absorb depends on the texture and colour of the surface.

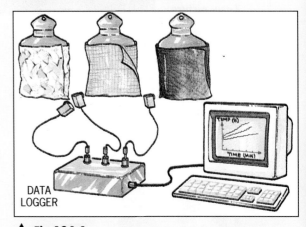

▲ **Fig 104.4**

Dull black surfaces are the best emitters and absorbers of infra-red radiation. Silvered surfaces are good reflectors of infra-red radiation.

Q6 Why are the glass walls of a vacuum flask silvered (see page 221)?

Q7 Explain why the cooling pipes at the back of a refrigerator are painted black (see page 219).

Q8 Why are marathon runners given an aluminium foil cape to wear when they have completed their race?

Q9 Infra-red beams are used to operate televisions and video recorders. If you have one at home, experiment to see which materials allow the infra-red radiation to pass through and which absorb it. What types of surface are good reflectors of infra-red radiation?

Solar panels

Solar panels use infra-red radiation from the Sun to heat water, fig 104.5.

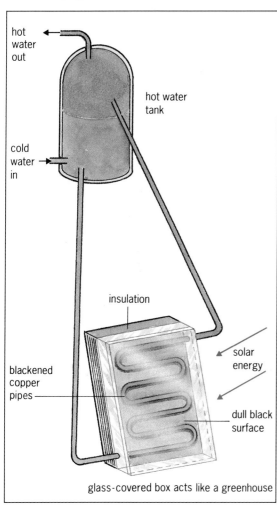

▲ **Fig 104.5 A solar panel uses the Sun's energy to heat water directly**

Water is pumped through blackened copper pipes which are fixed to a black base. The whole panel is covered in glass.

Q10 Explain how the design of the solar panel enables the maximum amount of energy to be absorbed.

Thermography

Thermography is a medical technique for producing an infra-red picture of a body or part of a body. Hot areas show up as different colours or brightness. The thermogram will show parts of the body which are cool due to poor blood circulation or hot areas where there are tumours or inflammation.

Q11 Study the thermogram shown in fig 104.6. Describe what you can deduce from the different colours which are shown.

Infra-red cameras

Cameras which are sensitive to infra-red radiation are used to take pictures at night. You may have seen television programmes which show the behaviour of nocturnal animals such as badgers.

Q12 Why do television pictures taken using infra-red cameras not show things in colour?

Q13 Explain how detectors of infra-red radiation are useful when there has been a disaster such as an earthquake.

Weather satellites

Weather satellites also detect infra-red radiation. The satellite picture in fig 104.7 shows that during the day the land is much warmer than the sea.

Q14 Describe how you would expect the image to change during the night.

The Earth cools down at night because it is giving out more infra-red radiation than it is receiving. On a cloudy night the clouds absorb the radiation and re-emit it in all directions, so a lot of it comes back to us.

Q15 Explain why a frosty night is more likely when the sky is clear than when it is cloudy.

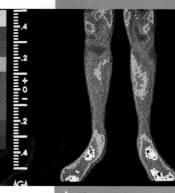

▲ **Fig 104.6 Thermogram of legs showing rheumatoid arthritis affecting the joints of the ankles and toes**

◄ **Fig 104.7 Infra-red satellite photographs show the different tempeatures of the land and sea**

By the end of this section you should be able to

- describe some of the uses of radio waves
- appreciate that the wavelength used for a particular application depends on the amount of spreading out which is required.

Fig 105.1 Microwaves are short wavelength radio waves, and are used for cooking

MICROWAVES

Radio waves have a vast range of wavelength, from centimetres to hundreds of metres. The shortest wavelength waves are called **microwaves**, and are used for radar and telecommunication as well as for cooking, fig 105.1.

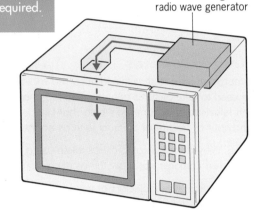

12 cm wavelength radio wave generator

Microwave cookers produce radio waves of wavelength about 12 cm. The waves are guided from the radio wave generator into the cooking chamber. Those that do not immediately go into the food are reflected from the walls and the inside of the door. The energy from the microwaves is absorbed by water molecules and salt in the food, causing an increase in the kinetic energy of these molecules which makes the food hot.

Q1 Name three foods which are good absorbers and three foods which are poor absorbers of microwave energy.

Q2 Calculate the frequency of the microwaves used in cooking (see page 253).

Q3 Microwave cookers have an efficiency of about 40%. Calculate the radio wave power produced by a microwave cooker which has an input power of 650 W.

RADAR

Reflections

The principle of **radar** is the same as echo sounding using ultrasound, page 250. A beam of radio waves is sent out and any reflections are detected. Fig 105.2 shows how only a small amount of the energy which is reflected by an aircraft returns to the radar detector, so the beam has to be

narrow to stop the energy from spreading out too much and becoming too weak to detect. A concave reflector is used behind the transmitting aerial to focus the beam.

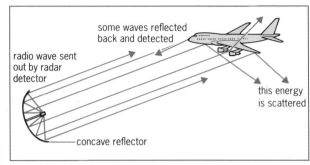

some waves reflected back and detected

radio wave sent out by radar detector

this energy is scattered

concave reflector

▲ **Fig 105.2 The radio waves are focused by the concave reflector or dish**

Reducing diffraction

To reduce the amount of spreading out of the radar beam the reflector has to be many wavelengths in diameter. The easiest way to achieve this is to use short wavelength waves rather than have a very large reflector. The waves used for radar have a wavelength of a few centimetres.

Fig 105.3 Radar apparatus on this oil tanker sends out a pulse of short wavelength radio waves and detects the 'echoes'

A ship's radar, fig 105.3, takes several seconds to do a complete sweep. While it is turning, short pulses of waves are sent out with a small time interval between each pulse and the next one. In the gap between sending out the pulses, the transmitting aerial acts as a receiving aerial to detect the reflections.

Q4 A ship's radar detects a reflection above the surface 80 μs after emitting a pulse. Calculate the distance between the ship and the object which caused the reflection. (The speed of radar is 3×10^8 m/s.)

Radar has one important advantage over sonar when large distances are involved – it is much faster. However, its range under water is very limited because the energy is absorbed by the water molecules, just as in a microwave cooker.

RADIO TRANSMISSIONS

One of the main uses of radio waves is to transmit information of all kinds, from telephone calls to television pictures.

Amplitude modulation

Long and medium wave radio broadcasts use **amplitude modulation** (AM) to carry the sound wave. This involves varying the amplitude of the radio wave so that the sound signal is superimposed on it, fig 105.4.

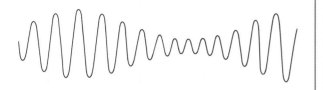

▲ **Fig 105.4 Amplitude modulation**

Radio receivers contain a demodulator circuit which extracts the information about the sound from the modulated radio wave.

Frequency modulation

VHF (very high frequency) radio transmissions use **frequency modulation** (FM), fig 105.5. Much more information can be sent on a frequency modulated wave, provided that the frequency of the carrier wave is high enough. High sound quality and stereo broadcasts are possible using FM.

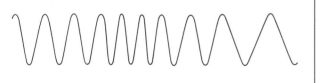

▲ **Fig 105.5 Frequency modulation**

Diffraction

The radio waves used by broadcasting stations are longer wavelength than the microwaves used in radar. They are intended to spread out from the transmitter, so diffraction is not a problem.

Polarisation

Radio waves from a transmitting aerial are **polarised** when they leave the aerial, which means that the oscillations are only in one direction, fig 105.6.

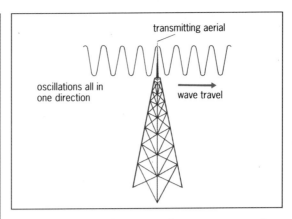

transmitting aerial

oscillations all in one direction

wave travel

In order to receive the waves, the receiving aerial needs to aligned with the direction of the oscillations. As the receiving aerial is rotated, the signal strength becomes less and is zero when the aerial has been turned through 90°.

Horizontal polarisation is used for most television transmissions but there are some areas where vertical polarisation is used. Look at your television aerial to see whether the rods on it are horizontal or vertical.

 Q5 What other sources give out radio waves, apart from transmitting aerials? Do you think that these radio waves are polarised?

Using microwaves for transmission

Not all radio communications are 'broadcast'. Telephone and satellite communications use a narrow beam to transmit from one aerial to another. Microwaves are used to avoid the spreading out due to diffraction, see page 266.

The dish aerials on the Telecom tower, fig 105.7, transmit microwaves which carry television signals and thousands of telephone calls. Each of the aerials transmits to a repeater tower, fig 105.8, which in turn transmits the signals to other repeater towers. These towers are built on high ground and are spaced at 30–40 km intervals.

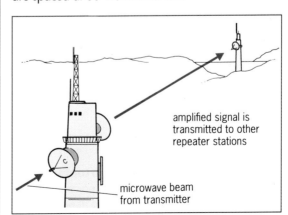

amplified signal is transmitted to other repeater stations

microwave beam from transmitter

▲ **Fig 105.8 Repeater towers amplify and transmit the signal**

◄ **Fig 105.6 Radio waves are polarised – the oscillations are all in one direction**

▲ **Fig 105.7 Transmitter aerials on the Telecom tower**

By the end of this section you should be able to

- describe how a change in direction of a wave is caused by a change in speed
- describe how mirrors and transparent substances cause images
- describe how a prism causes dispersion.

IMAGES CAUSED BY REFLECTION

Locating objects

Our eye–brain system works on the principle that light travels in straight lines in order to locate the position of things that we see. The light which is reflected from an object is scattered in all directions. With two eyes, we can detect the light in two of those directions. This enables the brain to pinpoint the position of an object, fig 106.1.

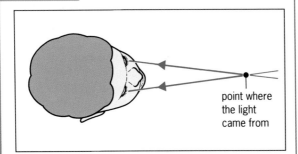

Fig 106.1 ▷
We assume that light travels in straight lines to work out the position of an object we see

point where the light came from

Mirror images

When the light does not travel in a straight line from an object to our eyes, the result is that our brain 'sees' something in the wrong place. This happens when we look at ourselves in a mirror, fig 106.2.

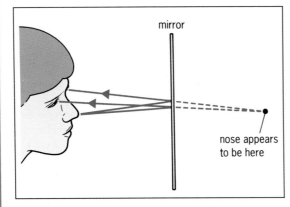

Fig 106.2 ▷
A mirror reflects the light rays, so they do not travel in a straight line

mirror

nose appears to be here

When we look in the mirror our eyes focus on a point behind the mirror. At this point we see a likeness, or **image**, of ourselves which differs in only one important aspect from the real thing.

Q1 What is the main difference between an object and the image of that object in a mirror?

The image in a mirror is called a **virtual image**. If you look behind the mirror at the point where it appears to be, there is nothing there. It only *appears* to be there because of the way in which light is reflected from the mirror.

Activity

In the middle of a piece of paper, draw a straight line to represent a mirror. Draw an arrow anywhere in front of the mirror. Use the **law of reflection** (angle of incidence = angle of reflection) to find the position of the image of the arrow. Compare the size and position of the image with those of the arrow you drew.

Periscopes

Periscopes use two mirrors. Each one turns the light round a corner, fig 106.3.

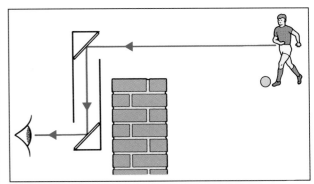

▲ Fig 106.3 A periscope uses two mirrors to reflect the light twice

A periscope is easy to make using two small mirror tiles and a cardboard tube.

IMAGES CAUSED BY REFRACTION

Virtual images are very common in our everyday lives. We often use mirrors. Images can also be made in different ways, as the following two examples show.

Activity

1 Look through a thick block of glass at some writing. Note the ways in which the writing looks to be the same or different.
2 Seat a friend down at a table. Place a coin in a suitable container so that it is just out of your friend's view, fig 106.4.

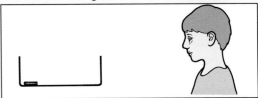

Fig 106.4

Now pour water into the container, taking care not to disturb the coin.

Bending light

Both of these examples involve looking at images which are nearer to you than the real object. The images are formed by the bending of the light as it crosses the surface from the water or glass into air, fig 106.5.

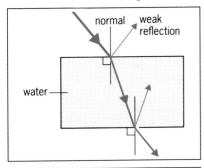

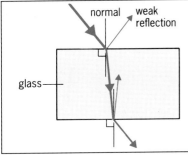

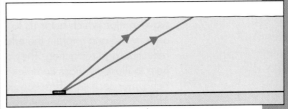

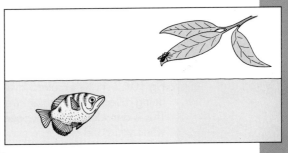

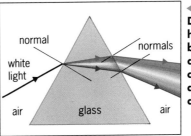

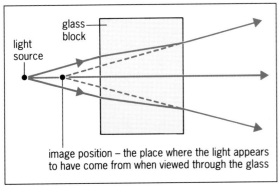

Fig 106.5 Water and glass bend light by refraction

A line drawn at right angles to the surface where the ray hits is called a **normal** line. The normal line gives a useful reference for describing the bending which occurs.

Light bends *towards* the normal line when it crosses the surface going into the water, and *away* from the normal when it comes out. The same thing happens when light passes through glass, but the effect is greater.

Forming the image

The virtual images seen when objects are viewed through a transparent material can be explained as being due to the bending which occurs when light crosses a boundary, fig 106.6.

▲ Fig 106.6 We assume the light has travelled in a straight line and see an image at a different place from the object position

Q2 Fig 106.7 shows two rays of light from a coin at the bottom of a swimming bath.

◀ Fig 106.7

Copy the diagram leaving space above it and draw in the approximate path of the rays as they emerge. Trace these back as straight lines to find where a person would see the coin.

Q3 The archer fish 'sees' things further away than they really are. Copy fig 106.8 and draw two rays of light to the water surface.

◀ Fig 106.8

Continue the rays into the water, making an estimate of the bending. Trace these rays back to show where the archer fish 'sees' the insect.

Refraction and colour

On page 252 you saw how a triangular prism can be used to split white light into its different colours. This is called **dispersion**. It happens because the different colours of light bend by different amounts as they enter and leave the prism. Fig 106.9 shows how some dispersion takes place both when the light goes into the prism and when it comes out again.

◀ Fig 106.9 Dispersion happens because different colours of light are refracted differently

Q4 Which colour is bent the most as the light goes into the prism? Which is bent the most as the light leaves the prism?

Q5 Where else can you commonly see dispersion? Is the order of colours the same as with the prism?

107 A WAVE MODEL

By the end of this section you should be able to

- use the wave model to describe reflection and refraction of waves
- relate the angles of incidence and refraction to the change in speed of the wave.

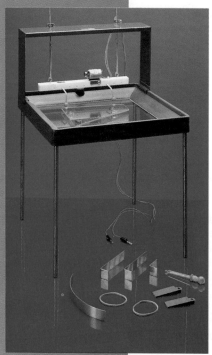

USING WATER WAVES

Water waves provide a model of wave motion which helps us to understand and explain the effects of reflection and refraction. They also help to illustrate more complex wave behaviour such as diffraction. Ripple tanks provide a convenient way of studying water waves, fig 107.1.

Making waves

Circular waves can be generated by using a water dropper or the end of a finger, while a vibrating beam can be used to produce a continuous stream of circular or straight waves.

REFLECTION

Reflection of circular waves

Fig 107.2 shows circular waves being reflected at a straight wall. This is a model of what happens when you stand close to a mirror – the light coming from each point of your face hits the mirror as a circular wave and is reflected.

Q1 Imagine that you could only see the reflected wave. Where does it seem to have come from, that is, where is the centre of the circle?

The point where the reflected wave seems to have originated is the image position.

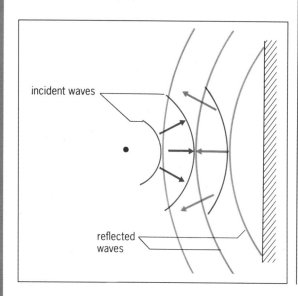

Fig 107.2 ▶
Reflection of a circular wave

Reflection of plane waves

The light which reaches the mirror from more distant objects is only a small part of a circular wave. Imagine a circle 5 m in radius. If you were to study 10 cm of the circumference of that circle, you would not notice very much curvature. Light from distant objects can be represented as a stream of plane (straight) waves. Fig 107.3 shows how such waves are reflected at a straight wall.

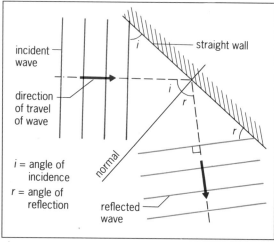

▲ **Fig 107.3 Reflection of a straight wave**

A stream of waves like this is a model of a single ray of light.

Q2 Measure the angles on the diagram. Do they correspond to the law of reflection for mirrors?

REFRACTION

Changing speed

Refraction is a change in speed when waves pass from one substance into another. The refraction of water waves can be seen by placing a perspex sheet in a ripple tank, creating a region of shallow water, fig 107.4.

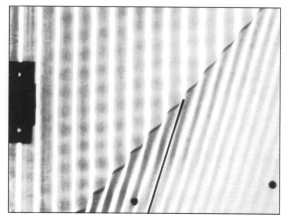

▲ **Fig 107.4 Refraction of water waves caused by a change in depth of the water**

Changing wavelength

The waves are slowed down as they enter the shallow water region. This causes the wave crests to get closer together so that the waves have a shorter wavelength. The frequency of the waves stays the same – the same number of waves pass each second in the shallow water as in the deep water.

Colour and frequency

The colour of light depends on the frequency of the waves, not the wavelength. If you look at an object under water it doesn't seem to have changed colour.

Q3 The speed of light in air is 3×10^8 m/s and in water is 2.3×10^8 m/s. Calculate the wavelength in air and in water of light which has a frequency of 6×10^{14} Hz.

How the change in speed causes bending

The bending of light as it passes into water and glass is caused by the change of speed at the boundary. Figs 107.4 and 107.5 show this bending.

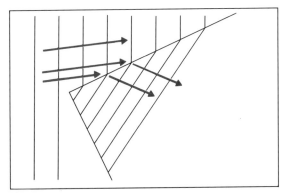

▲ **Fig 107.5 The change in direction happens because of a change in speed**

As the wave enters the shallow water at an angle, the part which enters first slows down first, and so it lags behind the rest of the wave. The wave cannot continue as a straight line when one part is travelling slower than the rest. Fig 107.6 shows what happens as the wave crosses the boundary.

Q4 Does the direction of bending shown figs 107.4 and 107.5 correspond to the bending of light as it goes into glass?

Q5 You saw on page 261 that light bends more when passing into glass than when passing into water. What does this tell you about the speed of light in water compared to its speed in glass?

SIZING THE ANGLES

For the same angle of incidence, glass bends light more than water does, fig 107.7. This is because the change of speed is greater. When light passes from air into a transparent substance the angles of incidence and refraction are related by the equation

$$\frac{\text{speed of light in air}}{\text{speed of light in substance}} = \frac{\text{sine (angle of incidence)}}{\text{sine (angle of refraction)}}$$

$$\frac{c_{air}}{c_{sub}} = \frac{\sin i}{\sin r}$$

The equation can be used when light travels between any two transparent substances.

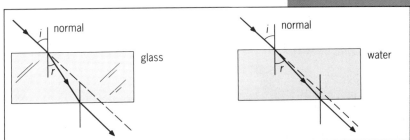

▲ **Fig 107.7 The angle of refraction is greater in water than in glass for the same angle of incidence**

The speed of light in air is 3×10^8 m/s and in water is 2.3×10^8 m/s. Light passes from air to water at an angle of incidence of 45°. Calculate the angle of refraction in water.

First rearrange the equation to give

$$\sin r = \frac{\sin i \times c_{water}}{c_{air}}$$

Substitute the numbers into the equation

$$\sin r = \frac{\sin 45° \times 2.3 \times 10^8}{3 \times 10^8}$$

$$= 0.542$$

To find the angle r, use your calculator to work out the inverse sine of 0.542, which is 33°.

Q6 Calculate the angle of refraction when light travelling from air into water meets the boundary at an angle of incidence of 58°. Use the speeds of light given above.

Q7 Light travels from air into glass. Use the speeds above (and $c_{glass} = 2.0 \times 10^8$ m/s to calculate the angle of incidence when the angle of refraction is **a** 20° **b** 30° **c** 40°.

Q8 Repeat the calculations of question 7 for light travelling from water into glass. Compare the amount of bending in each case. Can you explain this difference?

Fig 107.6 How a change in speed causes bending ▼
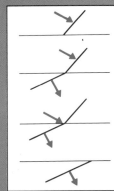

WAVES

263

108 LIGHT
ROUND THE BEND (2)

By the end of this section you should be able to

- understand the conditions necessary for light to be totally internally reflected
- describe applications of total internal reflection.

Some recent technological advances in medicine and communications have relied on trapping light in a plastic fibre, enabling it to travel round bends and over long distances with very little loss of energy. Everyday objects such as cats' eyes and bicycle reflectors use the same principle.

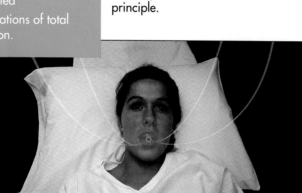

Fig 108.1
Optical fibres guide the laser beam to treat cancer in the throat

INTERNAL REFLECTION

Whenever waves cross a boundary from one material to another, there is some reflection, fig 108.2.

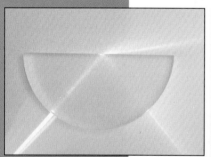

▲ **Fig 108.2**

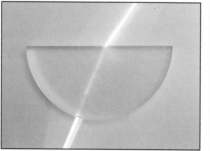

▲ **Fig 108.3**

At small angles of incidence the reflection is weak. Increasing the angle of incidence causes more light to be reflected and less emerges from the flat edge of the block. The dispersion of the light leaving the block becomes apparent when the angle of incidence is about 40°, and the internally reflected ray is now very bright, fig 108.3.

At a slightly greater angle, about 42° for glass and perspex, there is a change at the boundary. Instead of some light leaving and the rest being reflected, all the light is reflected inside the block. The angle at which the changeover occurs is called the **critical angle**. At all angles of incidence greater than this the light undergoes **total internal reflection**, fig 108.4.

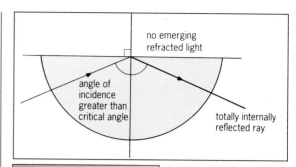

no emerging refracted light

angle of incidence greater than critical angle

totally internally reflected ray

▲ **Fig 108.4 Total internal reflection happens at an angle of incidence greater than 42°**

Using total internal reflection

Bicycle reflectors, prismatic binoculars and prismatic periscopes all use total internal reflection. In these devices triangular prisms are used as reflectors. Fig 108.5 shows a reflector. It contains hundreds of prisms in a single plastic moulding. Total internal reflection takes place at the inside surfaces of each prism.

▶ **Fig 108.5**
A bicycle reflector works by total internal reflection

Q1 Fig 108.6 shows the arrangement of two prisms in a periscope. Copy the diagram and trace the path of the two rays of light from the object to the eye.

Is the image seen by the eye upright or inverted?

Fig 108.6 ▶

264

Keeping the light inside

Light travels along optical fibres by being totally internally reflected when it hits the boundary (edge) of the fibre. In this way light can be made to go around corners and curves by being reflected many times, fig 108.7.

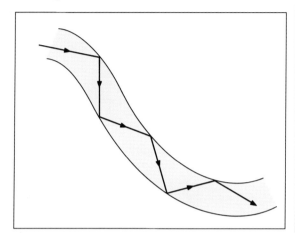

▲ **Fig 108.7 Light is totally internally reflected at the boundary of an optical fibre, so cannot escape**

In order to keep the light in the fibre, each time it meets the boundary the angle of incidence has to be bigger than the critical angle of the material.

Q2 Is it better to use a plastic which has a small critical angle or a large one? Explain your choice.

Endoscopy

An **endoscope** is a device used in medicine for looking inside patients, fig 108.8.

The endoscope tube contains two bundles of fibres. Light is shone down one bundle to light up part of the inside of the body. Reflected light then passes down the second bundle to create an image which can be photographed or viewed on a television screen, fig 108.9.

The endoscope also enables doctors to perform minor surgery without having to cut into the patient.

Laser surgery

Lasers are useful in medicine for delicate surgery where a lot of energy is required in a small area. Examples include treatment of ulcers and the retina of the eye. Optical fibres are used to guide the laser light to the precise location where it is needed.

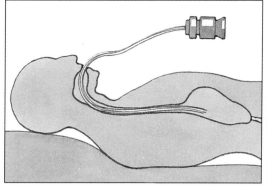

▲ **Fig 108.8 An endoscope enables a doctor to look inside a patient's body**

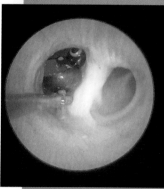

▲ **Fig 108.9 This endoscope picture shows the top of a cocktail stirrer in the trachea of a child who swallowed it accidentally**

Communications

Optical fibres are being increasingly used in communications for transmitting telephone conversations and other information. The energy loss is much less than when the information is sent as an electrical signal along copper wires. Using very pure glass, an optical signal can travel 100 km before it needs to be amplified, while an electrical signal has to be amplified every few kilometres. By using a process known as multiplexing, one narrow fibre can carry thousands of telephone calls at the same time.

Information can be transmitted very rapidly along the fibres if it is sent as a digital signal using binary code. Lasers are used as the light sources. They can be switched on and off very rapidly to produce the pulses of light which represent the binary digits, fig 108.10.

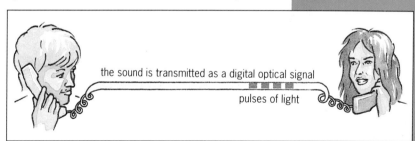

the sound is transmitted as a digital optical signal
pulses of light

▲ **Fig 108.10 Optical fibres are used for communication – they can transmit digital information very effectively**

Q3 Laser light is of a single wavelength. Why is this an advantage when sending information as a series of pulses which are very close together?

Q4 If a white light source were used, would the different wavelengths present all travel at the same speed?

Q5 A pulse of white light enters one end of an optical fibre which is 100 km long. If you could see the pulse arriving at the other end, how would it have been changed?

WAVES

By the end of this section you should be able to

- understand that diffraction is a property of all waves
- describe how diffraction of electromagnetic waves can be demonstrated
- appreciate how the effects of diffraction depend on the wavelength of the waves.

SPREADING LIGHT

You have already seen the effects of diffraction of sound and water waves, page 251. Diffraction is a wave property which affects all waves, but in the case of short wavelength waves the effects of diffraction are not very evident.

Diffraction and slit width

Fig 109.1 shows what happens when light passes through a 'narrow' slit 1 mm wide.

▼ **Fig 109.1 Light does not diffract through a 1mm slit**

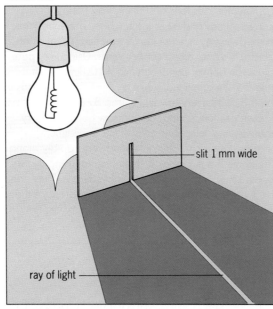

ray of light

slit 1 mm wide

No visible spreading occurs because the width of the slit is several thousand times the wavelength of light. In order to see the diffraction of light a much narrower slit has to be used.

A narrow slit can be made by using a pin to scratch a line down a microscope slide which has been painted black, fig 109.2.

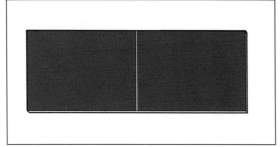

▲ **Fig 109.2 A scratched slide provides a narrower gap**

This slit is still many wavelengths wide, but some spreading occurs when light passes through it, fig 109.3.

▲ **Fig 109.3 Diffraction can be seen when light passes through a scratched slide**

One effect of the diffraction of light can be seen very easily. If you look at a light source through a slit made by holding two straight-edged pieces of paper close together you can see bright and dark lines in the gap.

The pattern of the lines changes as you change the width of the slit. A similar pattern can be seen by looking through the eye of a needle. These patterns are due to the spreading of the light when it goes through a narrow opening. The closer the gap size to the wavelength, the more the light is spread out.

Diffraction of microwaves

The spreading out of microwaves is easy to see if your school has a 3 cm microwave transmitter and receiver, fig 109.4.

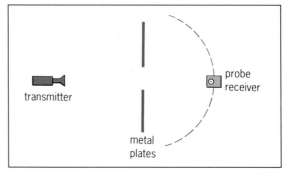

transmitter

probe receiver

metal plates

▲ **Fig 109.4 How the amount of spreading through different sizes of gap can be investigated**

SATELLITE TRANSMISSIONS

In satellite communications, the beam of microwaves has to travel thousands of kilometres to the receiving aerial, so it is important that the amount of spreading as it leaves the transmitter is as close to zero as possible. This can be achieved with a reflector of 2–3 m in diameter if the wavelength of the waves used is a few millimetres. Even so, the signal which arrives at the satellite is very much weaker than the one which is sent from the transmitter.

If the satellite is being used for telephone communications the beam which is sent back to Earth also needs to be very narrow, and aimed precisely at the receiving dish which focuses it onto the aerial, fig 109.5.

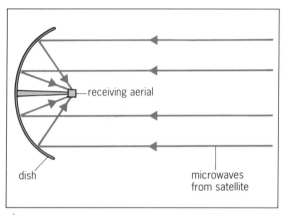

▲ **Fig 109.5 Focusing of microwaves by a dish**

Satellites used for television broadcasting need to transmit a beam with some spreading out so that the signals can be received over a large area, fig 109.6.

◀ **Fig 109.7 Satellites transmit microwaves which are focused by dishes very much bigger than their wavelength to reduce diffraction**

Q1 Explain why satellites need to amplify signals which they receive before sending them back to Earth.

Q2 How does a satellite obtain its electricity supply to power the amplifiers?

Q3 The wavelength of the waves used for normal television transmission in the UK is slightly different for the various channels, but in all cases is around 0.6 m.

a If you wished to transmit this to a satellite, how big a reflecting dish would be needed to ensure a narrow beam? Would this be practical?

b Explain why there is a maximum size to a reflector which is part of a satellite, and why waves with a wavelength of a few millimetres are used for satellite television broadcasts.

c Television sets are designed to 'tune in' to wavelengths of around 0.6 m. Explain why a decoder is needed to view transmissions from satellites.

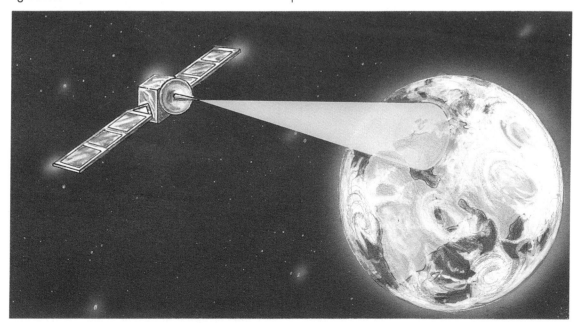

◀ **Fig 109.6 Sometimes diffraction is necessary, such as when transmitting television signals. The beam is designed to be received throughout Europe**

INTERFERENCE

By the end of this section you should be able to

- appreciate that interference is a wave property
- describe how interference of electromagnetic waves can be demonstrated
- understand polarisation of electromagnetic waves
- discuss the uses of polarised light.

The colours which can be seen in soap bubbles and oil films on puddles are caused by the **interference** of light. Interference takes place whenever two waves cross each other, but the effects of this are only noticeable in special circumstances.

The interference of water waves can be studied with a ripple tank, using two dippers vibrating in step. The interference pattern in fig 110.1 is caused by the waves from the two sources interfering with each other when they cross.

Fig 110.1 Interference pattern in water waves ▶

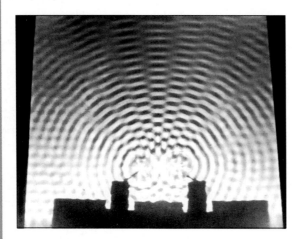

Destructive and constructive interference

The lines of calm water are caused by **destructive interference**, where a wave crest from one of the dippers meets a trough from the other one. The result is that they cancel each other out, as fig 110.2 shows.

Fig 110.2 Crest + trough results in flat water – destructive interference

▶

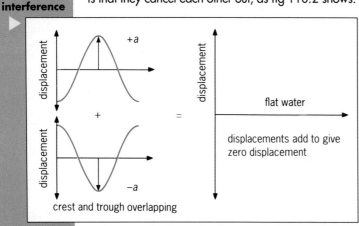

crest and trough overlapping

In between the lines of calm water, **constructive interference** occurs. Extra large crests and troughs are formed when two crests or two troughs come together, fig 110.3.

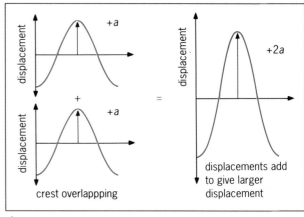
crest overlappping

▲ **Fig 110.3 Crest + crest and trough + trough results in larger waves – constructive interference**

Fig 110.4 shows the crests and troughs coming from each source. The crests are drawn in blue and the troughs in red. You should be able to pick out the lines of constructive and destructive interference.

Q1 Draw similar diagrams to show what happens to the interference pattern when
  a the dippers are moved closer together
  b the wavelength of the water waves is made shorter by increasing the frequency of the dippers.

It is only possible to see such a clear interference pattern when the two sources are producing waves of the same frequency.

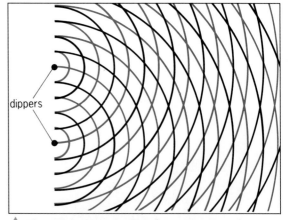
dippers

▲ **Fig 110.4 How an interference pattern is set up**

Interference of light waves

Interference is one of the properties which is common to all waves but, like diffraction, it is more difficult to see with waves of shorter wavelength because the lines of constructive and destructive interference become closer together and are hard to distinguish. To be able to see an interference pattern from light waves, two or more identical sources placed very close together are needed.

A **diffraction grating** uses the interference of light from hundreds of sources to give much clearer interference patterns.

Activity

If you view a sodium lamp through a diffraction grating you will see several images of the lamp, fig 110.5.

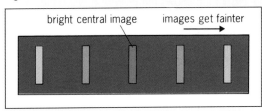
bright central image   images get fainter

▲ **Fig 110.5**

Each image corresponds to constructive interference occurring between the waves diffracted from each of the narrow gaps in the grating. A sodium lamp does not give out the range of wavelengths that come from a source of white light such as a tungsten filament. It gives two 'orange' wavelengths which are very close together. You may also see other colours of image which are due to other gases in the sodium lamp.

If you now look at a white light source you can see that each image is actually a spectrum.

POLARISATION

Polarising light

Unlike radio waves from transmitting aerials, page 259, light waves are not polarised when they leave a light source, so the oscillations are in different directions at different times, fig 110.6.

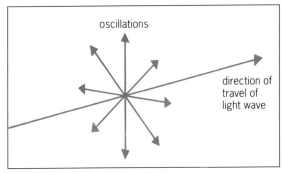
oscillations

direction of travel of light wave

▲ **Fig 110.6 Light waves are not polarised – the oscillations are in all directions**

Light can be polarised when it passes through some materials, and some polarisation also takes place when light is reflected. The most common and readily available polarising material is called polaroid. It is used to make lenses for some sunglasses, and for covering a liquid crystal display in a calculator. Fig 110.7 shows what happens when you look through a piece of polaroid.

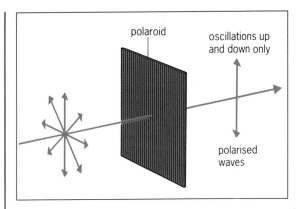
polaroid
oscillations up and down only
polarised waves

Things look darker when viewed through polaroid because it only allows about 30% of the energy to pass through. Polaroid can be used with light which is already polarised. To see the effect of this you need to look at a light source through two pieces of polaroid, fig 110.8.

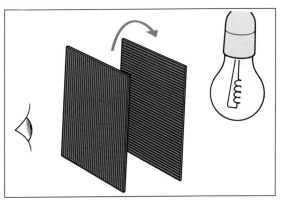

The light becomes darker and brighter if one of the pieces of polaroid is rotated. If the polaroids are crossed so that one only allows vertical oscillations through and the other only horizontal oscillations, then no light can get through.

Polaroid sunglasses

Photographers and manufacturers of sunglasses use polaroid to reduce the glare caused by reflections from glass and water, fig 110.9.

Light reflected from a water surface is mainly horizontally polarised. The polaroid in sunglasses only allows vertical oscillations to pass through it, so most of the reflected light does not get through. This is more effective at some viewing angles than others.

Q2 The figures on a calculator display appear as black on a lighter coloured background. If the polaroid is removed from the front of the display, the figures cannot be seen at all. Use the idea of polarisation to try to explain this.

Q3 Can sound waves be polarised? Explain your answer fully.

◄ **Fig 110.7 Polaroid polarises light – it lets through the oscillations in one direction only**

◄ **Fig 110.8 The amount of light getting through two pieces of polaroid varies depending on the angle between them**

▲ **Fig 110.9 Polaroid (bottom left) cuts down the glare by allowing only vertical oscillations through**

WAVES

269

By the end of this section you should be able to

■ explain the movement of projectiles and satellites

■ appreciate the benefits of artificial satellites.

PROJECTILES

Gravitational pull

All objects near the surface of the Earth experience a downward force of 10N for each kilogram of mass, page 228. Darts players need to take into account the downward motion of the darts between leaving the hand and arriving at the dart board. Fig 111.1 shows the path of a dart which is thrown horizontally and one which is thrown to compensate for the downward motion.

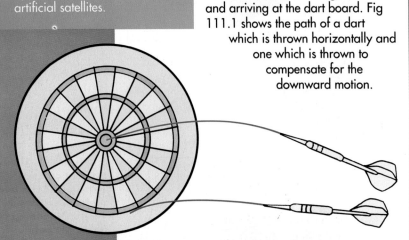

▲ **Fig 111.1 A darts player knows the dart will be accelerated downwards**

The 'monkey and hunter'

An object which is projected horizontally, a **projectile**, has the same pattern of downward motion as one which is released and allowed to fall vertically. Its free-fall acceleration is not affected by the horizontal motion. Fig 111.2 shows a demonstration of this, the 'monkey and hunter' experiment. The 'bullet' is fired horizontally and the 'monkey' is released at the same time. Does the 'monkey' get hit?

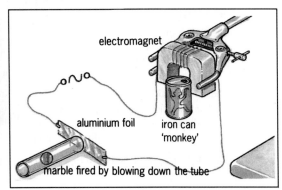

electromagnet

aluminium foil

iron can 'monkey'

marble fired by blowing down the tube

▲ **Fig 111.2 The marble breaks the circuit and so the 'monkey' starts to fall as the marble is fired – they are both released at the same time**

The path of a projectile

The effect of air resistance on a projectile travelling at low speed is small, so a ball which is thrown horizontally at 15m/s maintains that horizontal speed. In equal time intervals it travels equal distances horizontally, and increasing distances vertically. This explains why the path of a projectile gets steeper the longer it is in the air.

Q1 Fig 111.3 shows the path of a projectile which is projected horizontally at 15 m/s. Draw similar graphs to show the paths of projectiles with horizontal speeds of
a 10m/s **b** 25m/s.

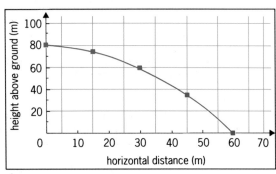

▲ **Fig 111.3**

Satellites

A projectile becomes a **satellite** when the curvature of its path exactly matches the curvature of the Earth, so that it is constantly falling towards the Earth but never getting any nearer, fig 111.4.

this projectile reaches the ground

this projectile is falling at the same rate as the ground is falling away

▲ **Fig 111.4 A projectile becomes a satellite when projected at such a speed that the rate of fall equals the curvature of the Earth's surface**

GOING ROUND IN CIRCLES

Whirling a rubber bung in a horizontal circle above your head requires a pulling force towards the centre of the circle (it must be a pull because you cannot push with a piece of string). If you let go of the string, the bung becomes a projectile and travels with a constant horizontal velocity. This is how water leaves washing which is in a spin dryer.

Unbalanced forces

To keep an object moving in a circle there has to be an unbalanced force acting towards the centre. When doing a loop on a fairground ride, you can feel a larger than normal force from your seat at the bottom of the loop, but this contact force almost disappears at the top of the loop as your weight provides the unbalanced force towards the centre of the loop, fig 111.5.

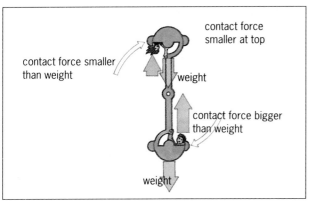

contact force smaller than weight

contact force smaller at top

weight

contact force bigger than weight

weight

▲ **Fig 111.5 To keep her moving in a circle there is an unbalanced force towards the centre**

When a car is going round a corner, the unbalanced force towards the centre comes from the friction between the tyres and the road. The faster the car is travelling, the bigger the force needed.

Q2 Draw diagrams to show the unbalanced force acting for each of the following examples of circular motion.
a a train going round a corner
b a child on a roundabout
c washing in a spin dryer
d a passenger inside a bus which is cornering.
In each case explain what causes the unbalanced force.

ARTIFICIAL SATELLITES

The force on a satellite

Artificial satellites are used to monitor weather conditions on the Earth and to enable worldwide communications through the media of telephone, radio and television. Because even low orbit satellites are well above the Earth's atmosphere, the only force acting on them is the gravitational pull. There is no air resistance.

Satellites are kept in orbit by the gravitational pull of the Earth which acts as the unbalanced force towards the centre of the circle, fig 111.6.

The speed of a satellite

The speed of a satellite in stable orbit depends only on its height above the Earth's surface. Satellites in high orbits travel slower than low orbit satellites.

Q3 What other factor determines the time it takes for a satellite to complete one orbit?

◄ **Fig 111.6 There is only one force acting on a satellite – the pull of the Earth**

Weather satellites

Some weather satellites are in low orbits, up to 1000 km. At these heights the orbit time is about 90 minutes. They transmit both visible light and infra-red (page 257) pictures back to Earth.

◄ **Fig 111.7 This image is made using both visible and infa-red radiation**

Q4 Suggest what the different colours on the land represent in the image.

Communications satellites

Communications satellites need to stay in the same place above the Earth's surface. To achieve this they are placed in an orbit which has an orbit time of 24 hours so that their rotation around the Earth matches the Earth's spin on its axis. The orbit height for this is 36 000 km above the Earth's surface.

Satellites allow communication between places which would normally be hidden from each other because of the Earth's curvature, fig 111.8.

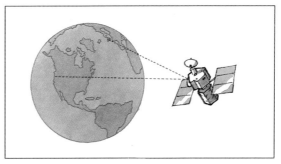

▲ **Fig 111.8 Satellites overcome the problem of the Earth's curvature**

Q5 Estimate the time delay between television pictures being transmitted from the UK and arriving in the USA by satellite transmission. Page 267 will help you. What implications does this have for a television interviewer who is talking to someone across the Atlantic?

By the end of this section you should be able to
- describe how rockets are propelled
- understand how a rocket can be put into orbit around the Earth and return to Earth.

ROCKET PROPULSION

Pushing back

When you walk, run, jump, ride a bicycle or swim, the force which pushes you forwards results from a backwards push on the ground or the water, fig 112.1.

Jet and rocket engines push back on the gases which are expelled from the exhaust. This is how a balloon is propelled when it is blown up and then released – the backwards push on the expelled air produces a force on the balloon which is equal in size but opposite in direction.

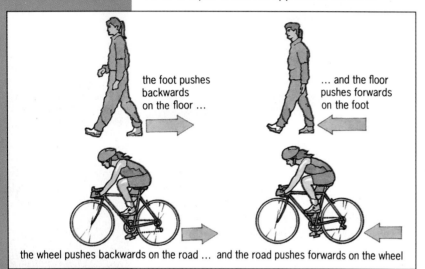

the foot pushes backwards on the floor …

… and the floor pushes forwards on the foot

the wheel pushes backwards on the road … and the road pushes forwards on the wheel

▲ **Fig 112.1 You move because the ground pushes you when you push the ground**

Fuelling rockets

Rockets have their own oxygen supply. In a solid fuel rocket, for example a firework rocket, this is in the form of an oxidising agent mixed in the correct proportions with the fuel. Liquid fuel rockets carry separate tanks of hydrogen and oxygen which are mixed together before being burned.

Q1 Explain why rockets need to carry their own oxygen supply.

THE LAUNCH

Getting into orbit

A lot of energy is needed to put a satellite into orbit so rockets need to carry a large amount of fuel. This in turn adds to the weight and the energy requirement. To avoid carrying extra weight further than necessary, rockets are built in stages so that the fuel containers can be jettisoned when they are empty.

▲ **Fig 112.2**

Launching the shuttle

The space shuttle has three main engines which use liquid fuel, and two solid fuel booster rockets which are only used in the early part of the launch. If it were not restrained, the shuttle would start to take off as soon as the upward force from the exhaust gases was greater than the weight. The shuttle is held back until the upward force is much greater than this.

Q2 The mass of the shuttle is 70 tonnes (1 tonne = 1000 kg). The liquid and solid fuel tanks, when full, have a total mass of 1300 tonnes.
  a What is the total weight which has to be lifted off the launch pad?
  b At launch the upward force produced by the rockets is 17 MN (1 MN = 1×10^6 N). What is the resultant upward force?
  c Calculate the acceleration which this force causes.

The acceleration which you calculated in question 2 does not seem very great, but it quickly increases as the force from the rockets is increased and the total mass decreases due to the fuel being burned.

Q3 Two minutes after launch, the solid fuel rockets are ditched. The speed is 1400 m/s. Calculate the average acceleration during the first two minutes.

Six minutes later the liquid fuel rockets are turned off and the fuel tank is released. The shuttle is now 100 km above the Earth's surface. It has sufficient kinetic energy to take it another 100 km into space and still be travelling at 8000 m/s, the speed required to maintain a stable orbit at a height of 200 km.

Q4 Describe the energy changes which take place during the launch of the space shuttle.

Q5 Assuming that the value of g remains constant at 10 N/kg, calculate the total energy, kinetic plus potential, of each kilogram of mass which is orbiting at a height of 200 km.

Falling at constant speed

The space shuttle can perform a variety of tasks. It is used to launch new satellites as well as to repair existing ones. Once in orbit the shuttle is well above the Earth's atmosphere so there is no force to slow it down. The shuttle and its contents maintain a constant speed, falling freely in the Earth's gravitational field. The engines are not used to maintain the speed.

Steering

Fig 112.3 The shuttle manoeuvres by firing its rockets in order to capture satellites

When capturing a satellite for repair, fig 112.3, the shuttle has to adjust its orbit to exactly match that of the satellite. This can be done by firing the rocket motors in short bursts, using fuel carried on the shuttle itself. Accelerating in space is not like travelling faster in a car on Earth – because there are no resistive forces, once the speed and position of the shuttle have been adjusted the motors are switched off again.

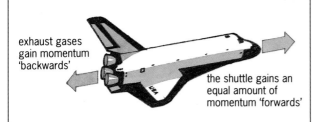

exhaust gases gain momentum 'backwards'

the shuttle gains an equal amount of momentum 'forwards'

▲ Fig 112.4 The principle of conservation of momentum is applied to the shuttle and exhaust gases

Space walks

The first 'space walks' were undertaken with the astronaut tied to the spacecraft with a cord. Without this cord, the slightest push against the spacecraft would have meant the astronaut and his vehicle parting company for ever.

 Q6 Use the idea of conservation of momentum to explain why this would happen.

The **manned manoeuvring device** enables astronauts to move around the spacecraft and to be able to make small adjustments to their speed and position. It uses compressed nitrogen as a 'fuel'. The gas can be squirted out from a number of jets which point in different directions.

Q7 Explain how the release of the nitrogen gas affects the speed and position of the astronaut.

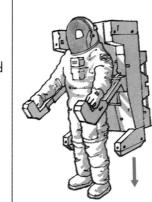

nitrogen squirted out like this causes the astronaut to gain momentum 'upwards'

▲ Fig 112.5 In the manned manoeuvring device, nitrogen is used as the 'exhaust gas'

Out of orbit

When in orbit, the shuttle is falling like a projectile. It does not get any closer to the Earth because the curvature of its path exactly matches the curvature of the Earth. To return to Earth the shuttle's horizontal speed is reduced by firing the motors to turn it round. This gives it a steeper path so it begins to approach the Earth, fig 112.6.

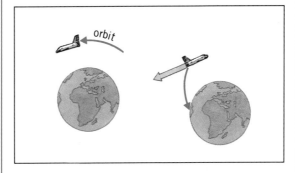

orbit

◄ Fig 112.6 To get out of orbit, the shuttle fires its motors and turns round to reduce the orbital velocity

Re-entry

As the shuttle loses height its vertical speed increases. The decrease in gravitational potential energy is balanced by an increase in kinetic energy. On entering the atmosphere the shuttle is subject to the frictional force of air resistance. This slows the shuttle down, but causes intense heating. Silica tiles are used to protect the shuttle from overheating.

Q8 What properties of silica make it a suitable material for protecting the shuttle?

Q9 Explain why the nose and leading edges of the wings are black.

GRAVITY

By the end of this section you should be able to
- describe the evidence which supports the 'big bang' theory
- understand the life cycle of a star.

THE BIG BANG

How the Universe began

Have there always been planets and stars and galaxies? Or was there a time when none of this existed? What happened when the Universe was created?

There are no answers to any of these questions, only theories based on our very limited knowledge of the state of the Universe.

In the 1920s Edwin Hubble observed that the galaxies are hurtling away from each other, and the further away a galaxy is from us, the faster it is receding. When the paths of the galaxies are plotted and traced back, they seem to have originated at the same place, fig 113.1.

Fig 113.1 The movement of the galaxies suggests they all started at the same place

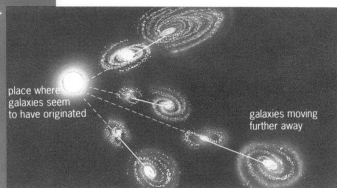

place where galaxies seem to have originated

galaxies moving further away

The 'big bang' theory

The theory of the 'big bang' describes how the Universe is the aftermath of an explosion, and the fragments are still moving away from where the explosion took place.

There is other evidence to support the 'big bang' theory. We know that the explosion of a large bomb releases a lot of radiant energy – initially light, and then infra-red as cooling takes place. Space is not cold – it is filled with microwave energy which gives it a temperature of about 3 K, so the evidence is that space itself is still cooling down from the effects of the the 'big bang'.

The 'bang' itself

What caused the bang, and what it grew out of, are matters of speculation, but whatever existed before the bang, it was not our Universe. The temperature of the compact Universe during the first seconds of its existence must have been very high and nuclei could not exist. Fusion of neutrons and protons could have formed some nuclei of deuterium, helium and lithium in subsequent minutes, fig 113.2.

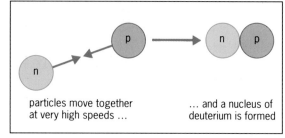

particles move together at very high speeds …

… and a nucleus of deuterium is formed

Fig 113.2 Fusion of neutrons and protons to form a nucleus

After the 'bang'

After the 'bang' the Universe continued to expand and cool. After millions of years it had cooled sufficiently for protons to capture electrons and become hydrogen atoms. At temperatures above 1000 °C the electrons have too much energy to be captured, but below this temperature hydrogen atoms can exist. Before any stars were formed, the Universe probably consisted of clouds of hydrogen gas, with some traces of other very light atoms.

A STAR IS BORN

Cooling continues

The hydrogen clouds broke into fragments and as the gas continued to cool, gravitational forces caused the clouds to condense. The contraction of the hydrogen caused heating in the centre of the clouds of gas, or **nebulae**, so that temperatures in the Universe once again reached millions of degrees. At these temperatures hydrogen nuclei fuse together to form helium nuclei, which releases vast amounts of energy.

Fig 113.3 Two young blue/white giant stars in a nebula of hydrogen

New stars are continually being formed in this way, from the shrinkage of clouds of gas and dust, fig 113.3. Our star, the Sun, is in its **main sequence**, a stable state which is expected to last for another 5000 million years while the hydrogen is being fused into helium.

The life cycle of a star

As the fusion reaction slows down, two things happen in a nebula. The outer zone of hydrogen expands and cools while the inner zone of helium shrinks and heats up. The temperature in the shrinking core reaches several million degrees. At this high temperature the helium nuclei are moving so fast that they now fuse together to produce carbon and oxygen nuclei. The pressure of the radiation emitted from the core causes the whole star to expand and become a **red giant**. The red giant's outer layers stream away from the star and form a nebula around it. Gravitational forces contract the core causing very high temperatures and further fusion reactions. The star is now a **white dwarf**. The fusion reactions gradually cease and the star cools.

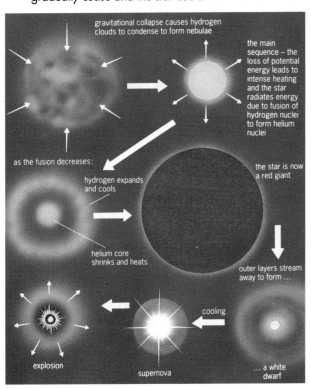

the main sequence – the loss of potential energy leads to intense heating and the star radiates energy due to fusion of hydrogen nuclei to form helium nuclei

gravitational collapse causes hydrogen clouds to condense to form nebulae

as the fusion decreases:

hydrogen expands and cools

helium core shrinks and heats

the star is now a red giant

outer layers stream away to form ...

cooling

... a white dwarf

explosion

supernova

▲ Fig 113.4 The life cycle of a star

What happens next depends on how massive the star is. A small star which is less than about 1.5 times the mass of our Sun eventually cools and stops giving out light – it is now a **black dwarf**. Larger stars, up to 3 times the mass of our Sun, condense to form **neutron stars** with densities of millions of tonnes per cubic centimetre. These emit pulses of radio waves and are sometimes called **pulsars**.

Even more massive stars go through a very bright stage called a **supernova**. As the star contracts and heats to a very high temperatures, iron and other metals are created by fusion reactions. These reactions eventually cease and the core of the star collapses while the outer part of the star explodes, fig 113.4.

After the supernova explodes

Second-generation stars can be formed from the outer layers of a supernova which are ejected into space. Our Sun is a second-generation star which started as a whirling cloud of fragments from an exploding supernova.

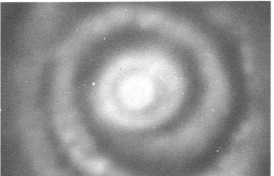

The composition of the cloud was largely hydrogen, but it also contained substantial amounts of carbon, oxygen and metals from the fusion reactions.

The remaining core of the supernova glows with a spectacular brilliance for a short period of time before collapsing into a neutron star or a **black hole**.

Black holes are formed from very massive stars. The density of the core which follows the supernova stage is greater than that of neutron stars. They are so dense that the escape velocity is greater than the speed of light. The very intense gravitational field which surrounds black holes prevents us from seeing parts of the Universe as light is pulled into the black hole.

THE FUTURE OF THE UNIVERSE

The Universe is currently expanding, but will it continue to expand, or will the gravitational forces cause it to contract, perhaps returning it to the state it was in at the beginning of time?

Nobody knows the answer – precise calculations about the future of the Universe are difficult because the amount of mass is not known.

Models of the Universe

The 'open' model of the Universe pictures it as continuing to expand for ever, while the 'closed' model predicts that eventually the galaxies will be pulled back together and there will be an enormous crash.

There is a third model of what may happen – the 'inflationary' model. This supposes that the density of matter in the Universe is not sufficient to cause it to collapse, but is just enough to stop it from expanding for ever. Whatever happens, it will be long after the Earth has been vaporised, so none of us will live to know the answer.

◄ **Fig 113.5 The Sun began to form in the centre of the whirling cloud of fragments from the explosion of a supernova**

By the end of this section you should be able to

- understand how the composition of the inner planets is related to the formation of the Solar System
- describe how the Moon causes tides and how these are influenced by the Sun.

THE SOLAR SYSTEM FORMS

About 5000 million years ago our Solar System formed from a cloud of gas and dust which came from an exploding supernova. Exactly how the Solar System formed is not known, but it seems likely that as the cloud rotated it flattened into a disc and eventually the core condensed to form the Sun, with the planets condensing and spinning around it.

Substances in the Solar System

The fusion reaction of the supernova created helium, oxygen, carbon and some metals. The nebula which became the Solar System contained compounds of these – water, methane, carbon dioxide and metal oxides. As the Sun began to shine the lighter gases were driven off the inner planets, leaving them with molten cores of metal oxides surrounded by atmospheres of the dense gases water, methane and carbon dioxide, fig 114.1.

gases driven off

▲ **Fig 114.1 Lighter gases were driven off the inner planets**

Asteroids and comets

The Solar System consists of much more than the nine known planets and the Sun. Rocky debris orbits the Sun in the **asteroid belt** and on the far reaches of the Solar System there are **comets**, collections of ice and dust which occasionally become visible as they pass sufficiently close to the Sun for the ice to vaporise.

THE INNER PLANETS

▲ **Fig 114.2 Mercury**

▲ **Fig 114.3 Venus**

▲ **Fig 114.4 Earth**

▲ **Fig 114.5 Mars**

Mercury

Being very close to the Sun, Mercury is very difficult to observe. It is about the size of our Moon with a density similar to that of the Earth. Mercury's iron core probably extends to about three-quarters of the diameter of the planet, and is covered in a single solid crust. We do not know whether the core is liquid, like the Earth's, or whether the smaller size of Mercury has allowed sufficient cooling for it to solidify. Its surface is covered in craters which were formed by meteorites colliding with it in the early life of the Solar System. Although it is too hot to keep an atmosphere of its own, it has a transitory atmosphere of mainly hydrogen and helium which blows past it from the outer layer of the Sun.

Venus

Venus is very similar in size and mass to the Earth, so it may have a similar composition. Its thick, dense atmosphere is mainly carbon dioxide but is also rich in sulphuric acid, probably as a result of volcanic activity in the past. The surface has ridges and valleys which could have been caused by horizontal movement of the planet's crust.

Earth

The Earth is the blue planet, with its delicate balance of water, atmosphere and temperature that allows such a rich variety of life. It has a hot, massive core and the surface is made up of plates which float on the core. Volcanoes and earthquakes show that it is still geologically active.

Mars

Mars has an atmosphere, made up mainly of carbon dioxide, and it has water which is now frozen into the surface but may have once formed rivers. Being the furthest from the Sun, it is the least dense of the inner planets. There are the remnants of enormous volcanoes, much bigger than those found on Earth, and it is probable that volcanoes will erupt in the future.

THE EARTH'S NATURAL SATELLITE

The Moon's composition is slightly different from that of the Earth. It is less abundant in elements which vaporise easily, so perhaps the Moon was once subjected to higher temperatures than the Earth.

Structure of the Moon

Although Moon rock brought back to the Earth is volcanic in origin, it is thought that geological activity ceased three billion years ago and the craters on the Moon, fig 114.6, are due to impacts from meteors.

▲ **Fig 114.6 Craters on the Moon were caused by meteors millions of years ago**

With no wind or weather on the Moon, dust is not blown about so these craters have been undisturbed since they were created, which was after the volcanic activity ceased.

Keeping the Moon in orbit

The Moon's orbit, like that of the planets of the Solar System, is not a perfect circle. Its movement around the Earth is due to the gravitational attraction between the Moon and the Earth in the same way as gravitational forces keep the planets in orbit around the Sun.

The Earth's gravitational field strength decreases with distance from the planet. At the surface of the Earth it is approximately 10 N/kg but at a distance of 380 000 km, the mean radius of the Moon's orbit, it is less than 3 mN/kg. This unbalanced force towards the Earth keeps the Moon in orbit.

Tides

Gravitational forces, like all other forces, act between pairs of objects. The Moon pulls the Earth with a force equal to that with which the Earth pulls the Moon, but because the Earth is a much more massive body the force has less effect on its motion.

The most noticeable effect that the Moon has on the Earth is that it causes tides. The water on the side of the Earth which is facing the Moon is pulled towards it the most, while the water on the opposite side is the least affected. This causes two bulges in the water over the Earth's surface, fig 114.7.

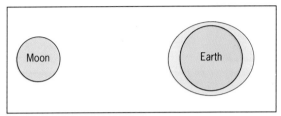

▲ **Fig 114.7 The gravitational force of the Moon pulls the water on the Earth towards the Moon. The water furthest from the Moon experiences the smallest amount of attraction**

If the Moon were stationary, the Earth's rotation about its axis would cause a high tide at each coast every 12 hours. The Moon's rotation around the Earth lengthens this to approximately 13 hours.

Q1 On a diagram similar to that in fig 114.7, draw the position of the Moon one day later. Use this to explain why the interval between high tides is 13 hours. Explain what would happen if the Moon's rotation around the Earth was in the opposite direction.

The Sun's gravitational field also has a small effect on the tides. Exceptionally high and low tides, called **spring tides**, are due to the Sun and the Moon creating bulges in the same places.

Less extreme tides, or **neap tides**, occur when the effect of the Sun's gravitational field 'flattens out' the bulges caused by the Moon, fig 114.8.

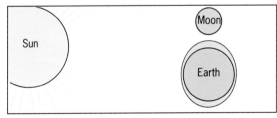

▲ **Fig 114.8 In this position the Sun's gravitational field opposes that of the Moon, causing neap tides**

Q2 Draw diagrams to show the other positions of the Moon and Sun which would cause spring and neap tides. How are the tides related to the phases of the Moon?

115 THE OUTER SOLAR SYSTEM

By the end of this section you should be able to

- describe how the composition of the outer planets is related to their distance from the Sun
- understand how gravitational force causes the motion of comets
- be able to relate surface gravitational field strength to the size and mass of a planet.

THE ASTEROID BELT

The inner planets all have a high concentration of metals, making them dense. Much of the lighter material in the nebula which became our Solar System was driven to the colder parts and formed larger, but less dense planets. Between the outer and inner planets lies the **asteroid belt**, pieces of rock and metal which are up to 100 km in diameter. Large asteroids have hit the Earth in the past and will do so in the future, causing immense craters, fig 115.1.

Fig 115.1 ▶
Meteor Crater, Arizona, USA is half a mile wide

It may have been dust thrown up from an asteroid collision which caused the cooling of the Earth and the death of the dinosaurs 65 million years ago. Many of the meteorites which reach the Earth, producing spectacular displays as they heat up when falling through the atmosphere, probably come from the asteroid belt.

THE COLD PLANETS

Jupiter

Fig 115.2 Jupiter ▶
with four of its moons. Io is on the far left

The low density of Jupiter suggests that its composition is probably similar to that of the nebula from which the Solar System formed. Beneath the upper atmosphere of hydrogen and helium, with traces of methane and ammonia, there is liquid hydrogen and helium, with a core of compressed hydrogen.

One of Jupiter's 16 known moons, Io, is the most geologically active body in the Solar System. Volcanic eruptions reach heights of hundreds of kilometres and cause enormous craters.

Saturn

Saturn is similar in composition to Jupiter, although it is smaller and less dense. Saturn's colour is due to clouds of ammonia. The remarkable wide, thin rings of Saturn are probably ice particles which can be seen by the reflection of sunlight.

▲ **Fig 115.3 Saturn**

Uranus and Neptune

Uranus and Neptune are denser than Saturn and Jupiter but less dense than the inner planets. They may consist of a rocky core surrounded by water with an atmosphere mainly composed of hydrogen and helium.

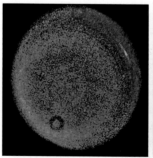 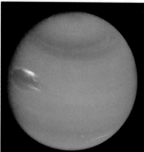

▲ **Fig 115.4 Uranus**   ▲ **Fig 115.5 Neptune**

Pluto

Pluto, except when it passes inside Neptune's orbit, is the most distant planet. It is also the smallest and most dense of the outer planets. It is probably a mixture of ice and rock, covered in frozen methane.

278

◀ **Fig 115.6 Space probes have not reached Pluto, so we only have pictures taken through a telescope**

COMETS

Comets provide spectacular sights when they are close enough to the Sun to be visible. Like the planets, comets go around the Sun in elliptical orbits, fig 115.7.

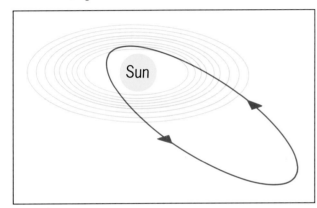

Sun

▲ **Fig 115.7 The path of a comet**

What is a comet?

The head of a comet is a collection of frozen gases and dust which are held together by a weak gravitational force. As a comet approaches the Sun, it speeds up due to the increasing gravitational force. The warming effect of the Sun causes evaporation of the frozen gases, which get blown away along with dust and form the tail of the comet. Comets can only be seen during the brief part of their orbit which is close to the Sun – the glowing gases make them appear as enormous regions of moving light, fig 115.8. A visible comet is losing mass all the time as its tail is blown away and replenished with material from its head.

Meteor showers

Space is littered with the debris of comets, causing **meteor showers** or **shooting stars** when the Earth passes through a mass of dust particles which have been left behind.

The comet Swift-Tuttle regularly crosses the Earth's orbit and dust left behind is responsible for the

Perseid meteor shower which occurs each August. It is due to pass very close to the Earth in 2126. The chances of a collision are small, but if it does happen the effects will be devastating.

Fig 115.8 Halley's comet ▶

PLANETARY GRAVITATION

The gravitational field strength of a planet depends on its mass and diameter. The more massive a planet is, the stronger its gravitational field. At the same time, gravitational field strength decreases with increasing distance from the centre of the planet so a large planet with the same mass as a smaller one would have a smaller gravitational field strength at its surface.

The table gives data about the nine planets and the Earth's moon.

Planet	Surface gravitational field strength (N/kg)	Mass (compared with Earth's mass)	Radius (compared with Earth's radius)
Mercury	3.7	0.06	0.38
Venus	8.8	0.81	0.95
Earth	9.8	1	1
Moon	1.6	0.01	0.27
Mars	3.7	0.11	0.53
Jupiter	26	318	11.2
Saturn	11.4	95	9.5
Uranus	10.9	14.6	4
Neptune	11.9	17.1	3.8
Pluto	4.6	0.03	0.18

Q1 With the exception of Pluto, the outer planets have greater gravitational field strengths than the inner ones. Explain why this is the case, and why Pluto is different.

Q2 The field strengths of Saturn, Uranus and Neptune are all similar, but Saturn is much more massive than the other two. Explain these observations.

Q3 The gravitational field strength of Uranus is similar in strength to that of the Earth, but the Earth is much more dense. Why are the gravitational fields of similar strength?

GRAVITY

EQUATIONS YOU SHOULD KNOW

You should learn the following equations as you may be expected to remember and apply them in examinations. These equations are printed in colour throughout the book.

LEVEL 6

- Pressure = $\dfrac{\text{force}}{\text{area}}$ $p = \dfrac{F}{A}$

- Speed = $\dfrac{\text{distance travelled}}{\text{time taken}}$ $v = \dfrac{s}{t}$

LEVEL 7

- The general gas equation for a fixed mass of gas: $\dfrac{p_1 V_1}{T_1} = \dfrac{p_2 V_2}{T_2}$

- Work done = force × distance moved in its own direction $W = Fd$

- Power = $\dfrac{\text{work done (or energy changed)}}{\text{time taken}}$ $p = \dfrac{W}{t}$

- The law of moments: in a balanced system the sum of the clockwise moments about a point equals the sum of the anticlockwise moments about that point

- Moment = size of force × perpendicular distance to pivot $M = Fd$

LEVEL 8

- Energy = current × potential difference × time $E = IVt$
- Energy change = mass × specific heat capacity × temperature change $E = mc\Delta T$
- Force = mass × acceleration $F = ma$
- Acceleration = $\dfrac{\text{increase in speed}}{\text{time taken}}$ $a = \dfrac{v}{t}$
- Wave speed = frequency × wavelength $v = f\lambda$

LEVEL 9

- Current = $\dfrac{\text{charge}}{\text{time}}$ $I = \dfrac{Q}{t}$

- Resistance = $\dfrac{\text{potential difference}}{\text{current}}$ $R = \dfrac{V}{I}$

- Power = current × potential difference $P = IV$
- Weight = mass × gravitational field strength $w = mg$
- Kinetic energy = $\frac{1}{2}$ × mass × (speed)^2 $KE = \frac{1}{2}mv^2$
- Change in gravitational potential energy = mass × gravitational field strength × change in height   g.p.e. = mgh

LEVEL 10

- Momentum = mass × velocity $p = mv$

INDEX

281